Microsoft

Visual C++ 5

Power Toolkit

For Windows 95 & Windows NT

Cutting-Edge Tools &
Techniques for Programmers

Richard C. Leinecker

VENTANA

Visual C++ 5 Power Toolkit
Copyright © 1997 by Richard C. Leinecker

Library of Congress Cataloging-in-Publication Data

Leinecker, Richard C.
     Visual C++ 5 power toolkit. / Rick Leinecker.
          p.   cm.
     Includes index.
     ISBN 1-56604-528-2
     1. C++ (Computer program language) 2. Microsoft Visual C++.
     I. Leinecker, Richard C. Visual C++ power toolkit. II. Title.
     QA76.73.C153L45 1997
     005.26'8—DC21   97-3503
                            CIP

First Edition 9 8 7 6 5 4 3 2 1

Printed in the United States of America

Ventana Communications Group
P.O. Box 13964
Research Triangle Park, NC 27709-3964
919.544.9404
FAX 919.544.9472
http://www.vmedia.com

Ventana Communications Group is a division of International Thomson Publishing.

President
Michael E. Moran

**Vice President of
Content Development**
Karen A. Bluestein

**Director of Acquisitions
and Development**
Robert Kern

Managing Editor
Lois J. Principe

Production Manager
John Cotterman

Art Director
Marcia Webb

**Technology Operations
Manager**
Kerry L. B. Foster

Brand Manager
Jamie Jaeger Fiocco

Creative Services Manager
Diane Lennox

Acquisitions Editor
Neweleen A. Trebnik

Project Editor
Judith F. Wilson

Development Editor
Michelle Corbin Nichols

Copy Editor
Marion Laird

CD-ROM Specialist
Ginny Phelps

Technical Reviewer
Russ Mullen

Desktop Publisher
Jaimie Livingston

Proofreader
Tom Collins

Indexer
Richard T. Evans, Infodex

Cover Illustrator
Laura Stalzer

ABOUT THE AUTHOR

Richard C. Leinecker has been writing computer programs since 1982. His first commercial software was published in 1985, and since then he's had a steady stream of published programs.

Besides writing software, he's written many books and magazine articles. For five years he wrote a column in *COMPUTE* magazine, along with many features and reviews. Other magazines he's written for include *Dr. Dobbs Journal*, *The Atari Journal*, and *Byte*. Besides this book, his most recent title to hit the shelves is *The Visual J++ Bible* (IDG).

As a programmer for CI Impressions in Greensboro, North Carolina, Richard specializes in image processing software. If he's not working, writing a book, or writing software, he's spending time with his family or serving as the musical director for the Rockingham County Theater Guild. Richard lives in Reidsville, North Carolina.

ACKNOWLEDGMENTS

Any book this size is the result of the efforts of many people.

The folks at Ventana are a class act. From Judy Wilson who steered the project, to Michelle Nichols who made sure everything made sense, to Russ Mullen who ensured the technical accuracy, to Marion Laird who spruced up my sentences, to Ginny Phelps who endured while I got the CD-ROM contents finalized, and to Neweleen Trebnik who made sure the entire project was on target—my gratitude goes out to all of them. Their expertise and hard work are what make the Ventana books so great.

Matt Wagner has been my agent for more than three years. For arranging this deal, I'm very grateful to him. Matt is skilled at keeping me busy, and that's music to an author's ears.

I'd like to especially thank Jamie Nye for his help with the Sound, Midi, CD Audio, and Video chapters. Jamie has always been someone I could rely on for good quality work.

My three children have been troopers. When I had to work through Saturdays and Sundays instead of playing games with them, they understood. They even occasionally offered to do extra chores to help out. Now those are good kids!

To my wife, I owe the biggest debt. Without her, I'd never be able to do projects such as this one. She manages household affairs and keeps things running smoothly. She's the biggest contributor to my success.

DEDICATION

This book is dedicated to my wonderful wife, Tammy. My achievements wouldn't be possible without her love and support.

Contents

Introduction

Visual C++ is one of the most powerful tools to come on the programming scene in this decade. It makes creating Windows applications easy. At the same time, it allows programmers to stay close to the Windows architecture, unlike many other development languages that insulate programmers from the Windows API. Programmers have the best of both worlds: quick startup code with tools to create dialog boxes, menus, and other Windows objects, and a language that allows complete control at the same time.

Visual C++ 5 takes this programming tool to a new level. It has better Microsoft Foundation classes (MFC). They're more efficient and robust, they're smaller, and they're easier to use. Added classes for things such as Internet access make MFC even more comprehensive than ever.

Visual C++ makes it easy to create an application. All a programmer has to do is run the App Wizard and answer some queries. Startup code is created, and many of the hooks for advanced features, such as ActiveX and Winsock, are already built in.

Once the application is created, MFC provides a rich set of class libraries with which a programmer can easily give an application additional functionality. The basics such as file I/O, string handling, dialog and user interface tools, graphics functions, and much more are available through MFC.

This book takes up where MFC left off. It adds functionality that MFC doesn't—you'll be grateful for the ability to load and display images. Communication over a modem is something else you get, and there's no support for that in MFC either.

Visual C++ is great, MFC is wonderful, but this book takes the suite to another level—the professional level.

Who Needs This Book?

If you program with Visual C++, there's a lot here for you. Whether you're a beginner or a seasoned veteran, this book provides a wealth of information and how-to that can take your application from average to excellent. You will, however, need to know the basics of Visual C++. Familiarity with the App Wizard and the Class Wizard are essential. Each chapter requires you to create sample hands-on projects, and without a foundation in the basics of Visual C++, you may feel somewhat overwhelmed.

Each chapter shows you how to do different things—such as load and display images and communicate over the Internet. With the class libraries that are included, you need only a few lines of code to perform these tasks. There are no headaches and there's virtually no learning curve for applications developers.

The class libraries that are included are royalty-free. If you purchased them commercially, the cost would probably be in the thousands of dollars. These libraries are worth many times the cost of the book.

Let's say a project you're working on calls for displaying images such as JPEG or GIF files. It's going to take you some time to do this. You could write the code yourself in about six months or lay out hundreds of dollars for a commercial library and spend two weeks learning how to use it. Or you can buy this book and have images loading into your application in less than a day. The choice is yours.

What's in the Book?

Chapter 1, "Images," tells you how to load and save image files. Five lines of code is all it takes to load and display an image in your application. This chapter focuses on adding visual appeal to your applications with very little effort on your part.

Chapter 2, "Screen Effects," helps you learn how to create cool screen effects—taking applications from mundane to dazzling. Users will love your software even more when you give them screens that fade into each other.

Chapter 3, "Image Point Processing," and Chapter 4, "Image Area Processing," introduce you to tools that allow you to create colorized and grayscale variations of your images. These and other enhancements you'll learn about can improve the appearance of many images. Processing also allows you to alter images you include with an application so that the images can be used more than once, thus saving disk space.

Chapter 5, "Splash Screens," gives you a class library that lets you easily add a fantastic splash screen to your application. The hands-on programs show you how to take this simple idea to new levels.

Chapter 6, "TWAIN Data Acquisition," brings you into the world of scanned images. With the class library in this chapter, you'll be able to get images from scanners and other TWAIN-compliant devices. These images can be loaded in, manipulated, and used with the class libraries presented in the first five chapters of this book.

Chapter 7, "Region Maps," shows you how to create and use region maps in your programs. These maps can obviously be used for geographical programs. But they can also be used to create presentations and advertising promotions.

Chapter 8, "Animation," gives you the tools to liven up your work with animated images. Programs with animation catch the attention of users. They also can convey ideas and information better than static text and still images.

Chapter 9, "Video," is all about adding live digitized video to your applications. You'll be able to bring up video clips, play them, pause them, and allow users to move through them at will.

Chapter 10, "Using the Class Library in Applications," gives you more real-life applications of the imaging class library. In this chapter, you'll learn how to print images. You'll also learn how to acquire images from the clipboard.

Chapter 11, "MIDI," shows you how to add music to your programs with MIDI playback. The class library that's presented in this chapter makes it a no-brainer to add MIDI music to your applications and take them from average to extraordinary.

Chapter 12, "Sound," offers a class library that plays sounds. With only two lines of code, you can play back a recording of Arnold saying "I'll be Back." This class library will truly enliven your programs to a degree you won't believe.

Chapter 13, "CD Audio," provides information and resources that are hard to find elsewhere. The class library in this chapter gives you the ability to easily play CD audio. You can write programs that play audio CDs, or write programs that take advantage of the ability to write CD audio to computer data CDs.

Chapter 14, "Modem, Network & Internet Connections," is an on-ramp to the information superhighway. You'll get a class library that makes it a snap to communicate over modems, Novell-compatible networks, and the Internet. This chapter may be one of the most popular in the book due to the desirability of having applications that can communicate with remote computers.

Chapter 15, "Data Compression," has a class library that allows you to save and load data to and from compressed files. This will save you disk space on your distribution disks. Your users will also be happy that they don't lose as much hard drive space after your application has been installed.

How To Use This Book

Each chapter starts with a summary of what the chapter has to offer and what you'll learn from it. A demo program for each chapter is also featured. You'll find out what it is and how to use it.

Some chapters offer background as well as descriptive information on the subject. For example, serial communications and Internet protocols are covered. In the imaging chapter you'll find detailed information on image formats.

There's a discussion of the respective class library in each chapter. Detailed descriptions help you understand each function, argument, and return type.

As we dissect the demo program, you'll read about its inner workings in detail and see how the class library is used throughout.

A series of hands-on exercises using the library instruct you in a step-by-step manner on how to create the programs. Every single step is spelled out, so you're practically guaranteed success in quickly mastering the class library.

We've also included valuable Web resources. Since there are so many sites that can be useful for programmers, a few of the most outstanding are shown and described.

About the Companion CD-ROM

The Companion CD-ROM that comes with the book has every class library that's covered in the book. Each one has both a release and a debug version. To use them, all you have to do is link them into your project and recompile.

Source code for the class libraries is on the Companion CD-ROM, too. You can modify the code if you want and then easily rebuild them.

Demo programs for each chapter are on the disk. Along with the complete project and source code, the executable files can be found in the project's directory.

There are a lot of shareware programs and commercial demos on the CD-ROM. You'll gain valuable information and ideas by using and viewing them.

USING THE CLASS LIBRARIES

The easiest way to use the class libraries is to create a directory on your hard drive for the library files and a directory for the include files. Then, you can add these directories to the list of directories Visual C++ searches when it compiles and links.

To do this, begin by creating a *lib* and an *include* directory. I suggest creating a directory off of the root named VCPTK. Inside of the VCPTK directory, create lib and include directories.

Copy the files from the CD-ROM that are in the lib directory to your newly created VCPTK\lib directory. Copy the files from the CD-ROM that are in the include directory to your newly created VCPTK\include directory.

Run Visual C++. Under the Tools menu, select Options. Click on the Directories tab. In the Show Directories for: combo box, select *include*. Add the VCPTK\include directory to the list. Now in the Show Directories for: combo box, select *lib*. Add the VCPTK\lib directory to the list.

When you want to link any of the class libraries into a project, simply select Settings from the Project menu. Click on the Link tab. Add the library to the Object/library modules: field. Note that there's a Settings for: combo box that determines whether you're adding a library to the release or the debug version of the project.

Most of the libraries on the CD-ROM have a release version and a debug version of the library (which has a "D" appended to the filename of the library). For instance, the ImageObject.lib release library has a debug counterpart that's named ImageObjectD.lib.

CONTACTING THE AUTHOR

I'd love to hear from you. I'd especially like to hear about the projects for which you've been able to use the class libraries. If you can, send me your application.

If you have suggestions for future modifications to the library, those are also welcome. I like to keep the best ideas I get from readers and use them in upcoming versions. If you make your own modifications that you find useful, please send the source code along with an explanation.

If you have problems, feel free to contact me. Sometimes it's possible to answer a question when given the details about the project and the problem. Other times, I need to see the source code. Many times I really can't solve a problem without the entire project.

I try to make time to answer e-mail. Sometimes, though, I'm at the end of a project and get bogged down. Although I'll usually answer e-mail within a day or two, don't lose patience if it takes me a few weeks when I'm in the midst of writing books and software to share with you.

The best way to get in touch with me is via e-mail at ivt-rcl@ interpath.com. You can also e-mail me on CompuServe at 74676,457.

Chapter 1

Images

Art is much less important than life,
but what a poor life without it.
—Robert Motherwell

Why use images? Your program performs the functions for which it was intended—isn't that enough? If you add visuals, does that mean you're placing too much importance on the appearance of your program?

An image is worth a thousand words. That's one reason Windows software is so popular. Attractive programs have an edge because we tend to equate pleasant, colorful screens with programs that are easy to use and powerful. Images can often convey information in a way that words can't. One image can replace many words and leave the viewer enlightened instead of confused.

I've downloaded plenty of shareware that worked well, but I usually end up using the programs that look good and have slick interfaces. Of the thousands of programs on the retail shelves, software authors need a way to pull out of the pack. Of course, the first requirement is a useful program that works well. But what catches the consumer's eye are the graphics and art. More programs have been sold that *look good* than programs that *work well*. I'm not recommending that you favor appearance over functionality, but you should spend enough time so that the "look" of your program doesn't detract from its usefulness.

While it's true that writing computer programs requires above-average technical skills, the creative process during software development is much the same as it is in writing a novel. If you approach your programming as an integrated presentation of information and art, you'll be able to produce software that appeals to the widest possible audience.

Besides the "edge" graphic images give a program that's competing commercially, there's great satisfaction when you can point to a program that looks great and say, "I created that." To help you realize your creative goals, the ImageObject class that comes with this book provides a quick yet powerful tool for adding images to any Windows 95 or Windows NT application. With almost no effort, you can make your programs shine.

THE IMAGEOBJECT CLASS LIBRARY

The ImageObject class library can be linked in with any Visual C++ project. A dynamic link library (DLL) named ImageLoad must be in the application's program directory, your Windows directory, or your Windows\System directory. Six file formats are supported: BMP, GIF, JPG, PCX, TGA, and TIF. With just a few lines of code, you can load and display an image file. You don't need to know anything about the image files or the intricacies. The class library does all the work for you.

Images can be saved, too. You can modify a loaded image and overwrite the old disk file, save it as a different file, then change picture file formats and save it as a new picture file. Don't worry about displaying the image either. The class library will do all of the extra stuff it takes to display a bitmap—such as creating a device context, selecting the bitmap, and doing a BitBlt. A single call replaces the entire bitmap display procedure.

Many different pictures have different dimensions, different numbers of colors, and different ways of storing information. All of that is handled in a way that's transparent to a program. Of course, if you want to get down-and-dirty and twiddle the bits, the source code is included on the Companion CD-ROM. Otherwise, enjoy the simplicity of a few lines of code that load and display a picture.

All source code and support files to rebuild ImageObject.lib can be found in the IMAGES\ImageObject directory on the Companion CD-ROM that comes with this book.

Image File Formats

The six image file formats supported by the CImageObject class library, BMP, GIF, JPG, PCX, TGA, and TIF, all have advantages and disadvantages. For this reason, you should give some thought to which one you'll use for a given application. Here's a brief description of each file format.

BMP

The Microsoft Windows Bitmap (BMP) file format is one of several graphics file formats supported by the Microsoft Windows operating environment. BMP is the native bitmap format of Windows and is used to store virtually any type of bitmap data. Most graphics and imaging applications running under Microsoft Windows support the creation and display of BMP files.

BMP files support all of the screen resolutions and color combinations that Windows supports. For this reason, it's always possible to create a BMP file that exactly matches a screen format.

BMP files are almost always completely uncompressed. This makes them very large. A screen capture of a screen that's 800 by 600 and a color resolution of 24 bits will create a file that's 2,743,545 bytes. As you can see, if disk space is a consideration, this file format isn't a good choice.

GIF

GIF stands for Graphics Interchange Format. Its major feature is its great compression capability, achieved by using LZW compression. After being converted to a color resolution of 8 bits, the same BMP image that's 800 by 600 with a color resolution of 24 bits can be as small as 20 kilobytes.

In view of today's demand for high color resolution, one disadvantage of using the GIF format is its limitation of 8 bits of color resolution. For most applications this is enough. For applications requiring photographic-quality images, it's not adequate.

JPG

JPG (JPEG) is one of the newest file formats to become popular. Its major feature is great compression, far greater even than GIF's. It achieves this degree of compression, though, at the expense of image integrity.

Many times, losing a small amount of image quality won't be noticed. In cases such as this, JPG is a good choice because of the fantastic image compression. The same BMP image that's 800 by 600 with a color resolution of 24 bits can be as small as 5 kilobytes.

JPEGs are usually used for photographic images. That's because the small amount of image degradation can rarely be detected in a photographic image. The trade-off between file size and an unperceived loss in quality weighs in on the side of smaller file sizes.

PCX

PCX was developed by Zsoft many years ago in order to provide their own paint program, PC Paint, with an image file format that offered some compression. The compression is better than an uncompressed file, but the run-length-encoding scheme it uses can still produce large image files.

One problem with PCX files is their limitation of 8 bits of color resolution. This, combined with the fact that the compression is not very good, has PCX files fading fast from the PC scene.

TGA

TGA (Targa) files were developed to support hardware devices that capture video images. The Targa file format makes it easy to store many of the video captures to disk, since very little data manipulation is required.

Targa offers some compression schemes, but normally the images are stored in an uncompressed format. One big advantage that Targa files have had for some time is their support for images ranging from monochrome to those of 32-bit color resolution.

TIF

TIF, or tagged image file format, was designed as the file format that would be everything to everybody. As a result, the file format became difficult to maintain. Many vendors and third parties added their own tags, or modifications, making it hard to keep up with the changes in the file format.

It's still used in many desktop publishing applications because it handles many photometric values that are necessary when manipulating the images. It offers several compression schemes, but TIF files are found uncompressed more often than not.

Most TIF files are stored without compression. Files without compression load and save faster than those with compression. If you're planning to do any image manipulation, you may consider saving your files as TIFs initially until you're done with any manipulations you want to do. Then, you can save them in a format with compression.

The ImageView Demo

We've built a simple demonstration program that shows what the class library can do. The program can be found in the IMAGES\ImageView directory on the CD-ROM. Using File Manager or Program Manager, run the program named ImageView.exe. It's a multiple-document program. When it first runs, all you'll see is an empty application window as pictured in Figure 1-1.

Figure 1-1: When ImageView first runs, you see an empty application with no view windows showing.

To load and display an image file, select Open from the File menu. A file selector appears from which you can select the file you want loaded and displayed. The list of file types includes BMP, GIF, JPG, PCX, TGA, and TIF. (There are several sample files in the IMAGES\ImageView directory.) Any of these will successfully load. You can open as many child windows with pictures as your system has memory for. If, for some reason, the picture doesn't load successfully, you'll be notified of the error. Figure 1-2 shows ImageView with multiple images loaded.

Figure 1-2: You can load multiple images into ImageView.

If you're loading multiple images into ImageView and they have different palettes, it won't take you long to realize that pictures in the background don't always have the correct colors. That's because each picture can have its own palette. When you click the mouse on any of the loaded pictures, the palette will change to that of the picture that has the focus.

Try saving a loaded picture. Select Save As from the File menu. A file selector appears, from which you can select the file name and type you'd like to save the image to. Make sure you're not trying to save the image to the CD-ROM that comes with the book. If you try this, you'll get an error message saying that the save operation wasn't successful, as shown in Figure 1-3.

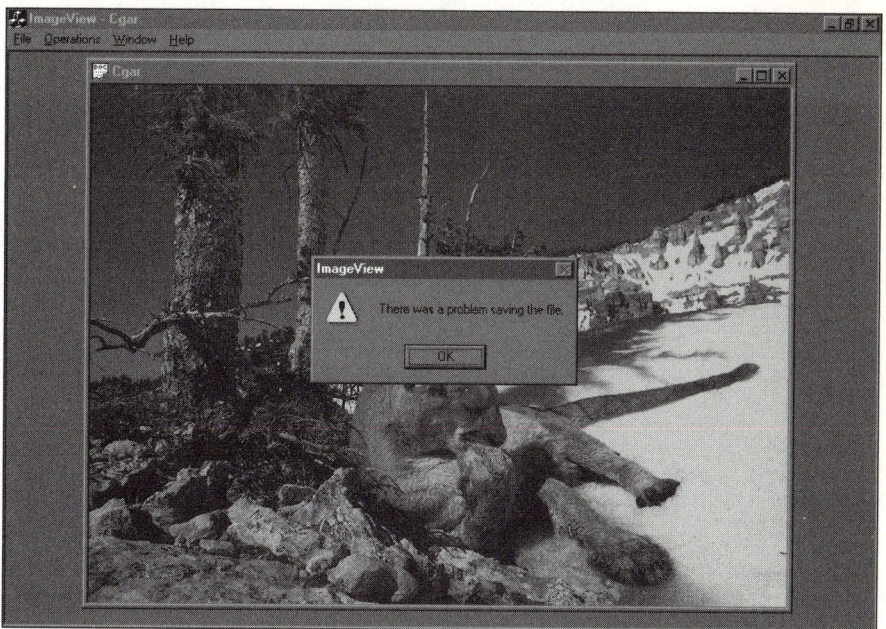

Figure 1-3: ImageView gives you error messages when problems occur during save and load operations.

CIMAGEOBJECT CLASS LIBRARY FUNCTION CALLS

This section is provided as a reference to the public function calls offered by the ImageObject class library. Since the class library was designed with simplicity as a major goal, the calls are simple and easy to use. That's good, because to load and save a picture is easy—it just takes a few lines of code.

You may want to skip over this section and read the section entitled "Behind ImageView," which shows how the calls are used. For some people, it's better to look at the usage of function calls before actually studying the syntax.

CImageObject()

Prototype: `CImageObject( void );`

Purpose: This is the constructor that takes no arguments. It simply creates a CImageObject class and initializes its internal variables.

Arguments: None

Returns: Nothing

CImageObject()

Prototype: `CImageObject( const char *pszFilename, CDC *pDC, int nX,`
`  int nY );`

Purpose: This constructs a CImageObject. The only argument that's required is the filename. If the CDC argument is given, the image will be drawn once it's loaded. If nX or nY are given, their values will be stored and the image will be drawn to that location. Otherwise, the image will always be drawn to coordinates 0, 0.

Arguments: const char *pszFilename
CDC *pDC, Defaults to NULL
int nX, Defaults to -1
int nY, Defaults to -1

Returns: Nothing

Load()

Prototype: `BOOL Load( const char *pszFilename, CDC *pDC, int nX, int nY );`

Purpose: This function loads a file into the CImageObject. The only argument required is the filename. If the CDC argument is given, the image will be drawn once it's loaded. If nX or nY are given, their values will be stored and the image will be drawn to that location. Otherwise, the image will always be drawn to coordinates 0, 0.

Arguments: const char *pszFilename
CDC *pDC, Defaults to NULL
int nX, Defaults to -1
int nY, Defaults to -1

Returns: BOOL: TRUE for success, FALSE for FAIL

GetLastError()

Prototype: `int GetLastError( void );`

Purpose: This function returns the last CImageObject error that occurred. See the Errors.h include file for details.

Arguments: None

Returns: int nErrorNumber

Save()

Prototype: `BOOL Save( const char *pszFilename, int nType );`

Purpose: This function saves the image that currently resides in the CImageObject class. (See GetImageType() for the image type defines.)

Arguments: const char *pszFilename
int nType, Defaults to -1

Returns: BOOL: TRUE for success, FALSE for FAIL

GetWidth()

Prototype: `int GetWidth( void );`

Purpose: This function returns the pixel width of the image.

Arguments: None

Returns: int nWidth

GetHeight()

Prototype: `int GetHeight( void );`

Purpose: This function returns the pixel height of the image.

Arguments: None

Returns: int nHeight

GetNumBits()

Prototype: `int GetNumBits( void );`

Purpose: This function returns the number of pixels for the image: 1, 4, 8, 16, 24, or 32.

Arguments: None

Returns: int nBits

GetNumColors()

Prototype: `int GetNumColors( void );`

Purpose: This function returns the number of colors in the palette. For an image of 16 bits or greater, this value will be zero.

Arguments: None

Returns: int nColors

GetPaletteData()

Prototype: `BOOL GetPaletteData( RGBQUAD *pRGBPalette );`

Purpose: This function fills in the point that's passed in with the current RGB palette data. Nothing will be filled in for images of 16 bits or greater.

Arguments: RGBQUAD *pRGBPalette

Returns: BOOL: TRUE for success, FALSE for FAIL

GetPaletteData()

Prototype: `RGBQUAD *GetPaletteData( void );`

Purpose: This function returns a pointer to the CImageObject's list of palette data. This will return NULL for images of 16 bits or greater.

Arguments: None

Returns: RGBQUAD *PaletteList

GetImageType()

Prototype: `int GetImageType( const char *pFilename );`

Purpose: This function returns the image type. Image types are defined as follows:

```
#define IMAGETYPE_NONE 0
#define IMAGETYPE_BMP  1
#define IMAGETYPE_GIF  2
#define IMAGETYPE_PCX  3
#define IMAGETYPE_TGA  4
#define IMAGETYPE_JPG  5
#define IMAGETYPE_TIF  6
```

Arguments: const char *pFilename

Returns: int nImageType

GetImageInfo()

Prototype: `BOOL GetImageInfo(const char *pszFilename,int *pnWidth, int *pnHeight, int *pnPlanes,int *pnBitsPerPixel, int *pnNumColors );`

Purpose: This function retrieves the image width, height, number of bit planes, number of bits per pixel, and number of colors. Any arguments that are NULL will not be filled in.

Arguments: const char *pszFilename
int *pnWidth, Defaults to NULL
int *pnHeight, Defaults to NULL
int *pnPlanes, Defaults to NULL
int *pnBitsPerPixel, Defaults to NULL
int *pnNumColors, Defaults to NULL

Returns: BOOL: TRUE for success, FALSE for FAIL

Draw()

Prototype: `BOOL Draw( CDC *pDC, int nX, int nY );`

Purpose: This function draws the image to the device context. If the X- and Y-coordinates are not given, the image will be drawn to either 0, 0 or the last valid coordinates that were passed in.

Arguments: CDC *pDC
int nX, Defaults to -1
int nY, Defaults to -1

Returns: BOOL: TRUE for success, FALSE for FAIL

SetPalette()

Prototype: `BOOL SetPalette( CDC *pDC );`

Purpose: This function sets the palette of the device context to that of the image. The palette information is stored in the CImageObject class when the image loads.

Arguments: CDC *pDC

Returns: BOOL: TRUE for success, FALSE for FAIL

SetPaletteCreationType()

Prototype: `void SetPaletteCreationType( int nType );`

Purpose: This function sets the method of palette creation when color reduction to a palettized image is desired. The possible values are defined as follows:

```
define POPULARITY_PALETTE 0
#define MEDIAN_CUT_PALETTE 1
#define FIXED_PALETTE 2
```

Arguments: int nType

Returns: Nothing

GetPaletteCreationType()

Prototype:	`int GetPaletteCreationType( );`
Purpose:	This function returns the palette creation type that will be used on the next color reduction operation.
Arguments:	None
Returns:	int nPaletteCreationType

IsLoaded()

Prototype:	`BOOL IsLoaded( void );`
Purpose:	This function reports whether an image has been loaded or not.
Arguments:	None
Returns:	BOOL: TRUE for success, FALSE for FAIL

Crop()

Prototype:	`BOOL Crop( int nX1, int nY1, int nX2,int nY2 );`
Purpose:	This function crops an image to the given coordinates.
Arguments:	int nX1 int nY1 int nX2 int nY2
Returns:	BOOL: TRUE for success, FALSE for FAIL

Stretch()

Prototype:	`BOOL Stretch( int nNewWidth, int nNewHeight );`
Purpose:	This function stretches (or shrinks) the image to the given width and height.
Arguments:	int nNewWidth int nNewHeight
Returns:	BOOL: TRUE for success, FALSE for FAIL

Rotate()

Prototype: `BOOL Rotate( int nDegrees );`

Purpose: This function rotates the image. Valid arguments are 90, 180, and 270.

Arguments: int nDegrees

Returns: BOOL: TRUE for success, FALSE for FAIL

Invert()

Prototype: `BOOL Invert( void );`

Purpose: This function inverts an image.

Arguments: None

Returns: BOOL: TRUE for success, FALSE for FAIL

Reverse()

Prototype: `BOOL Reverse( void );`

Purpose: This function reverses an image.

Arguments: None

Returns: BOOL: TRUE for success, FALSE for FAIL

ChangeFormat()

Prototype: `BOOL ChangeFormat( int nNewBitsPerPixel );`

Purpose: This function changes an image from its current pixel resolution to the given pixel resolution.

Arguments: int nNewBitsPerPixel

Returns: BOOL: TRUE for success, FALSE for FAIL

GetDib()

Prototype: `HGLOBAL GetDib( void );`

Purpose: This function returns the Dib handle of the currently loaded image.

Arguments: None

Returns: HGLOBAL hDib

GetPalette()

Prototype: `CPalette *GetPalette( void );`

Purpose: This function returns a pointer to the Cpalette class.

Arguments: None

Returns: CPalette *Palette

BEHIND IMAGEVIEW

ImageView displays image files that are in BMP, GIF, JPG, PCX, TGA, or TIF format. You can open as many windows as your system has memory for. You can change attributes of the images, then save them to disk.

ImageView was created with the Visual C++ AppWizard with the following settings:

- ❏ Multiple document interface
- ❏ English language
- ❏ No database support
- ❏ No compound document support
- ❏ No automation or ActiveX control support
- ❏ 3D controls, but no other features
- ❏ Yes source file comments
- ❏ MFC linked as a static library

Opening a File

The file open code can be found in the main application class. It's easier to create a view class from the main application class than from the CMainFrame class. The reason it's easier is that there's a protected OnFileNew() function that can only be called from the main application class. That makes loading an image and creating a new view class easier. Before actually loading the image to display, the code that calls the CFileDialog() common dialog box and creates the view class follows:

The OnFileOpen() Code

```
char szFilter[] = "BMP Files(*.BMP)|*.BMP|GIF
Files(*.GIF)|*.GIF|PCX Files(*.PCX)|*.PCX|Targa
Files(*.TGA)|*.TGA|Jpeg Files(*.JPG)|*.JPG|Tif
Files(*.TIF)|*.TIF||";

void CImageViewApp::OnFileOpen()
{
 static int nIndex = 1;

 CFileDialog FileDlg( TRUE, NULL, NULL,
  OFN_HIDEREADONLY, szFilter );
 FileDlg.m_ofn.nFilterIndex = (DWORD) nIndex;

 if( FileDlg.DoModal() == IDOK ){
  CString PathName = FileDlg.GetPathName();
  PathName.MakeUpper();
  OpenDocumentFile( PathName );
  nIndex = (int) FileDlg.m_ofn.nFilterIndex;
 }

}
```

Saving a File

Saving an image to a file is relatively easy. The first thing to do is use the CFileDialog() common dialog box to let the user select a filename.

One thing that's checked is the bit resolution of the image. The CImageObject class library does not save JPEG images that don't have 24 bits of color resolution. If JPEG is selected and the image isn't a 24-bit image, the process is aborted and the no view window is created.

If the image is to be saved as a JPEG, the quality must be set. A dialog box comes up allowing the user to set the quality if the image will be saved as a JPEG image.

Before the actual image save code is called, the filename must have the correct extension. For instance, if you selected GIF as the file format to which the image will be saved, the filename must have a GIF extension.

After all the preliminaries, the image is saved with the CImageObject class's Save() function. The child window's caption text is set to reflect the new filename. Finally, if the image is a JPEG, it's reloaded so that the saved quality is reflected in what's seen on the screen.

The OnFileSaveAs() Code

```
extern char szFilter[];

void CImageViewDoc::OnFileSaveAs()
{
 static int nIndex = 1;

 CFileDialog FileDlg( FALSE, NULL, NULL,
  OFN_HIDEREADONLY, szFilter );
 FileDlg.m_ofn.nFilterIndex = (DWORD) nIndex;

 if( FileDlg.DoModal() == IDOK ){
 nIndex = (int) FileDlg.m_ofn.nFilterIndex;
 CMainFrame *pFrame =
  (CMainFrame *) AfxGetMainWnd();
 CChildFrame *pChild =
 (CChildFrame *) pFrame->MDIGetActive();
 CImageViewView *pView =
 (CImageViewView *) pChild->GetActiveView();

 if( nIndex == 5 ){
 if(pView->m_pImageObject->GetNumBits()!=24){
   AfxMessageBox( "The image must be 24 bits\
        of color resolution to save as JPEG" );
   return;
   }
 CBrightness Brightness;
 strcpy(Brightness.m_szTitle,"Set Quality");
 strcpy( Brightness.m_szLabel, "Quality" );
 if( Brightness.DoModal() != IDOK ) return;
 if( pView->m_pImageObject != NULL )
  pView->m_pImageObject->SetQuality(
    Brightness.m_nBrightness / 2 );
 }
```

```
    if( pView->m_pImageObject != NULL ){

  CString PathName = FileDlg.GetPathName();
  int nFindIndex = PathName.Find( "." );
  if( nFindIndex != -1 )
   PathName = PathName.Left( nFindIndex );
  PathName +=
   CImageObject::szExtensions[nIndex-1];
  if(!pView->m_pImageObject->Save(PathName))
   AfxMessageBox( "There was a problem\
       saving the file." );
  else{
   CString FileName = FileDlg.GetFileName();
   nFindIndex = FileName.Find( "." );
   if( nFindIndex != -1 )
    FileName = FileName.Left( nFindIndex );
   FileName +=
    CImageObject::szExtensions[nIndex-1];
   FileName.MakeUpper();
   pChild->SetWindowText( FileName );

   SetPathName( PathName );

   if( nIndex == 5 ){
    pView->m_pImageObject->Load( PathName );
    pView->InvalidateRect( NULL, FALSE );
    pView->UpdateWindow();
    }
   }
  }
 }

 }
```

Drawing

All of the image drawing and loading happens in the view class's
OnDraw() function. A member variable of the view class named
m_bImageLoaded keeps track of whether an image has been loaded. If
an attempt to load the image hasn't already been made, it's done here in
the OnDraw() function. Loading an image couldn't be easier: the only
thing required is to create a new CImageClass with the new operator and
pass the filename. It initializes itself, loads the image, and makes any
adjustments necessary. Message boxes are displayed if the CImageObject
class couldn't be created or if the image wasn't successfully loaded.

The view window is then given the image size so that the scroll bars know how to respond to window resizing. A SetWindowPos() function is made so that the child window will resize to be exactly large enough to accommodate the image. If the image is too big for the screen itself, an adjustment is made so that the child window doesn't exceed the size of the physical screen. (That adjustment is made in the CChildFrm class.)

The last thing in the OnDraw() function is the actual image drawing code. An attempt is made each time to reset the palette. For most images today with 16, 24, and 32 bits of color resolution, the palette won't be set. This will only happen for 256-color images.

The OnDraw() Code

```
void CImageViewView::OnDraw(CDC* pDC)
{
CImageViewDoc* pDoc = GetDocument();
ASSERT_VALID(pDoc);

if( !m_bImageLoaded ){

 CString PathName = pDoc->GetPathName ();

 BeginWaitCursor ();
 m_pImageObject =
  new CImageObject( PathName.GetBuffer( 3 ),
  pDC );
 EndWaitCursor ();
 if( m_pImageObject == NULL ){
 AfxMessageBox( "Could not create image!" );
 return;
 }
 if( m_pImageObject->GetDib() == NULL ){
 AfxMessageBox( "Could not load image!" );
 return;
 }

 CSize SizeTotal;
 SizeTotal.cx = m_pImageObject->GetWidth();
 SizeTotal.cy = m_pImageObject->GetHeight();
 SetScrollSizes (MM_TEXT, SizeTotal);

 CMainFrame *pFrame =
 (CMainFrame *) AfxGetMainWnd();
 CChildFrame *pChild =
 (CChildFrame *) pFrame->MDIGetActive();
```

```
pChild->m_nWidth =
 m_pImageObject->GetWidth();
pChild->m_nHeight =
 m_pImageObject->GetHeight();
pChild->SetWindowPos( NULL, 0, 0, 2500,
 2500, SWP_NOZORDER | SWP_NOMOVE );

m_bImageLoaded = TRUE;
 }

OnPrepareDC (pDC);
if( GetFocus() == this )
 m_pImageObject->SetPalette( pDC );
m_pImageObject->Draw( pDC );

if( m_pTracker != NULL && m_bCropBoxShowing )
 m_pTracker->Draw( pDC );
}
```

LOADING & DISPLAYING IMAGES IN A NUTSHELL

In order to load an image, the following code is all you need:

```
CImageObject *pImageObject;
ImageObject =
 new CImageObject( "IMAGE.BMP" );
```

Make sure the CImageObject variable isn't local or it'll go out of scope and you won't be able to use it again. Make sure you delete the CImageObject before leaving the application, too.

Displaying an image that's already been loaded is also simple. Assuming you're doing it from the OnDraw() function, you'll already have a device context pointer. Here's the code you need:

```
pImageObject->Draw( pDC );
```

Optional second and third parameters let you specify the X- and Y-coordinates to which the image will be drawn. For instance, the following code would be used to draw an image at screen coordinates of 10, 20:

```
pImageObject->Draw( pDC, 10, 20 );
```

If you're not drawing from the OnDraw() function, you'll need to get a device context. The code for drawing from any other function of the view class follows:

```
CClientDC ClientDC( this );
pImageObject->Draw( &ClientDC );
```

CREATING PROGRAMS THAT USE IMAGES

The following five hands-on exercises will get you warmed up so that you can move on to create your own masterpieces. Going through them won't take very long, and the investment of time will be well worth it, since you'll then have mastered loading and displaying images.

You may be asking why you should type in the code for each exercise. Why not just load the project from the CD-ROM? Take my word for it, you learn by doing, not just reading.

Hands-On 1: Loading & Displaying an Image

The first thing to do is simply load the program and display an image. The fancy stuff can come later. But for now, this first exercise keeps things really simple.

The program you'll create uses the CImageObject class constructor to initialize the image class and load the image. The CImageObject's SetPalette() function is used from the View class's OnDraw() function so that the palette is always correct if this View window is in focus. The last of the CImageObject function calls used is the Draw() function.

Follow the steps correctly and you'll be amazed at how easy it is to load and display an image. Figure 1-4 shows what the program looks like when it runs.

Figure 1-4: The first hands-on exercise will get you up and going with a simple program that loads and displays a single image.

1. Create a Visual C++ project named HandsOn1_1 with the following attributes:

   ❑ Single-document interface

   ❑ English language

   ❑ No database support

   ❑ No compound document support

   ❑ No automation or ActiveX control support

   ❑ 3D controls, but no other features

   ❑ No source file comments

   ❑ Link MFC as a static library

2. Select Settings from the Project menu. Choose the Link tab. Add the following libraries to the Object/library modules field. The libraries for the release and debug versions are different. Both are listed below.

Release Project Libraries	Debug Project Libraries
ImageLoad.lib	ImageLoad.lib
ImageObject.lib	ImageObjectD.lib

3. Set the Active Configuration to Win32 Release.

4. Copy the file BIRDPIC1.BMP from the \IMAGES\Samples directory on the CD to the newly created project directory.

5. Add the following includes to the HandsOn1_1View.h file:

```
#include "ImageObject.h"
```

6. Add the following variable declarations to the CHandsOn1_1View class in the HandsOn1_1View.h file:

```
public:
 CImageObject *m_pImageObject[4];
```

7. Add the following code to the CHandsOn1_1View constructor:

```
CHandsOn1_1View::CHandsOn1_1View()
{
 m_pImageObject = NULL;
}
```

8. Add the following code to the CHandsOn1_1View destructor:

```
CHandsOn1_1View::~CHandsOn1_1View()
{
 if( m_pImageObject != NULL )
  delete m_pImageObject;
}
```

9. Edit the OnDraw function in the CHandsOn1_1View class in the HandsOn1_1View.cpp file as follows:

```
void CHandsOn1_1View::OnDraw(CDC* pDC)
{
 CHandsOn1_1Doc* pDoc = GetDocument();
 ASSERT_VALID(pDoc);

 if( m_pImageObject == NULL ){

  BeginWaitCursor ();
  m_pImageObject =
   new CImageObject( "BIRDPIC1.BMP", pDC );
  EndWaitCursor ();
  if( m_pImageObject == NULL ){
   AfxMessageBox( "Could not create image!" );
   return;
  }

 }

 if( m_pImageObject != NULL ){
  if( GetFocus() == this )
   m_pImageObject->SetPalette( pDC );
  m_pImageObject->Draw( pDC );
 }
}
```

10. Compile and run the program.

When the program runs, you'll see an image appear in the view window as shown in Figure 1-4. When the window resizes and moves, the image redraws as it should. If the image has an associated palette, the palette is set when the image is redrawn.

Hands-On 2: Loading Four Images

In this exercise you'll load four images. Only one will be displayed at a time, though. To change the image that's displayed, simply click the left mouse button in the view window. The first picture comes up by default, as shown in Figure 1-5. This exercise differs from the first in that it loads four images into an array of four CImageObject classes.

Figure 1-5: The first picture is all you see when the program first runs.

1. Create a Visual C++ project named HandsOn1_2 with the following attributes:

   ❏ Single-document interface

   ❏ English language

   ❏ No database support

   ❏ No compound document support

   ❏ No automation or ActiveX control support

   ❏ 3D controls, but no other features

   ❏ No source file comments

   ❏ Link MFC as a static lib

2. Select Settings from the Project menu. Choose the Link tab. Add the following libraries to the Object/library modules field. The libraries for the release and debug versions are different. Both are listed below.

Release Project Libraries	Debug Project Libraries
ImageLoad.lib	ImageLoad.lib
ImageObject.lib	ImageObjectD.lib

3. Set the Active Configuration to Win32 Release.

4. Copy the following files from the IMAGES\Samples directory on the CD to the newly created project directory:

```
PIC1.BMP
PIC2.BMP
PIC3.BMP
PIC4.BMP
```

5. Add the following include to the HandsOn1_2View.h file:

```
#include "ImageObject.h"
```

6. Add the following variable declarations to the CHandsOn1_2View class in the HandsOn1_2View.h file:

```
public:
 CImageObject *m_pImageObject[4];
 int m_nWhichImage;
```

7. Add the following code to the CHandsOn1_2View constructor:

```
CHandsOn1_2View::CHandsOn1_2View()
{
 m_nWhichImage = 0;

 for( int i=0; i<4; i++ )
  m_pImageObject[i] = NULL;
}
```

8. Add the following code to the CHandsOn1_2View destructor:

```
CHandsOn1_2View::~CHandsOn1_2View()
{
 for( int i=0; i<4; i++ )
  if( m_pImageObject[i] != NULL )
    delete m_pImageObject[i];
}
```

9. Edit the OnDraw function in the CHandsOn1_2View class in the HandsOn1_2View.cpp file as follows:

```
void CHandsOn1_2View::OnDraw(CDC* pDC)
{
 CHandsOn1_2Doc* pDoc = GetDocument();
 ASSERT_VALID(pDoc);

 static char *szFileNames[] = {
  "PIC1.BMP", "PIC2.BMP",
  "PIC3.BMP", "PIC4.BMP"
  };

 int i;

 for( i=0; i<4; i++ ){
  if( m_pImageObject[i] == NULL ){
   BeginWaitCursor();
   m_pImageObject[i] =
    new CImageObject( szFileNames[i] );
   EndWaitCursor();
   }
  }

 if( m_pImageObject[m_nWhichImage] != NULL ){
  if( GetFocus() == this )
    m_pImageObject[m_nWhichImage]->SetPalette(
     pDC );
  m_pImageObject[m_nWhichImage]->Draw( pDC );
  }

}
```

10. Add the following function with the Class Wizard to the CHandsOn1_2View class in the HandsOn1_2View.h file:

```
Name:OnLButtonDown()   Message:WM_LBUTTONDOWN
```

11. Edit the OnLButtonDown function in the CHandsOn1_2View class in the HandsOn1_2View.cpp file as follows:

```
void CHandsOn1_2View::OnLButtonDown(UINT nFlags, CPoint point)
{
 m_nWhichImage++;
 m_nWhichImage &= 3;
 InvalidateRect( NULL, FALSE );
 UpdateWindow( );
 CView::OnLButtonDown(nFlags, point);
}
```

12. Compile and run the program.

When the program runs, you'll see the image shown in Figure 1-5. Click the mouse in the view window twice (being careful not to quickly double-click), and you'll see the image that's pictured in Figure 1-6.

Figure 1-6: Clicking the mouse twice shows you the third picture, a mountain scene.

27

Hands-On 3: Loading Images Into Multiple View Windows

This hands-on exercise randomly loads one of four images into the child view windows. The images are displayed in the view class's OnDraw() function.

If you're loading images with palettes (images of color resolution less than 16 bits), the images will be displayed in the wrong palette when they're not the active window.

When the program runs, a single window will open with one of four images. The image that appears in the window is selected randomly. Figure 1-7 shows the application when it first runs. This exercise differs from the previous two in that it loads each image into a separate view window.

Figure 1-7: The application displays a single randomly selected image when it first runs.

1. Create a Visual C++ project named HandsOn1_3 with the following attributes:

   ❏ Multiple-document interface

   ❏ English language

   ❏ No database support

❒ No compound document support

❒ No automation or ActiveX control support

❒ 3D controls, but no other features

❒ No source file comments

❒ Link MFC as a static library

2. Select Settings from the Project menu. Choose the Link tab. Add the following libraries to the Object/library modules field. The libraries for the release and debug versions are different. Both are listed below.

Release Project Libraries	Debug Project Libraries
ImageLoad.lib	ImageLoad.lib
ImageObject.lib	ImageObjectD.lib

3. Set the Active Configuration to Win32 Release.

4. Copy the following files from the IMAGES\Samples directory on the CD to the newly created project directory:

```
PIC1.BMP
PIC2.BMP
PIC3.BMP
PIC4.BMP
```

5. Add the following variable declarations to the CHandsOn1_3View class in the HandsOn1_3View.h file:

```
public:
 CImageObject *m_pImageObject;
```

6. Add the following code to the CHandsOn1_3View constructor:

```
CHandsOn1_3View::CHandsOn1_3View()
{
 m_pImageObject = NULL;
}
```

7. Add the following code to the CHandsOn1_3View destructor:

```
CHandsOn1_3View::~CHandsOn1_3View()
{
 if( m_pImageObject != NULL )
  delete m_pImageObject;
}
```

8. Edit the OnDraw function in the CHandsOn1_3View class in the HandsOn1_3View.cpp file as follows:

```
void CHandsOn1_3View::OnDraw(CDC* pDC)
{
CHandsOn1_3Doc* pDoc = GetDocument();
ASSERT_VALID(pDoc);

static char *szFileNames[] = {
"PIC1.BMP", "PIC2.BMP",
"PIC3.BMP", "PIC4.BMP"
};

if( m_pImageObject == NULL ){
BeginWaitCursor();
m_pImageObject =
 new CImageObject( szFileNames[rand()&3] );
EndWaitCursor();
}

if( m_pImageObject != NULL ){
if( GetFocus() == this )
 m_pImageObject->SetPalette( pDC );
m_pImageObject->Draw( pDC );
}

}
```

9. Compile and run the program.

When the application runs, the initial window can be seen. To create new windows, select New from the File menu. The image that's displayed in each newly created window is selected at random. Figure 1-8 shows the application with four windows.

Figure 1-8: The application supports multiple windows. In this example, four have been created.

 ## Hands-On 4: Inverting & Reversing Images

This hands-on exercise loads four images. One of four images can be selected by pressing the 1, 2, 3, or 4 key. To draw an image to the view window, click the left mouse button in the view window. The currently selected image will be drawn.

The biggest difference between this exercise and the previous three is that this one allows users to alter the image. The previous ones simply displayed images.

You can reverse the currently selected image by pressing the R key. You can invert the currently selected image by pressing the I key. The images are restored to their original state when you press the number key corresponding to the image. For instance, you may have image 2 selected as the active image. You can reverse it by pressing the R key. Now you might press the 3 key and the I key, selecting image 3 and inverting it. If you then press the 2 key to get back to image 2, the Z key restores image 2 to its original unreversed state. Figure 1-9 shows an image that's been reversed and drawn to the right of the original image.

Figure 1-9: This shows an image with its reversed counterpart.

1. Create a Visual C++ project named HandsOn1_4 with the following attributes:

   ❐ Single-document interface

   ❐ English language

   ❐ No database support

   ❐ No compound document support

   ❐ No automation or ActiveX control support

   ❐ 3D controls, but no other features

   ❐ No source file comments

   ❐ Link MFC as a static library

2. Select Settings from the Project menu. Choose the Link tab. Add the following libraries to the Object/library modules field. The libraries for the release and debug versions are different. Both are listed below.

Release Project Libraries	Debug Project Libraries
ImageLoad.lib	ImageLoad.lib
ImageObject.lib	ImageObjectD.lib

3. Set the Active Configuration to Win32 Release.

4. Copy the following files from the IMAGES\Samples directory on the CD to the newly created project directory:

```
PIC5.BMP
PIC6.BMP
PIC7.BMP
PIC8.BMP
```

5. Add the following include to the HandsOn1_4View.h file:

```
#include "ImageObject.h"
```

6. Add the following variable declarations to the CHandsOn1_4View class in the HandsOn1_4View.h file:

```
public:
 CImageObject *m_pImageObject[4];
 CImageObject *m_pImage;
 int m_nWhichImage;
```

7. Add the following code to the CHandsOn1_4View constructor:

```
CHandsOn1_4View::CHandsOn1_4View()
{
 m_nWhichImage = 0;

 m_pImage = NULL;

 for( int i=0; i<4; i++ )
  m_pImageObject[i] = NULL;
}
```

8. Add the following code to the CHandsOn1_4View destructor:

```
CHandsOn1_4View::~CHandsOn1_4View()
{
 if( m_pImage )
  delete m_pImage;

 for( int i=0; i<4; i++ )
  if( m_pImageObject[i] != NULL )
   delete m_pImageObject[i];
}
```

9. Edit the OnDraw function in the CHandsOn1_4View class in the HandsOn1_4View.cpp file as follows:

```
void CHandsOn1_4View::OnDraw(CDC* pDC)
{
 CHandsOn1_4Doc* pDoc = GetDocument();
 ASSERT_VALID(pDoc);

 static char *szFileNames[] = {
  "PIC5.BMP", "PIC6.BMP",
  "PIC7.BMP", "PIC8.BMP"
  };

 int i;

 for( i=0; i<4; i++ ){
  if( m_pImageObject[i] == NULL ){
   BeginWaitCursor();
   m_pImageObject[i] =
    new CImageObject( szFileNames[i] );
   EndWaitCursor();
   }
  }

 if( m_pImage == NULL ){
  m_pImage = new CImageObject();
  if( m_pImage != NULL ){
   if( m_pImageObject[m_nWhichImage] != NULL){
    *m_pImage =
      *m_pImageObject[m_nWhichImage];
    }
   }
  }

}
```

10. Add the following functions with the Class Wizard to the CHandsOn1_4View class in the HandsOn1_4View.h file:

```
Name:OnLButtonDown()  Message:WM_LBUTTONDOWN
Name:OnChar()  Message:WM_CHAR
```

11. Edit the OnLButtonDown function in the CHandsOn1_4View class in the HandsOn1_4View.cpp file as follows:

```
void CHandsOn1_4View::OnLButtonDown(UINT nFlags, CPoint point)
{
 if( m_pImage != NULL ){
  CClientDC ClientDC( this );
  int x, y;
  x = point.x - m_pImage->GetWidth() / 2;
  y = point.y - m_pImage->GetHeight() / 2;
  m_pImage->Draw( &ClientDC, x, y );
  }

 CView::OnLButtonDown(nFlags, point);
}
```

12. Edit the OnChar function in the CHandsOn1_4View class in the
    HandsOn1_4View.cpp file as follows:

```
void CHandsOn1_4View::OnChar(UINT nChar, UINT nRepCnt, UINT nFlags)
{

 if( nChar == '1' ){
  m_nWhichImage = 0;
  bChangeImage = TRUE;
  }
 else if( nChar == '2' ){
  m_nWhichImage = 1;
  bChangeImage = TRUE;
  }
 else if( nChar == '3' ){
  m_nWhichImage = 2;
  bChangeImage = TRUE;
  }
 else if( nChar == '4' ){
  m_nWhichImage = 3;
  bChangeImage = TRUE;
  }
 else if( toupper( nChar ) == 'R' ){
  if( m_pImage != NULL ){
   m_pImage->Reverse();
   }
  }
 else if( toupper( nChar ) == 'I' ){
  if( m_pImage != NULL ){
   m_pImage->Invert();
   }
  }
```

```
if( m_pImage != NULL && bChangeImage ){
 if( m_pImageObject[m_nWhichImage] != NULL ){
  *m_pImage = *m_pImageObject[m_nWhichImage];
  }
 }

CView::OnChar(nChar, nRepCnt, nFlags);
}
```

13. Compile and run the program.

When the application runs, you can click anywhere in the view window to draw one of the four pictures. Figure 1-10 shows an image and its inverted counterpart drawn below it.

Figure 1-10: You can invert images for interesting effects.

Hands-On 5: Cropping & Resizing Images

The last hands-on exercise in this chapter crops and resizes a single image in a loop controlled by a timer. This exercise adds the ability for users to crop and resize.

1. Create a Visual C++ project named HandsOn1_5 with the following attributes:

    ❏ Single-document interface

    ❏ English language

    ❏ No database support

    ❏ No compound document support

    ❏ No automation or ActiveX control support

    ❏ 3D controls, but no other features

    ❏ No source file comments

    ❏ Link MFC as a static library

2. Set the Active Configuration to Win32 Release.

3. Add the following include to the HandsOn1_5View.h file:

    ```
    #include "ImageObject.h"
    ```

4. Add the following variable declarations to the CHandsOn1_5View class in the HandsOn1_5View.h file:

    ```
    public:
     CImageObject *m_pImageObject;
     CImageObject *m_pImage;
     int m_nCropOrStretch;
     int m_nStep;
    ```

5. Add the following code to the CHandsOn1_5View constructor:

    ```
    CHandsOn1_5View::CHandsOn1_5View()
    {
     m_pImageObject = NULL;
     m_pImage = NULL;
     m_nCropOrStretch = 0;
     m_nStep = 1;
    }
    ```

6. Add the following code to the CHandsOn1_5View destructor:

```
CHandsOn1_5View::~CHandsOn1_5View()
{
 if( m_pImageObject != NULL )
  delete m_pImageObject;
 if( m_pImage != NULL )
  delete m_pImage;
}
```

7. Edit the OnDraw function in the CHandsOn1_5View class in the HandsOn1_5View.cpp file as follows:

```
void CHandsOn1_5View::OnDraw(CDC* pDC)
{
 CHandsOn1_5Doc* pDoc = GetDocument();
 ASSERT_VALID(pDoc);

 if( m_pImageObject == NULL ){
  m_pImageObject =
   new CImageObject( "PIC9.BMP" );
  }

 if( m_pImage != NULL ){
  if( GetFocus() == this )
   m_pImage->SetPalette( pDC );
  m_pImage->Draw( pDC );
  }

}
```

8. Add the following functions with the Class Wizard to the CHandsOn1_5View class in the HandsOn1_5View.h file:

```
Name:OnCreate()  Message:WM_CREATE
Name:OnTimer()  Message:WM_TIMER
```

9. Edit the OnCreate function in the CHandsOn1_5View class in the HandsOn1_5View.cpp file as follows:

```
int CHandsOn1_5View::OnCreate(LPCREATESTRUCT lpCreateStruct)
{
return -1;
   SetTimer( 1, 1000, NULL );
return 0;
}
```

10. Edit the OnTimer function in the CHandsOn1_5View class in the HandsOn1_5View.cpp file as follows:

```cpp
void CHandsOn1_5View::OnTimer(UINT nIDEvent)
{
 if( m_pImageObject != NULL ){

  if( m_pImage != NULL )
   delete m_pImage;

  m_pImage = new CImageObject();
  if( m_pImage == NULL ) goto BailOut;

  *m_pImage = *m_pImageObject;
  int nWidth = m_pImageObject->GetWidth();
  int nHeight = m_pImageObject->GetHeight();

  int nWidthCenter, nHeightCenter;

  int nNewWidth = ( nWidth * m_nStep ) / 5;
  int nNewHeight = ( nHeight * m_nStep ) / 5;

  if( m_nCropOrStretch == 0 ){
   nWidthCenter = nWidth / 2;
   nHeightCenter = nHeight / 2;
   m_pImage->Crop(
    nWidthCenter - ( nNewWidth / 2 ),
    nHeightCenter - ( nNewHeight / 2 ),
    nWidthCenter + ( nNewWidth / 2 ),
    nHeightCenter + ( nNewHeight / 2 ) );
   }

  else m_pImage->Stretch( nNewWidth * 2,
   nNewHeight * 2 );
  }

 m_nStep++;
 if( m_nStep > 5 ){
  m_nStep = 1;
  m_nCropOrStretch ^= 1;
  }

 InvalidateRect( NULL, TRUE );
 UpdateWindow();
```

```
BailOut:
 CView::OnTimer(nIDEvent);
}
```

11. Compile and run the program.

ON THE WEB

There are many Web sites dedicated to supporting programmers who use images in their programs. Here's a short sampling:

Softel vdm

Softel vdm is a developer and publisher of programmer productivity tools for Windows, specializing in ActiveX and DLL-based custom controls and development tools for the professional Windows programmer. (See Figure 1-11.)

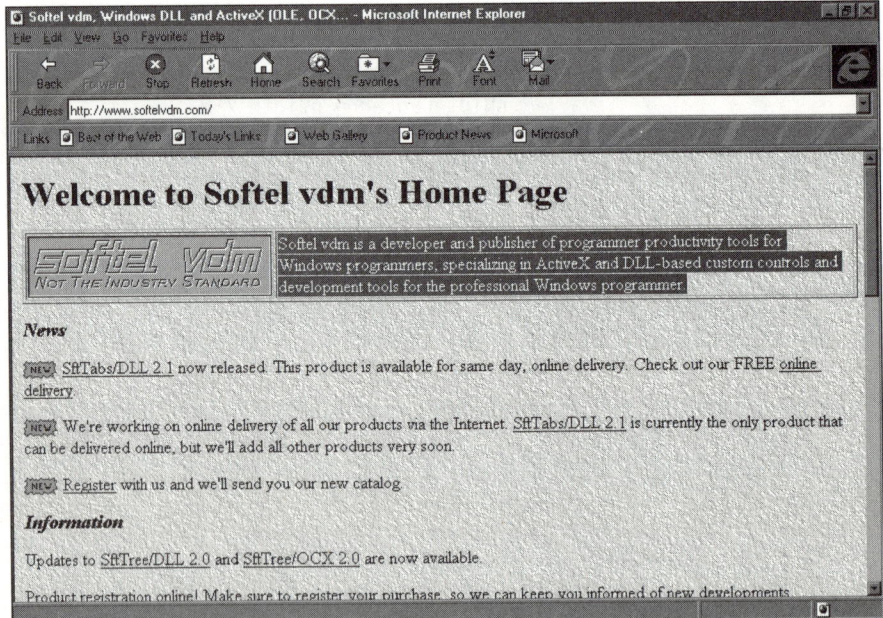

Figure 1-11: Softel vdm offers a variety of products related to images.

LeadTools Pro 6.0 for Windows

LeadTools offers several programming libraries in one toolkit. It offers everything developers need to integrate black-and-white, grayscale, and color images into their applications. The toolkit contains a variety of run times depending upon the package you choose. See Figure 1-12.

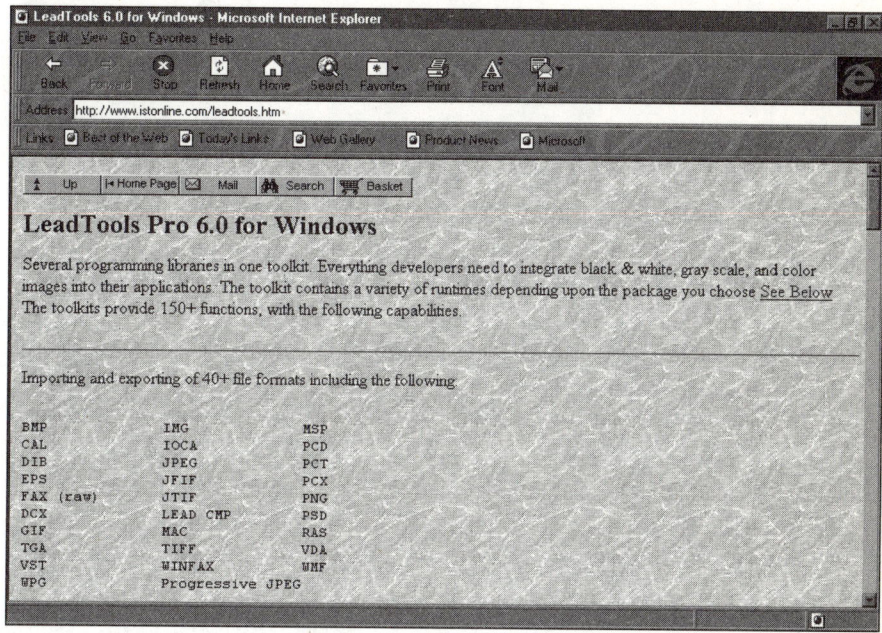

Figure 1-12: LeadTools offers toolkits that do everything but wash windows.

AccuSoft

AccuSoft Corporation is in its second decade of excellence in imaging toolkits. AccuSoft is a software development company specializing in high-performance imaging technologies used in thousands of applications by companies such as Microsoft, America Online, Kodak, Corel, Micron, Softkey, and Hewlett-Packard. See Figure 1-13.

Figure 1-13: AccuSoft, one of the industry leaders, has much to offer at its Web site.

SHAREWARE & COMMERCIAL DEMOS

You may at some point outgrow the CImageObject class library that comes with this book. For this reason, we're showing two commercial packages you can buy and use.

ImageGear

This package is published by AccuSoft and does more than I can ever imagine using. The demo can be found in the IMAGES\demos directory with the filename SETUP1.EXE. See Figure 1-14.

LeadTools Demo

Another great package is published by LeadTools. A fantastic demo can be found in the IMAGES\demos directory with the filename DEMO32.ZIP. See Figure 1-15.

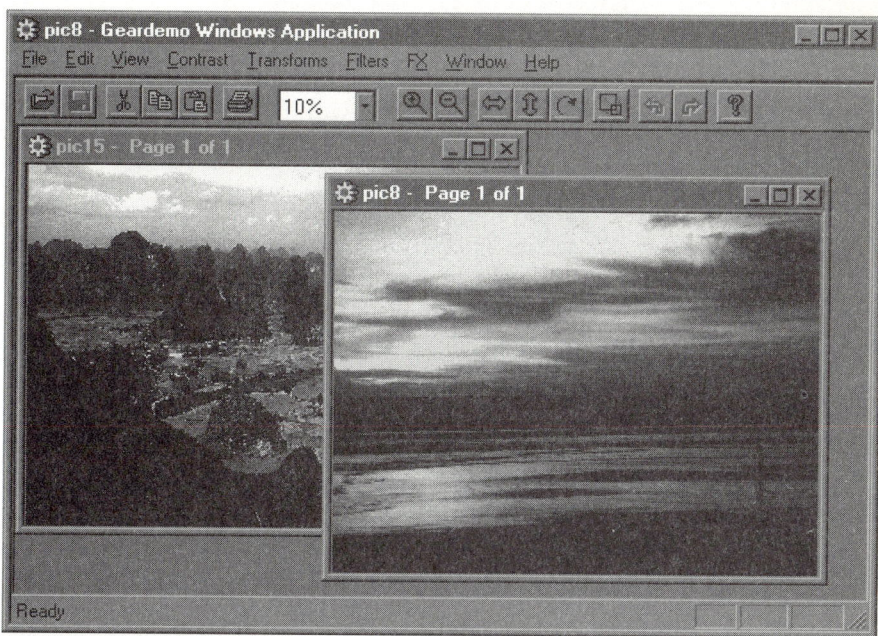

Figure 1-14: AccuSoft's ImageGear is one of the best imaging packages available.

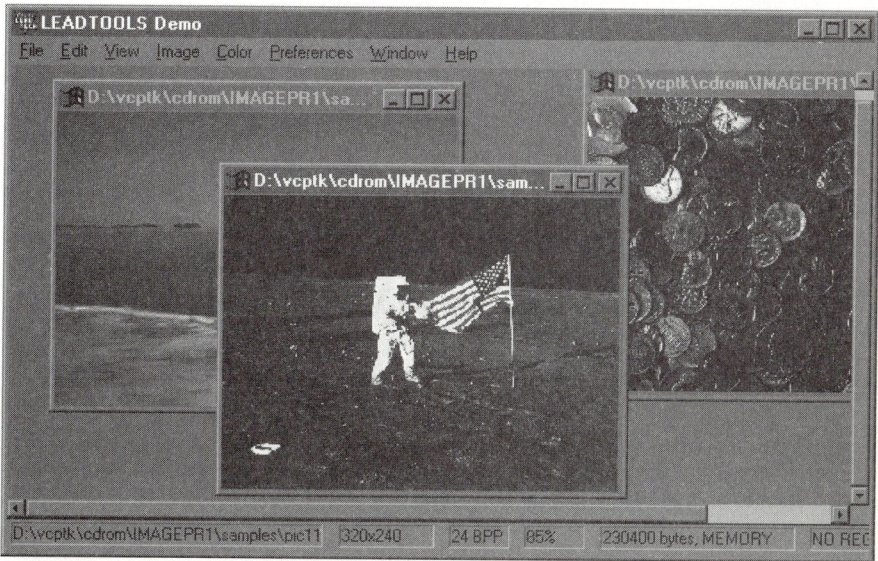

Figure 1-15: LeadTools's programmer's toolkit offers the full gamut of image tools, as illustrated in their demo.

Moving On

Images will make your application look great. You'll have the competitive edge you need. And displaying images has never been as easy. Just link in the CImageObject library class and add a few lines of code to your program.

And that's not the end. The next two chapters talk about image processing. They show you how to take loaded images and manipulate them so you can get much more use out of every single image.

Send me your applications at ivt-rcl@interpath.com. I'd love to see what you can come up with.

Chapter 2

Screen Effects

Delight in splendor is no more than happiness with little, for both have their appeal.

-Euripedes

I love fireworks. I love the vivid colors and the powerful explosions. Most people feel the same way. Each July fourth when I take my children to the local fireworks display, I hear the oohs and ahs all across the park.

Screen effects in software applications are similar to fireworks in many ways. They're not necessary, but most people love them. I often demonstrate applications of my own creation to computer professionals. The predictable reactions are, "Nice idea," or "The interface is easy to use." But if I insert a screen effect where the program changes gears, going from one screen to another, I get a much more enthusiastic reaction—even from seasoned computer professionals.

In today's markets, both commercial and shareware, applications are very sophisticated and advanced. With all of these programs competing for attention, you need a way to be noticed—to make your demonstrations memorable. And if you try to sell your product (or get registrations), screen effects may be the edge you need.

THE SCREENEFFECTS CLASS LIBRARY

The ScreenEffects class library requires the ImageObject library. The ImageObject library loads the images and then sends them on to the ScreenEffects library; therefore, the ScreenEffects library doesn't have to have all of the additional code necessary for loading images.

The ScreenEffects library is simple to use. A few lines of code will create and perform screen effects. There are enough options to choose from so that your programs won't be boring. You can wipe left, right, up, and down. You can create spiral effects. You can fade in and out of images.

 All source code and support files to rebuild the ScreenEffects library can be found in the SEFFECTS\ScreenLibrary directory on the CD-ROM that comes with this book.

The ScreenEffects Demo

 We've built a simple demonstration program that shows what the ScreenEffects class library can do. The program can be found in the SEFFECTS\ScreenEffectsDemo directory on the CD-ROM. Using File Manager or Program Manager, run the program named ScreenEffects-Demo.EXE. It's a multiple-document program. When it first runs, all you'll see is an empty application window as shown in Figure 2-1.

Figure 2-1: When ScreenEffectsDemo first runs, you'll see an empty application window.

To start an effect, select New from the File menu. You'll see the mouse cursor change to a "wait" shape while the images are loaded. Once all the images are loaded, the jet will scroll across the screen and the window will have a full-size image once it's done. Additional effect windows can be opened. Any additional effect windows you open will use the previously loaded images that were loaded when the first effect window was opened.

The Effect menu lets you select the effect type you want; it also lets you start and stop the effects. There are only five effects featured in the demo program, but there are more in the class library. When you select Start Immediate from the Effect menu, the effect starts and retains control of your application until it's done. When you select Start Background from the Effect menu, the effect starts and is serviced in the background while Windows continues to process your application's messages.

Figure 2-2: You can select the effect type and start it in either immediate or background mode.

The effect alternates between a large number of options for each graphic (see Figure 2-3). Sixteen are background colors and four are images. You can select each of the two graphic types with the Graphic 1 and Graphic 2 menus.

Figure 2-3: The effect demo alternates between the graphic types you select.

CScreenEffect Class Library
Function Calls

This section is provided as a reference for the public function calls offered by the CScreenEffect class library. Since the class library was designed with simplicity as a major goal, the calls are simple and easy to use. That's good, because to load and save a picture is easy—it just takes a few lines of code.

You may want to skip over this section and read the section entitled "Behind ScreenEffectsDemo," which shows how the calls are used. For some people, it's better to look at the usage of fucntion calls before actually studying the syntax.

CScreenEffect()

Prototype: `CScreenEffect( int nWidth, int nHeight, Cbitmap *pBitmap, COLORREF`
`Color, CDC *pDC, int nType, int nFlags );`

Purpose: This is the class constructor. It creates the class based on all of the parameters that it is passed, including the bitmap, color, and dimensions.

Arguments: int nWidth
int nHeight
Cbitmap *pBitmap
COLORREF Color
CDC *pDC
int nType (defined as follows)

```
#define NO_EFFECT 0
#define WIPE_RIGHT 1
#define WIPE_LEFT 2
#define WIPE_UP 3
#define WIPE_DOWN 4
#define WIPE_SPIRALIN 5
#define WIPE_SPIRALOUT 6
#define FADE_IN 7
#define FADE_OUT 8
#define BLEND_IN 9
#define TILE_RIGHT 10
#define TILE_LEFT 11
```

int nFlags (defined as follows)

```
#define IMMEDIATE 1
#define START_NOW 2
```

Returns: Nothing

Maintain()

Prototype: `void Maintain( CDC *pDC );`

Purpose: Maintains the screen effect's operation. If the screen effect has been completed, nothing happens. (You can check the public m_bDone variable to see if the screen effect has been completed.)

Arguments: CDC *pDC

Returns: Nothing

49

Redraw()

Prototype: `void Redraw( CDC *pDC );`

Purpose: Redraws the screen effect in its current state. This is usually needed from the view class's OnDraw() function.

Arguments: `CDC *pDC`

Returns: Nothing

InProgress()

Prototype: `BOOL InProgress( void );`

Purpose: This function can be used to determine whether the screen effect is still in progress or it's done.

Arguments: None

Returns: BOOL TRUE is still in progress, FALSE if done

Pause()

Prototype: `void Pause( void );`

Purpose: This function pauses the screen effect so that Maintain() will not advance it any further. The Redraw() function still operates normally, redrawing the screen effect in its current state.

Arguments: None

Returns: Nothing

Halt()

Prototype: `void Halt( void );`

Purpose: This function halts the screen effect. Once halted, it will report being finished.

Arguments: None

Returns: Nothing

Start()

Prototype: `void Start( int Width, int Height, Cbitmap *Bitmap, COLORREF Color, CDC *pDC, int Type, int Flags );`

Purpose: This function starts the screen effect.

Arguments:
int Width
int Height
CBitmap *Bitmap
COLORREF Color
CDC *pDC
int Type, Defaults to WIPE_RIGHT
int Flags, Defaults to IMMEDIATE | START_NOW

Returns: Nothing

ChangeGraphic()

Prototype: `void ChangeGraphic( Cbitmap *pBitmap, COLORREF Color );`

Purpose: This function changes the graphic the screen effect will use.

Arguments:
Cbitmap *pBitmap
COLORREF Color

Returns: Nothing

BEHIND SCREENEFFECTSDEMO

ScreenEffectsDemo was created with the Visual C++ AppWizard with the following settings:

- ❏ Multiple-document interface
- ❏ English language
- ❏ No database support
- ❏ No compound document support
- ❏ No automation or ActiveX control support
- ❏ 3D controls, but no other features
- ❏ Yes source file comments
- ❏ MFC linked as a static library

Drawing the Image

The images are drawn in the program's view class's OnDraw() function. It's much more convenient to perform graphics operations from the OnDraw() function, since a device context pointer is passed in. You don't have to declare a device context object; you can just use the one that comes with the OnDraw() function.

The initial picture loading happens in the OnDraw() function when the first child window is opened. The bitmaps are only loaded once and used for each screen effect class that's created. All variables for the bitmaps, including the ImageObject classes, are static in the MAINFRM.CPP module. The ImageObject classes are deleted in the CMainFrame class destructor. The Cbitmap objects delete the GDI object in their own destructors.

Four images, PIC1.BMP, PIC2.BMP, PIC3.BMP, and PIC4.BMP, are loaded into CImageObject classes. If the bitmaps haven't been loaded, the OnDraw() function simply loops through four times and creates all four CImageObject classes.

There's code in OnDraw() that matches the 16 color values to the closest system palette colors it can find. This code ensures that the brushes are solid colors and not dithered.

Two screen effect classes are created. The program then alternates between these two screen effects each time users start an effect (whether it's immediate or background). Most of the information needed by the screen effect is given in the constructor. The screen width and height, the bitmap class pointer, the color value, the device context pointer, the effect type, and the flags are all passed to the constructor. When the program first starts, the first effect seen is the one that wipes the jet to the right.

If the screen effects have already been created, then the OnDraw() function is called when a redraw message has been generated. To redraw the screen from a CScreenEffect class, you simply call Redraw() and the screen effect class does the rest.

The OnDraw() Code

```
void CScreenEffectsDemoView::OnDraw(CDC* pDC)
{
CScreenEffectsDemoDoc* pDoc = GetDocument();
ASSERT_VALID(pDoc);

if( !g_bBitmapsLoaded ){
 BeginWaitCursor();
```

```
static char *szPictureNames[] = {
 "PIC1.PCX", "PIC2.PCX",
 "PIC3.PCX", "PIC4.PCX" };

for( int i=0; i<4; i++ ){
 g_pImageObject[i] =
  new CImageObject( szPictureNames[i] );
 if( g_pImageObject[i] == NULL ){
  AfxMessageBox( "Could not create image!");
  i = 4;
  }
 else{
  CDC WorkDC;
  WorkDC.CreateCompatibleDC( pDC );
  g_Bitmap[i].CreateCompatibleBitmap( pDC,
   g_pImageObject[i]->GetWidth(),
   g_pImageObject[i]->GetHeight() );
  CBitmap *pOldBitmap =
(CBitmap *)WorkDC.SelectObject(&g_Bitmap[i]);
  g_pImageObject[i]->Draw( &WorkDC );
  WorkDC.SelectObject( pOldBitmap );
  }
 }

for( int j=0; j<16; j++ )
 Colors[j]=pDC->GetNearestColor(Colors[j]);

EndWaitCursor();
g_bBitmapsLoaded = TRUE;
 }

if( !m_bEffectsCreated ){
 if( pDoc->m_nEffect[0] < 16 )
  m_pEffect[0] = new CScreenEffect( 640, 480,
   NULL, Colors[pDoc->m_nEffect[0]], pDC,
   pDoc->m_nEffectType, IMMEDIATE|START_NOW);
 else m_pEffect[0] = new CScreenEffect( 640,
   480, &g_Bitmap[pDoc->m_nEffect[0]-16], 0,
pDC,pDoc->m_nEffectType,IMMEDIATE|START_NOW);
 if( pDoc->m_nEffect[1] < 16 )
  m_pEffect[1] = new CScreenEffect( 640, 480,
  NULL, Colors[pDoc->m_nEffect[1]], pDC,
  pDoc->m_nEffectType, 0 );
 else m_pEffect[1] = new CScreenEffect( 640,
  480, &g_Bitmap[pDoc->m_nEffect[1]-16], 0,
```

53

```
     pDC, pDoc->m_nEffectType, 0 );
  m_nCurrentEffect ^= 1;
  m_bEffectsCreated = TRUE;
  }
 else{
  if( m_pEffect[0]->m_bDone &&
   m_pEffect[1]->m_bDone ){
   m_pEffect[m_nCurrentEffect^1]->Redraw(pDC);
   }
  else if( m_pEffect[0]->m_bDone &&
   !m_pEffect[1]->m_bDone ){
   m_pEffect[0]->Redraw( pDC );
   m_pEffect[1]->Redraw( pDC );
   }
  else{
   m_pEffect[1]->Redraw( pDC );
   m_pEffect[0]->Redraw( pDC );
   }
  }

 }
```

Pausing the Effect

At some point, you may want to pause the screen effect. There are many reasons your users might want to do this. You might even want to pause the screen effect in response to some external events such as incoming modem data. The CScreenEffect's Pause() function can be used just for this purpose—to pause the animation.

This code is called in response to a menu-generated message. The Pause() function call toggles the state of the screen effect between paused and unpaused. The first time this call is made, it pauses; the next time it unpauses; the next it pauses; and so forth.

The OnEffectPause() Code

```
void CScreenEffectsDemoView::OnEffectPause()
{

    if(m_pEffect[m_nCurrentEffect]->m_bStarted)
    m_pEffect[m_nCurrentEffect]->Pause();

}
```

Starting the Effect

Users who run the ScreenEffectsDemo program will need to start the screen effect. There are two menu items that let them start the effects. One can be found in the Start Immediate menu entry in the Effect menu.

This code is called in response to a menu-generated message. It starts the currently selected effect. This can be either effect 0 or effect 1. The effect number alternates each time a screen effect is executed.

When the OnEffectStart() code is called, it calls theCScreenEffect function Start(). This routine needs all of the information to correctly carry out the screen effect. The screen width and height, the bitmap class pointer, the color value, the device context pointer, the effect type, and the flags are all passed to the Start() function.

The OnEffectStart() Code

```
void CScreenEffectsDemoView::OnEffectStart()
{
    CScreenEffectsDemoDoc* pDoc =
  GetDocument ();
    CClientDC dc( this );

  if( pDoc->m_nEffect[m_nCurrentEffect] < 16)
  m_pEffect[m_nCurrentEffect]->Start( 640,
  480, NULL,
  Colors[pDoc->m_nEffect[m_nCurrentEffect]],
  &dc, pDoc->m_nEffectType,
  IMMEDIATE | START_NOW );
  else m_pEffect[m_nCurrentEffect]->Start(640,
  480,
    &g_Bitmap[pDoc->m_nEffect[m_nCurrentEffect]-16],
  0, &dc, pDoc->m_nEffectType,
  IMMEDIATE | START_NOW );
    m_nCurrentEffect ^= 1;
  m_pEffect[m_nCurrentEffect]-
>InvalidateEffect();
}
```

Starting the Effect in the Background

Another way to start a screen effect is to select Start Background from the Effect menu. This causes the effect to be started, then the CScreenEffect class maintains it in the background so that your application can go about its other business.

This code is called in response to a menu-generated message. It starts the currently selected effect. This can be either effect 0 or effect 1. The effect number alternates each time a screen effect is executed.

When the OnEffectStart() code is called, it calls the screen effect function Start(). This routine needs all of the information to correctly carry out the screen effect. The screen width and height, the bitmap class pointer, the color value, the device context pointer, the effect type, and the flags are all passed to the Start() function. The differences between this call and the one in OnEffectStart() are the flags that are passed in Start(). In InEffectStart() the flags were IMMEDIATE | START_NOW. Here they are just START_NOW. The screen effect class will perform only the very first draw operation of the effect as a result of this Start() call.

The OnEffectStartBackground() Code

```
void
CScreenEffectsDemoView::OnEffectStartbackground( )
{
    CScreenEffectsDemoDoc* pDoc =
    GetDocument ();
    CClientDC dc( this );

    if( pDoc->m_nEffect[m_nCurrentEffect] < 16)
    m_pEffect[m_nCurrentEffect]->Start( 640,
    480, NULL,
    Colors[pDoc->m_nEffect[m_nCurrentEffect]],
    &dc, pDoc->m_nEffectType, START_NOW );
     else m_pEffect[m_nCurrentEffect]->Start(
    640, 480,
    &g_Bitmap[pDoc->m_nEffect[m_nCurrentEffect]-16],
    0, &dc, pDoc->m_nEffectType, START_NOW );

}
```

Stopping the Effect

Your users might want to stop the screen effect altogether. By selecting Stop from the Effect menu, the current screen effect will stop executing.

This code is called in response to a menu-generated message. It stops the currently executing screen effect.

The OnEffectStop() Code

```
void CScreenEffectsDemoView::OnEffectStop()
{
 m_pEffect[m_nCurrentEffect]->Halt();
}
```

Changing the Graphic

You can change the graphic that the screen effect uses. There are four different images that load when the application first runs. There are also 16 solid colors that can be selected as the graphic for a screen effect.

If you change the graphic type (such as changing from a bitmap to a solid color or changing from one bitmap to another), you need to let the screen effect class know about it. The class function call ChangeGraphic() must be called so that the class will know how to draw the next time an effect is started.

The ChangeGraphic() Code

```
void CScreenEffectsDemoView::ChangeGraphic( void )
{
    CScreenEffectsDemoDoc* pDoc =
  GetDocument();

    if( pDoc->m_nEffect[0] < 16 )
    m_pEffect[0]->ChangeGraphic( NULL,
    Colors[pDoc->m_nEffect[0]] );
    else m_pEffect[0]->ChangeGraphic(
  &g_Bitmap[pDoc->m_nEffect[0]-16], 0 );
    if( pDoc->m_nEffect[1] < 16 )
    m_pEffect[1]->ChangeGraphic( NULL,
    Colors[pDoc->m_nEffect[1]] );
    else m_pEffect[1]->ChangeGraphic(
  &g_Bitmap[pDoc->m_nEffect[1]-16], 0 );

}
```

The Timer

The CScreenEffect class must be maintained on a periodic basis. The best way to do this is from a timer. A timer function will be called regularly (in the case of this program, every 250 milliseconds), and the screen effect will be updated.

This code is called in response to a timer message. It calls the code that maintains the screen effect. If the effect has finished, the variable that keeps track of which effect is being played (0 or 1) is toggled. If the user has selected *continuous* from the menu, then the next screen effect is started.

The OnTimer() Code

```
void CScreenEffectsDemoView::OnTimer(UINT nIDEvent)
{

 if( !m_pEffect[m_nCurrentEffect]->m_bDone ){
  CClientDC dc( this );
  m_pEffect[m_nCurrentEffect]->Maintain( &dc);
  if( m_pEffect[m_nCurrentEffect]->m_bDone ){
   m_nCurrentEffect ^= 1;
   CScreenEffectsDemoDoc* pDoc =
    GetDocument ();
   if( pDoc->m_bContinuous ){
    if( pDoc->m_nEffect[m_nCurrentEffect] <16)
     m_pEffect[m_nCurrentEffect]->Start( 640,
       480, NULL,
     Colors[pDoc->m_nEffect[m_nCurrentEffect]],
       &dc, pDoc->m_nEffectType, START_NOW );
    else m_pEffect[m_nCurrentEffect]->Start(
      640, 480,
      &g_Bitmap[pDoc->m_nEffect[m_nCurrentEffect]-16],
      0, &dc, pDoc->m_nEffectType, START_NOW );
    }
   }
  }

 CView::OnTimer(nIDEvent);
}
```

Screen Effects in a Nutshell

Using the CScreenEffects class is easy. The first thing that must be done is
to load an image with the CImageObject class and then convert it into a
Cbitmap object. Here's a function that loads an image and returns an
allocated Cbitmap class:

```
Cbitmap *LoadAndAllocate( char *pszFilename )
{
// Create the CImageObject and Cbitmap
// classes (the CImageObject constructor
// loads the file...
CImageObject ImageObject( pszFilename );
Cbitmap *pBitmap = new CBitmap;

// Create a working DC and create the bitmap
CClientDC ClientDC( this );
CDC WorkDC;
WorkDC.CreateCompatibleDC( &ClientDC );
pBitmap->CreateCompatibleBitmap( &ClientDC,
  ImageObject.GetWidth(),
  ImageObject.GetHeight() );

// Select the bitmap and draw the image into
// the bitmap
CBitmap *pOldBitmap =
  (CBitmap *) WorkDC.SelectObject( pBitmap );
ImageObject,Draw( &WorkDC );
WorkDC.SelectObject( pOldBitmap );

return( pBitmap );

}
```

With a Cbitmap object, now it's easy to perform a screen effect in
immediate mode. Here's all you have to do:

```
Cbitmap *pBitmap = LoadAndAllocate("PIC.BMP");
CScreenEffect ScreenEffect( 640, 480, pBitmap,
  0, &ClientDC, WIPE_LEFT,
  IMMEDIATE | START_NOW );
```

CREATING PROGRAMS THAT USE SCREEN EFFECTS

The next few sections will give you a series of hands-on exercises, after which you'll have no trouble using the CScreenEffects library in your own applications. They cover all of the functions and show you how to use them.

These sections were written so that every single step is explicitly spelled out. We decided it was better to enable everyone to work through the examples, with almost no chance of going astray, than to cater to those few who never make mistakes.

Hands-On 1: A Simple Screen Effect

It's time to create your own application that displays a screen effect. Follow the creation and implementation steps exactly as they're listed. Your program will work like a charm, and you'll see an application that wipes an image across the application's view window, as shown in Figure 2-4.

Figure 2-4: This example program simply loads the image file named PIC1.BMP and displays it with a screen effect that wipes right.

1. Create a Visual C++ project named HandsOn2_1 with the following attributes:

   ❐ Single-document interface

   ❐ English language

   ❐ No database support

   ❐ No compound document support

   ❐ No automation or ActiveX control support

   ❐ 3D controls, but no other features

   ❐ No source file comments

   ❐ Link MFC as a static library

2. Select Settings from the Project menu. Choose the Link tab. Add the following libraries to the Object/library modules field. The libraries for the release and debug versions are different; both are listed below.

Release Project Libraries	Debug Project Libraries
ImageLoad.lib	ImageLoad.lib
ImageObject.lib	ImageObjectD.lib
ScreenEffects.lib	ScreenEffectsD.lib

3. Set the Active Configuration to Win32 Release.

4. Copy the file PIC1.BMP from the \SEFFECTS\SAMPLES directory on the CD to the newly created project directory.

5. Add the following includes to the HandsOn2_1View.h file:

```
#include "ImageObject.h"
#include "ScreenEffects.h"
```

6. Add the following include to the HandsOn2_1View.h file:

```
#include "MAINFRM.h"
```

7. Add the following variable declarations to the CHandsOn2_1View class in the HandsOn2_1View.h file:

```
public:
 CImageObject *m_pImageObject;
 CScreenEffect *m_pScreenEffect;
 CBitmap m_Bitmap;
```

8. Add the following code to the CHandsOn2_1View constructor:

```
CHandsOn2_1View::CHandsOn2_1View()
{
 m_pImageObject = NULL;
 m_pScreenEffect = NULL;
}
```

9. Add the following code to the CHandsOn2_1View destructor:

```
CHandsOn2_1View::~CHandsOn2_1View()
{
 if( m_pImageObject != NULL )
  delete m_pImageObject;
 if( m_pScreenEffect != NULL )
  delete m_pScreenEffect;
}
```

10. Edit the OnDraw function in the CHandsOn2_1View class in the HandsOn2_1View.cpp file as follows:

```
void CHandsOn2_1View::OnDraw(CDC* pDC)
{
 CHandsOn2_1Doc* pDoc = GetDocument();
 ASSERT_VALID(pDoc);

 if( m_pImageObject == NULL ){

  CMainFrame *pFrame =
   (CMainFrame *) AfxGetMainWnd();
  pFrame->SetWindowPos( NULL, 0, 0,
   326, 275, SWP_NOZORDER | SWP_NOMOVE );

  BeginWaitCursor ();
  m_pImageObject =
   new CImageObject( "PIC1.BMP" );
  EndWaitCursor ();
  if( m_pImageObject == NULL ){
   AfxMessageBox( "Could not create image!" );
   return;
   }
  else if( m_pImageObject->GetDib() == NULL ){
   AfxMessageBox( "Could not load image!" );
   return;
   }
```

```
    CDC WorkDC;
    WorkDC.CreateCompatibleDC( pDC );
    m_Bitmap.CreateCompatibleBitmap( pDC,
     m_pImageObject->GetWidth(),
     m_pImageObject->GetHeight() );
    CBitmap *pOldBitmap =
    (CBitmap *) WorkDC.SelectObject( &m_Bitmap);
    m_pImageObject->Draw( &WorkDC );
    WorkDC.SelectObject( pOldBitmap );

    m_pScreenEffect = new CScreenEffect( 320,
     240, &m_Bitmap, 0, pDC,
     WIPE_RIGHT, IMMEDIATE | START_NOW );

    }

  if( m_pScreenEffect != NULL ){
   if( GetFocus() == this )
    m_pImageObject->SetPalette( pDC );
   m_pScreenEffect->Redraw( pDC );
   }

  }
```

11. Compile and run the program.

When the program runs, you'll see a single image wipe across the screen. It won't do anything else after that. This is, after all, the simplest example in this section. The image will redraw from inside the view class's OnDraw() function.

Hands-On 2: Using Colors for Effects

The next exercise is even easier than the first, since it doesn't load any images. Instead, it simply uses solid colors for its screen effects. It cycles through the first 16 system colors, so the colors you see won't dazzle you. Figure 2-5 shows the program as it wipes across the screen.

This exercise will teach you how to use solid colors for screen effects. Many times this is more desirable for a program, since it doesn't require any loaded images or the time it takes to load the image files.

Figure 2-5: This hands-on exercise is simple because it just uses solid colors for its effects.

1. Create a Visual C++ project named HandsOn2_2 with the following attributes:

   ❏ Single-document interface

   ❏ English language

   ❏ No database support

   ❏ No compound document support

   ❏ No automation or ActiveX control support

   ❏ 3D controls, but no other features

   ❏ No source file comments

   ❏ Link MFC as a static library

2. Select Settings from the Project menu. Choose the Link tab. Add the following libraries to the Object/library modules field. The libraries for the release and debug versions are different; both are listed below.

Release Project Libraries	Debug Project Libraries
ImageLoad.lib	ImageLoad.lib
ImageObject.lib	ImageObjectD.lib
ScreenEffects.lib	ScreenEffectsD.lib

3. Set the Active Configuration to Win32 Release.

4. Add the following include to the HandsOn2_2View.h file:

```
#include "ScreenEffects.h"
```

5. Add the following include to the HandsOn2_2View.h file:

```
#include "MAINFRM.h"
```

6. Add the following variable declarations to the CHandsOn2_2View class in the HandsOn2_2View.h file:

```
public:
 CScreenEffect *m_pScreenEffect;
 int m_nCurrentColor;
```

7. Add the following code to the CHandsOn2_2View constructor:

```
CHandsOn2_2View::CHandsOn2_2View()
{
 m_pScreenEffect = NULL;
 m_nCurrentColor = 1;
}
```

8. Add the following code to the CHandsOn2_2View destructor:

```
CHandsOn2_2View::~CHandsOn2_2View()
{
 if( m_pScreenEffect != NULL )
  delete m_pScreenEffect;
}
```

9. Edit the OnDraw function in the CHandsOn2_2View class in the HandsOn2_2View.cpp file as follows:

```
void CHandsOn2_2View::OnDraw(CDC* pDC)
{
 CHandsOn2_2Doc* pDoc = GetDocument();
 ASSERT_VALID(pDoc);
```

```
if( m_pScreenEffect == NULL ){

  CMainFrame *pFrame =
   (CMainFrame *) AfxGetMainWnd();
  pFrame->SetWindowPos( NULL, 0, 0,
   646, 515, SWP_NOZORDER | SWP_NOMOVE );

  m_pScreenEffect =
   new CScreenEffect( 640, 480,
    NULL, RGB( 0, 0, 0 ), pDC, WIPE_LEFT,
    START_NOW );
   }
  else m_pScreenEffect->Redraw( pDC );

}
```

10. Add the following functions with the Class Wizard to the CHandsOn2_2View class in the HandsOn2_2View.h file:

```
Name:OnCreate()  Message:WM_CREATE
Name:OnTimer()  Message:WM_TIMER
```

11. Edit the OnCreate function in the CHandsOn2_2View class in the HandsOn2_2View.cpp file as follows:

```
int CHandsOn2_2View::OnCreate(LPCREATESTRUCT lpCreateStruct)
{
  return -1;

  SetTimer( 1, 200, NULL );

  return 0;
}
```

12. Edit the OnTimer function in the CHandsOn2_2View class in the HandsOn2_2View.cpp file as follows:

```
void CHandsOn2_2View::OnTimer(UINT nIDEvent)
{
 if( m_pScreenEffect != NULL ){
  CClientDC ClientDC( this );
  m_pScreenEffect->Maintain( &ClientDC );
  if( m_pScreenEffect->m_bDone ){
   m_pScreenEffect->Start( 640, 480,
    NULL,
    GetSysColor( m_nCurrentColor ),
    &ClientDC, WIPE_LEFT,
```

```
        START_NOW );
      m_nCurrentColor++;
      if( m_nCurrentColor >= 10 )
        m_nCurrentColor = 0;
      }
    }

    CView::OnTimer(nIDEvent);
  }
```

13. Compile and run the program.

When the program runs, you'll see 16 system colors take their turn and wipe across the screen. It could make an interesting effect for a program, or it might just be fun to watch the system colors.

 ## Hands-On 3: Using an Image & a Color

This third hands-on exercise combines an image with a color. The image is one of a table full of coins. The color is bright red. Both the image and the solid red color alternately wipe right across the screen as shown in Figure 2-6.

This exercise is valuable because you'll gain experience in mixing images and colors. More complications arise when you do this. Using only images or only colors is much easier, since you can always take the graphic type of the image for granted.

Figure 2-6: This program alternates between an image and a solid color.

1. Create a Visual C++ project named HandsOn2_3 with the following attributes:
   - ❏ Single-document interface
   - ❏ English language
   - ❏ No database support
   - ❏ No compound document support
   - ❏ No automation or ActiveX control support
   - ❏ 3D controls, but no other features
   - ❏ No source file comments
   - ❏ Link MFC as a static library

2. Select Settings from the Project menu. Choose the Link tab. Add the following libraries to the Object/library modules field. The libraries for the release and debug versions are different; both are listed below.

Release Project Libraries	Debug Project Libraries
ImageLoad.lib	ImageLoad.lib
ImageObject.lib	ImageObjectD.lib
ScreenEffects.lib	ScreenEffectsD.lib

3. Set the Active Configuration to Win32 Release.

4. Copy the file PIC2.BMP from the \SEFFECTS\SAMPLES directory on the CD to the newly created project directory.

5. Add the following includes to the HandsOn2_3View.h file:

```
#include "ScreenEffects.h"
#include "ImageObject.h"
```

6. Add the following include to the HandsOn2_3View.h file:

```
#include "MAINFRM.h"
```

7. Add the following variable declarations to the CHandsOn2_3View class in the HandsOn2_3View.h file:

```
public:
 CImageObject *m_pImageObject;
 CScreenEffect *m_pScreenEffect;
 CBitmap m_Bitmap;
 BOOL m_bDisplayingColor;
```

8. Add the following code to the CHandsOn2_3View constructor:

```
CHandsOn2_3View::CHandsOn2_3View()
{
 m_pImageObject = NULL;
 m_pScreenEffect = NULL;
 m_bDisplayingColor = FALSE;
}
```

9. Add the following code to the CHandsOn2_3View destructor:

```
CHandsOn2_3View::~CHandsOn2_3View()
{
 if( m_pImageObject != NULL )
  delete m_pImageObject;
 if( m_pScreenEffect != NULL )
  delete m_pScreenEffect;
}
```

10. Edit the OnDraw function in the CHandsOn2_3View class in the HandsOn2_3View.cpp file as follows:

```
void CHandsOn2_3View::OnDraw(CDC* pDC)
{
 CHandsOn2_3Doc* pDoc = GetDocument();
 ASSERT_VALID(pDoc);

 if( m_pImageObject == NULL ){

  CMainFrame *pFrame =
   (CMainFrame *) AfxGetMainWnd();
  pFrame->SetWindowPos( NULL, 0, 0,
   326, 275, SWP_NOZORDER | SWP_NOMOVE );

  BeginWaitCursor ();
  m_pImageObject =
   new CImageObject( "PIC2.BMP" );
  EndWaitCursor ();
  if( m_pImageObject == NULL ){
   AfxMessageBox( "Could not create image!" );
   return;
  }
  else if( m_pImageObject->GetDib() == NULL ){
   AfxMessageBox( "Could not load image!" );
   return;
  }
```

```
CDC WorkDC;
WorkDC.CreateCompatibleDC( pDC );
m_Bitmap.CreateCompatibleBitmap( pDC,
 m_pImageObject->GetWidth(),
 m_pImageObject->GetHeight() );
CBitmap *pOldBitmap =
(CBitmap *) WorkDC.SelectObject( &m_Bitmap);
m_pImageObject->Draw( &WorkDC );
WorkDC.SelectObject( pOldBitmap );

m_pScreenEffect = new CScreenEffect( 320,
 240, &m_Bitmap, RGB( 255, 0, 0 ), pDC,
 WIPE_RIGHT, START_NOW );

}

if( m_pScreenEffect != NULL ){
 if( GetFocus() == this )
  m_pImageObject->SetPalette( pDC );
 m_pScreenEffect->Redraw( pDC );
 }

}
```

11. Add the following functions with the Class Wizard to the
    CHandsOn2_3View class in the HandsOn2_3View.h file:

    ```
    Name:OnCreate()  Message:WM_CREATE
    Name:OnTimer()  Message:WM_TIMER
    ```

12. Edit the OnCreate function in the CHandsOn2_3View class in the
    HandsOn2_3View.cpp file as follows:

    ```
    int CHandsOn2_3View::OnCreate(LPCREATESTRUCT lpCreateStruct)
    {
      return -1;

     SetTimer( 1, 200, NULL );

     return 0;
    }
    ```

13. Edit the OnTimer function in the CHandsOn2_3View class in the HandsOn2_3View.cpp file as follows:

```
void CHandsOn2_3View::OnTimer(UINT nIDEvent)
{
 if( m_pScreenEffect != NULL ){
  CClientDC ClientDC( this );
  m_pScreenEffect->Maintain( &ClientDC );
  if( m_pScreenEffect->m_bDone ){
   m_bDisplayingColor = !m_bDisplayingColor;
   CBitmap *pBitmap = NULL;
   if( !m_bDisplayingColor )
    pBitmap = &m_Bitmap;
   m_pScreenEffect->ChangeGraphic( pBitmap,
    RGB( 255, 0, 0 ) );
   m_pScreenEffect->Start( 320, 240,
    pBitmap,
    RGB( 255, 0, 0 ),
    &ClientDC, WIPE_RIGHT,
    START_NOW );
  }
 }

 CView::OnTimer(nIDEvent);
}
```

14. Compile and run the program.

When the program runs, you'll see an image of coins wipe right. Solid red will wipe right after that's done. And then it goes back to the coins image.

Hands-On 4: Multiple Screen Effects

The program that you're about to create in this exercise may be your favorite. That's because it has multiple windows, and each one has a randomly selected image and a randomly selected screen effect. Figure 2-7 shows the program when it runs with a single window opened.

This exercise is probably what you'll strive for in your own applications. Multiple screen effects are the best way to give your applications interest and attractiveness.

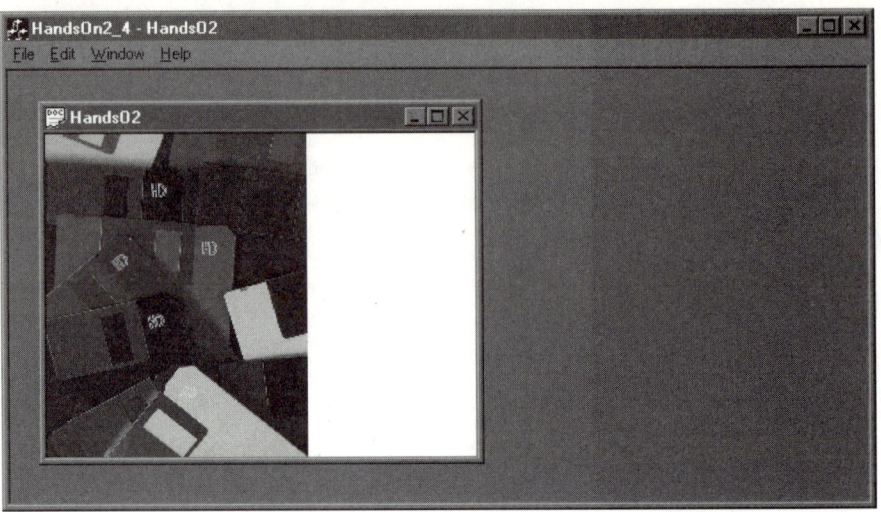

Figure 2-7: You can keep things simple and open a single window to watch one effect.

1. Create a Visual C++ project named HandsOn2_4 with the following attributes:
   - ❑ Multiple-document interface
   - ❑ English language
   - ❑ No database support
   - ❑ No compound document support
   - ❑ No automation or ActiveX control support
   - ❑ 3D controls, but no other features
   - ❑ No source file comments
   - ❑ Link MFC as a static library

2. Select Settings from the Project menu. Choose the Link tab. Add the following libraries to the Object/library modules field. The libraries for the release and debug versions are different; both are listed below.

Release Project Libraries	Debug Project Libraries
ImageLoad.lib	ImageLoad.lib
ImageObject.lib	ImageObjectD.lib
ScreenEffects.lib	ScreenEffectsD.lib

3. Set the Active Configuration to Win32 Release.

4. Copy the following files from the \SEFFECTS\SAMPLES directory on the CD to the newly created project directory:

```
PIC3.BMP
PIC4.BMP
PIC5.BMP
PIC6.BMP
```

5. Add the following includes to the HandsOn2_4View.h file:

```
#include "ScreenEffects.h"
#include "ImageObject.h"
```

6. Add the following includes to the HandsOn2_4View.h file:

```
#include "MAINFRM.h"
#include "CHILDFRM.h"
```

7. Add the following variable declarations to the CHandsOn2_4View class in the HandsOn2_4View.h file:

```
public:
 CImageObject *m_pImageObject;
 CScreenEffect *m_pScreenEffect;
 CBitmap m_Bitmap;
 BOOL m_bDisplayingColor;
 COLORREF m_Color;
 int m_nWhichEffect;
```

8. Add the following code to the CHandsOn2_4View constructor:

```
CHandsOn2_4View::CHandsOn2_4View()
{
 m_pImageObject = NULL;
 m_pScreenEffect = NULL;
 m_bDisplayingColor = FALSE;
 srand( GetTickCount() );
 m_Color = GetSysColor( rand() & 15 );
 do{
  m_nWhichEffect = ( rand() & 7 ) + 1;
  } while( m_nWhichEffect > 6 );
}
```

9. Add the following code to the CHandsOn2_4View destructor:

```
CHandsOn2_4View::~CHandsOn2_4View()
{
 if( m_pImageObject != NULL )
  delete m_pImageObject;
 if( m_pScreenEffect != NULL )
  delete m_pScreenEffect;
}
```

10. Edit the OnDraw function in the CHandsOn2_4View class in the HandsOn2_4View.cpp file as follows:

```
void CHandsOn2_4View::OnDraw(CDC* pDC)
{
 CHandsOn2_4Doc* pDoc = GetDocument();
 ASSERT_VALID(pDoc);

 if( m_pImageObject == NULL ){

  CMainFrame *pFrame =
   (CMainFrame *) AfxGetMainWnd();
  pFrame->SetWindowPos( NULL, 0, 0,
   640, 480, SWP_NOZORDER | SWP_NOMOVE );

  CChildFrame *pChild =
   (CChildFrame *) pFrame->MDIGetActive();
  pChild->SetWindowPos( NULL, 0, 0,
   326, 270, SWP_NOZORDER | SWP_NOMOVE );

  static char *szPics[] = { "PIC3.BMP",
   "PIC4.BMP", "PIC5.BMP", "PIC6.BMP" };

  BeginWaitCursor ();
  m_pImageObject =
   new CImageObject( szPics[rand()&3] );
  EndWaitCursor ();
  if( m_pImageObject == NULL ){
   AfxMessageBox( "Could not create image!" );
   return;
   }
```

```
      else if( m_pImageObject->GetDib() == NULL ){
      AfxMessageBox( "Could not load image!" );
      return;
      }

      CDC WorkDC;
      WorkDC.CreateCompatibleDC( pDC );
      m_Bitmap.CreateCompatibleBitmap( pDC,
       m_pImageObject->GetWidth(),
       m_pImageObject->GetHeight() );
      CBitmap *pOldBitmap =
       (CBitmap *) WorkDC.SelectObject(&m_Bitmap);
      m_pImageObject->Draw( &WorkDC );
      WorkDC.SelectObject( pOldBitmap );

      m_pScreenEffect = new CScreenEffect( 320,
       240, &m_Bitmap, m_Color, pDC,
       m_nWhichEffect, START_NOW );

      }

     if( m_pScreenEffect != NULL ){
     if( GetFocus() == this )
      m_pImageObject->SetPalette( pDC );
     m_pScreenEffect->Redraw( pDC );
     }
}
```

11. Add the following functions with the Class Wizard to the
    CHandsOn2_4View class in the HandsOn2_4View.h file:

    ```
    Name:OnCreate()  Message:WM_CREATE
    Name:OnTimer()  Message:WM_TIMER
    ```

12. Edit the OnCreate function in the CHandsOn2_4View class in the
    HandsOn2_4View.cpp file as follows:

    ```
    int CHandsOn2_4View::OnCreate(LPCREATESTRUCT lpCreateStruct)
    {
      return -1;

     SetTimer( 1, 200, NULL );

      return 0;
    }
    ```

75

13. Edit the OnTimer function in the CHandsOn2_4View class in the HandsOn2_4View.cpp file as follows:

```
void CHandsOn2_4View::OnTimer(UINT nIDEvent)
{
 if( m_pScreenEffect != NULL ){
  CClientDC ClientDC( this );
  m_pScreenEffect->Maintain( &ClientDC );
  if( m_pScreenEffect->m_bDone ){
   m_bDisplayingColor = !m_bDisplayingColor;
   CBitmap *pBitmap = NULL;
   if( !m_bDisplayingColor )
    pBitmap = &m_Bitmap;
   m_pScreenEffect->ChangeGraphic( pBitmap,
    RGB( 255, 0, 0 ) );
   m_pScreenEffect->Start( 320, 240,
    pBitmap,
    m_Color,
    &ClientDC, m_nWhichEffect,
    START_NOW );
  }
 }

 CView::OnTimer(nIDEvent);
}
```

14. Compile and run the program.

When the program first runs, you'll see a blank application window. Select New from the File menu to open up a window with an effect. Open up several and enjoy watching the activity. Figure 2-8 shows the program with three windows opened.

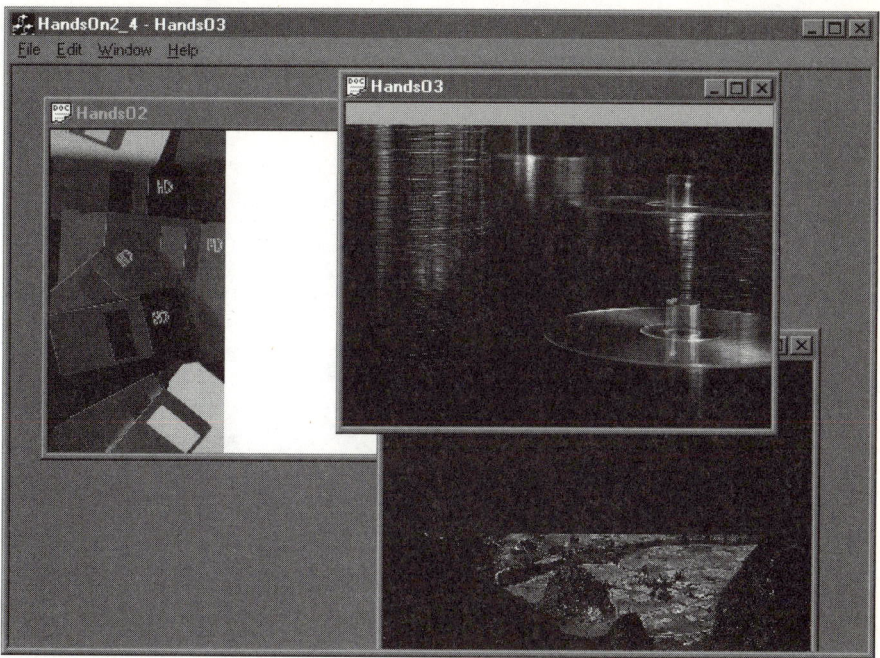

Figure 2-8: Three screen effect windows may be just about all you can keep track of as you watch them perform.

Hands-On 5: Interactive Screen Effects

It's time to get interactive. This hands-on exercise displays an effect then waits for the user to click before it shows the next effect. If you click at the top of the screen, the effect wipes up. If you click at the bottom of the screen, the effect wipes down. If you click at the right of the screen, the effect wipes right. And if you click at the left of the screen, the effect wipes left.

There are four images loaded, and the effects cycle through the four images. Figure 2-9 shows what happens after clicking at the top of the screen—it wipes up.

Figure 2-9: Clicking at the top of the screen causes the screen effect to wipe up.

1. Create a Visual C++ project named HandsOn2_5 with the following attributes:

   ❑ Single-document interface

   ❑ English language

   ❑ No database support

   ❑ No compound document support

   ❑ No automation or ActiveX control support

   ❑ 3D controls, but no other features

   ❑ No source file comments

   ❑ Link MFC as a static library

2. Select Settings from the Project menu. Choose the Link tab. Add the following libraries to the Object/library modules field. The libraries for the release and debug versions are different; both are listed below.

Release Project Libraries	Debug Project Libraries
ImageLoad.lib	ImageLoad.lib
ImageObject.lib	ImageObjectD.lib
ScreenEffects.lib	ScreenEffectsD.lib

3. Set the Active Configuration to Win32 Release.

4. Copy the following files from the \SEFFECTS\SAMPLES directory on the CD to the newly created project directory:

```
PIC3.BMP
PIC4.BMP
PIC5.BMP
PIC6.BMP
```

5. Add the following includes to the HandsOn2_5View.h file:

```
#include "ScreenEffects.h"
#include "ImageObject.h"
```

6. Add the following include to the HandsOn2_5View.h file:

```
#include "MAINFRM.h"
```

7. Add the following variable declarations to the CHandsOn2_5View class in the HandsOn2_5View.h file:

```
public:
 CImageObject *m_pImageObject[4];
 CScreenEffect *m_pScreenEffect;
 CBitmap m_Bitmap[4];
 int m_nWhichBitmap;
 int m_nWhichEffect;
```

8. Add the following code to the CHandsOn2_5View constructor:

```
CHandsOn2_5View::CHandsOn2_5View()
{
 for( int i=0; i<4; i++ )
  m_pImageObject[i] = NULL;
 m_pScreenEffect = NULL;
 m_nWhichBitmap = 0;
 m_nWhichEffect = WIPE_LEFT;
}
```

9. Add the following code to the CHandsOn2_5View destructor:

```
CHandsOn2_5View::~CHandsOn2_5View()
{
 for( int i=0; i<4; i++ )
  if( m_pImageObject[i] != NULL )
   delete m_pImageObject[i];
 if( m_pScreenEffect != NULL )
  delete m_pScreenEffect;
}
```

10. Edit the OnDraw function in the CHandsOn2_5View class in the HandsOn2_5View.cpp file as follows:

```
void CHandsOn2_5View::OnDraw(CDC* pDC)
{
 CHandsOn2_5Doc* pDoc = GetDocument();
 ASSERT_VALID(pDoc);

 for( int i=0; i<4; i++ ){
  if( m_pImageObject[i] == NULL ){

   if( i == 0 ){
    CMainFrame *pFrame =
     (CMainFrame *) AfxGetMainWnd();
    pFrame->SetWindowPos( NULL, 0, 0,
     326, 275, SWP_NOZORDER | SWP_NOMOVE );
    }

   static char *szPics[] = { "PIC3.BMP",
    "PIC4.BMP", "PIC5.BMP", "PIC6.BMP" };

   BeginWaitCursor ();
   m_pImageObject[i] =
    new CImageObject( szPics[i] );
   EndWaitCursor ();
```

```
if( m_pImageObject[i] != NULL &&
 m_pImageObject[i]->GetDib() != NULL ){
 CDC WorkDC;
 WorkDC.CreateCompatibleDC( pDC );
 m_Bitmap[i].CreateCompatibleBitmap( pDC,
  m_pImageObject[i]->GetWidth(),
  m_pImageObject[i]->GetHeight() );
 CBitmap *pOldBitmap =
(CBitmap *)WorkDC.SelectObject(&m_Bitmap[i]);
 m_pImageObject[i]->Draw( &WorkDC );
 WorkDC.SelectObject( pOldBitmap );
 }
}

m_pScreenEffect = new CScreenEffect( 320,
 240, &m_Bitmap[0], RGB( 0, 0, 0 ), pDC,
 m_nWhichEffect, START_NOW );

}

if( m_pScreenEffect != NULL ){
 if( GetFocus() == this )
 m_pImageObject[0]->SetPalette( pDC );
 m_pScreenEffect->Redraw( pDC );
 }

}
```

11. Add the following functions with the Class Wizard to the
    CHandsOn2_5View class in the HandsOn2_5View.h file:

```
Name:OnCreate()  Message:WM_CREATE
Name:OnLButtonDown()  Message:WM_LBUTTONDOWN
Name:OnTimer()  Message:WM_TIMER
```

12. Edit the OnCreate function in the CHandsOn2_5View class in the HandsOn2_5View.cpp file as follows:

```
int CHandsOn2_5View::OnCreate(LPCREATESTRUCT lpCreateStruct)
{
  return -1;

 SetTimer( 1, 200, NULL );

 return 0;
}
```

13. Edit the OnLButtonDown function in the CHandsOn2_5View class in the HandsOn2_5View.cpp file as follows:

```
void CHandsOn2_5View::OnLButtonDown(UINT nFlags, CPoint point)
{
 if( m_pScreenEffect != NULL ){
  if( point.x < 80 )
   m_nWhichEffect = WIPE_LEFT;
  else if( point.x > 240 )
   m_nWhichEffect = WIPE_RIGHT;
  else if( point.y < 60 )
   m_nWhichEffect = WIPE_UP;
  else if( point.y > 180 )
   m_nWhichEffect = WIPE_DOWN;
  m_nWhichBitmap++;
  m_nWhichBitmap &= 3;
  CBitmap *pBitmap =
   &m_Bitmap[m_nWhichBitmap];
  m_pScreenEffect->Halt();
  CClientDC ClientDC( this );
  m_pScreenEffect->ChangeGraphic( pBitmap,
   RGB( 0, 0, 0 ) );
  m_pScreenEffect->Start( 320, 240,
   pBitmap,
   RGB( 0, 0, 0 ),
   &ClientDC, m_nWhichEffect,
   START_NOW );
  }

 CView::OnLButtonDown(nFlags, point);
}
```

14. Edit the OnTimer function in the CHandsOn2_5View class in the HandsOn2_5View.cpp file as follows:

```
void CHandsOn2_5View::OnTimer(UINT nIDEvent)
{
 if( m_pScreenEffect != NULL &&
  !m_pScreenEffect->m_bDone ){
  CClientDC ClientDC( this );
  m_pScreenEffect->Maintain( &ClientDC );
  }

  CView::OnTimer(nIDEvent);
}
```

15. Compile and run the program.

When the program first runs, you'll see the first image wipe across the screen. Then, if you click in the left portion of the screen as shown in Figure 2-10, the next image will wipe left.

Figure 2-10: Clicking in the left side of the screen causes the next image to wipe left.

On the Web

If you search the Web, you're bound to find screen effect information. Here's a short sampling:

A few Web sites try to show you how to perform screen effects in your programs. Figure 2-11 shows a site that does just that.

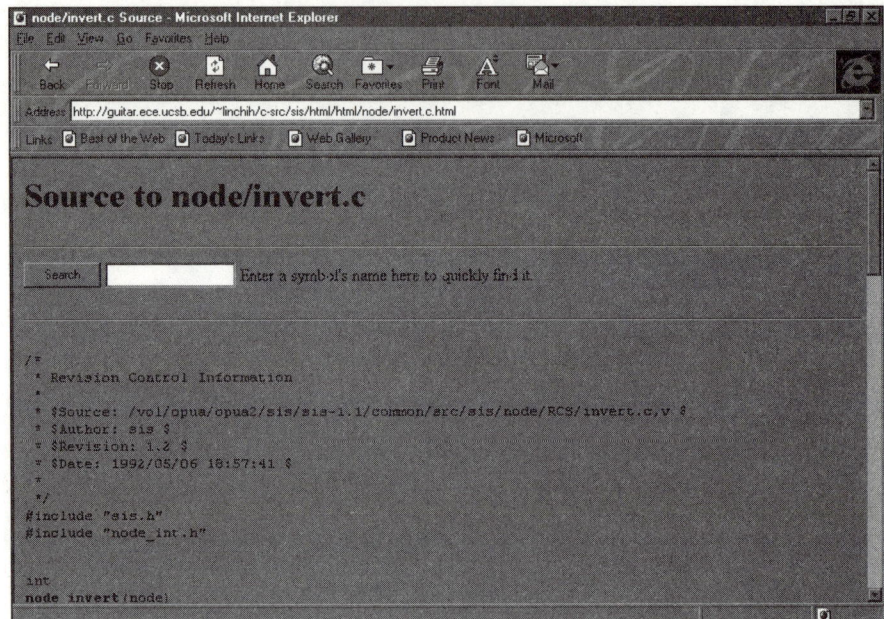

Figure 2-11: You can find source code that shows you how to perform screen effects.

You can create nice screen effects by translating, rotating, and scaling images. A site that presents ways to do this is shown in Figure 2-12.

One of the easiest ways to create a screen effect is to change the palette. In Figure 2-13, a site is pictured that shows you how to implement such a screen effect.

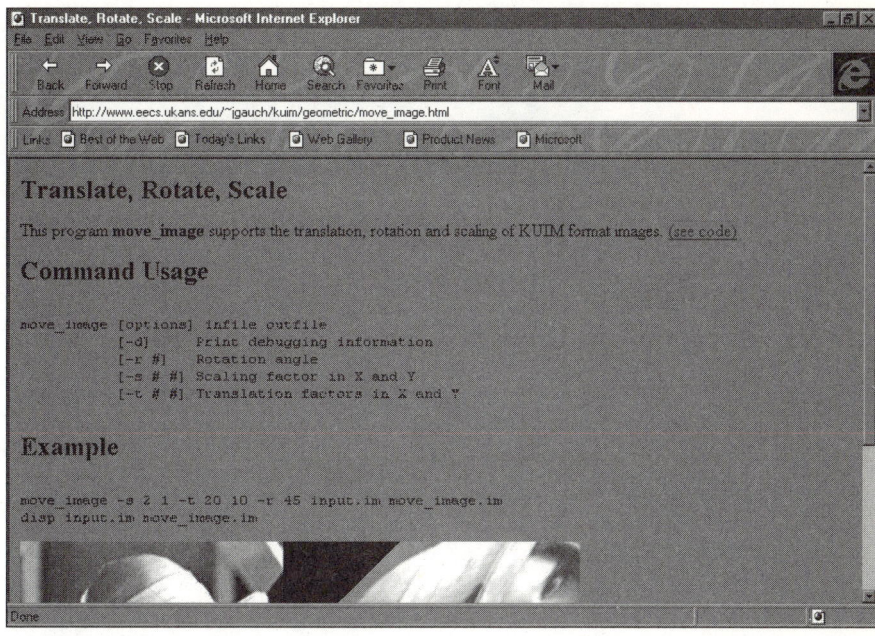

Figure 2-12: Translating, rotating, and scaling all make for interesting screen effects.

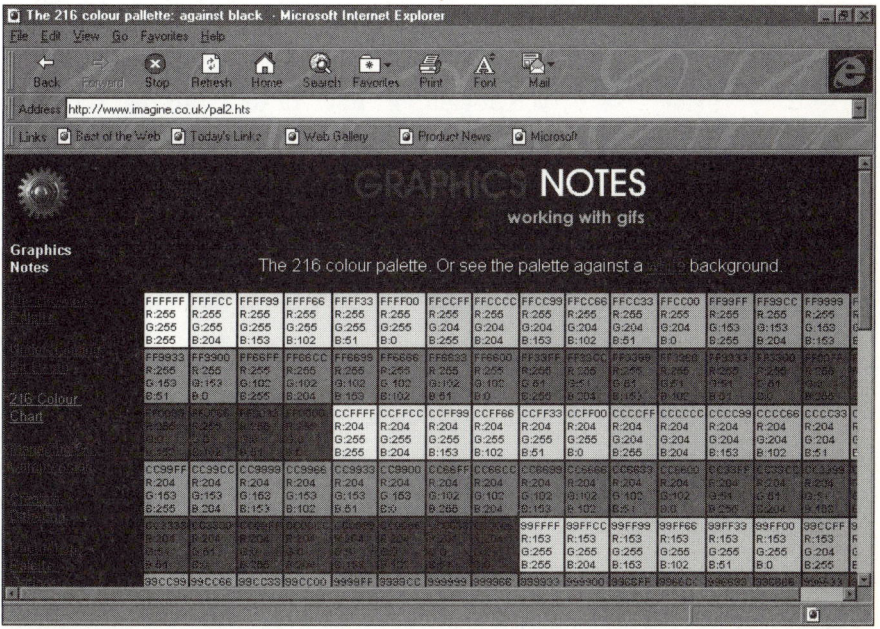

Figure 2-13: Palettes can be changed for easy screen effects.

The father of all Internet browsers, Netscape, has some features that let you get a variation in screens (see Figure 2-14).

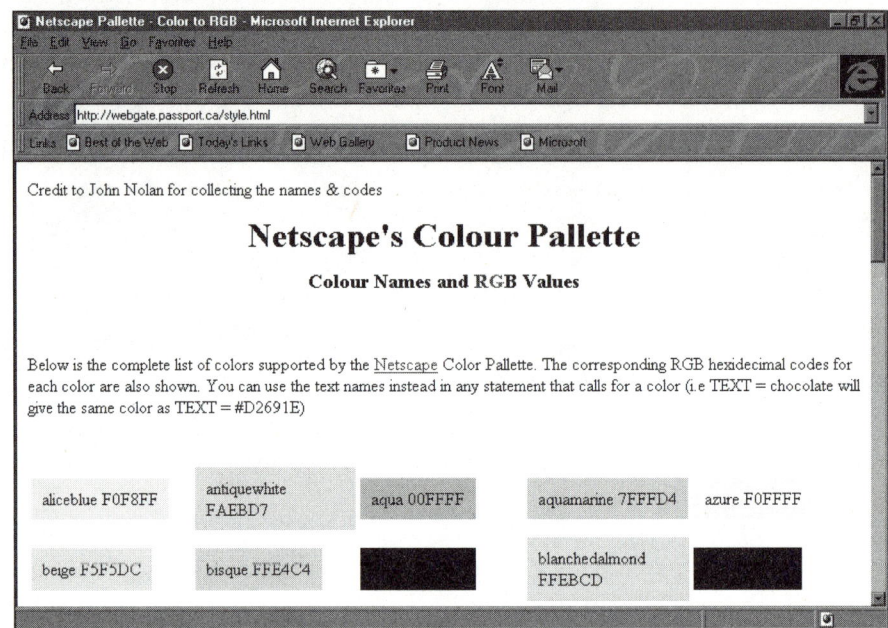

Figure 2-14: Even Netscape has palette adjustments for variation in screen effects.

Web developers have figured out that screen effects catch people's attention. The site shown in Figure 2-15 is a good example of effective use of screen effects.

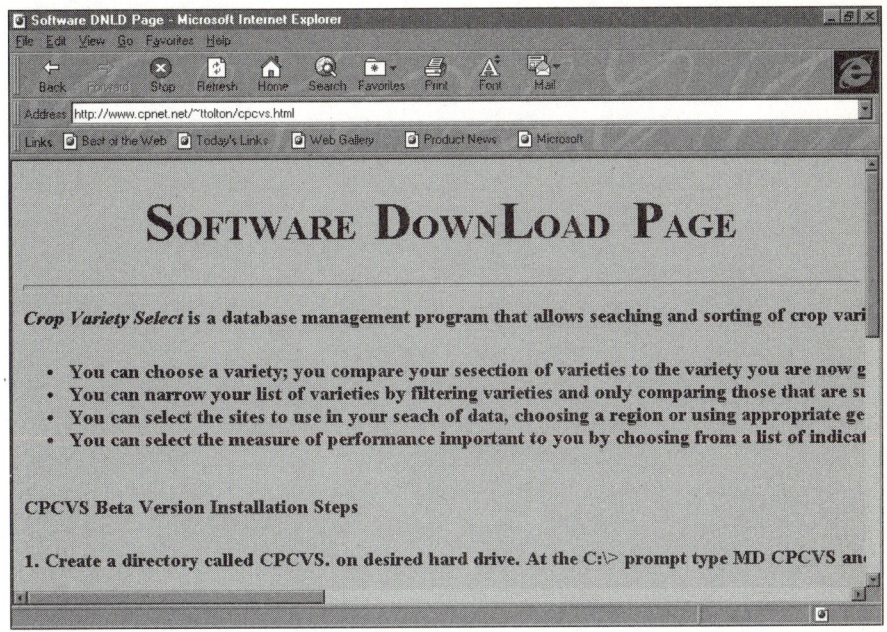

Figure 2-15: Some Web pages use screen effects to get your attention for boring subjects such as databases.

MOVING ON

Screen effects are easy to do with the CScreenEffects class library that comes with this book. It's a technique that has gone by the wayside for many people. Don't let that happen to you.

I remember the first time I saw Hypercard in 1988. The one thing that stuck in my mind was the cool screen effects you could use. Make your programs memorable—use screen effects!

Chapter 3

Image Point Processing

The color of the World is changing day by day.
—Les Miserables

If you work with images in your programs, you'll quickly notice how much disk space they consume. Even a CD gets full rather quickly when the graphics get intensive.

It's not just images that your programs need, it's images plus variations of those same images. For instance, a program might highlight a rectangular region of the screen when the mouse cursor moves over it. This can be done by Exclusive Oring (XORing) a color to the region, but that produces unpredictable results. Another way to highlight is to colorize the region with red. Most people use a paint program, create the colorized image, and then use it in their program just as any other image.

This chapter shows you how to produce your own colorized versions of images that are loaded. It also shows you other useful techniques such as converting images to grayscale. All of the processes in this chapter fall into the category of point processes.

Point processes are techniques that are performed on single pixels. Since single pixels are all considered points of an image, the term point processes is used to describe operations to single pixels.

Point processes are fundamental image processing operations. They are the simplest and probably the most frequently used of the image processing algorithms. Because they are less complex than other image processing algorithms, they are a natural starting place for this book's image processing libraries.

Point processes are algorithms that modify a pixel's value in an image based solely upon that pixel's value (and sometimes its location). No other pixel values are involved in the transformation. Individual pixels are replaced with new values that are algorithmically related to the pixel's original value. As a result of the algorithmic relationship between the original and the new pixel value, point processes can generally be reversed.

THE IMAGEPOINTPROCESSES CLASS LIBRARY

The ImagePointProcesses class library provides you with functions to perform operations such as colorization, brightness alterations, and grayscale conversion. The source code for the library can be found in the IMAGEPR1\ImagePointProcesses directory on the Companion CD-ROM.

The ImagePointProcesses Demo

Since loading images is an important part of image processing, this demo program takes the ImageView demo program of Chapter 1 and adds the image point processes. That way, you'll have a program with more functionality than one that simply performs image point processes.

When the program first runs, you'll see an empty application window. Load an image by selecting Open from the File menu. You can then choose an image to load in. Figure 3-1 shows an image with a rose loaded into the program.

For most of the point processes, you can perform the operation to the entire image or to a smaller rectangular region. In order to perform the operation to a smaller region, you must show the crop box by selecting Show Crop Box from the Operations menu. You can then move the crop box around to the region upon which you want to perform the operation. Figure 3-2 shows two identical images. One is completely brightened and the other has only a portion brightened.

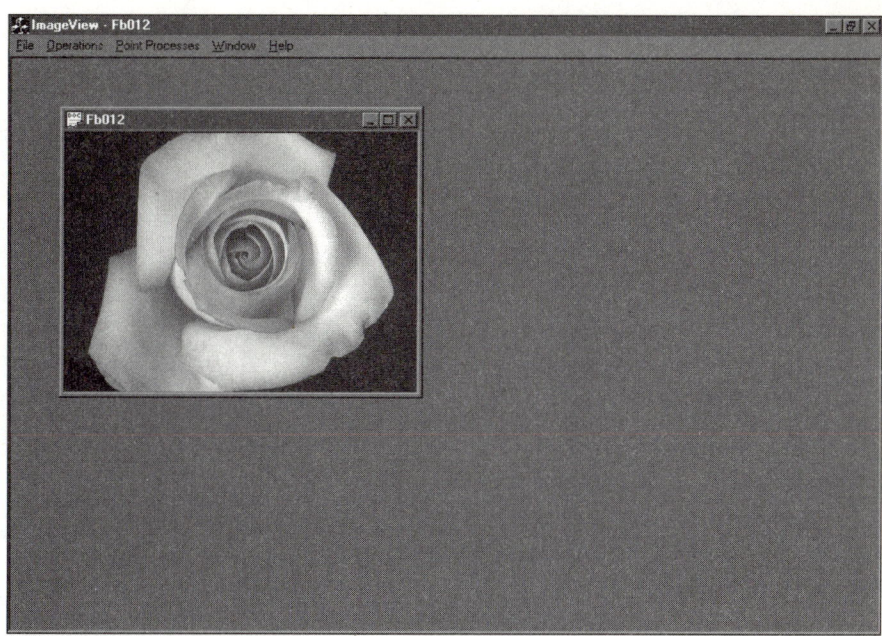

Figure 3-1: The ImagePointProcesses demo loads images into child windows.

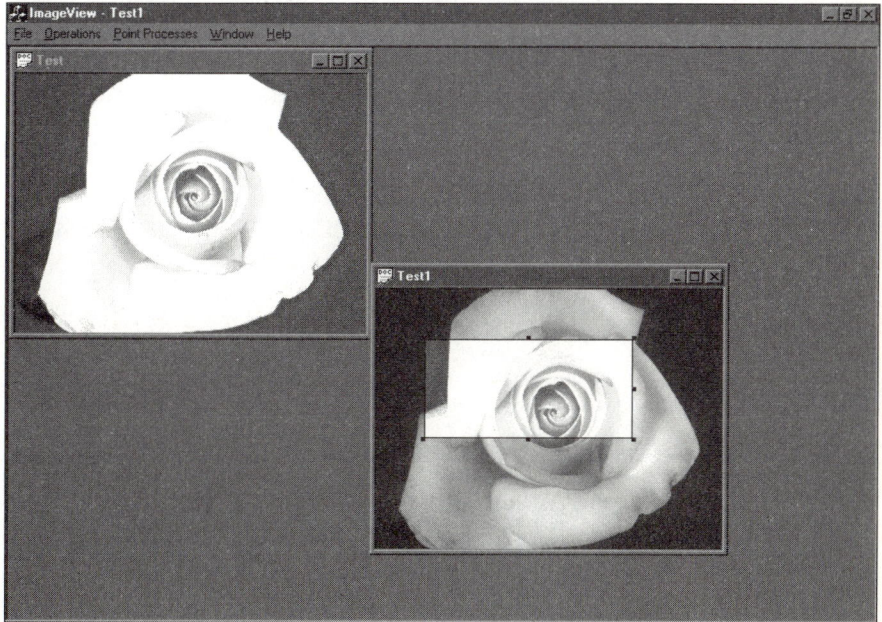

Figure 3-2: You can perform most of the image point processes on either the entire image or a smaller section.

Another interesting feature of the program is that you can see a histogram of the various color components of the image. This is a good way to locate the range of colors that exists in the image. Figure 3-3 shows a histogram of the grayscale values of the rose image.

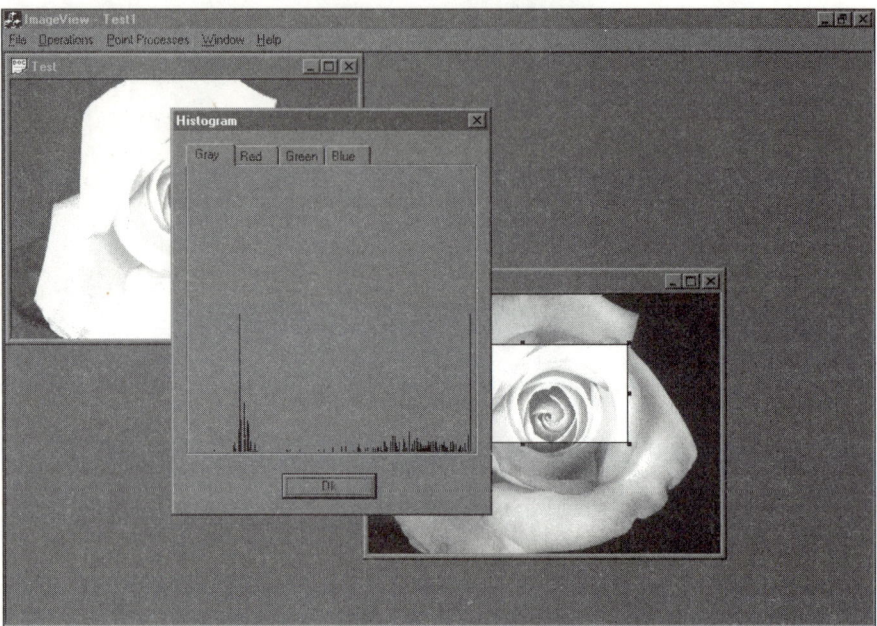

Figure 3-3: You can view a histogram of grayscale, red, green, or blue values.

CIMAGEPOINTPROCESSES CLASS LIBRARY FUNCTION CALLS

This section is provided as a reference for the public function calls offered by the CImagePointProcesses class library. Since the class library was designed with simplicity as a major goal, the calls are simple and easy to use. That's good, because to load and save a picture is easy—it just takes a few lines of code.

You may want to skip over this section and read the section entitled "Behind the ImagePointProcesses (ImageView) Demo Program," which shows how the calls are used. For some people, it's better to look at the usage of fucntion calls before actually studying the syntax.

CImagePointProcesses()

Prototype: `CImagePointProcesses( CImageObject *pImageObject );`

Purpose: This constructs a CImagePointProcesses class and initializes all internal variables. Since there is a CImageObject class in this version of the constructor, one does not need to be supplied for other CImagePointProcesses functions that are used.

Arguments: CImageObject *pImageObject

Returns: Nothing

CImagePointProcesses()

Prototype: `CImagePointProcesses( void );`

Purpose: This constructs a CImagePointProcesses class and initializes all internal variables. Since there is no CImageObject class in this version of the constructor, one must be supplied for other CImagePointProcesses functions that are used.

Arguments: None

Returns: Nothing

ChangeBrightness()

Prototype: `BOOL ChangeBrightness( int nBrightness, int nX1, int nY1, int nX2, int nY2, CImageObject *pImageObject );`

Purpose: This function changes the brightness of the image that's in the attached CImageObject class. If a CImageObject class point has not been specified before making this call, one must be specified when the call is made. Any coordinates that are not passed and that default to -1, will be assigned the minimum or maximum value of the image. The variables nX1 and nY1 will become 0, nX2 will become the image width -1, and nY2 will become the image height -1. The best way to perform the operation on the entire image is to not pass nX1, nY1, nX2, and mY2. This way, they will default to include the entire image.

93

Arguments: int nBrightness
int nX1, Defaults to -1
int nY1, Defaults to -1
int nX2, Defaults to -1
int nY2, Defaults to -1
CImageObject *pImageObject, Defaults to NULL

Returns: BOOL: TRUE for success, FALSE for FAIL

ReverseColors()

Prototype:
```
BOOL ReverseColors( int nX1, int nY1, int nX2, int nY2, CImageObject
    *pImageObject );
```

Purpose: This function reverses the colors of the image that's in the attached CImageObject class. If a CImageObject class point has not been specified before making this call, one must be specified when the call is made. Any coordinates that are not passed and that default to -1 will be assigned the minimum or maximum value of the image. The variables nX1 and nY1 will become 0, nX2 will become the image width -1, and nY2 will become the image height -1. The best way to perform the operation on the entire image is to not pass nX1, nY1, nX2, and mY2. This way, they will default to include the entire image.

Arguments: int nX1, Defaults to -1
int nY1, Defaults to -1
 int nX2, Defaults to -1
int nY2, Defaults to -1
CImageObject *pImageObject, Defaults to NULL

Returns: BOOL: TRUE for success, FALSE for FAIL

MakeGray()

Prototype:
```
BOOL MakeGray( BOOL bSetPalette, CImageObject *pImageObject );
```

Purpose: This function makes a color image into a grayscale image for the image that's in the attached CImageObject class. If a CImageObject class point has not been specified before making this call, one must be specified when the call is made.

Arguments: BOOL bSetPalette, Defaults to TRUE
CImageObject *pImageObject, Defaults to NULL

Returns: BOOL: TRUE for success, FALSE for FAIL

Colorize()

Prototype:

```
BOOL Colorize( int nX1, int nY1, int nX2, int nY2, CImageObject
    *pImageObject );
```

Purpose: This function colorizes the pixels of the image that's in the attached CImageObject class. If a CImageObject class point has not been specified before making this call, one must be specified at the time the call is made. Any coordinates that are not passed and that default to -1, will be assigned the minimum or maximum value of the image. The variables nX1 and nY1 will become 0, nX2 will become the image width -1 and nY2 will become the image height -1. The best way to perform the operation on the entire image is to not pass nX1, nY1, nX2, and mY2. This way they will default to include the entire image.

Arguments: int nX1, Defaults to -1
int nY1, Defaults to -1
int nX2, Defaults to -1
int nY2, Defaults to -1
CImageObject *pImageObject, Defaults to NULL

Returns: BOOL: TRUE for success, FALSE for FAIL

BEHIND IMAGEPOINTPROCESSES (IMAGEVIEW)

This program is based on the ImageView program that was originally built for Chapter 1. As a result, the actual filenames are the same as those from the ImageView program in the images directory. Additions have been made that add the area image processing procedures. All source code for this version of ImageView can be found in the imagepr2\ImageView directory on the Companion CD-ROM.

The ImagePointProcesses demo program shares a lot of code with the ImageView program of Chapter 1. For this reason, only four functions unique to the ImagePointProcesses demo program will be covered.

Changing Brightness

One of the things everyone does with their television set is to change the brightness. Individual tastes vary, and the brightness of the television picture changes accordingly.

Some computer images just need their brightness changed because they've been acquired through maladjusted hardware or during less-than-optimal circumstances.

By selecting Change Brightness from the Point Processes menu, you can adjust the brightness of an image. Before the image brightness is changed, you'll get a dialog box with a slider that lets you set the value from 1 to 200. These values are in terms of percentage. At 100 percent, you'll get the same image you started with. At 200 percent, you get an image twice as bright as what you started with.

You have to be careful. If you start with an image that's fairly bright, increasing the brightness by very much will cause many of the colors to oversaturate. Figure 3-4 shows an original image, Figure 3-5 shows an image with a small amount (15 percent) of brightening, and Figure 3-6 shows an image with a large amount of brightening (60 percent), which makes many of the colors oversaturate.

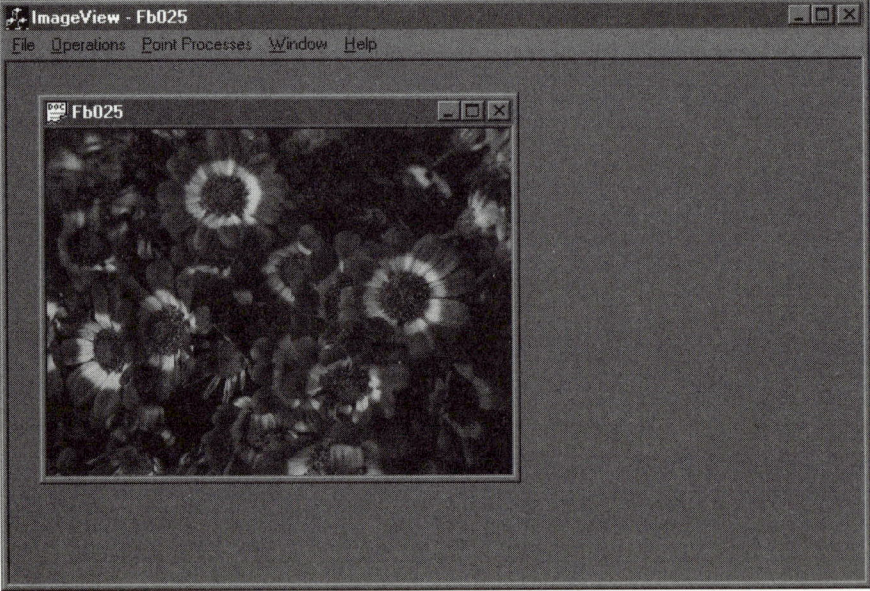

Figure 3-4: The original image.

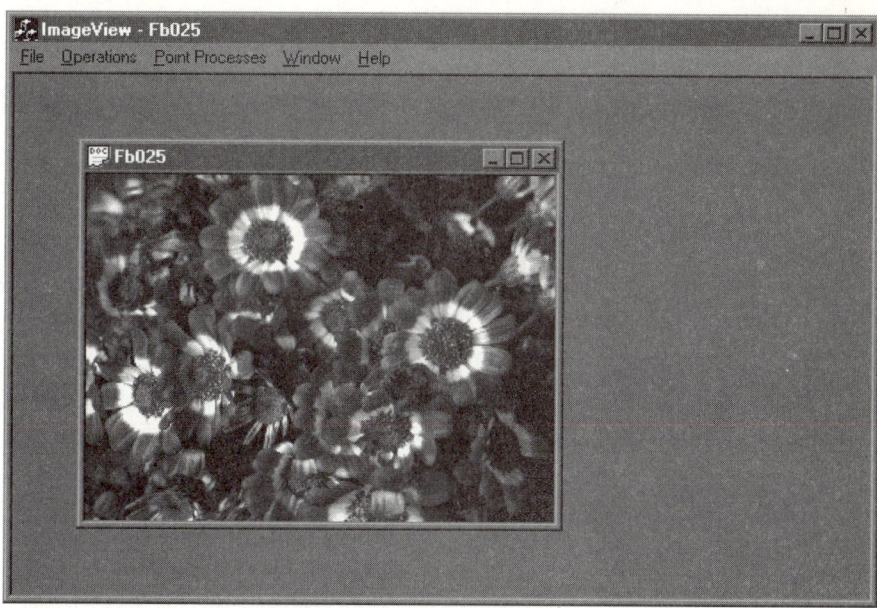

Figure 3-5: The original image 15 percent brighter.

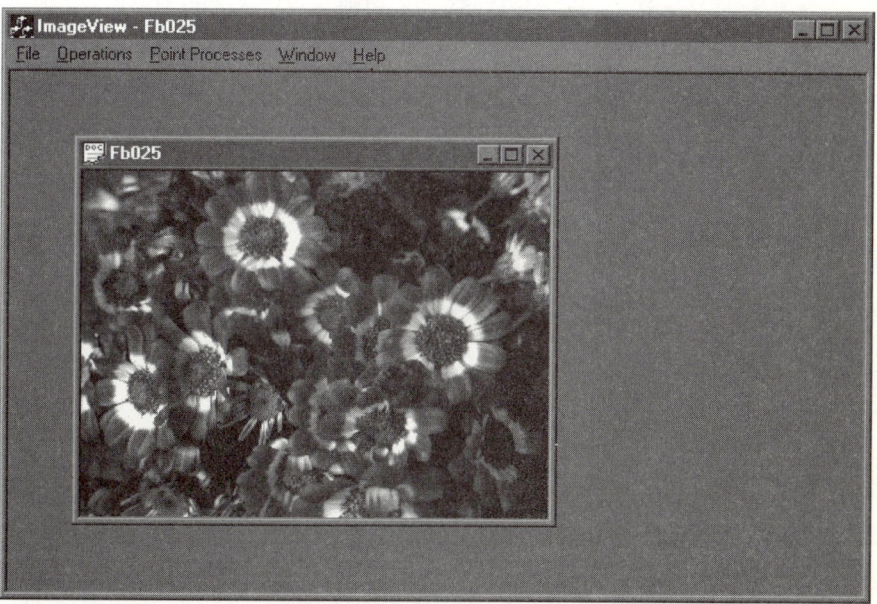

Figure 3-6: The original image 60 percent brighter.

The majority of code in the function is devoted to making sure the CRectTracker object class's coordinates are all within a valid range. A dialog allows users to select the new brightness. After that it's a simple matter of attaching the CImageObject to a CImagePointProcesses object and making a single function call. The image is then redrawn with the new brightness.

The OnPointProcessesChangebrightness() Code

```
void CImageViewView::
OnPointprocessesChangebrightness()
{

if( m_pTracker == NULL ||
 m_pImageObject == NULL ) return;

int nX1 = m_pTracker->m_rect.left;
int nY1 = m_pTracker->m_rect.top;
int nX2 = m_pTracker->m_rect.right;
int nY2 = m_pTracker->m_rect.bottom;

if( nX1 < 0 ) nX1 = 0;
if( nX1 > m_pImageObject->GetWidth() - 1 )
 nX1 = m_pImageObject->GetWidth() - 1;
if( nY1 < 0 ) nY1 = 0;
if( nY1 > m_pImageObject->GetHeight() - 1 )
 nY1 = m_pImageObject->GetHeight() - 1;
if( nX2 < 0 ) nX2 = 0;
if( nX2 > m_pImageObject->GetWidth() - 1 )
 nX2 = m_pImageObject->GetWidth() - 1;
if( nY2 < 0 ) nY2 = 0;
if( nY2 > m_pImageObject->GetHeight() - 1 )
 nY2 = m_pImageObject->GetHeight() - 1;

if( !m_bCropBoxShowing ){
 nX1 = nY1 = 0;
 nX2 = m_pImageObject->GetWidth() - 1;
 nY2 = m_pImageObject->GetHeight() - 1;
 }

CBrightness Brightness;
if( Brightness.DoModal() != IDOK ) return;
```

```
CImagePointProcesses
 PointProcesses( m_pImageObject );
BeginWaitCursor();
PointProcesses.ChangeBrightness(
 Brightness.m_nBrightness, nX1, nY1,nX2,nY2);
EndWaitCursor();

InvalidateRect( NULL, FALSE );
UpdateWindow();

}
```

Colorizing

The best use I've found for image colorization is highlighting a region of an image over which the mouse is pointing. It lets users know that the mouse is now pointing to a hot spot. Clicking a mouse button will result in some action.

Figure 3-7 shows just such an image, with one of the buttons highlighted.

Figure 3-7: Colorizing a region can let users know the mouse is over a hot spot.

The OnPointProcessesColorize() Code

```
void CImageViewView::
OnPointprocessesColorize()
{

 if( m_pTracker == NULL ||
 m_pImageObject == NULL ) return;

 int nX1 = m_pTracker->m_rect.left;
 int nY1 = m_pTracker->m_rect.top;
 int nX2 = m_pTracker->m_rect.right;
 int nY2 = m_pTracker->m_rect.bottom;

 if( nX1 < 0 ) nX1 = 0;
 if( nX1 > m_pImageObject->GetWidth() - 1 )
  nX1 = m_pImageObject->GetWidth() - 1;
 if( nY1 < 0 ) nY1 = 0;
 if( nY1 > m_pImageObject->GetHeight() - 1 )
  nY1 = m_pImageObject->GetHeight() - 1;
 if( nX2 < 0 ) nX2 = 0;
 if( nX2 > m_pImageObject->GetWidth() - 1 )
  nX2 = m_pImageObject->GetWidth() - 1;
 if( nY2 < 0 ) nY2 = 0;
 if( nY2 > m_pImageObject->GetHeight() - 1 )
  nY2 = m_pImageObject->GetHeight() - 1;

 if( !m_bCropBoxShowing ){
  nX1 = nY1 = 0;
  nX2 = m_pImageObject->GetWidth() - 1;
  nY2 = m_pImageObject->GetHeight() - 1;
  }

 CColorDialog ColorDialog;
 if( ColorDialog.DoModal() != IDOK ) return;
 CImagePointProcesses
  PointProcesses( m_pImageObject );
 BeginWaitCursor();
 PointProcesses.Colorize( nX1, nY1, nX2, nY2,
  ColorDialog.GetColor() );
 EndWaitCursor();

 InvalidateRect( NULL, FALSE );
 UpdateWindow();

 }
```

Converting to Grayscale

This function makes a call to the CImagePointProcesses class library that converts a color image to a grayscale image. It's simpler than the other functions discussed in the program, since it converts the entire image, thereby eliminating the possibility of converting a subportion.

Converting to grayscale is the same as taking a color picture to the photo shop and having it printed in black and white. While we call these photographs black and white, they're really many shades of gray.

The OnPointprocessesMakegray() Code

```
void CImageViewView::
OnPointprocessesMakegray()
{

 if( m_pImageObject == NULL ) return;

CImagePointProcesses
  PointProcesses( m_pImageObject );
PointProcesses.MakeGray( TRUE );

 InvalidateRect( NULL, FALSE );
 UpdateWindow();

}
```

Reversing Colors

Reversing colors gives you a negative image. It's the same as what you'd expect when comparing your developed film prints to the negatives included in the package.

There are times when reversing colors can be a great way to get attention or alert users to a control they need to be aware of. Sometimes it's just fun to display images of people you dislike in reversed colors.

The OnPointprocessesReversecolors() Code

```
void CImageViewView::
OnPointprocessesReversecolors()
{

 if( m_pTracker == NULL ||
 m_pImageObject == NULL ) return;
```

```
int nX1 = m_pTracker->m_rect.left;
int nY1 = m_pTracker->m_rect.top;
int nX2 = m_pTracker->m_rect.right;
int nY2 = m_pTracker->m_rect.bottom;

if( nX1 < 0 ) nX1 = 0;
if( nX1 > m_pImageObject->GetWidth() - 1 )
 nX1 = m_pImageObject->GetWidth() - 1;
if( nY1 < 0 ) nY1 = 0;
if( nY1 > m_pImageObject->GetHeight() - 1 )
 nY1 = m_pImageObject->GetHeight() - 1;
if( nX2 < 0 ) nX2 = 0;
if( nX2 > m_pImageObject->GetWidth() - 1 )
 nX2 = m_pImageObject->GetWidth() - 1;
if( nY2 < 0 ) nY2 = 0;
if( nY2 > m_pImageObject->GetHeight() - 1 )
 nY2 = m_pImageObject->GetHeight() - 1;

if( !m_bCropBoxShowing ){
 nX1 = nY1 = 0;
 nX2 = m_pImageObject->GetWidth() - 1;
 nY2 = m_pImageObject->GetHeight() - 1;
 }
CImagePointProcesses
 PointProcesses( m_pImageObject );
BeginWaitCursor();
PointProcesses.ReverseColors( nX1, nY1, nX2,
 nY2 );
EndWaitCursor();

InvalidateRect( NULL, FALSE );
UpdateWindow();

}
```

IMAGE POINT PROCESSING IN A NUTSHELL

Performing image point processing is very easy. It requires an image to be loaded into a CImageObject class object first, though. Once you have the image loaded, a single call does the work.

There are four image point processes supported in the CImagePointProcesses class. Each one is described separately below.

ChangeBrightness()

This example makes an image 50 percent brighter. The brightness argument is the first. A value of 100 means you're changing to a brightness of 100 percent. The image won't change in this case. But if you're changing to a brightness of 150 percent, that means you're making the image 50 percent brighter. That's what this example does. Once the operation is performed, the next time the image is drawn it'll be brighter.

```
CImageObject ImageObject( "PIC.BMP" );
CImagePointProcesses
 ImagePointProcess( &ImageObject );
ImagePointProcess.ChangeBrightness( 150 );
```

Let's say you only want to brighten part of the image. You can specify the coordinates of a rectangular region to which you want the operation applied. The following example brightens a region bounded by the coordinates 10, 10 and 120, 120. With no coordinates specified, the entire image is brightened.

```
CImageObject ImageObject( "PIC.BMP" );
CImagePointProcesses
 ImagePointProcess( &ImageObject );
ImagePointProcess.ChangeBrightness( 150, 10,
 10, 120, 120 );
```

Colorize()

This example colorizes an image with pure red. The color value that's passed in is always of a COLORREF type. For this reason, this and other chapters use the RGB macro to create the value. For instance, a COLORREF value of pure red can be formed with RGB(255, 0, 0); one of pure green by RGB(0, 255, 0); and one of pure blue by RGB(0, 0, 255). This example uses RGB(255, 0, 0) for pure red. Once the operation is performed, the next time the image is drawn it'll be colorized with red.

```
CImageObject ImageObject( "PIC.BMP" );
CImagePointProcesses
 ImagePointProcess( &ImageObject );
ImagePointProcess.ChangeBrightness(
 RGB( 255, 0, 0 ) );
```

Let's say you only want to colorize part of the image. You can specify the coordinates of a rectangular region to which you want the operation performed. The following example colorizes a region bounded by the coordinates 10, 10 and 120, 120. With no coordinates specified, the entire image is colorized.

```
CImageObject ImageObject( "PIC.BMP" );
CImagePointProcesses
 ImagePointProcess( &ImageObject );
ImagePointProcess.ChangeBrightness(
 RGB( 255, 0, 0 ), 10, 10, 120, 120 );
```

MakeGray()

Many times it's desirable to convert an image to grayscale. You get a better idea of how it'll look printed to a black-and-white printer when you convert to grayscale. This example shows how to load an image and convert it to grayscale. This operation can't be performed to a portion of the image, only to the entire image.

```
CImageObject ImageObject( "PIC.BMP" );
CImagePointProcesses
 ImagePointProcess( &ImageObject );
ImagePointProcess.MakeGray();
```

ReverseColors()

This example reverses the colors of an image. It's like creating the photographic negative from the original image. Once the operation is performed, the next time the image is drawn it'll be drawn in reverse colors.

```
CImageObject ImageObject( "PIC.BMP" );
CImagePointProcesses
 ImagePointProcess( &ImageObject );
ImagePointProcess.RevsersColors();
```

Let's say you want to reverse the colors of only a part of the image. You can specify the coordinates of a rectangular region to which you want the operation applied. The following example reverses the colors of a region bounded by the coordinates 10, 10 and 120, 120. With no coordinates specified, the entire image is reversed.

```
CImageObject ImageObject( "PIC.BMP" );
CImagePointProcesses
 ImagePointProcess( &ImageObject );
ImagePointProcess.ReverseColors( 10, 10,
 120, 120 );
```

CREATING PROGRAMS THAT CREATE IMAGES

This section provides you with five hands-on exercises that'll walk you through the image point processes. After you work through the exercises, you'll be able to go on to more advanced uses of the CImagePointProcesses class library.

Since the class library is on the Companion CD-ROM and can be found in the IMAGEPR1\ImagePointProcesses directory, you have full access to the source code. You can add your own point processes if you have the need. And you can start with the functions that are already there and just modify them for your own functions. If you create your own image point process to add to the library, please send it to me at ivt-rcl@interpath.com. I'll probably use it myself, and with your permission I'll make it available to others.

Hands-On 1: Changing the Brightness of an Image

The first hands-on exercise in this chapter shows you how to create a program that lets users interactively brighten and dim an image. With the mouse inside of the application's view window, its Y-coordinate changes the brightness. The higher in the view window the mouse is, the brighter the image (with a limit of 200 percent). Figure 3-8 shows the image in its brightest form. The lower in the view window the mouse is, the dimmer the image (with a limit of 1 percent). Figure 3-9 shows the image in a very dim form.

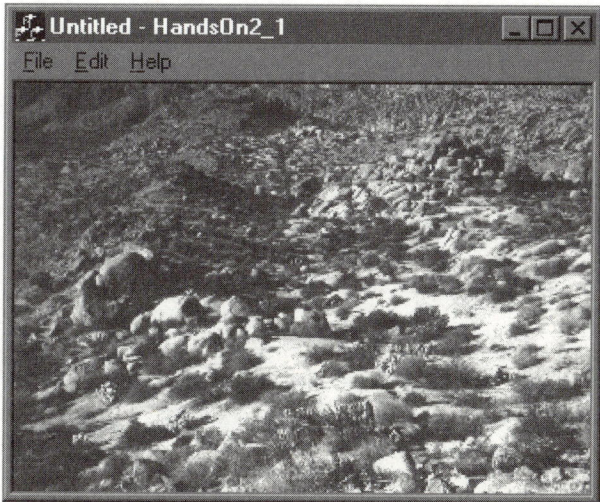

Figure 3-8: The image brightens when the mouse moves higher in the view window.

105

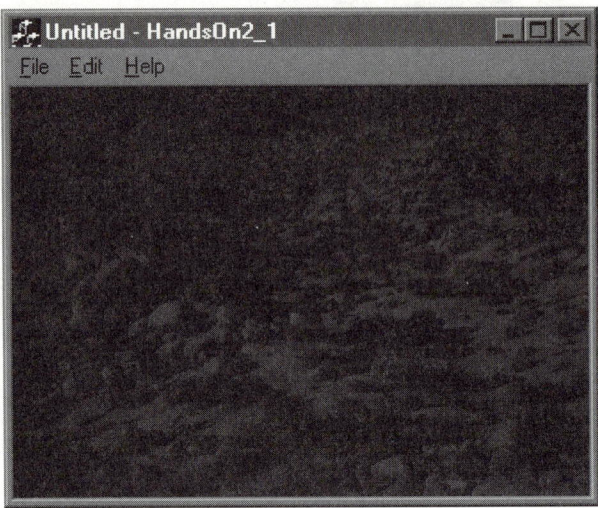

Figure 3-9: The image dims when the mouse moves lower in the view window.

1. Create a Visual C++ project named HandsOn3_1 with the following attributes:

   ❏ Single-document interface

   ❏ English language

   ❏ No database support

   ❏ No compound document support

   ❏ No automation or ActiveX control support

   ❏ 3D controls, but no other features

   ❏ No source file comments

   ❏ Link MFC as a static library

2. Select Settings from the Project menu. Choose the Link tab. Add the following libraries to the Object/library modules field. The libraries for the release and debug versions are different; both are listed below.

Release Project Libraries	Debug Project Libraries
ImageLoad.lib	ImageLoad.lib
ImageObject.lib	ImageObjectD.lib
ImagePointProcesses.lib	ImagePointProcessesD.lib

CD-ROM

3. Set the Active Configuration to Win32 Release.

4. Copy the file PIC1.BMP from the \IMAGEPR1\SAMPLES directory on the Companion CD-ROM to the newly created project directory.

5. Add the following includes to the HandsOn3_1View.h file:

```
#include "ImagePointProcesses.h"
```

6. Add the following include to the HandsOn3_1View.h file:

```
#include "MAINFRM.h"
```

7. Add the following variable declarations to the CHandsOn3_1View class in the HandsOn3_1View.h file:

```
public:
 CImageObject *m_pImageObject;
 CImageObject *m_pImage;
```

8. Add the following code to the CHandsOn3_1View constructor:

```
CHandsOn3_1View::CHandsOn3_1View()
{
 m_pImageObject = NULL;
 m_pImage = NULL;
}
```

9. Add the following code to the CHandsOn3_1View destructor:

```
CHandsOn3_1View::~CHandsOn3_1View()
{
 if( m_pImageObject != NULL )
  delete m_pImageObject;
 if( m_pImage != NULL )
  delete m_pImage;
}
```

10. Edit the OnDraw function in the CHandsOn3_1View class in the HandsOn3_1View.cpp file as follows:

```
void CHandsOn3_1View::OnDraw(CDC* pDC)
{
 CHandsOn3_1Doc* pDoc = GetDocument();
 ASSERT_VALID(pDoc);

 if( m_pImageObject == NULL ){

  CMainFrame *pFrame =
   (CMainFrame *) AfxGetMainWnd();
```

107

```
        pFrame->SetWindowPos( NULL, 0, 0,
         326, 275, SWP_NOZORDER | SWP_NOMOVE );

        BeginWaitCursor ();
        m_pImageObject =
         new CImageObject( "PIC1.BMP", pDC );
        EndWaitCursor ();
        if( m_pImageObject == NULL ){
         AfxMessageBox( "Could not create image!" );
         return;
         }

        m_pImage = new CImageObject();
        *m_pImage = *m_pImageObject;

        }

     if( m_pImage != NULL ){
      if( GetFocus() == this )
       m_pImage->SetPalette( pDC );
      m_pImage->Draw( pDC );
      }

     }
```

11. Add the following function with the Class Wizard to the CHandsOn3_1View class in the HandsOn3_1View.h file:

```
Name:OnMouseMove( )  Message:WM_MOUSEMOVE
```

12. Edit the OnMouseMove function in the CHandsOn3_1View class in the HandsOn3_1View.cpp file as follows:

```
void CHandsOn3_1View::OnMouseMove(UINT nFlags, CPoint point)
{
 if( y > 239 ) y = 239;
 y = 239 - y;
 int nBrightness = ( y * 100 ) / 120;

 if( m_pImage != NULL )
  delete m_pImage;
 m_pImage = new CImageObject();
 *m_pImage = *m_pImageObject;
 CImagePointProcesses *pImagePointProcess;
 pImagePointProcess =
  new CImagePointProcesses( m_pImage );
```

```
if( pImagePointProcess != NULL ){
 pImagePointProcess->ChangeBrightness(
  nBrightness );
 InvalidateRect( NULL, FALSE );
 UpdateWindow();
 delete pImagePointProcess;
 }

 CView::OnMouseMove(nFlags, point);
}
```

13. Compile and run the program.

When the program runs, you'll see the original image appear in the view window in its original brightness. Move the mouse into the view window. Now move it higher and lower and watch it brighten and dim.

One important thing to notice about the program that you've just created: if you brighten an image, some hues reach a saturation point. If you take the same brightened image and then dim it back to its original brightness, the image won't be the same. That's because if colors oversaturate when the image is brightened, they get clipped to the highest value of 255. For this reason, when an image is oversaturated, it loses its integrity.

The same thing happens to an image when it's dimmed. It loses its integrity in the opposite way. In order to retain the image integrity for this program, a copy of the original image is retained in memory. Before performing a ChangeBrightness() operation, a new CImageObject object is created with the original image. This way, each ChangeBrightness() operation acts on the original image and not on one of the altered versions of the image.

Hands-On 2: Brighten & Dim Simultaneously

This exercise is similar to the last one because it uses the ChangeBrightness() function. The difference, though, is that it performs the operation on two different rectangular regions of the image.

The left region is exactly like the last exercise. The higher the mouse is in the view window, the brighter the image. The right region is the exact opposite. The lower the mouse is in the view window, the brighter the image. Figure 3-10 shows the program with both regions of opposite brightening.

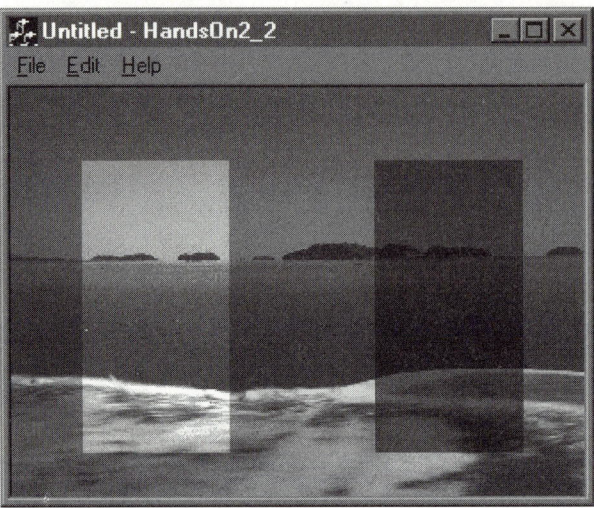

Figure 3-10: Both regions react in opposite manners. One brightens when the mouse moves higher; the other dims.

1. Create a Visual C++ project named HandsOn3_2 with the following attributes:

   ❑ Single-document interface

   ❑ English language

   ❑ No database support

   ❑ No compound document support

   ❑ No automation or ActiveX control support

   ❑ 3D controls, but no other features

   ❑ No source file comments

   ❑ Link MFC as a static library

2. Select Settings from the Project menu. Choose the Link tab. Add the following libraries to the Object/library modules field. The libraries for the release and debug versions are different. Both are listed below.

Release Project Libraries	Debug Project Libraries
ImageLoad.lib	ImageLoad.lib
ImageObject.lib	ImageObjectD.lib
ImagePointProcesses.lib	ImagePointProcessesD.lib

3. Set the Active Configuration to Win32 Release.

4. Copy the file PIC2.BMP from the \IMAGEPR1\SAMPLES directory on the Companion CD-ROM to the newly created project directory.

5. Add the following include to the HandsOn3_2View.h file:

```
#include "ImagePointProcesses.h"
```

6. Add the following include to the HandsOn3_2View.h file:

```
#include "MAINFRM.h"
```

7. Add the following variable declarations to the CHandsOn3_2View class in the HandsOn3_2View.h file:

```
public:
 CImageObject *m_pImageObject;
 CImageObject *m_pImage;
```

8. Add the following code to the CHandsOn3_2View constructor:

```
CHandsOn3_2View::CHandsOn3_2View()
{
 m_pImageObject = NULL;
 m_pImage = NULL;
}
```

9. Add the following code to the CHandsOn3_2View destructor:

```
CHandsOn3_2View::~CHandsOn3_2View()
{
 if( m_pImageObject != NULL )
  delete m_pImageObject;
 if( m_pImage != NULL )
  delete m_pImage;
}
```

10. Edit the OnDraw function in the CHandsOn3_2View class in the HandsOn3_2View.cpp file as follows:

```
void CHandsOn3_2View::OnDraw(CDC* pDC)
{
 CHandsOn3_2Doc* pDoc = GetDocument();
 ASSERT_VALID(pDoc);

 if( m_pImageObject == NULL ){

  CMainFrame *pFrame =
   (CMainFrame *) AfxGetMainWnd();
```

```
pFrame->SetWindowPos( NULL, 0, 0,
 326, 275, SWP_NOZORDER | SWP_NOMOVE );

BeginWaitCursor ();
m_pImageObject =
 new CImageObject( "PIC2.BMP", pDC );
EndWaitCursor ();
if( m_pImageObject == NULL ){
 AfxMessageBox( "Could not create image!" );
 return;
 }

m_pImage = new CImageObject();
*m_pImage = *m_pImageObject;

 }

if( m_pImage != NULL ){
 if( GetFocus() == this )
  m_pImage->SetPalette( pDC );
 m_pImage->Draw( pDC );
 }

}
```

11. Add the following functions with the Class Wizard to the CHandsOn3_2View class in the HandsOn3_2View.h file:

```
Name:OnMouseMove()  Message:WM_MOUSEMOVE
```

12. Edit the OnMouseMove function in the CHandsOn3_2View class in the HandsOn3_2View.cpp file as follows:

```
void CHandsOn3_2View::OnMouseMove(UINT nFlags, CPoint point)
{
if( y > 239 ) y = 239;
y = 239 - y;
int nBrightness = ( y * 100 ) / 120;

if( m_pImage != NULL )
 delete m_pImage;
m_pImage = new CImageObject();
```

```
*m_pImage = *m_pImageObject;
CImagePointProcesses *pImagePointProcess;
pImagePointProcess =
 new CImagePointProcesses( m_pImage );
if( pImagePointProcess != NULL ){
 pImagePointProcess->ChangeBrightness(
  nBrightness, 40, 40, 120, 200 );
 pImagePointProcess->ChangeBrightness(
  200 - nBrightness, 200, 40, 280, 200 );
 InvalidateRect( NULL, FALSE );
 UpdateWindow();
 delete pImagePointProcess;
 }

 CView::OnMouseMove(nFlags, point);
}
```

13. Compile and run the program.

When the program runs, you'll see the image drawn in the view window in its normal state. Move the mouse into the view window. Move it up and down inside of the view window and watch both regions change brightness.

This program, like the last one, keeps the original image in memory, and the operations are performed on the original image to retain the image integrity.

Hands-On 3: Reverse Colors

This hands-on exercise reverses the colors for a square region of the image. To reverse the colors of a square, simply point the mouse to the center of the square you want to reverse, and press the left mouse button. Figure 3-11 shows the image after a square region has been reversed.

While the reversed image isn't likely to be very attractive, it might be just what you want in the way of calling attention to a region of the screen. Some color schemes are more attractive than others, though, and their reversed colors might be nice looking.

113

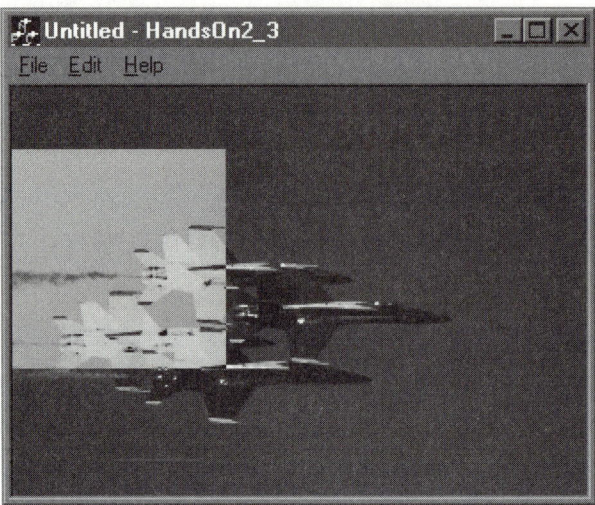

Figure 3-11: Point the mouse and click the left mouse button to reverse a square region of the image.

1. Create a Visual C++ project named HandsOn3_3 with the following attributes:

   ❏ Single-document interface

   ❏ English language

   ❏ No database support

   ❏ No compound document support

   ❏ No automation or ActiveX control support

   ❏ 3D controls, but no other features

   ❏ No source file comments

   ❏ Link MFC as a static library

2. Select Settings from the Project menu. Choose the Link tab. Add the following libraries to the Object/library modules field. The libraries for the release and debug versions are different. Both are listed below.

Release Project Libraries	Debug Project Libraries
ImageLoad.lib	ImageLoad.lib
ImageObject.lib	ImageObjectD.lib
ImagePointProcesses.lib	ImagePointProcessesD.lib

3. Set the Active Configuration to Win32 Release.

4. Copy the file PIC3.BMP from the \IMAGEPR1\SAMPLES directory on the Companion CD-ROM to the newly created project directory.

5. Add the following include to the HandsOn3_3View.h file:

```
#include "ImagePointProcesses.h"
```

6. Add the following include to the HandsOn3_3View.h file:

```
#include "MAINFRM.h"
```

7. Add the following variable declarations to the CHandsOn3_3View class in the HandsOn3_3View.h file:

```
public:
 CImageObject *m_pImageObject;
 int m_nSize;
```

8. Add the following code to the CHandsOn3_3View constructor:

```
CHandsOn3_3View::CHandsOn3_3View()
{
 m_pImageObject = NULL;
 m_nSize = 3;
}
```

9. Add the following code to the CHandsOn3_3View destructor:

```
CHandsOn3_3View::~CHandsOn3_3View()
{
 if( m_pImageObject != NULL )
  delete m_pImageObject;
}
```

10. Edit the OnDraw function in the CHandsOn3_3View class in the HandsOn3_3View.cpp file as follows:

```
void CHandsOn3_3View::OnDraw(CDC* pDC)
{
 CHandsOn3_3Doc* pDoc = GetDocument();
 ASSERT_VALID(pDoc);

 if( m_pImageObject == NULL ){
  CMainFrame *pFrame =
   (CMainFrame *) AfxGetMainWnd();
  pFrame->SetWindowPos( NULL, 0, 0,
   326, 275, SWP_NOZORDER | SWP_NOMOVE );
```

```
BeginWaitCursor ();
m_pImageObject =
 new CImageObject( "PIC3.BMP", pDC );
EndWaitCursor ();
if( m_pImageObject == NULL ){
 AfxMessageBox( "Could not create image!" );
 return;
 }
}


if( m_pImageObject != NULL ){
 if( GetFocus() == this )
  m_pImageObject->SetPalette( pDC );
 m_pImageObject->Draw( pDC );
 }
}
```

11. Add the following functions with the Class Wizard to the CHandsOn3_3View class in the HandsOn3_3View.h file:

```
Name:OnChar()  Message:WM_CHAR
Name:OnLButtonDown()  Message:WM_LBUTTONDOWN
```

12. Edit the OnChar function in the CHandsOn3_3View class in the HandsOn3_3View.cpp file as follows:

```
void CHandsOn3_3View::OnChar(UINT nChar, UINT nRepCnt, UINT nFlags)
{
 if( nChar == '1' ) m_nSize = 1;
 else if( nChar == '2' ) m_nSize = 2;
 else if( nChar == '3' ) m_nSize = 3;
 else if( nChar == '4' ) m_nSize = 4;
 else if( nChar == '5' ) m_nSize = 5;

 CView::OnChar(nChar, nRepCnt, nFlags);
}
```

13. Edit the OnLButtonDown function in the CHandsOn3_3View class in the HandsOn3_3View.cpp file as follows:

```
void CHandsOn3_3View::OnLButtonDown(UINT nFlags, CPoint point)
{
 if( m_pImageObject != NULL ){
  CImagePointProcesses *pImagePointProcess;
  pImagePointProcess =
   new CImagePointProcesses( m_pImageObject );
```

```
if( pImagePointProcess != NULL ){
 int nHalfWidth = m_nSize * 20;
 pImagePointProcess->ReverseColors(
  point.x - nHalfWidth,
  point.y - nHalfWidth,
  point.x  + nHalfWidth,
  point.y + nHalfWidth );
 InvalidateRect( NULL, FALSE );
 UpdateWindow();
 delete pImagePointProcess;
 }
}

 CView::OnLButtonDown(nFlags, point);
}
```

14. Compile and run the program.

When the program first runs, you'll see the image in its original state. You can change the size of the square that's reversed by pressing the 1, 2, 3, 4, or 5 key. The 1 key will reverse the smallest area, the 5 key will reverse the largest area. There is no key that reverts the image to its original state, since all the reverse operations are reversible. Figure 3-12 shows the image with the smallest square area reversed and the largest square area reversed.

Figure 3-12: You can reverse different-size squares by pressing the 1, 2, 3, 4, or 5 key.

Hands-On 4: Colorize an Image

The program you're about to create lets you colorize square regions of an image. To colorize a square, simply point the mouse to the center of the square you want to colorize, and press the left mouse button. You can colorize with pure red, green, or blue. Press the R key for red, the G key for green, and the B key for blue. Figure 3-13 shows the image after a square region has been colorized with green.

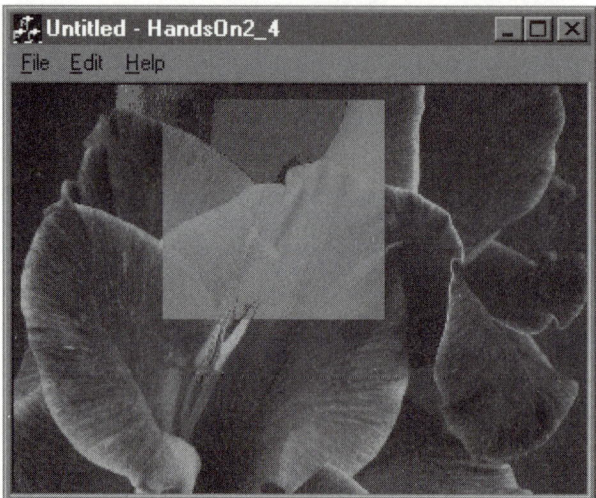

Figure 3-13: Point the mouse and click the left mouse button to colorize a square region of the image.

1. Create a Visual C++ project named HandsOn3_4 with the following attributes:

   ❏ Single-document interface

   ❏ English language

   ❏ No database support

   ❏ No compound document support

   ❏ No automation or ActiveX control support

   ❏ 3D controls, but no other features

   ❏ No source file comments

   ❏ Link MFC as a static library

2. Select Settings from the Project menu. Choose the Link tab. Add the following libraries to the Object/library modules field. The libraries for the release and debug versions are different; both are listed below.

Release Project Libraries	Debug Project Libraries
ImageLoad.lib	ImageLoad.lib
ImageObject.lib	ImageObjectD.lib
ImagePointProcesses.lib	ImagePointProcessesD.lib

3. Set the Active Configuration to Win32 Release.

4. Copy the file PIC4.BMP from the \IMAGEPR1\SAMPLES directory on the Companion CD-ROM to the newly created project directory.

5. Add the following include to the HandsOn3_4View.h file:

```
#include "ImagePointProcesses.h"
```

6. Add the following include to the HandsOn3_4View.h file:

```
#include "MAINFRM.h"
```

7. Add the following variable declarations to the CHandsOn3_4View class in the HandsOn3_4View.h file:

```
public:
 CImageObject *m_pImageObject;
 CImageObject *m_pImage;
 int m_nSize;
 COLORREF m_Color;
```

8. Add the following code to the CHandsOn3_4View constructor:

```
CHandsOn3_4View::CHandsOn3_4View()
{
 m_pImageObject = NULL;
 m_pImage = NULL;
 m_Color = RGB( 255, 0, 0 );
 m_nSize = 3;
}
```

9. Add the following code to the CHandsOn3_4View destructor:

```
CHandsOn3_4View::~CHandsOn3_4View()
{
 if( m_pImageObject != NULL )
  delete m_pImageObject;
```

```
   if( m_pImage != NULL )
    delete m_pImage;
  }
```

10. Edit the OnDraw function in the CHandsOn3_4View class in the HandsOn3_4View.cpp file as follows:

```
void CHandsOn3_4View::OnDraw(CDC* pDC)
{
 CHandsOn3_4Doc* pDoc = GetDocument();
 ASSERT_VALID(pDoc);

 if( m_pImageObject == NULL ){

   CMainFrame *pFrame =
    (CMainFrame *) AfxGetMainWnd();
   pFrame->SetWindowPos( NULL, 0, 0,
    326, 275, SWP_NOZORDER | SWP_NOMOVE );

   BeginWaitCursor ();
   m_pImageObject =
    new CImageObject( "PIC4.BMP", pDC );
   EndWaitCursor ();
   if( m_pImageObject == NULL ){
    AfxMessageBox( "Could not create image!" );
    return;
    }

   m_pImage = new CImageObject();
   *m_pImage = *m_pImageObject;
   }

 if( m_pImage != NULL ){
  if( GetFocus() == this )
   m_pImage->SetPalette( pDC );
  m_pImage->Draw( pDC );
  }
 }
```

11. Add the following functions with the Class Wizard to the CHandsOn3_4View class in the HandsOn3_4View.h file:

```
Name:OnChar()  Message:WM_CHAR
Name:OnLButtonDown()  Message:WM_LBUTTONDOWN
```

12. Edit the OnChar function in the CHandsOn3_4View class in the HandsOn3_4View.cpp file as follows:

```
void CHandsOn3_4View::OnChar(UINT nChar, UINT nRepCnt, UINT nFlags)
{
 if( nChar == '1' ) m_nSize = 1;
 else if( nChar == '2' ) m_nSize = 2;
 else if( nChar == '3' ) m_nSize = 3;
 else if( nChar == '4' ) m_nSize = 4;
 else if( nChar == '5' ) m_nSize = 5;
 else if( toupper( nChar ) == 'R' )
  m_Color = RGB( 255, 0, 0 );
 else if( toupper( nChar ) == 'G' )
  m_Color = RGB( 0, 255, 0 );
 else if( toupper( nChar ) == 'B' )
  m_Color = RGB( 0, 0, 255 );
 else if( toupper( nChar ) == 'Z' ){
  *m_pImage = *m_pImageObject;
  InvalidateRect( NULL, FALSE );
  UpdateWindow();
  }

 CView::OnChar(nChar, nRepCnt, nFlags);
}
```

13. Edit the OnLButtonDown function in the CHandsOn3_4View class in the HandsOn3_4View.cpp file as follows:

```
void CHandsOn3_4View::OnLButtonDown(UINT nFlags, CPoint point)
{
 if( m_pImageObject != NULL ){
  CImagePointProcesses *pImagePointProcess;
  pImagePointProcess =
   new CImagePointProcesses( m_pImage );
  if( pImagePointProcess != NULL ){
   int nHalfWidth = m_nSize * 20;
   pImagePointProcess->Colorize(
    point.x - nHalfWidth,
    point.y - nHalfWidth,
    point.x  + nHalfWidth,
    point.y + nHalfWidth, m_Color );
   InvalidateRect( NULL, FALSE );
   UpdateWindow();
   delete pImagePointProcess;
   }
  }

 CView::OnLButtonDown(nFlags, point);
}
```

14. Compile and run the program.

When the program first runs, you'll see the image in its original state. You can change the size of the square that's being colorized by pressing the 1, 2, 3, 4, or 5 key. The 1 key will colorize the smallest area; the 5 key will colorize the largest area. The Z key reverts the image back to its original state. Figure 3-14 shows the image with the smallest square area colorized in blue and the largest square area colorized in red.

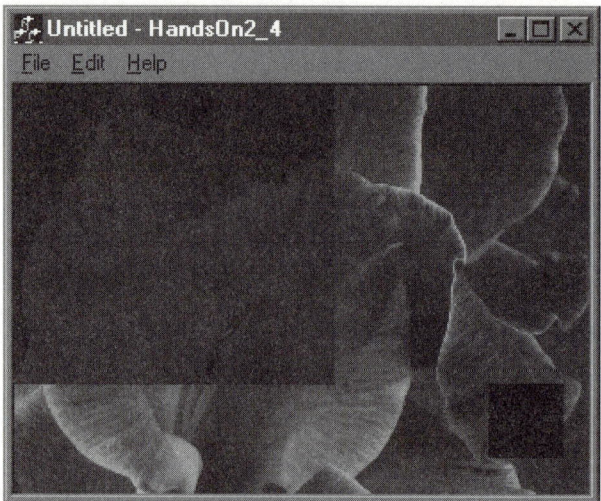

Figure 3-14: You can colorize different-size squares by pressing the 1, 2, 3, 4, or 5 key.

Hands-On 5: Convert an Image to Grayscale

This is the simplest exercise in this chapter. There's no user interaction—it simply converts an image to grayscale and displays it as shown in Figure 3-15.

Figure 3-15: The simplest point process is converting a color image to a grayscale image.

1. Create a Visual C++ project named HandsOn3_5 with the following attributes:

   ❑ Single-document interface

   ❑ English language

   ❑ No database support

   ❑ No compound document support

   ❑ No automation or ActiveX control support

   ❑ 3D controls, but no other features

   ❑ No source file comments

   ❑ Link MFC as a static library

2. Select Settings from the Project menu. Choose the Link tab. Add the following libraries to the Object/library modules field. The libraries for the release and debug versions are different; both are listed below.

Release Project Libraries	Debug Project Libraries
ImageLoad.lib	ImageLoad.lib
ImageObject.lib	ImageObjectD.lib
ImagePointProcesses.lib	ImagePointProcessesD.lib

3. Set the Active Configuration to Win32 Release.

4. Copy the file PIC5.BMP from the \IMAGEPR1\SAMPLES directory on the Companion CD-ROM to the newly created project directory.

5. Add the following include to the HandsOn3_5View.h file:

```
#include "ImagePointProcesses.h"
```

6. Add the following include to the HandsOn3_5View.h file:

```
#include "MAINFRM.h"
```

7. Add the following variable declarations to the CHandsOn3_5View class in the HandsOn3_5View.h file:

```
public:
 CImageObject *m_pImageObject;
```

8. Add the following code to the CHandsOn3_5View constructor:

```
CHandsOn3_5View::CHandsOn3_5View()
{
 m_pImageObject = NULL;
}
```

9. Add the following code to the CHandsOn3_5View destructor:

```
CHandsOn3_5View::~CHandsOn3_5View()
{
 if( m_pImageObject != NULL )
  delete m_pImageObject;
}
```

10. Edit the OnDraw function in the CHandsOn3_5View class in the HandsOn3_5View.cpp file as follows:

```
void CHandsOn3_5View::OnDraw(CDC* pDC)
{
 CHandsOn3_5Doc* pDoc = GetDocument();
 ASSERT_VALID(pDoc);

 if( m_pImageObject == NULL ){
```

```
CMainFrame *pFrame =
 (CMainFrame *) AfxGetMainWnd();
pFrame->SetWindowPos( NULL, 0, 0,
 326, 275, SWP_NOZORDER | SWP_NOMOVE );

BeginWaitCursor ();
m_pImageObject =
 new CImageObject( "PIC5.BMP", pDC );
EndWaitCursor ();
if( m_pImageObject == NULL ){
 AfxMessageBox( "Could not create image!" );
 return;
 }

CImagePointProcesses *pImagePointProcess;
pImagePointProcess =
 new CImagePointProcesses( m_pImageObject );
if( pImagePointProcess != NULL ){
 pImagePointProcess->MakeGray();
 delete pImagePointProcess;
 }
 }

if( m_pImageObject != NULL ){
 if( GetFocus() == this )
  m_pImageObject->SetPalette( pDC );
 m_pImageObject->Draw( pDC );
 }

}
```

11. Compile and run the program.

When the program runs, you won't get too excited since all you'll see is an image with flowers that has been converted to grayscale.

125

ON THE WEB

Several sites around the Web are devoted to graphics and image processing. Here's a sampling of a few.

One way of getting the most out of images is to use them more than once. You can use a single image many times if you perform image processing techniques on it so that it's different. The site in Figure 3-16 does this admirably, reducing the amount of transfer time so that users who hit the site have less waiting time.

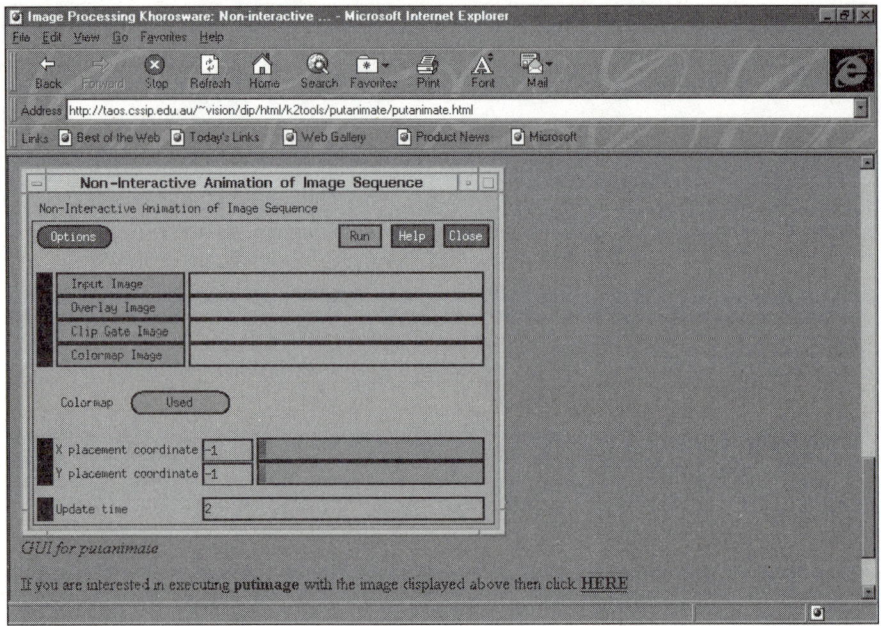

Figure 3-16: This site animates a sequence of images but processes them before it uses them.

Black-and-white images that are colorized can provide strikingly vivid results. The site in Figure 3-17 colorizes black-and-white images. This technique is very useful for situations in which users are given choices.

If you want to find out about current research and development in the field of image processing, the Web has some examples. One in particular is sponsored by the University of California at Berkeley. Figure 3-18 shows this site and some of what it has to offer.

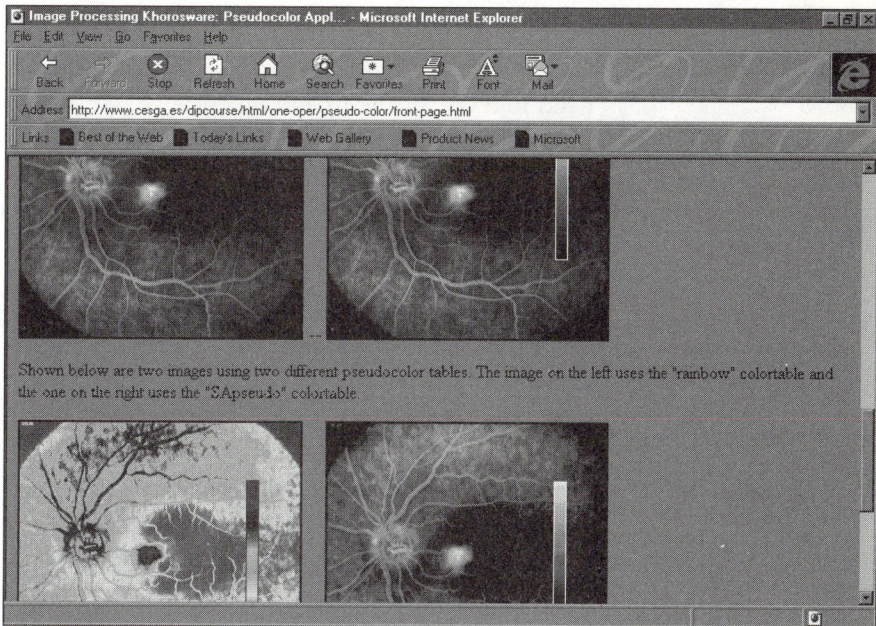

Figure 3-17: This site covers colorization of black-and-white images.

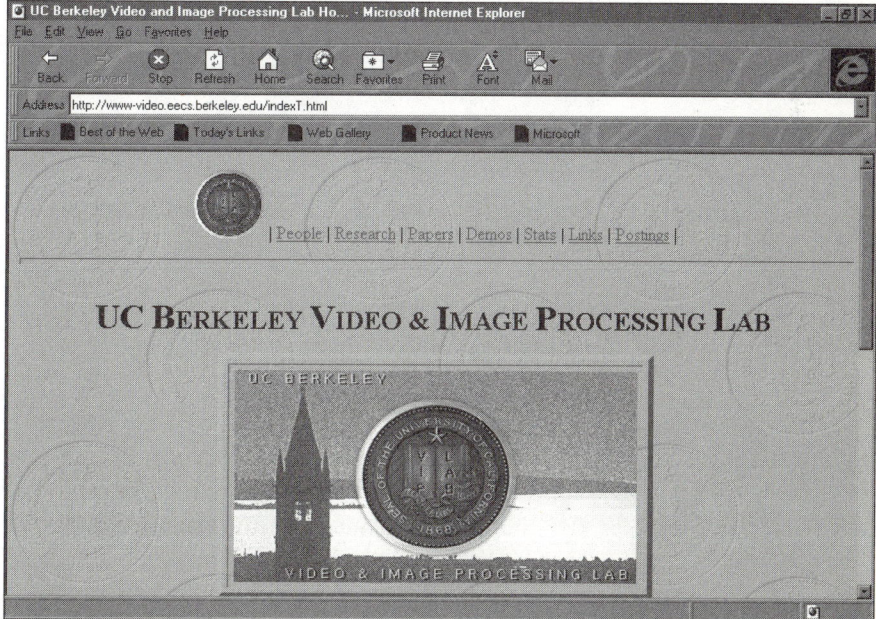

Figure 3-18: Many universities, such as the University of California at Berkeley, have Web pages devoted to image processing.

SHAREWARE

Vidfun v2.2 is a fantastic program that'll give you most everything you need in the realm of image processing (see Figure 3-19). You can load images of almost any format. Then, you can alter them by cropping, stretching, and color reducing.

It also boasts a wide variety of image processing options such as colorization and filtering.

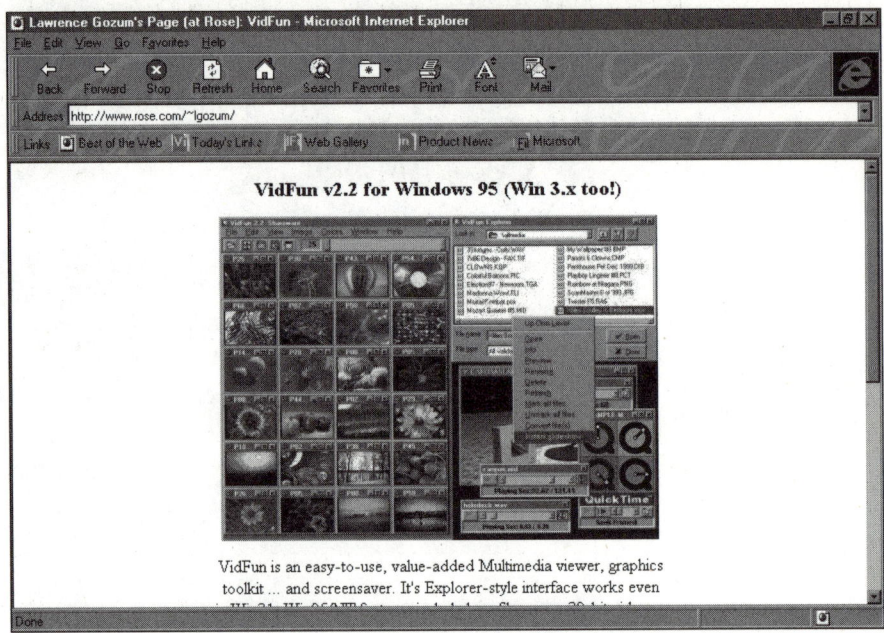

Figure 3-19: VidFun v2.2 is one of the best programs around for image processing.

MOVING ON

Image processing can save a lot of disk space and memory. You can use a single, original image and change its appearance for many purposes. This is the way to go if you have an interest in conserving system resources.

Besides the practical side of image processing, many people think it's just plain fun to manipulate and change images. I hope you're in this camp, because I'd love for you to send me your image point process functions.

The next chapter moves on to area processes. Unlike point processes, they perform operations on entire regions of pixels, or areas. These are just as useful, and just as much fun.

Chapter 4

Image Area Processing

One of the main causes of the fall of the Roman Empire was that, lacking zero, they had no way to indicate successful termination of their C programs.

—Robert Firth

The previous chapter showed you how to perform point processes on images. It's a great way to get more use out of a single image. You can colorize images to indicate a hot spot, convert to grayscale for a black-and-white photograph effect, or brighten an image to make it more appealing.

This chapter is similar, since it teaches image processing techniques. The difference, though, is that all of the processes in this chapter are *area* processes. They don't act on pixels based on a single pixel's value. They act on pixels based on the value of the pixels in the adjacent area.

These techniques are more useful for enhancing images than altering images. For instance, performing a median filter operation can remove many extraneous marks that are undesirable in an image.

Area processes, also referred to in some texts as group processes, use groups of pixels to derive information about an image. The group of pixels used in area processes is referred to as "the neighborhood." The neighborhood is generally a two-dimensional matrix of pixel values with each dimension having an odd number of elements. The pixel of interest (the pixel whose old value is being replaced by its new value as a result of an algorithmic computation) resides at the center of the neighborhood. Having a cluster of pixels in the neighborhood around the pixel of interest furnishes brightness trend information (in two dimensions) that is utilized by most area processes. Another, more proper, term for brightness trend information is *spatial frequency*.

Spatial frequency is defined as the rate of change of pixel brightness or intensity divided by the distance over which the change occurred. Spatial frequency has components in both the horizontal and vertical directions in an image. An image with high spatial frequency content contains large, closely spaced changes in pixel values. An image of a black and white checkerboard would contain a high spatial frequency content. The smaller the squares, the higher the frequency content. An image with low spatial frequency contains large areas of constant or slowly changing pixel values. Images of clouds generally have a low spatial frequency content.

Having access to the spatial frequency information allows area processes to act as filters for removing or enhancing selective frequency components found in an image. Many area processes thus fall into the general category of spatial filters. Like spatial filters found in electronic engineering, spatial filters in software have a firm basis in mathematics.

Spatial filtering has many applications in image processing. It can be used, for example, for extraction of image features (edge enhancement and detection), for sharpening an image, for smoothing an image, for blurring an image, and for removal of random noise present in an image. These aspects of spatial filtering will be demonstrated in this chapter.

THE CIMAGEAREAPROCESSES CLASS LIBRARY

The CImageAreaProcesses class library is used to perform image processing on instances of the CImageObject class. In order to use this class, an image must be loaded into a CImageObject class. Then the CImageObject class is attached to the CImageAreaProcesses class when it's created, or when an operation is performed.

Area processes are based on values derived for entire groups of pixels. For instance, if you want to perform a filter operation on a certain pixel, you'd look in its general vicinity. You'd then calculate a value based on the pixels in its general vicinity. The real term for a pixel's general vicinity is a pixel's *kernel*. The size and shape of the kernel can vary according to how the operation is structured.

The ImageProcess2 Demo

Once again this program builds upon the ImageView demo program of Chapter 1 and the ImageProcess1, and adds the image area processes. That way, you'll have a program with more functionality than one that simply performs image area processes.

The operations that the program adds are contrast change, contrast equalization, edge enhancement, high-pass filtering, low-pass filtering, and median filtering. These operations are the most common area processes and will give you a good sampling of that category of image processing.

When the program first runs, you'll see an empty application window. Load an image by selecting Open from the File menu. You can then choose an image to load in. Figure 4-1 shows an image of the earth that was taken by Apollo 7.

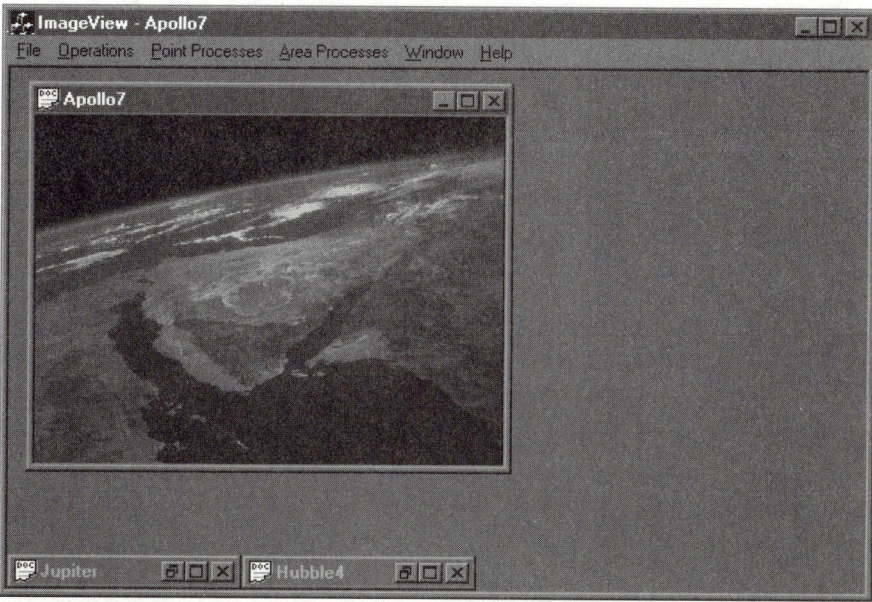

Figure 4-1: Astronomical images often are the subjects of image processing.

There may be many times (especially in cases of surveillance) when the edges of an image must be enhanced. The ImageProcess2 program can perform this operation. The image shown in Figure 4-1 can be seen in Figure 4-2 with the edges enhanced.

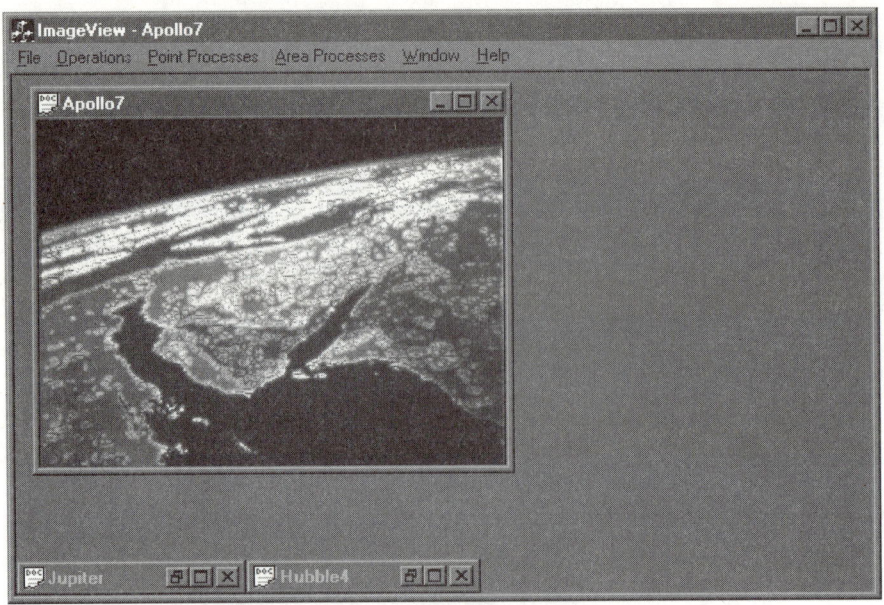

Figure 4-2: ImageProcess2 can enhance the edges of an image.

Other images may come in with imperfections. Figure 4-3 shows an image of Jupiter with imperfections.

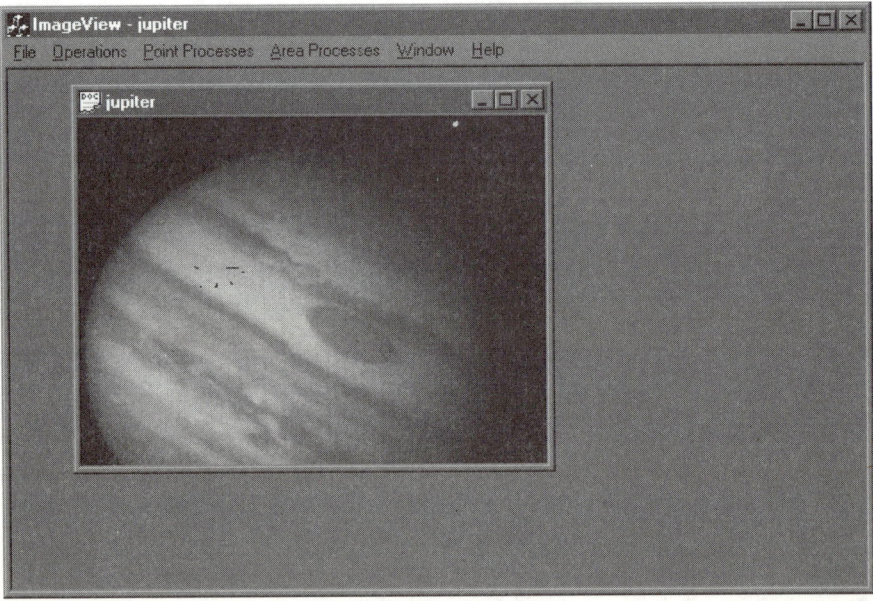

Figure 4-3: This image of Jupiter has imperfections that may have resulted from transmission noise.

Median filtering can fix many image imperfections. Figure 4-4 is the previous image of Jupiter with a median filter process performed. The imperfections are removed as a result.

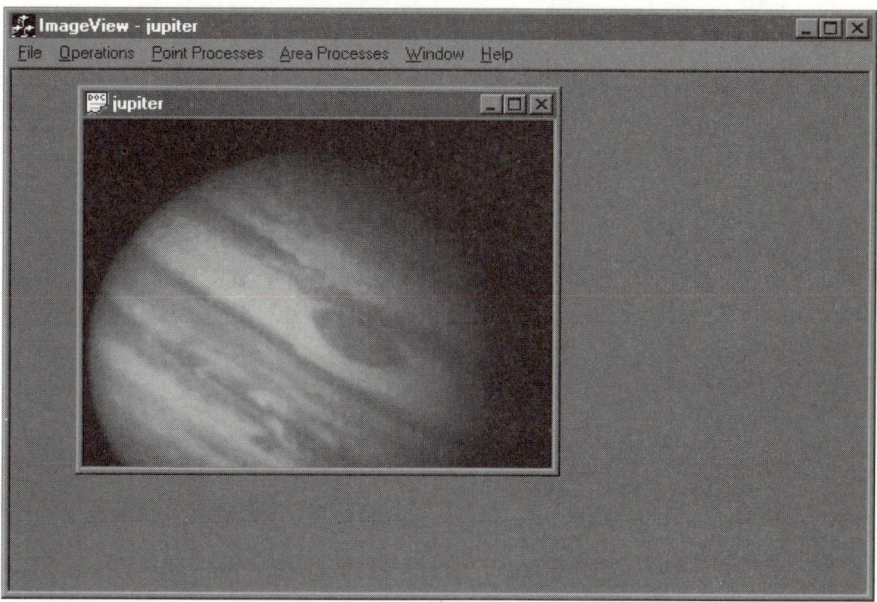

Figure 4-4: This image was median-filtered to remove imperfections.

CImageAreaProcesses Class Library Function Calls

CImageAreaProcesses()

Prototype: `CImageAreaProcesses( void );`

Purpose: This version of the CImageAreaProcesses class constructs the class without attaching a CImageObject class. The first call to an image processing function must include a CImageObject pointer in order for the function to have something upon which it can operate.

Arguments: None

Returns: Nothing

CImageAreaProcesses()

Prototype: `CImageAreaProcesses( CImageObject *pImageObject );`

Purpose: This version of the CImageAreaProcesses class constructs the class and attaches a CImageObject class. Every operation will refer to the CImageObject class that was attached until another is passed in as a function argument to one of the image processing functions.

Arguments: None

Returns: Nothing

MedianFilter()

Prototype: `BOOL MedianFilter( int nX1, int nY1, int nX2, int nY2, CImageObject *pImageObject);`

Purpose: This function performs a median filtering operation on the image that's attached. Any coordinate that's not specified and is allowed to default to -1 will revert to the edge of the image. For instance, nX1 and nY1 will become 0; nX2 and nY2 will become the width and height of the image. The best way to median-filter the entire image is not to pass any arguments. By not specifying a CImageObject pointer, the function will use the CImageObject that's been previously attached.

Arguments: int nX1, Defaults to -1
int nY1, Defaults to -1
int nX2, Defaults to -1
int nY2, Defaults to -1
CImageObject *pImageObject, Defaults to NULL

Returns: BOOL:TRUE for success, FALSE for FAIL

ChangeContrast()

Prototype: `BOOL ChangeContrast( int nContrast, int nX1, int nY1, int nX2, int nY2, CImageObject *pImageObect );`

Purpose: This function changes the contrast for the image that's attached. Any coordinate that's not specified and is allowed to default to -1 will revert to the edge of the image. For instance, nX1 and nY1 will become 0; nX2 and nY2 will become the width and height of the image. The best way to change the contrast for the entire image is not to pass any arguments. By not specifying a CImageObject pointer, the function will use the CImageObject that's been previously attached. Contrast values should range from 1 to 200.

Arguments:
int nContrast
int nX1, Defaults to -1
int nY1, Defaults to -1
int nX2, Defaults to -1
int nY2, Defaults to -1
CImageObject *pImageObject, Defaults to NULL

Returns:
BOOL:TRUE for success, FALSE for FAIL

EqualizeContrast()

Prototype:
```
BOOL EqualizeContrast( int nX1, int nY1, int nX2, int nY2, int
    nThresholdFactor );
```

Purpose:
This function equalizes the contrast for the image that's attached. Any coordinate that's not specified and is allowed to default to -1 will revert to the edge of the image. For instance, nX1 and nY1 will become 0; nX2 and nY2 will become the width and height of the image. The best way to equalize the contrast for the entire image is not to pass any arguments. By not specifying a CImageObject pointer, the function will use the CImageObject that's been previously attached.

Arguments:
int nX1, Defaults to -1
int nY1, Defaults to -1
int nX2, Defaults to -1
int nY2, Defaults to -1
int nThresholdFactor, Defaults to -1
CImageObject *pImageObject, Defaults to NULL

Returns:
BOOL:TRUE for success, FALSE for FAIL

HighpassFilter()

Prototype:
```
BOOL HighpassFilter( int nX1, int nY1, int nX2, int nY2, CImageObject
    *pImageObject);
```

Purpose:
This function performs a high-pass filtering operation on the image that's attached. Any coordinate that's not specified and is allowed to default to -1 will revert to the edge of the image. For instance, nX1 and nY1 will become 0; nX2 and nY2 will become the width and height of the

image. The best way to high-pass-filter the entire image is not to pass any arguments. By not specifying a CImageObject pointer, the function will use the CImageObject that's been previously attached.

Arguments: int nX1, Defaults to -1
int nY1, Defaults to -1
int nX2, Defaults to -1
int nY2, Defaults to -1
CImageObject *pImageObject, Defaults to NULL

Returns: BOOL:TRUE for success, FALSE for FAIL

LowpassFilter()

Prototype: BOOL LowpassFilter(int nX1, int nY1, int nX2, int nY2, DWORD
*dwFact);

Purpose: This function performs a low-pass filtering operation on the image that's attached. Any coordinate that's not specified and is allowed to default to -1 will revert to the edge of the image. For instance, nX1 and nY1 will become 0; nX2 and nY2 will become the width and height of the image. The best way to low-pass-filter the entire image is not to pass any arguments. By not specifying a CImageObject pointer, the function will use the CImageObject that's been previously attached.

Arguments: int nX1, Defaults to -1
int nY1, Defaults to -1
int nX2, Defaults to -1
int nY2, Defaults to -1
DWORD *dwFact, Defaults to NULL
CImageObject *pImageObject, Defaults to NULL

Returns: BOOL:TRUE for success, FALSE for FAIL

EdgeEnhance()

Prototype: BOOL EdgeEnhance(int nX1, int nY1, int nX2, int nY2, CImageObject
*pImageObject);

Purpose: This function performs an edge-enhancement operation on the image that's attached. Any coordinate that's not specified and is allowed to default to -1 will revert to the edge of the image. For instance, nX1 and nY1 will become 0; nX2 and nY2 will become the width and height of the image. The best way to edge-enhance the entire image is not to pass any arguments. By not specifying a CImageObject pointer, the function will use the CImageObject that's been previously attached.

Arguments: int nX1, Defaults to -1
               int nY1, Defaults to -1
               int nX2, Defaults to -1
               int nY2, Defaults to -1
               CImageObject *pImageObject, Defaults to NULL

Returns: BOOL:TRUE for success, FALSE for FAIL

BEHIND AREAPOINTPROCESSDEMO (IMAGEVIEW)

This program is based on the ImageView program that was originally built for Chapter 1. As a result, the actual filenames are the same as those from the ImageView program in the images directory. Additions have been made that add the area image processing procedures. All source code for this version of ImageView can be found in the imagepr2\ImageView directory on the Companion CD-ROM.

Below are explanations for the ImageView sections. Explanations for the parts of the program that relate to the area image processing techniques can be found later in this chapter under "Area Image Processing in a Nutshell."

Changing Contrast

Many times, your picture will improve with a change in contrast. Sometimes you can tell visually if there needs to be more contrast. A useful tool that's included in the program is a histogram viewer. If the majority of the histogram data is contained within a small area, the image would probably be enhanced if the contrast was increased. Figure 4-5 shows the histogram of an image with low contrast; Figure 4-6 shows the histogram of an image with broad contrast.

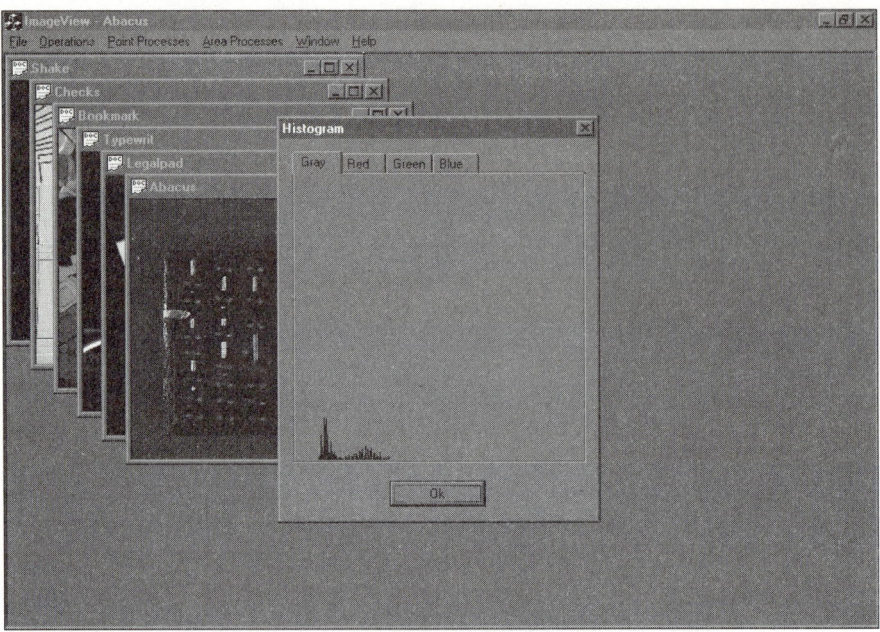

Figure 4-5: You can see from this histogram that this image has low contrast.

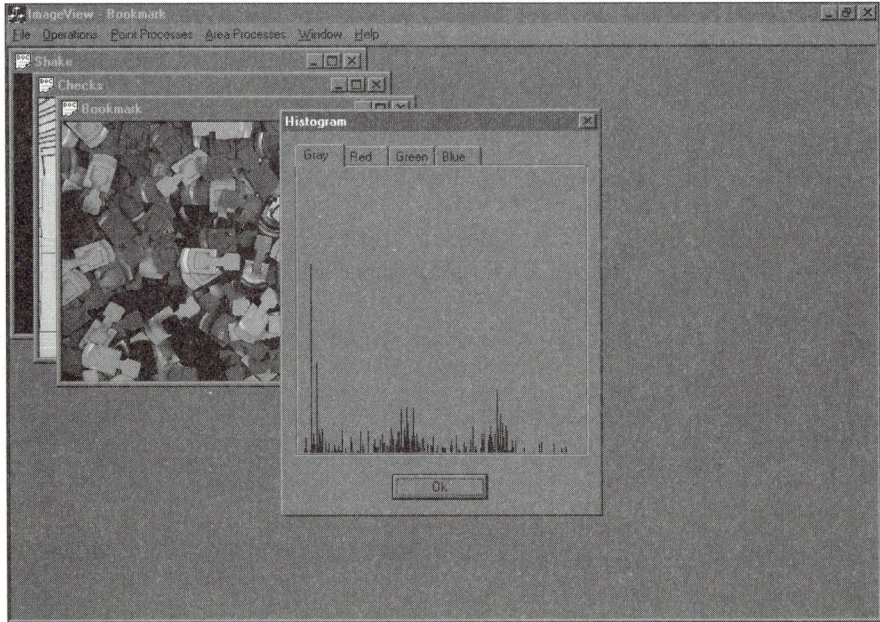

Figure 4-6: You can see from this histogram that this image has broad contrast.

If a crop box is showing, the OnAreaprocessChangecontrast() function makes sure that the coordinates of the CRectTracker object are in range. It makes adjustments if any of the vertices are outside of the image.

A dialog box allowing the user to specify a contrast value from 0 to 200 then appears. This value will be used to alter the contrast when the ChangeContrast() function is called.

The OnAreaprocessChangecontrast() Code

```
void CImageViewView::
OnAreaprocessesChangecontrast()
{

 if( m_pTracker == NULL ||
  m_pImageObject == NULL ) return;

 int nX1 = m_pTracker->m_rect.left;
 int nY1 = m_pTracker->m_rect.top;
 int nX2 = m_pTracker->m_rect.right;
 int nY2 = m_pTracker->m_rect.bottom;

 if( nX1 < 0 ) nX1 = 0;
 if( nX1 > m_pImageObject->GetWidth() - 1 )
  nX1 = m_pImageObject->GetWidth() - 1;
 if( nY1 < 0 ) nY1 = 0;
 if( nY1 > m_pImageObject->GetHeight() - 1 )
  nY1 = m_pImageObject->GetHeight() - 1;
 if( nX2 < 0 ) nX2 = 0;
 if( nX2 > m_pImageObject->GetWidth() - 1 )
  nX2 = m_pImageObject->GetWidth() - 1;
 if( nY2 < 0 ) nY2 = 0;
 if( nY2 > m_pImageObject->GetHeight() - 1 )
  nY2 = m_pImageObject->GetHeight() - 1;

 if( !m_bCropBoxShowing ){
  nX1 = nY1 = 0;
  nX2 = m_pImageObject->GetWidth() - 1;
  nY2 = m_pImageObject->GetHeight() - 1;
  }

 CBrightness Brightness;
 strcpy( Brightness.m_szTitle,
  "Set Contrast" );
 strcpy( Brightness.m_szLabel, "Contrast" );
 if( Brightness.DoModal() != IDOK ) return;
```

139

```
CImageAreaProcesses
 AreaProcesses( m_pImageObject );
BeginWaitCursor();
AreaProcesses.ChangeContrast(
 Brightness.m_nBrightness, nX1, nY1,nX2,nY2);
EndWaitCursor();

InvalidateRect( NULL, FALSE );
UpdateWindow();
}
```

Edge Enhancing

There are many times that the edges of objects within images must be enhanced. Good examples of this occur when satellite images are being studied. The edges of continents, countries, and other geographical objects can be seen better if their edges are enhanced.

If a crop box is showing, the OnAreaprocessEdgeenhance() function makes sure that the coordinates of the CRectTracker object are in range. It makes adjustments if any of the vertices are outside of the image.

The OnAreaprocessEdgeenhance() Code

```
void CImageViewView::OnAreaprocessesEdgeenhance()
{

if( m_pTracker == NULL ||
 m_pImageObject == NULL ) return;

int nX1 = m_pTracker->m_rect.left;
int nY1 = m_pTracker->m_rect.top;
int nX2 = m_pTracker->m_rect.right;
int nY2 = m_pTracker->m_rect.bottom;

if( nX1 < 0 ) nX1 = 0;
if( nX1 > m_pImageObject->GetWidth() - 1 )
 nX1 = m_pImageObject->GetWidth() - 1;
if( nY1 < 0 ) nY1 = 0;
if( nY1 > m_pImageObject->GetHeight() - 1 )
 nY1 = m_pImageObject->GetHeight() - 1;
if( nX2 < 0 ) nX2 = 0;
if( nX2 > m_pImageObject->GetWidth() - 1 )
 nX2 = m_pImageObject->GetWidth() - 1;
if( nY2 < 0 ) nY2 = 0;
if( nY2 > m_pImageObject->GetHeight() - 1 )
 nY2 = m_pImageObject->GetHeight() - 1;
```

```
if( !m_bCropBoxShowing ){
 nX1 = nY1 = 0;
 nX2 = m_pImageObject->GetWidth() - 1;
 nY2 = m_pImageObject->GetHeight() - 1;
 }
CImageAreaProcesses
 AreaProcesses( m_pImageObject );
BeginWaitCursor();
AreaProcesses.EdgeEnhance( nX1, nY1,nX2,nY2);
EndWaitCursor();

InvalidateRect( NULL, FALSE );
UpdateWindow();
}
```

Equalizing Contrast

You can change the contrast of an image with the CImageAreaProcesses class's ChangeContrast() function. You can also let the contrast of an image be equalized automatically, finding the best contrast for the image.

Taking the image for which a histogram was shown in Figure 4-5, we can equalize the contrast and get a histogram as shown in Figure 4-7.

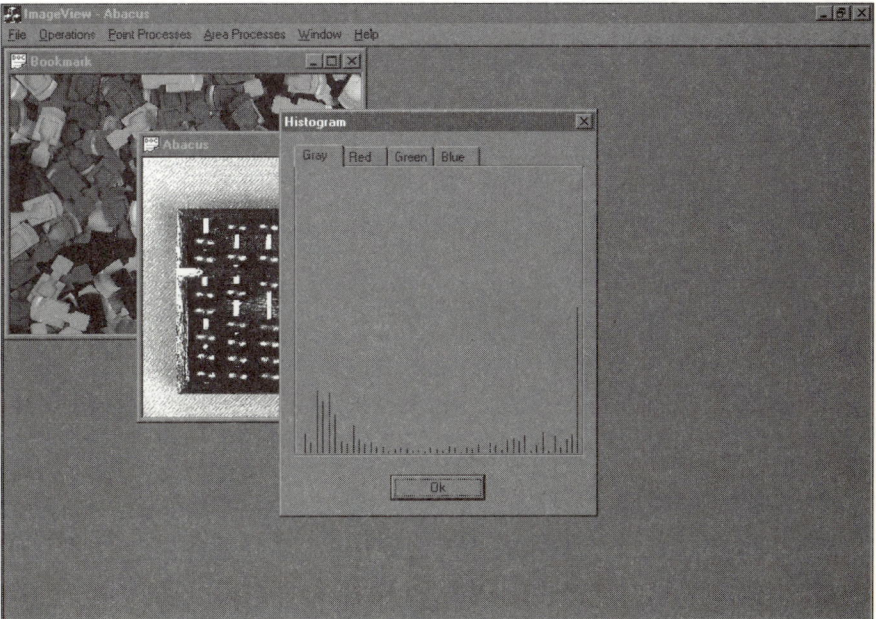

Figure 4-7: The histogram after an image with poor contrast underwent a contrast equalization procedure.

Viewing histograms is one thing; seeing the before-and-after images is another. Figure 4-8 shows the image before the contrast equalization; Figure 4-9 shows it after.

Figure 4-8: An image with poor contrast.

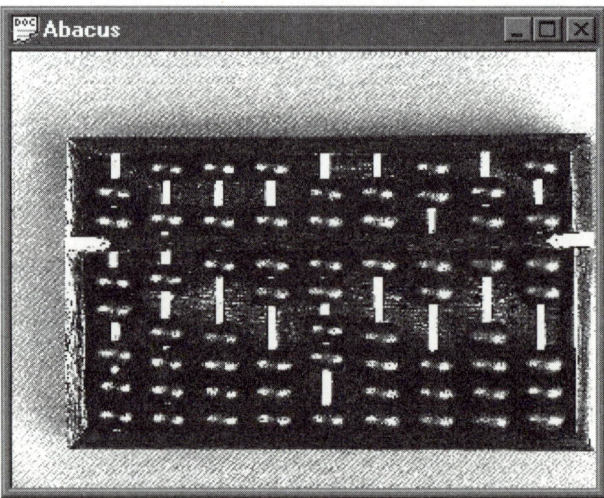

Figure 4-9: An image with poor contrast has much better contrast after contrast equalization.

Once again, if a crop box is showing, the OnAreaprocessEqualizecontrast() function makes sure that the coordinates of the CRectTracker object are in range. It makes adjustments if any of the vertices are outside of the image.

The OnAreaprocessEqualizecontrast() Code

```
void CImageViewView::
OnAreaprocessesEqualizecontrast()
{
 if( m_pTracker == NULL ||
  m_pImageObject == NULL ) return;

 int nX1 = m_pTracker->m_rect.left;
 int nY1 = m_pTracker->m_rect.top;
 int nX2 = m_pTracker->m_rect.right;
 int nY2 = m_pTracker->m_rect.bottom;

 if( nX1 < 0 ) nX1 = 0;
 if( nX1 > m_pImageObject->GetWidth() - 1 )
  nX1 = m_pImageObject->GetWidth() - 1;
 if( nY1 < 0 ) nY1 = 0;
 if( nY1 > m_pImageObject->GetHeight() - 1 )
  nY1 = m_pImageObject->GetHeight() - 1;
 if( nX2 < 0 ) nX2 = 0;
 if( nX2 > m_pImageObject->GetWidth() - 1 )
  nX2 = m_pImageObject->GetWidth() - 1;
 if( nY2 < 0 ) nY2 = 0;
 if( nY2 > m_pImageObject->GetHeight() - 1 )
  nY2 = m_pImageObject->GetHeight() - 1;

 if( !m_bCropBoxShowing ){
  nX1 = nY1 = 0;
  nX2 = m_pImageObject->GetWidth() - 1;
  nY2 = m_pImageObject->GetHeight() - 1;
  }
 CImageAreaProcesses
  AreaProcesses( m_pImageObject );
 BeginWaitCursor();
 AreaProcesses.EqualizeContrast( nX1, nY1,
  nX2, nY2 );
 EndWaitCursor();

 InvalidateRect( NULL, FALSE );
 UpdateWindow();
}
```

143

High-Pass Filtering

High-pass filters accentuate the high-frequency details of an image while leaving the low-frequency content intact. Relative to the high-frequency content, the low-frequency content is attenuated, or reduced. High-pass filtering is used whenever objects with high spatial frequency content need to be examined. The higher frequency portions of an image will be highlighted (become brighter), while the lower frequency portions become black. Image sharpness is sometimes enhanced with high-pass filtering at the expense of accentuated image noise. Edge enhancement of an image is also possible with the application of high-pass filtering.

The large center kernel coefficient (the size of the neighboring pixel area) holds the key to the operation of high-pass filters. As the large center coefficient moves across a portion of an image with high spatial frequency content (meaning a large-step change in pixel intensity), the new value of the pixel of interest is multiplied many times in value. The smaller negative coefficients in the kernel clustered around the large center value work to reduce the effect of the large weighting factor. The net effect is that large changes in pixel intensity are intensified, while areas of constant pixel intensity are left alone. In other words, areas of constant pixel intensity (areas of low spatial frequencies) are not affected by this transformation.

The OnAreaprocessHighpassfilter() Code

```
void CImageViewView::
OnAreaprocessesHighpassfilter()
{

 if( m_pTracker == NULL ||
  m_pImageObject == NULL ) return;

 int nX1 = m_pTracker->m_rect.left;
 int nY1 = m_pTracker->m_rect.top;
 int nX2 = m_pTracker->m_rect.right;
 int nY2 = m_pTracker->m_rect.bottom;

 if( nX1 < 0 ) nX1 = 0;
 if( nX1 > m_pImageObject->GetWidth() - 1 )
  nX1 = m_pImageObject->GetWidth() - 1;
 if( nY1 < 0 ) nY1 = 0;
 if( nY1 > m_pImageObject->GetHeight() - 1 )
  nY1 = m_pImageObject->GetHeight() - 1;
 if( nX2 < 0 ) nX2 = 0;
```

```
if( nX2 > m_pImageObject->GetWidth() - 1 )
 nX2 = m_pImageObject->GetWidth() - 1;
if( nY2 < 0 ) nY2 = 0;
if( nY2 > m_pImageObject->GetHeight() - 1 )
 nY2 = m_pImageObject->GetHeight() - 1;

if( !m_bCropBoxShowing ){
 nX1 = nY1 = 0;
 nX2 = m_pImageObject->GetWidth() - 1;
 nY2 = m_pImageObject->GetHeight() - 1;
 }
CImageAreaProcesses
 AreaProcesses( m_pImageObject );
BeginWaitCursor();
AreaProcesses.HighpassFilter( nX1, nY1, nX2,
 nY2 );
EndWaitCursor();

InvalidateRect( NULL, FALSE );
UpdateWindow();

}
```

Low-Pass Filtering

Low-pass spatial filters leave the low-frequency content of an image intact while attenuating the high-frequency content. Low-pass filters are good at reducing the visual noise contained in an image. They are also used to remove the high-frequency content of an image so that the low-frequency content can be examined more closely. With the high frequencies gone, more subtle low-frequency changes can be identified. The cutoff frequency of a low-pass filter is determined by the size of the kernel and the kernel coefficients.

Consider a portion of an image without high-frequency content. This means that the pixel values are of constant value or that they are changing slowly. As a low-pass kernel is passed over this portion of the image, the new value for the pixel of interest (the pixel centered under the kernel) is calculated as the sum of the kernel coefficients times the neighborhood pixel values. If all the neighborhood pixel values are the same (constant), the new pixel value is the same as the old value. This is the reason the sum of the coefficients is chosen to be 1. Low-frequency content has been preserved. As the kernel is moved over the portion of the image with high-frequency content, any rapid changes in intensity get averaged out with the remaining pixels in the neighborhood, thereby

145

lowering the high-frequency content. The visual result of low-pass filtering is a slight blur of the image. This blur results because any sharp pixel transitions are averaged with other surroundings as the high-frequency content is attenuated.

Contrary as it sounds, low-pass filtering can be used to sharpen the appearance of an image. If a low-pass filtered image is subtracted from the original image, the result is a relative increase in high-frequency information content without an increase in image noise. Subjectively, the resultant image appears sharper than the original. This could be used to highlight portions of an image that are obscured by haze or clouds. This technique might even be able to make an image of Los Angeles look good on a smoggy day.

The OnAreaprocessLowpassfilter() Code

```
void CImageViewView::OnAreaprocessesLowpassfilter()
{

if( m_pTracker == NULL ||
 m_pImageObject == NULL ) return;

int nX1 = m_pTracker->m_rect.left;
int nY1 = m_pTracker->m_rect.top;
int nX2 = m_pTracker->m_rect.right;
int nY2 = m_pTracker->m_rect.bottom;

if( nX1 < 0 ) nX1 = 0;
if( nX1 > m_pImageObject->GetWidth() - 1 )
 nX1 = m_pImageObject->GetWidth() - 1;
if( nY1 < 0 ) nY1 = 0;
if( nY1 > m_pImageObject->GetHeight() - 1 )
 nY1 = m_pImageObject->GetHeight() - 1;
if( nX2 < 0 ) nX2 = 0;
if( nX2 > m_pImageObject->GetWidth() - 1 )
 nX2 = m_pImageObject->GetWidth() - 1;
if( nY2 < 0 ) nY2 = 0;
if( nY2 > m_pImageObject->GetHeight() - 1 )
 nY2 = m_pImageObject->GetHeight() - 1;

if( !m_bCropBoxShowing ){
 nX1 = nY1 = 0;
 nX2 = m_pImageObject->GetWidth() - 1;
 nY2 = m_pImageObject->GetHeight() - 1;
 }
```

```
CImageAreaProcesses
 AreaProcesses( m_pImageObject );
BeginWaitCursor();
AreaProcesses.LowpassFilter( nX1, nY1, nX2,
 nY2 );
EndWaitCursor();

InvalidateRect( NULL, FALSE );
UpdateWindow();

}
```

Median Filtering

Median filtering is different than low- and high-pass filtering. It uses the values of pixels contained in the pixel neighborhood to determine the new value given to a pixel. However, it does not algorithmically calculate the new pixel value from the pixels in the neighborhood. Instead, it sorts the pixels in the neighborhood into ascending order and picks the middle or median pixel value as the new value for the pixel.

The result of median filtering is that any random noise contained in an image will be effectively eliminated. This is because any random, abrupt change in pixel intensity within a pixel neighborhood will be sorted out. That is, it will be placed at either the top or the bottom of the sorted neighborhood values and will be ignored because the median value is always picked for the new pixel value.

The OnAreaprocessMedianfilter() Code

```
void CImageViewView::OnAreaprocessesMedianfilter()
{

if( m_pTracker == NULL ||
 m_pImageObject == NULL ) return;

int nX1 = m_pTracker->m_rect.left;
int nY1 = m_pTracker->m_rect.top;
int nX2 = m_pTracker->m_rect.right;
int nY2 = m_pTracker->m_rect.bottom;

if( nX1 < 0 ) nX1 = 0;
if( nX1 > m_pImageObject->GetWidth() - 1 )
 nX1 = m_pImageObject->GetWidth() - 1;
if( nY1 < 0 ) nY1 = 0;
```

147

```
            if( nY1 > m_pImageObject->GetHeight() - 1 )
             nY1 = m_pImageObject->GetHeight() - 1;
            if( nX2 < 0 ) nX2 = 0;
            if( nX2 > m_pImageObject->GetWidth() - 1 )
             nX2 = m_pImageObject->GetWidth() - 1;
            if( nY2 < 0 ) nY2 = 0;
            if( nY2 > m_pImageObject->GetHeight() - 1 )
             nY2 = m_pImageObject->GetHeight() - 1;

            if( !m_bCropBoxShowing ){
             nX1 = nY1 = 0;
             nX2 = m_pImageObject->GetWidth() - 1;
             nY2 = m_pImageObject->GetHeight() - 1;
             }
            CImageAreaProcesses
             AreaProcesses( m_pImageObject );
            BeginWaitCursor();
            AreaProcesses.MedianFilter( nX1, nY1, nX2,
             nY2 );
            EndWaitCursor();

            InvalidateRect( NULL, FALSE );
            UpdateWindow();

            }
```

AREA IMAGE PROCESSING IN A NUTSHELL

Performing image area processing is very easy. It requires an image to be loaded into a CImageObject class object first, though. Once you have the image loaded, a single call does the work.

There are six image area processes supported in the CImageAreaProcesses class. Each one is described below.

ChangeContrast()

This example makes the contrast of an image 15 percent greater. The contrast argument is the first. A value of 100 means you're changing to a contrast of 100 percent. The image won't change in this case. But if you're changing to a contrast of 115 percent, that means you're making the contrast 15 percent greater. That's what this example does. Once the operation is performed, the next time the image is drawn it'll have a slightly greater contrast.

```
CImageObject ImageObject( "PIC.BMP" );
CImageAreaProcesses
 ImageAreaProcess( &ImageObject );
ImageAreaProcess.ChangeContrast( 115 );
```

Let's say you only want to change the contrast for part of the image. You can specify the coordinates of a rectangular region to which you want the operation applied. The following example changes the contrast for a region bounded by the coordinates 10, 10 and 120, 120. With no coordinates specified, the entire image is changed.

```
CImageObject ImageObject( "PIC.BMP" );
CImageAreaProcesses
 ImageAreaProcess( &ImageObject );
ImageAreaProcess.ChangeContrast( 115, 10,
 10, 120, 120 );
```

EqualizeContrast()

This example equalizes the contrast of an image. Once the operation is performed, the next time the image is drawn it'll have a contrast that has been equalized.

```
CImageObject ImageObject( "PIC.BMP" );
CImageAreaProcesses
 ImageAreaProcess( &ImageObject );
ImageAreaProcess.EqualizeContrast();
```

Let's say you only want to equalize the contrast for part of the image. You can specify the coordinates of a rectangular region to which you want the operation applied. The following example equalizes the contrast for a region bounded by the coordinates 10, 10 and 120, 120. With no coordinates specified, the entire image is changed.

```
CImageObject ImageObject( "PIC.BMP" );
CImageAreaProcesses
 ImageAreaProcess( &ImageObject );
ImageAreaProcess.EqualizeContrast( 10, 10,
 120, 120 );
```

MedianFilter()

This example performs a median filter on an image. Once the operation is performed, the next time the image is drawn it'll appear with the results of the median filter.

```
CImageObject ImageObject( "PIC.BMP" );
CImageAreaProcesses
 ImageAreaProcess( &ImageObject );
ImageAreaProcess.MedianFilter();
```

Let's say you only want to filter part of the image. You can specify the coordinates of a rectangular region to which you want the operation applied. The following example median-filters a region bounded by the coordinates 10, 10 and 120, 120. With no coordinates specified, the entire image is changed.

```
CImageObject ImageObject( "PIC.BMP" );
CImageAreaProcesses
 ImageAreaProcess( &ImageObject );
ImageAreaProcess.MedianFilter( 10, 10,
 120, 120 );
```

LowpassFilter()

This example performs a low-pass filter on an image. Once the operation is performed, the next time the image is drawn it'll appear with the results of the low-pass filter.

```
CImageObject ImageObject( "PIC.BMP" );
CImageAreaProcesses
 ImageAreaProcess( &ImageObject );
ImageAreaProcess.LowpassFilter();
```

Let's say you only want to filter part of the image. You can specify the coordinates of a rectangular region to which you want the operation applied. The following example low-pass-filters a region bounded by the coordinates 10, 10 and 120, 120. With no coordinates specified, the entire image is changed.

```
CImageObject ImageObject( "PIC.BMP" );
CImageAreaProcesses
 ImageAreaProcess( &ImageObject );
ImageAreaProcess.LowpassFilter( 10, 10,
 120, 120 );
```

HighpassFilter()

This example performs a high-pass filter on an image. Once the operation is performed, the next time the image is drawn it'll appear with the results of the high-pass filter.

```
CImageObject ImageObject( "PIC.BMP" );
CImageAreaProcesses
 ImageAreaProcess( &ImageObject );
ImageAreaProcess.HighpassFilter();
```

Let's say you only want to filter part of the image. You can specify the coordinates of a rectangular region to which you want the operation applied. The following example high-pass-filters a region bounded by the coordinates 10, 10 and 120, 120. With no coordinates specified, the entire image is changed.

```
CImageObject ImageObject( "PIC.BMP" );
CImageAreaProcesses
 ImageAreaProcess( &ImageObject );
ImageAreaProcess.HighpassFilter( 10, 10,
 120, 120 );
```

EdgeEnhance()

This example performs an edge enhancement on an image. Once the operation is performed, the next time the image is drawn it'll appear with the results of the enhancement.

```
CImageObject ImageObject( "PIC.BMP" );
CImageAreaProcesses
 ImageAreaProcess( &ImageObject );
ImageAreaProcess.EdgeEnhance();
```

Let's say you only want to edge-enhance part of the image. You can specify the coordinates of a rectangular region to which you want the operation applied. The following example edge-enhances a region bounded by the coordinates 10, 10 and 120, 120. With no coordinates specified, the entire image is changed.

```
CImageObject ImageObject( "PIC.BMP" );
CImageAreaProcesses
 ImageAreaProcess( &ImageObject );
ImageAreaProcess.EdgeEnhance( 10, 10,
 120, 120 );
```

CREATING PROGRAMS THAT USE AREA IMAGE PROCESSING

This section provides you with five hands-on exercises that'll walk you through the image area processes. After you work through the exercises, you'll be able to go on to more advanced uses of the CImageAreaProcesses class library.

Since the class library is on the Companion CD-ROM and can be found in the IMAGEPR2\ImageAreaProcesses directory, you have full access to the source code. You can add your own area processes if you have the need. And you can start with the functions that are already there and just modify them for your own functions. If you create your own image area process to add to the library, please send it to me at ivt-rcl@interpath.com. I'll probably use it myself, and with your permission I'll make it available to others.

Hands-On 1: Median-Filtering an Image

Our first hands-on exercise starts off with a median filter program. The program allows you to median-filter square regions of the screen. You can change the size of the area that'll be filtered by pressing the 1, 2, 3, 4, or 5 key. The Z key restores the image to its original state. Figure 4-10 shows an image with an upper left quadrant that's been median-filtered.

Figure 4-10: This image has had its upper left quadrant median-filtered.

1. Create a Visual C++ project named HandsOn4_1 with the following attributes:

   ❒ Single-document interface

   ❒ English language

   ❒ No database support

   ❒ No compound document support

   ❒ No automation or ActiveX control support

   ❒ 3D controls, but no other features

   ❒ No source file comments

   ❒ Link MFC as a static library

2. Select Settings from the Project menu. Choose the Link tab. Add the following libraries to the Object/library modules field. The libraries for the release and debug versions are different; both are listed below.

Release Project Libraries	Debug Project Libraries
ImageLoad.lib	ImageLoad.lib
ImageObject.lib	ImageObjectD.lib
ImageAreaProcesses.lib	ImageAreaProcessesD.lib

3. Set the Active Configuration to Win32 Release.

4. Copy the file PIC1.BMP from the \IMAGEPR2\SAMPLES directory on the CD-ROM to the newly created project directory.

5. Add the following include to the HandsOn4_1View.h file:

```
#include "ImageAreaProcesses.h"
```

6. Add the following include to the HandsOn4_1View.h file:

```
#include "MAINFRM.h"
```

7. Add the following variable declarations to the CHandsOn4_1View class in the HandsOn4_1View.h file:

```
public:
 CImageObject *m_pImageObject;
 CImageObject *m_pImage;
 int m_nSize;
```

8. Add the following code to the CHandsOn4_1View constructor:

```
CHandsOn4_1View::CHandsOn4_1View()
```

```
{
m_pImageObject = NULL;
m_pImage = NULL;
m_nSize = 3;
}
```

9. Add the following code to the CHandsOn4_1View destructor:

```
CHandsOn4_1View::~CHandsOn4_1View()
{
if( m_pImageObject != NULL )
 delete m_pImageObject;
if( m_pImage != NULL )
 delete m_pImage;
}
```

10. Edit the OnDraw function in the CHandsOn4_1View class in the HandsOn4_1View.cpp file as follows:

```
void CHandsOn4_1View::OnDraw(CDC* pDC)
{
CHandsOn4_1Doc* pDoc = GetDocument();
ASSERT_VALID(pDoc);

if( m_pImageObject == NULL ){

 CMainFrame *pFrame =
  (CMainFrame *) AfxGetMainWnd();
 pFrame->SetWindowPos( NULL, 0, 0,
  326, 275, SWP_NOZORDER | SWP_NOMOVE );

 BeginWaitCursor ();
 m_pImageObject =
  new CImageObject( "PIC1.BMP", pDC );
 EndWaitCursor ();
 if( m_pImageObject == NULL ){
  AfxMessageBox( "Could not create image!" );
  return;
  }

 m_pImage = new CImageObject();
 *m_pImage = *m_pImageObject;

 }
```

```
if( m_pImage != NULL ){
 if( GetFocus() == this )
  m_pImage->SetPalette( pDC );
 m_pImage->Draw( pDC );
 }

}
```

11. Add the following functions with the Class Wizard to the CHandsOn4_1View class in the HandsOn4_1View.h file:

```
Name:OnChar()  Message:WM_CHAR
Name:OnLButtonDown()  Message:WM_LBUTTONDOWN
```

12. Edit the OnChar function in the CHandsOn4_1View class in the HandsOn4_1View.cpp file as follows:

```
void CHandsOn4_1View::OnChar(UINT nChar, UINT nRepCnt, UINT nFlags)
{
 if( nChar == '1' ) m_nSize = 1;
 else if( nChar == '2' ) m_nSize = 2;
 else if( nChar == '3' ) m_nSize = 3;
 else if( nChar == '4' ) m_nSize = 4;
 else if( nChar == '5' ) m_nSize = 5;
 else if( toupper( nChar ) == 'Z' ){
  *m_pImage = *m_pImageObject;
  InvalidateRect( NULL, FALSE );
  UpdateWindow();
  }

 CView::OnChar(nChar, nRepCnt, nFlags);
}
```

13. Edit the OnLButtonDown function in the CHandsOn4_1View class in the HandsOn4_1View.cpp file as follows:

```
void CHandsOn4_1View::OnLButtonDown(UINT nFlags, CPoint point)
{
 if( m_pImageObject != NULL ){
  CImageAreaProcesses *pImageAreaProcess;
  pImageAreaProcess =
   new CImageAreaProcesses( m_pImage );
  if( pImageAreaProcess != NULL ){
   int nHalfWidth = m_nSize * 20;
```

```
pImageAreaProcess->MedianFilter(
 point.x - nHalfWidth,
 point.y - nHalfWidth,
 point.x  + nHalfWidth,
 point.y + nHalfWidth );
InvalidateRect( NULL, FALSE );
UpdateWindow();
delete pImageAreaProcess;
 }
 }

 CView::OnLButtonDown(nFlags, point);
 }
```

14. Compile and run the program.

When the program runs, you'll see the flower image appear in the view window. By clicking the mouse inside of the view window, you can median-filter the image in square regions.

Median-filtering is an excellent way to remove noise from an image. Figure 4-11 shows an image with noise that was introduced by transmission difficulties. Figure 4-12 shows the same image, fixed using median filtering.

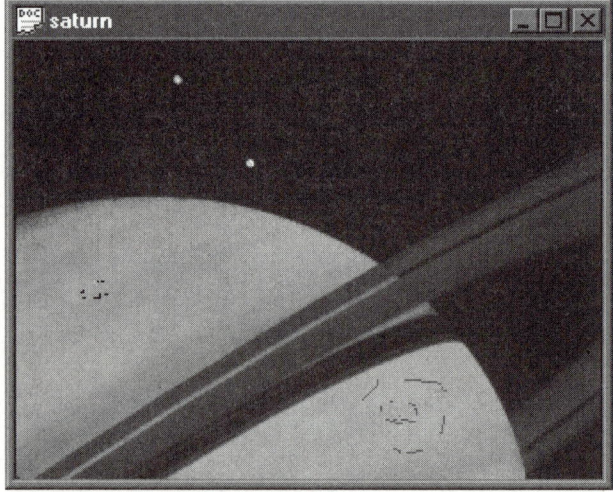

Figure 4-11: This image has noise that was introduced during transmission.

Figure 4-12: This image has had the noise fixed with median filtering.

Hands-On 2: High-Pass-Filter an Image

This hands-on exercise allows you to perform high-pass filter operations on square regions of an image. You can change the size of the area that'll be filtered by pressing the 1, 2, 3, 4, or 5 key. The Z key restores the image to its original state. Figure 4-13 shows the sunset image before any operations have been performed.

The changes in the image will vary from those you get in the first hands-on exercise where you perform median filtering. Here, you'll see the detail of the image attenuate while the median filter will blur images.

Figure 4-13: A sunset image appears upon which you can perform high-pass filter operations.

1. Create a Visual C++ project named HandsOn4_2 with the following attributes:
   ❏ Single-document interface
   ❏ English language
   ❏ No database support
   ❏ No compound document support
   ❏ No automation or ActiveX control support
   ❏ 3D controls, but no other features
   ❏ No source file comments
   ❏ Link MFC as a static library

2. Select Settings from the Project menu. Choose the Link tab. Add the following libraries to the Object/library modules field. The libraries for the release and debug versions are different; both are listed below.

Release Project Libraries	Debug Project Libraries
ImageLoad.lib	ImageLoad.lib
ImageObject.lib	ImageObjectD.lib
ImageAreaProcesses.lib	ImageAreaProcessesD.lib

3. Set the Active Configuration to Win32 Release.

4. Copy the file PIC2.BMP from the \IMAGEPR2\SAMPLES directory on the CD-ROM to the newly created project directory.

5. Add the following include to the HandsOn4_2View.h file:

```
#include "ImageAreaProcesses.h"
```

6. Add the following include to the HandsOn4_2View.h file:

```
#include "MAINFRM.h"
```

7. Add the following variable declarations to the CHandsOn4_2View class in the HandsOn4_2View.h file:

```
public:
 CImageObject *m_pImageObject;
 CImageObject *m_pImage;
 int m_nSize;
```

8. Add the following code to the CHandsOn4_2View constructor:

```
CHandsOn4_2View::CHandsOn4_2View()
{
 m_pImageObject = NULL;
 m_pImage = NULL;
 m_nSize = 3;
}
```

9. Add the following code to the CHandsOn4_2View destructor:

```
CHandsOn4_2View::~CHandsOn4_2View()
{
 if( m_pImageObject != NULL )
  delete m_pImageObject;
 if( m_pImage != NULL )
  delete m_pImage;
}
```

10. Edit the OnDraw function in the CHandsOn4_2View class in the HandsOn4_2View.cpp file as follows:

```
void CHandsOn4_2View::OnDraw(CDC* pDC)
{
 CHandsOn4_2Doc* pDoc = GetDocument();
 ASSERT_VALID(pDoc);
```

```
if( m_pImageObject == NULL ){

  CMainFrame *pFrame =
   (CMainFrame *) AfxGetMainWnd();
  pFrame->SetWindowPos( NULL, 0, 0,
   326, 275, SWP_NOZORDER | SWP_NOMOVE );

  BeginWaitCursor ();
  m_pImageObject =
   new CImageObject( "PIC2.BMP", pDC );
  EndWaitCursor ();
  if( m_pImageObject == NULL ){
   AfxMessageBox( "Could not create image!" );
   return;
   }

  m_pImage = new CImageObject();
  *m_pImage = *m_pImageObject;

  }

 if( m_pImage != NULL ){
  if( GetFocus() == this )
   m_pImage->SetPalette( pDC );
  m_pImage->Draw( pDC );
  }

}
```

11. Add the following functions with the Class Wizard to the CHandsOn4_2View class in the HandsOn4_2View.h file:

```
Name:OnChar()  Message:WM_CHAR
Name:OnLButtonDown()  Message:WM_LBUTTONDOWN
```

12. Edit the OnChar function in the CHandsOn4_2View class in the HandsOn4_2View.cpp file as follows:

```
void CHandsOn4_2View::OnChar(UINT nChar, UINT nRepCnt, UINT nFlags)
{
 if( nChar == '1' ) m_nSize = 1;
 else if( nChar == '2' ) m_nSize = 2;
 else if( nChar == '3' ) m_nSize = 3;
 else if( nChar == '4' ) m_nSize = 4;
 else if( nChar == '5' ) m_nSize = 5;
 else if( toupper( nChar ) == 'Z' ){
```

```
*m_pImage = *m_pImageObject;
InvalidateRect( NULL, FALSE );
UpdateWindow();
}


CView::OnChar(nChar, nRepCnt, nFlags);
}
```

13. Edit the OnLButtonDown function in the CHandsOn4_2View class in the HandsOn4_2View.cpp file as follows:

```
void CHandsOn4_2View::OnLButtonDown(UINT nFlags, CPoint point)
{
 if( m_pImageObject != NULL ){
  CImageAreaProcesses *pImageAreaProcess;
  pImageAreaProcess =
   new CImageAreaProcesses( m_pImage );
  if( pImageAreaProcess != NULL ){
   int nHalfWidth = m_nSize * 20;
   pImageAreaProcess->HighpassFilter(
    point.x - nHalfWidth,
    point.y - nHalfWidth,
    point.x + nHalfWidth,
    point.y + nHalfWidth );
   InvalidateRect( NULL, FALSE );
   UpdateWindow();
   delete pImageAreaProcess;
  }
 }

 CView::OnLButtonDown(nFlags, point);
}
```

14. Compile and run the program.

When the program first runs, you'll see the sunset image appear. By clicking in the view window, you can perform high-pass operations on square regions of the image.

Figure 4-14 shows the sunset image with its lower left quadrant altered after a high-pass operation.

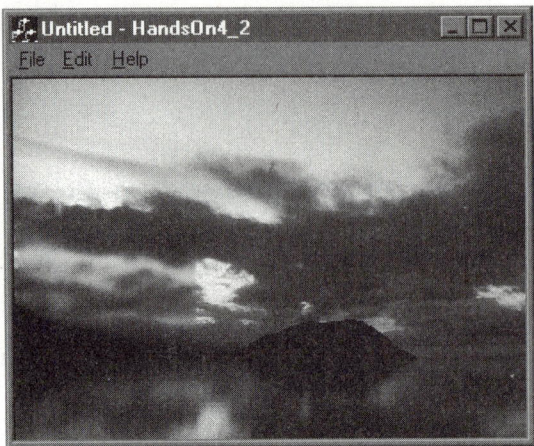

Figure 4-14: The sunset image has had a high-pass operation performed to its lower left quadrant.

Hands-On 3: Low-Pass-Filter an Image

This hands-on exercise allows you to perform low-pass operations on square regions of an image. You can change the size of the area that'll be filtered by pressing the 1, 2, 3, 4, or 5 key. The Z key restores the image to its original state. Figure 4-15 shows the sunset image before any operations have been performed.

This image processing operation will incrementally remove low-frequency image components. Eventually, the detail of the image will sharpen.

Figure 4-15: A sunset image appears upon which you can perform low-pass filter operations.

1. Create a Visual C++ project named HandsOn4_3 with the following attributes:
   - ❏ Single-document interface
   - ❏ English language
   - ❏ No database support
   - ❏ No compound document support
   - ❏ No automation or ActiveX control support
   - ❏ 3D controls, but no other features
   - ❏ No source file comments
   - ❏ Link MFC as a static library

2. Select Settings from the Project menu. Choose the Link tab. Add the following libraries to the Object/library modules field. The libraries for the release and debug versions are different; both are listed below.

Release Project Libraries	Debug Project Libraries
ImageLoad.lib	ImageLoad.lib
ImageObject.lib	ImageObjectD.lib
ImageAreaProcesses.lib	ImageAreaProcessesD.lib

3. Set the Active Configuration to Win32 Release.

4. Copy the file PIC3.BMP from the \IMAGEPR2\SAMPLES directory on the CD-ROM to the newly created project directory.

5. Add the following include to the HandsOn4_3View.h file:

   ```
   #include "ImageAreaProcesses.h"
   ```

6. Add the following include to the HandsOn4_3View.h file:

   ```
   #include "MAINFRM.h"
   ```

7. Add the following variable declarations to the CHandsOn4_3View class in the HandsOn4_3View.h file:

   ```
   public:
    CImageObject *m_pImageObject;
    CImageObject *m_pImage;
    int m_nSize;
   ```

8. Add the following code to the CHandsOn4_3View constructor:

```
CHandsOn4_3View::CHandsOn4_3View()
{
 m_pImageObject = NULL;
 m_pImage = NULL;
 m_nSize = 3;
}
```

9. Add the following code to the CHandsOn4_3View destructor:

```
CHandsOn4_3View::~CHandsOn4_3View()
{
 if( m_pImageObject != NULL )
  delete m_pImageObject;
 if( m_pImage != NULL )
  delete m_pImage;
}
```

10. Edit the OnDraw function in the CHandsOn4_3View class in the HandsOn4_3View.cpp file as follows:

```
void CHandsOn4_3View::OnDraw(CDC* pDC)
{
 CHandsOn4_3Doc* pDoc = GetDocument();
 ASSERT_VALID(pDoc);

 if( m_pImageObject == NULL ){

  CMainFrame *pFrame =
   (CMainFrame *) AfxGetMainWnd();
  pFrame->SetWindowPos( NULL, 0, 0,
   326, 275, SWP_NOZORDER | SWP_NOMOVE );

  BeginWaitCursor ();
  m_pImageObject =
   new CImageObject( "PIC3.BMP", pDC );
  EndWaitCursor ();
  if( m_pImageObject == NULL ){
   AfxMessageBox( "Could not create image!" );
   return;
   }

  m_pImage = new CImageObject();
  *m_pImage = *m_pImageObject;

  }
```

```
 if( m_pImage != NULL ){
  if( GetFocus() == this )
   m_pImage->SetPalette( pDC );
  m_pImage->Draw( pDC );
  }

}
```

11. Add the following functions with the Class Wizard to the CHandsOn4_3View class in the HandsOn4_3View.h file:

```
Name:OnChar()  Message:WM_CHAR
Name:OnLButtonDown()  Message:WM_LBUTTONDOWN
```

12. Edit the OnChar function in the CHandsOn4_3View class in the HandsOn4_3View.cpp file as follows:

```
void CHandsOn4_3View::OnChar(UINT nChar, UINT nRepCnt, UINT nFlags)
{
 if( nChar == '1' ) m_nSize = 1;
 else if( nChar == '2' ) m_nSize = 2;
 else if( nChar == '3' ) m_nSize = 3;
 else if( nChar == '4' ) m_nSize = 4;
 else if( nChar == '5' ) m_nSize = 5;
 else if( toupper( nChar ) == 'Z' ){
  *m_pImage = *m_pImageObject;
  InvalidateRect( NULL, FALSE );
  UpdateWindow();
  }

 CView::OnChar(nChar, nRepCnt, nFlags);
}
```

13. Edit the OnLButtonDown function in the CHandsOn4_3View class in the HandsOn4_3View.cpp file as follows:

```
void CHandsOn4_3View::OnLButtonDown(UINT nFlags, CPoint point)
{
 if( m_pImageObject != NULL ){
  CImageAreaProcesses *pImageAreaProcess;
  pImageAreaProcess =
   new CImageAreaProcesses( m_pImage );
  if( pImageAreaProcess != NULL ){
   int nHalfWidth = m_nSize * 20;
   pImageAreaProcess->LowpassFilter(
    point.x - nHalfWidth,
```

```
         point.y - nHalfWidth,
         point.x  + nHalfWidth,
         point.y + nHalfWidth );
        InvalidateRect( NULL, FALSE );
        UpdateWindow();
        delete pImageAreaProcess;
        }
      }

    CView::OnLButtonDown(nFlags, point);
    }
```

14. Compile and run the program.

   When the program first runs, you'll see the sunset image appear. By clicking in the view window, you can perform low-pass operations on square regions of the image.

   Figure 4-16 shows the sunset image with its lower left quadrant altered after a low-pass operation.

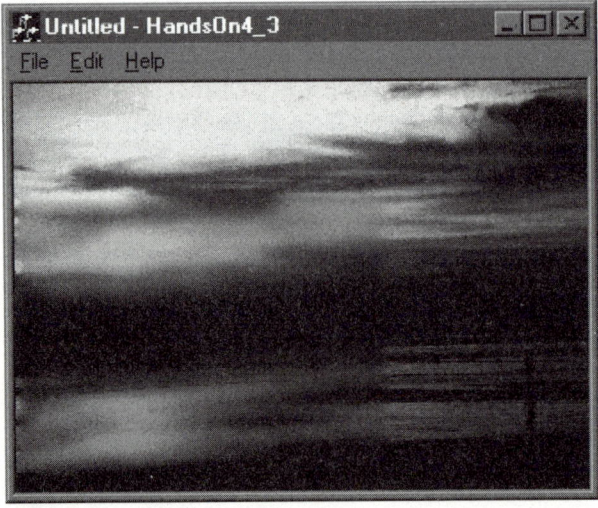

Figure 4-16: The sunset image has had a low-pass operation performed to its lower left quadrant.

Hands-On 4: Equalize the Contrast of an Image

This hands-on exercise allows you to equalize the contrast of square regions of an image. You can change the size of the area that'll be equalizes by pressing the 1, 2, 3, 4, or 5 key. The Z key restores the image to its original state. Figure 4-17 shows the triplane image before any operations have been performed.

This exercise will cause the image to equalize its contrast. Since the sample image was selected as one that doesn't have a large contrast range, the first time you perform the operation, the image's appearance will improve.

Figure 4-17: A triplane image appears upon which you can perform contrast equalization operations.

1. Create a Visual C++ project named HandsOn4_4 with the following attributes:

   ❏ Single-document interface

   ❏ English language

   ❏ No database support

   ❏ No compound document support

   ❏ No automation or ActiveX control support

   ❏ 3D controls, but no other features

   ❏ No source file comments

   ❏ Link MFC as a static library

2. Select Settings from the Project menu. Choose the Link tab. Add the following libraries to the Object/library modules field. The libraries for the release and debug versions are different; both are listed below.

Release Project Libraries	Debug Project Libraries
ImageLoad.lib	ImageLoad.lib
ImageObject.lib	ImageObjectD.lib
ImageAreaProcesses.lib	ImageAreaProcessesD.lib

3. Set the Active Configuration to Win32 Release.

4. Copy the file PIC4.BMP from the \IMAGEPR2\SAMPLES directory on the CD-ROM to the newly created project directory.

5. Add the following include to the HandsOn4_4View.h file:

```
#include "ImageAreaProcesses.h"
```

6. Add the following include to the HandsOn4_4View.h file:

```
#include "MAINFRM.h"
```

7. Add the following variable declarations to the CHandsOn4_4View class in the HandsOn4_4View.h file:

```
public:
 CImageObject *m_pImageObject;
 CImageObject *m_pImage;
 int m_nSize;
```

8. Add the following code to the CHandsOn4_4View constructor:

```
CHandsOn4_4View::CHandsOn4_4View()
{
 m_pImageObject = NULL;
 m_pImage = NULL;
 m_nSize = 3;
}
```

9. Add the following code to the CHandsOn4_4View destructor:

```
CHandsOn4_4View::~CHandsOn4_4View()
{
 if( m_pImageObject != NULL )
  delete m_pImageObject;
 if( m_pImage != NULL )
  delete m_pImage;
}
```

10. Edit the OnDraw function in the CHandsOn4_4View class in the
    HandsOn4_4View.cpp file as follows:

```
void CHandsOn4_4View::OnDraw(CDC* pDC)
{
CHandsOn4_4Doc* pDoc = GetDocument();
ASSERT_VALID(pDoc);

if( m_pImageObject == NULL ){

  CMainFrame *pFrame =
   (CMainFrame *) AfxGetMainWnd();
  pFrame->SetWindowPos( NULL, 0, 0,
   326, 275, SWP_NOZORDER | SWP_NOMOVE );

  BeginWaitCursor ();
  m_pImageObject =
   new CImageObject( "PIC4.BMP", pDC );
  EndWaitCursor ();
  if( m_pImageObject == NULL ){
   AfxMessageBox( "Could not create image!" );
   return;
   }

  m_pImage = new CImageObject();
  *m_pImage = *m_pImageObject;

 }

 if( m_pImage != NULL ){
  if( GetFocus() == this )
   m_pImage->SetPalette( pDC );
  m_pImage->Draw( pDC );
  }

}
```

11. Add the following functions with the Class Wizard to the
    CHandsOn4_4View class in the HandsOn4_4View.h file:

```
Name:OnChar()  Message:WM_CHAR
Name:OnLButtonDown()  Message:WM_LBUTTONDOWN
```

12. Edit the OnChar function in the CHandsOn4_4View class in the HandsOn4_4View.cpp file as follows:

```
void CHandsOn4_4View::OnChar(UINT nChar, UINT nRepCnt, UINT nFlags)
{
 if( nChar == '1' ) m_nSize = 1;
 else if( nChar == '2' ) m_nSize = 2;
 else if( nChar == '3' ) m_nSize = 3;
 else if( nChar == '4' ) m_nSize = 4;
 else if( nChar == '5' ) m_nSize = 5;
 else if( toupper( nChar ) == 'Z' ){
 *m_pImage = *m_pImageObject;
 InvalidateRect( NULL, FALSE );
 UpdateWindow();
 }

 CView::OnChar(nChar, nRepCnt, nFlags);
}
```

13. Edit the OnLButtonDown function in the CHandsOn4_4View class in the HandsOn4_4View.cpp file as follows:

```
void CHandsOn4_4View::OnLButtonDown(UINT nFlags, CPoint point)
{
 if( m_pImageObject != NULL ){
 CImageAreaProcesses *pImageAreaProcess;
 pImageAreaProcess =
  new CImageAreaProcesses( m_pImage );
 if( pImageAreaProcess != NULL ){
  int nHalfWidth = m_nSize * 20;
  pImageAreaProcess->EqualizeContrast(
   point.x - nHalfWidth,
   point.y - nHalfWidth,
   point.x + nHalfWidth,
   point.y + nHalfWidth );
  InvalidateRect( NULL, FALSE );
  UpdateWindow();
  delete pImageAreaProcess;
  }
 }

 CView::OnLButtonDown(nFlags, point);
}
```

14. Compile and run the program.

When the program first runs, you'll see the triplane image appear. By clicking in the view window, you can perform contrast equalization operations on square regions of the image.

Figure 4-18 shows the triplane image with its upper left quadrant altered after a contrast equalization operation.

Figure 4-18: The triplane image has had a contrast equalization operation performed to its upper left quadrant.

 ## Hands-On 5: Edge-Enhance an Image

This hands-on exercise allows you to perform an edge-enhancement operation to square regions of an image. You can change the size of the area that'll be edge-enhanced by pressing the 1, 2, 3, 4, or 5 key. The Z key restores the image to its original state. Figure 4-19 shows an Apollo 7 image before any operations have been performed.

In this exercise, edges in the image will become more prominent. The more times you perform the operation, the more pronounced they will become.

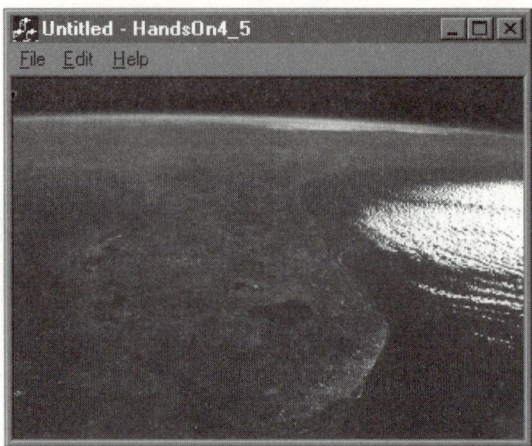

Figure 4-19: An Apollo 7 image appears upon which you can perform edge enhancement operations.

1. Create a Visual C++ project named HandsOn4_5 with the following attributes:

   ❑ Single-document interface

   ❑ English language

   ❑ No database support

   ❑ No compound document support

   ❑ No automation or ActiveX control support

   ❑ 3D controls, but no other features

   ❑ No source file comments

   ❑ Link MFC as a static library

2. Select Settings from the Project menu. Choose the Link tab. Add the following libraries to the Object/library modules field. The libraries for the release and debug versions are different; both are listed below.

Release Project Libraries	Debug Project Libraries
ImageLoad.lib	ImageLoad.lib
ImageObject.lib	ImageObjectD.lib
ImageAreaProcesses.lib	ImageAreaProcessesD.lib

3. Set the Active Configuration to Win32 Release.

4. Copy the file PIC5.BMP from the \IMAGEPR2\SAMPLES directory on the CD-ROM to the newly created project directory.

5. Add the following include to the HandsOn4_5View.h file:

```
#include "ImageAreaProcesses.h"
```

6. Add the following include to the HandsOn4_5View.h file:

```
#include "MAINFRM.h"
```

7. Add the following variable declarations to the CHandsOn4_5View class in the HandsOn4_5View.h file:

```
public:
 CImageObject *m_pImageObject;
 CImageObject *m_pImage;
 int m_nSize;
```

8. Add the following code to the CHandsOn4_5View constructor:

```
CHandsOn4_5View::CHandsOn4_5View()
{
 m_pImageObject = NULL;
 m_pImage = NULL;
 m_nSize = 3;
}
```

9. Add the following code to the CHandsOn4_5View destructor:

```
CHandsOn4_5View::~CHandsOn4_5View()
{
 if( m_pImageObject != NULL )
  delete m_pImageObject;
 if( m_pImage != NULL )
  delete m_pImage;
}
```

10. Edit the OnDraw function in the CHandsOn4_5View class in the HandsOn4_5View.cpp file as follows:

```
void CHandsOn4_5View::OnDraw(CDC* pDC)
{
 CHandsOn4_5Doc* pDoc = GetDocument();
 ASSERT_VALID(pDoc);

 if( m_pImageObject == NULL ){
  CMainFrame *pFrame =
   (CMainFrame *) AfxGetMainWnd();
```

173

```
pFrame->SetWindowPos( NULL, 0, 0,
 326, 275, SWP_NOZORDER | SWP_NOMOVE );

BeginWaitCursor ();
m_pImageObject =
 new CImageObject( "PIC5.BMP", pDC );
EndWaitCursor ();
if( m_pImageObject == NULL ){
 AfxMessageBox( "Could not create picture class!" );
 return;
 }

m_pImage = new CImageObject();
*m_pImage = *m_pImageObject;
 }

if( m_pImage != NULL ){
 if( GetFocus() == this )
  m_pImage->SetPalette( pDC );
 m_pImage->Draw( pDC );
 }
}
```

11. Add the following functions with the Class Wizard to the CHandsOn4_5View class in the HandsOn4_5View.h file:

```
Name:OnChar()  Message:WM_CHAR
Name:OnLButtonDown()  Message:WM_LBUTTONDOWN
```

12. Edit the OnChar function in the CHandsOn4_5View class in the HandsOn4_5View.cpp file as follows:

```
void CHandsOn4_5View::OnChar(UINT nChar, UINT nRepCnt, UINT nFlags)
{
 if( nChar == '1' ) m_nSize = 1;
 else if( nChar == '2' ) m_nSize = 2;
 else if( nChar == '3' ) m_nSize = 3;
 else if( nChar == '4' ) m_nSize = 4;
 else if( nChar == '5' ) m_nSize = 5;
```

```
else if( toupper( nChar ) == 'Z' ){
*m_pImage = *m_pImageObject;
InvalidateRect( NULL, FALSE );
UpdateWindow( );
}

CView::OnChar(nChar, nRepCnt, nFlags);
}
```

13. Edit the OnLButtonDown function in the CHandsOn4_5View class in the HandsOn4_5View.cpp file as follows:

```
void CHandsOn4_5View::OnLButtonDown(UINT nFlags, CPoint point)
{
if( m_pImageObject != NULL ){
CImageAreaProcesses *pImageAreaProcess;
pImageAreaProcess =
 new CImageAreaProcesses( m_pImage );
if( pImageAreaProcess != NULL ){
int nHalfWidth = m_nSize * 20;
pImageAreaProcess->EdgeEnhance(
 point.x - nHalfWidth,
 point.y - nHalfWidth,
 point.x  + nHalfWidth,
 point.y + nHalfWidth );
InvalidateRect( NULL, FALSE );
UpdateWindow( );
delete pImageAreaProcess;
}
}

CView::OnLButtonDown(nFlags, point);
}
```

14. Compile and run the program.

When the program first runs, you'll see the Apollo 7 image appear. By clicking in the view window, you can perform edge-enhancement operations on square regions of the image.

Figure 4-20 shows the Apollo 7 image with its middle section having had an edge enhancement operation performed.

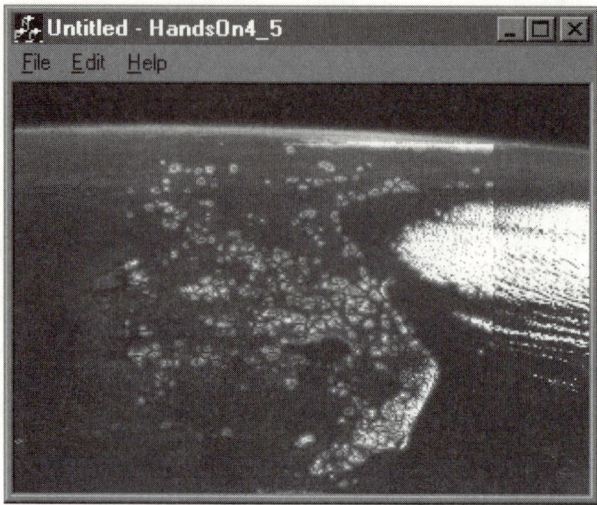

Figure 4-20: The middle section of the Apollo 7 image has had an edge enhancement operation performed.

ON THE WEB

There's a wealth of resources on the Web in the realm of image processing. Since this chapter talks about area processes, we'll show some sites of interest.

There are several Web sites that offer information about image processing. The site shown in Figure 4-21 has more information about area image processes than anything else. You'll find it useful if you're looking for more information.

For a Web site that offers real-time image processing techniques, check out the one shown in Figure 4-22.

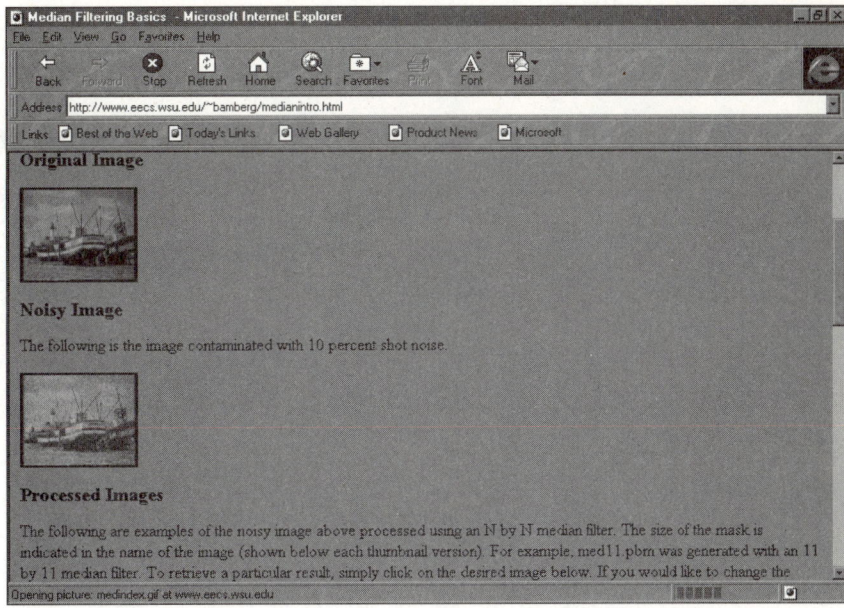

Figure 4-21: Washington State University features an Interactive Image Processing Project.

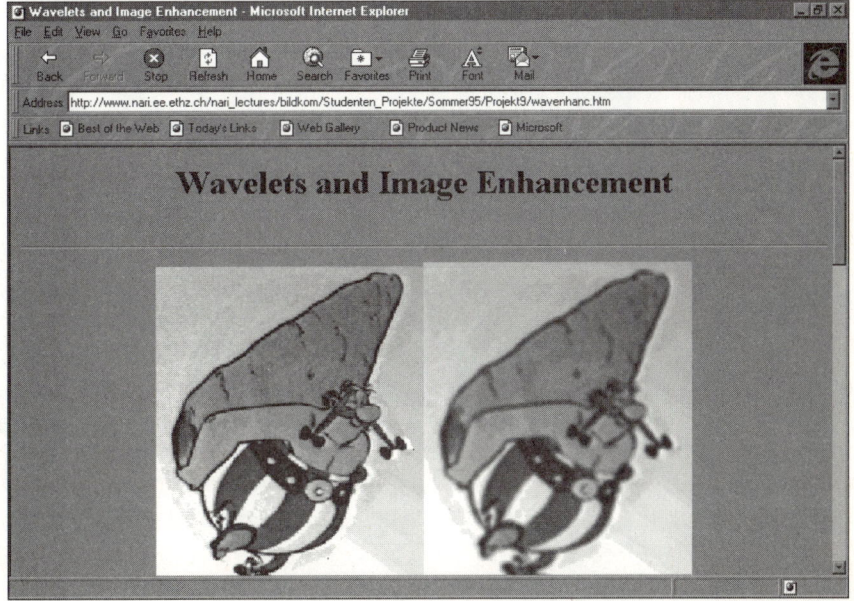

Figure 4-22: There's an intriguing Web site at http://www.nari.ee.ethz.ch/ nari_lectures/bildkom/Studenten_Projekte/Sommer95/Projekt9/wavenhanc.htm.

For a down-to-earth and practical explanation of using edge enhancement, check out David Cyganski's site (see Figure 4-23). He brings the subject to a practical level.

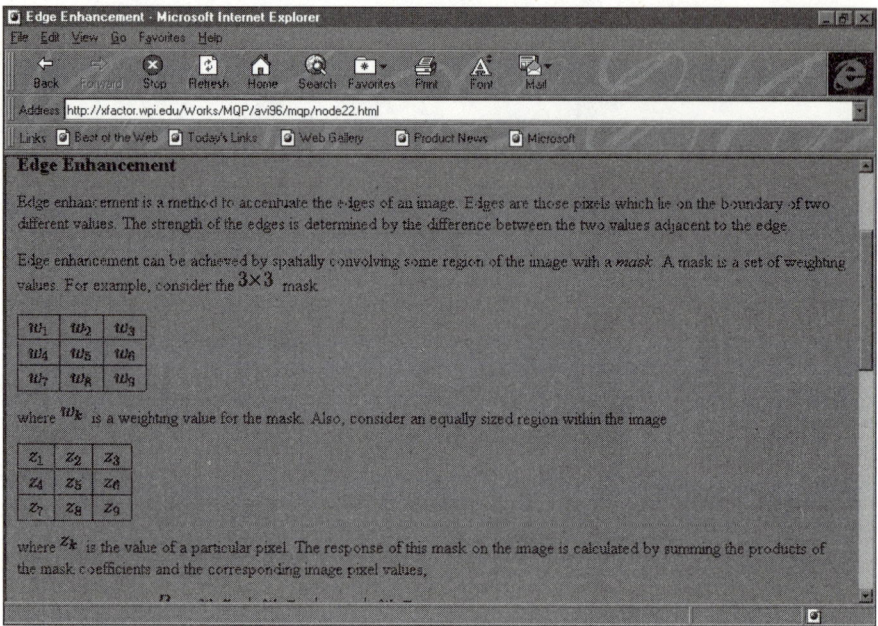

Figure 4-23: An excellent graphical explanation of edge enhancement (among other things) can be seen as part of David Cyganski's passive automatic vehicle identification (AVI) system.

SHAREWARE

There's no shortage of shareware tools to help you with your imaging needs. One of the best that you'll find, though, is WinJPEG (see Figure 4-24). Besides loading and saving images, it offers a wide variety of image processing, especially in the area processing realm. A list of filters such as median and low-pass are among those in its arsenal.

Figure 4-24: WinJPEG opens more than JPG files; it opens most other bitmap files too.

MOVING ON

Area image processing is something you'll find very useful. If you already use it, the class library in this chapter will help you in your endeavors. If you're looking for code to use, you've found what you need.

Area image processing is the most challenging of the image-processing categories, so I'd appreciate hearing anything you come up with that's cool. E-mail your creations to me at ivt-rcl@interpath.com.

Chapter 5

Splash Screens

*The stroke of the brush as you splash color
onto a naked canvas. The feel of rough fiber
as it meets your skin. All of these sensations
are possible in the world of art.*
—*Alex Canas*

When you start most commercial applications, the first display you see is a splash screen. There are several reasons why programmers should seriously consider bringing up a splash screen first when their applications run.

One reason is to show program and copyright information. In this day of legalese and litigation, it's best to display copyright information immediately instead of leaving it in an "About Box" that users may not even look at.

Another reason to add a splash screen is that it's a good way to add visual appeal. This might be especially important for applications that don't have many graphics. A splash screen with interesting graphics makes a lasting impression, even after the splash screen disappears.

Probably the most important reason to use a splash screen, though, is to give your viewer something to look at during the time needed for the application to load files and initialize. If an attractive splash screen is visible during this time, users rarely get annoyed with load and initialization delays. But try it without a splash screen and you may get nasty letters and calls to the tech support department.

THE CSplashScreen Class Library

This class library takes the worry out of splash screens. Unlike what's available through the component gallery, this class allows you to display high-color and 256-color images. What's more, you'll have the source code, so modifications for special effects will be easy.

 The class library that's included on the Companion CD-ROM takes care of all the details necessary to display a splash screen. This makes it much easier to incorporate splash screens in your programs.

All source code and support files to rebuild the SplashLib.lib file can be found in the splash\SplashLib directory on the Companion CD-ROM.

THE SplashDemo

We've built a simple demonstration program that displays a splash screen. After three seconds, the splash screen disappears. (Also, if the user clicks the mouse in the splash screen window, it disappears.) Figure 5-1 shows the application with the splash screen on top of it.

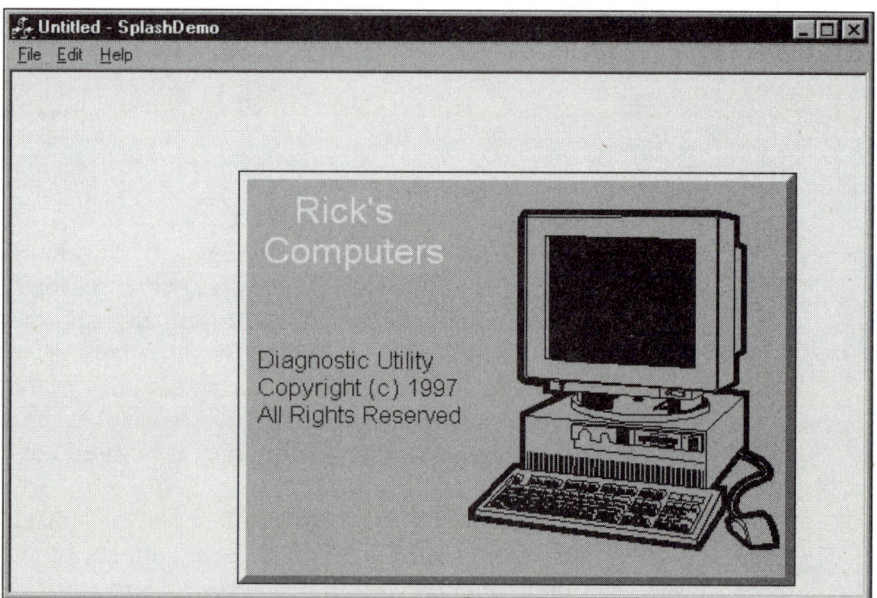

Figure 5-1: Something similar to this simple splash screen might be just what your program needs when it first runs.

CSplashScreen Class Library Function Calls

This section is provided as a reference to the public function calls the SplashLib class library offers. Since the library was designed with simplicity as a major goal, there aren't many calls. That's good, because to display a splash screen is easy—it just takes a few lines of code.

You may want to skip over this section and read the section entitled "Behind SplashDemo," which shows how the calls are used (some people prefer to see how the function calls are used before studying the syntax).

CSplashScreen()

Prototype:	`CSplashScreen( void );`
Purpose:	This is the constructor for the CSplashScreen class.
Arguments:	None
Returns:	Nothing

CSplashScreen()

Prototype:	`CSplashScreen( const char *pszFilename );`
Purpose:	This is the constructor for the CSplashScreen object. This overloaded version allows you to pass an image filename. The CSplashScreen object will then load the image file and display it in the splash screen window.
Arguments:	const char *pszFilename
Returns:	Nothing

SetFilename()

Prototype:	`void SetFilename( const char *pszFilename );`
Purpose:	This function allows you to set the filename for an image file. If the splash screen hasn't been displayed yet, the filename you pass to this function determines the image file that'll be loaded when the splash screen first appears.

```
CSplashScreen *pSplash =
new CSplashScreen();
pSplash->SetFilename("IMAGE.BMP");
```

is equivalent to:

```
CSplashScreen *pSplash = new CSplashScreen("IMAGE.BMP");
```

Arguments: const char *pszFilename

Returns: Nothing

ChangeFile()

Prototype: `void ChangeFile( const char *pszFilename );`

Purpose: This function changes the image file that the CSplashScreen object has loaded in. It releases the memory from the old image and loads the new image. You must remember, though, that the window will not be resized. For that reason, images of identical size should be loaded with the ChangeFile() function.

Arguments: const char *pszFilename

Returns: Nothing

SaveImage()

Prototype: `void SaveImage( void );`

Purpose: This saves the currently loaded image into a holding CImageObject class. The reason you would want to do this is so that you can alter the image that's loaded in the CSplashScreen object, display it, then later restore it.

Arguments: None

Returns: Nothing

RestoreImage()

Prototype: `void RestoreImage( void );`

Purpose: This function restores the CImageObject that was previously saved with the SaveImage() function.

Arguments: None

Returns: Nothing

GetImage()

Prototype: `CImageObject *GetImage( void );`

Purpose: This function returns a pointer to the CImageObject class that contains the current image.

Arguments: None

Returns: CImageObject *m_pCurrentImage

SetImage()

Prototype: `void SetImage( CImageObject * );`

Purpose: This function sets the current CImageObject class to contain the image that's in the class that's passed in. The CSplashScreen object creates a copy of the image, so the caller must take care of maintaining and deleting the CImageObject that's passed in.

Arguments: None

Returns: Nothing

Redraw()

Prototype: `void Redraw( void );`

Purpose: This causes the current image to be redrawn in the splash screen window.

Arguments: None

Returns: Nothing

BEHIND SPLASHDEMO

SplashDemo was created with the Visual C++ AppWizard. It has a single-document interface and no initial toolbar. After creating the program, the ImageObject, ImageLoad, and SplashLib libraries were added to the linker.

ImageView was created with the Visual C++ AppWizard with the following settings:

- ❏ Multiple-document interface
- ❏ English language
- ❏ No database support
- ❏ No compound document support
- ❏ No automation or ActiveX control support
- ❏ 3D controls, but no other features
- ❏ Yes source file comments
- ❏ MFC linked as a static library

All of the code that has anything to do with the scanner library is in SplashDemo.cpp. That file, along with the SplashDemo.h file, is shown below.

SplashDemo.cpp

```
#include "stdafx.h"
#include "SplashDemo.h"
#include "MainFrm.h"
#include "SplashDemoDoc.h"
#include "SplashDemoView.h"

#ifdef _DEBUG
#define new DEBUG_NEW
#undef THIS_FILE
static char THIS_FILE[] = __FILE__;
#endif

/////////////////////////////////////////////
// CSplashDemoApp

BEGIN_MESSAGE_MAP(CSplashDemoApp, CWinApp)
 //{{AFX_MSG_MAP(CSplashDemoApp)
 ON_COMMAND(ID_APP_ABOUT, OnAppAbout)
 //}}AFX_MSG_MAP
 // Standard file based document commands
 ON_COMMAND(ID_FILE_NEW, CWinApp::OnFileNew)
 ON_COMMAND(ID_FILE_OPEN, CWinApp::OnFileOpen)
END_MESSAGE_MAP()

/////////////////////////////////////////////
```

```
// CSplashDemoApp construction

CSplashDemoApp::CSplashDemoApp()
{
 m_pSplashScreen = NULL;
}

/////////////////////////////////////////
// The one and only CSplashDemoApp object

CSplashDemoApp theApp;

/////////////////////////////////////////
// CSplashDemoApp initialization

BOOL CSplashDemoApp::InitInstance()
{

 m_pSplashScreen = new CSplashScreen;
 m_pSplashScreen->SetFilename( "IMAGE1.BMP" );
 m_pSplashScreen->Create();
 m_pSplashScreen->ShowWindow( SW_SHOW );
 m_pSplashScreen->UpdateWindow();

 // Standard initialization

#ifdef _AFXDLL
 Enable3dControls();    // Call this when using MFC in a shared DLL
#else
 Enable3dControlsStatic(); // Call this when linking to MFC
                              // statically
#endif

 // Change the registry key under which our settings are stored.
 SetRegistryKey(_T("Local AppWizard-Generated Applications"));

 LoadStdProfileSettings();  // Load standard
          // INI file options (including MRU)

 // Register document templates

 CSingleDocTemplate* pDocTemplate;
 pDocTemplate = new CSingleDocTemplate(
  IDR_MAINFRAME,
  RUNTIME_CLASS(CSplashDemoDoc),
```

```
     RUNTIME_CLASS(CMainFrame), // main SDI frame
     RUNTIME_CLASS(CSplashDemoView));
    AddDocTemplate(pDocTemplate);

    // Parse command line for standard shell
    // commands, DDE, file open
    CCommandLineInfo cmdInfo;
    ParseCommandLine(cmdInfo);

    // Dispatch commands specified on the command
    // line
    if (!ProcessShellCommand(cmdInfo))
     return FALSE;
    m_pMainWnd->ShowWindow(SW_SHOW);
    m_pMainWnd->UpdateWindow();

    m_dwSplashTime = GetCurrentTime();

    return TRUE;
    }

    /////////////////////////////////////////////
    // CAboutDlg dialog used for App About

    class CAboutDlg : public CDialog
    {
    public:
     CAboutDlg();

    // Dialog Data
     //{{AFX_DATA(CAboutDlg)
     enum { IDD = IDD_ABOUTBOX };
     //}}AFX_DATA

     // ClassWizard generated virtual function
     // overrides
     //{{AFX_VIRTUAL(CAboutDlg)
     protected:
     virtual void
      DoDataExchange(CDataExchange* pDX);
      // DDX/DDV support
     //}}AFX_VIRTUAL

    // Implementation
    protected:
     //{{AFX_MSG(CAboutDlg)
```

```
  // No message handlers
 //}}AFX_MSG
 DECLARE_MESSAGE_MAP()
};

CAboutDlg::CAboutDlg() : CDialog(CAboutDlg::IDD)
{
 //{{AFX_DATA_INIT(CAboutDlg)
 //}}AFX_DATA_INIT
}

void CAboutDlg::DoDataExchange(CDataExchange* pDX)
{
 CDialog::DoDataExchange(pDX);
 //{{AFX_DATA_MAP(CAboutDlg)
 //}}AFX_DATA_MAP
}

BEGIN_MESSAGE_MAP(CAboutDlg, CDialog)
 //{{AFX_MSG_MAP(CAboutDlg)
  // No message handlers
 //}}AFX_MSG_MAP
END_MESSAGE_MAP()

// App command to run the dialog
void CSplashDemoApp::OnAppAbout()
{
 CAboutDlg aboutDlg;
 aboutDlg.DoModal();
}

/////////////////////////////////////////////
// CSplashDemoApp commands

BOOL CSplashDemoApp::PreTranslateMessage(MSG* pMsg)
{

 if( m_pSplashScreen != NULL ){
    if( ( pMsg->message == WM_KEYDOWN ||
  pMsg->message == WM_SYSKEYDOWN ||
  pMsg->message == WM_LBUTTONDOWN ||
  pMsg->message == WM_RBUTTONDOWN ||
  pMsg->message == WM_MBUTTONDOWN ||
  pMsg->message == WM_NCLBUTTONDOWN ||
  pMsg->message == WM_NCRBUTTONDOWN ||
```

```
     pMsg->message == WM_NCMBUTTONDOWN ) &&
     m_pSplashScreen->m_bOkToKill ){
     if( pMsg->hwnd == m_pSplashScreen->m_hWnd )
      m_dwSplashTime -=
       m_pSplashScreen->m_dwSplashTime;
     else{
      m_pSplashScreen->DestroyWindow();
      delete m_pSplashScreen;
      m_pSplashScreen = NULL;
       }
      }
     }

  return CWinApp::PreTranslateMessage(pMsg);
 }

BOOL CSplashDemoApp::OnIdle(LONG lCount)
{
 BOOL bRet;

 bRet = CWinApp::OnIdle(lCount);

 if( m_pSplashScreen != NULL ){
  if( GetCurrentTime() - m_dwSplashTime >=
   m_pSplashScreen->m_dwSplashTime ){
   m_pSplashScreen->DestroyWindow();
   delete m_pSplashScreen;
   m_pSplashScreen = NULL;
    }
  bRet = TRUE;
   }

 return( bRet );

 }
```

SplashDemo.h

```
#if
!defined(AFX_SPLASHDEMO_H__8378F7C3_8026_11D0_A555_00A024771373__INCLUDED_)
#define
AFX_SPLASHDEMO_H__8378F7C3_8026_11D0_A555_00A024771373__INCLUDED_

#ifndef __AFXWIN_H__
 #error include 'stdafx.h' before including this file for PCH
#endif
```

```
#include "resource.h"        // main symbols
#include "SplashLib.h"

/////////////////////////////////////////////
// CSplashDemoApp:
// See SplashDemo.cpp for the implementation of this class
//

class CSplashDemoApp : public CWinApp
{
public:
 CSplashDemoApp();

 CSplashScreen *m_pSplashScreen;
 DWORD m_dwSplashTime;

// Overrides
 // ClassWizard generated virtual function overrides
 //{{AFX_VIRTUAL(CSplashDemoApp)
 public:
 virtual BOOL InitInstance();
 virtual BOOL PreTranslateMessage(MSG* pMsg);
 virtual BOOL OnIdle(LONG lCount);
 //}}AFX_VIRTUAL

// Implementation

 //{{AFX_MSG(CSplashDemoApp)
 afx_msg void OnAppAbout();
 //}}AFX_MSG
 DECLARE_MESSAGE_MAP()
};

/////////////////////////////////////////////

//{{AFX_INSERT_LOCATION}}
// Microsoft Developer Studio will insert additional declarations
// immediately before the previous line.

#endif //
!defined(AFX_SPLASHDEMO_H__8378F7C3_8026_11D0_A555_00A024771373__INCLUDED_)
```

191

DISPLAYING A SPLASH SCREEN IN A NUTSHELL

The first thing you must do to display a splash screen with an image is create an image. For this example, the image is called "SPLASH.BMP."

The next thing you'll have to do is add PreTranslateMessage() and OnIdle() functions, using the App Wizard, to your main application source code file.

Next, you must add SplashLib.lib, ImageLoad.lib, and ImageObject.lib to your project.

Add the following include to the main application include file:

```
#include "RgnMapLib.h"
```

Add the following declarations to the main application include file:

```
CSplashScreen *m_pSplashScreen;
DWORD m_dwSplashTime;
```

Add the following code to the top of the main application source code file's InitInstance() function:

```
m_pSplashScreen =
    new CSplashScreen( "SPLASH.BMP" );
m_pSplashScreen->Create();
m_pSplashScreen->ShowWindow( SW_SHOW );
m_pSplashScreen->UpdateWindow();
```

Add the following code to the very end of the InitInstance() function, just before the function returns:

```
m_dwSplashTime = GetCurrentTime();
```

Edit the OnIdle() function to look like the following:

```
BOOL CSplashDemoApp::OnIdle(LONG lCount)
{
 BOOL bRet;

 bRet = CWinApp::OnIdle(lCount);

 if( m_pSplashScreen != NULL ){
  if( GetCurrentTime() - m_dwSplashTime >=
  m_pSplashScreen->m_dwSplashTime ){
  m_pSplashScreen->DestroyWindow();
  delete m_pSplashScreen;
  m_pSplashScreen = NULL;
  }
 bRet = TRUE;
```

```
    }
   return( bRet );
  }
```

If you want users to be able to click on the splash screen and make it disappear, edit the PreTranslateMessage() function so that it looks like the following:

```
BOOL CSplashDemoApp::PreTranslateMessage(MSG* pMsg)
{
 if( m_pSplashScreen != NULL ){
  if( ( pMsg->message == WM_KEYDOWN ||
   pMsg->message == WM_SYSKEYDOWN ||
   pMsg->message == WM_LBUTTONDOWN ||
   pMsg->message == WM_RBUTTONDOWN ||
   pMsg->message == WM_MBUTTONDOWN ||
   pMsg->message == WM_NCLBUTTONDOWN ||
   pMsg->message == WM_NCRBUTTONDOWN ||
   pMsg->message == WM_NCMBUTTONDOWN ) &&
   m_pSplashScreen->m_bOkToKill ){
   if( pMsg->hwnd == m_pSplashScreen->m_hWnd )
    m_dwSplashTime -=
     m_pSplashScreen->m_dwSplashTime;
   else{
    m_pSplashScreen->DestroyWindow();
    delete m_pSplashScreen;
    m_pSplashScreen = NULL;
    }
   }
  }

 return CWinApp::PreTranslateMessage(pMsg);
}
```

CREATING APPLICATIONS WITH SPLASH SCREENS

The following five hands-on exercises will get you warmed up so that you can move on to create your own applications with splash screens. Going through them won't take very long, and the investment of time will be well worth it, since you'll then have mastered splash screens with the CSplashLib class library.

You may be wondering why you should type in the code for each exercise: why not just load the project from disk? The answer is, you'll learn more by doing than just by reading.

Hands-On 1: Creating an Application With a Simple Splash Screen

This first exercise is the simplest example possible. It displays a splash screen for three seconds. There's no PreTranslateMessage() function to look for keypresses and mouse clicks. That means the user can't click on the splash screen and get it to disappear as in the demo program. Follow the steps and your splash screen will work like magic.

1. Create a Visual C++ project named HandsOn5_1 with the following attributes:

   ❐ Single-document interface

   ❐ English language

   ❐ No database support

   ❐ No compound document support

   ❐ No automation or ActiveX control support

   ❐ 3D controls, but no other features

   ❐ No source file comments

   ❐ Link MFC as a shared DLL

2. Select Settings from the Project menu. Choose the Link tab. Add ImageObject.lib, ImageLoad.lib, and SplashLib.lib to the Object/library modules field. Make sure you add them to the release and debug versions.

3. Copy the file splash1.bmp from the \samples directory on the Companion CD-ROM to the newly created project directory.

4. Add the following include to the HandsOn5_1.h file

   ```
   #include "SplashLib.h"
   ```

5. Add the following variable declarations to the HandsOn5_1App class in the HandsOn5_1.h file:

   ```
   DWORD m_dwSplashTime;
   CSplashScreen *m_pSplashScreen;
   ```

6. Add the following code at the top of the InitInstance() function in the HandsOn5_1App class in the HandsOn5_1.cpp file:

```
m_pSplashScreen =
    new CSplashScreen( "SPLASH1.BMP" );
m_pSplashScreen->Create();
m_pSplashScreen->ShowWindow( SW_SHOW );
m_pSplashScreen->UpdateWindow();
```

7. Add the following code to the bottom of the InitInstance() function in the HandsOn5_1App class in the HandsOn5_1.cpp file:

```
m_dwSplashTime = GetCurrentTime();
```

8. Add the following functions with the Class Wizard to the HandsOn5_1App class in the HandsOn5_1.h file:

```
Function: OnIdle()
```

9. Edit the OnIdle() function in the HandsOn5_1App class in the HandsOn5_1.cpp file as follows:

```
BOOL CHandsOn5_1App::OnIdle(LONG lCount)
{
 BOOL bRet;

 bRet = CWinApp::OnIdle(lCount);

 if( m_pSplashScreen != NULL ){
  if( GetCurrentTime() - m_dwSplashTime >=
   m_pSplashScreen->m_dwSplashTime ){
   m_pSplashScreen->DestroyWindow();
   delete m_pSplashScreen;
   m_pSplashScreen = NULL;
   }
  bRet = TRUE;
  }

 return( bRet );
}
```

10. Compile and run the program.

When the program runs, you'll see a splash screen with flowers and the text "Joe's Floral Design," as shown in Figure 5-2.

Figure 5-2: This is a simple splash screen that can be added to your application.

Hands-On 2: Creating an Application With Multiple Images for the Splash Screen

This exercise is almost as easy as the last one. It displays four splash screen images, each for three seconds. There's no PreTranslateMessage() function to look for keypresses and mouse clicks. Follow the steps and your splash screen will function with no trouble.

1. Create a Visual C++ project named HandsOn5_2 with the following attributes:

- ❐ Single-document interface
- ❐ English language
- ❐ No database support
- ❐ No compound document support
- ❐ No automation or ActiveX control support
- ❐ 3D controls, but no other features
- ❐ No source file comments
- ❐ Link MFC as a shared DLL

2. Select Settings from the Project menu. Choose the Link tab. Add ImageObject.lib, ImageLoad.lib, and SplashLib.lib to the Object/library modules field. Make sure you add them to the release and debug versions.

3. Copy the files image1.bmp, image2.bmp, image3.bmp, and image4.bmp from the \samples directory on the Companion CD-ROM to the newly created project directory.

4. Add the following include to the HandsOn5_2.h file

```
#include "SplashLib.h"
```

5. Add the following variable declarations to the HandsOn5_2App class in the HandsOn5_2.h file:

```
DWORD m_dwSplashTime;
CSplashScreen *m_pSplashScreen;
```

6. Add the following variable declaration to the top of the HandsOn5_2.cpp file:

```
static char szFilename[] = "IMAGE1.BMP";
```

7. Add the following code at the top of the InitInstance() function in the HandsOn5_2App class in the HandsOn5_2.cpp file:

```
m_pSplashScreen =
    new CSplashScreen( "IMAGE1.BMP" );
m_pSplashScreen->Create();
m_pSplashScreen->ShowWindow( SW_SHOW );
m_pSplashScreen->UpdateWindow();
```

8. Add the following code to the bottom of the InitInstance() function in the HandsOn5_2App class in the HandsOn5_2.cpp file:

```
m_dwSplashTime = GetCurrentTime();
```

9. Add the following functions with the Class Wizard to the HandsOn5_2App class in the HandsOn5_2.h file:

```
Function: OnIdle()
```

10. Edit the OnIdle() function in the HandsOn5_2App class in the HandsOn5_2.cpp file as follows:

```
BOOL CHandsOn5_1App::OnIdle(LONG lCount)
{
BOOL bRet;
bRet = CWinApp::OnIdle(lCount);
```

```
if( m_pSplashScreen != NULL ){
 if( GetCurrentTime() - m_dwSplashTime >=
  m_pSplashScreen->m_dwSplashTime ){
  szFilename[5]++;
  if( szFilename[5] > '4' ){
     m_pSplashScreen->DestroyWindow();
   delete m_pSplashScreen;
   m_pSplashScreen = NULL;
   }
  else{
   m_pSplashScreen->ChangeFile( szFilename );
   m_dwSplashTime = GetCurrentTime();
   }
  }
 bRet = TRUE;
 }
 return( bRet );
}
```

11. Compile and run the program.

When the program runs, you'll see a splash screen with lions, as shown in Figure 5-3. After three seconds you'll see another image. There are four images altogether that'll be displayed before the splash screen disappears.

Figure 5-3: This splash screen is simple, but it cycles through four image files before disappearing.

Hands-On 3: Creating an Application That Uses Image Processing to Blur a Splash Screen Image

The biggest difference between this exercise and the last two is that this one uses the CImageAreaProcesses class to perform a median filter on the splash screen's image. After doing so several times, the image becomes blurry. This is a special effect you might find useful at times.

1. Create a Visual C++ project named HandsOn5_3 with the following attributes:

   ❒ Single-document interface

   ❒ English language

   ❒ No database support

   ❒ No compound document support

   ❒ No automation or ActiveX control support

   ❒ 3D controls, but no other features

   ❒ No source file comments

   ❒ Link MFC as a shared DLL

2. Select Settings from the Project menu. Choose the Link tab. Add ImageObject.lib, ImageLoad.lib, ImagePointProcesses.lib, and SplashLib.lib to the Object/library modules field. Make sure you add them to the release and debug versions.

3. Copy the file splash2.bmp from the \samples directory on the Companion CD-ROM to the newly created project directory.

4. Add the following includes to the HandsOn5_3.h file:

   ```
   #include "SplashLib.h"
   #include "ImageAreaProcesses.h"
   ```

5. Add the following variable declarations to the HandsOn5_3App class in the HandsOn5_3.h file:

   ```
   DWORD m_dwSplashTime;
   CSplashScreen *m_pSplashScreen;
   int m_nCount;
   ```

6. Add the following code at the top of the InitInstance() function in the HandsOn5_3App class in the HandsOn5_3.cpp file:

```
m_pSplashScreen =
new CSplashScreen( "SPLASH2.BMP" );
m_pSplashScreen->Create();
m_pSplashScreen->ShowWindow( SW_SHOW );
m_pSplashScreen->UpdateWindow();
```

7. Add the following code to the bottom of the InitInstance() function in the HandsOn5_3App class in the HandsOn5_3.cpp file:

```
m_dwSplashTime = GetCurrentTime();
m_nCount = 0;
```

8. Add the following function with the Class Wizard to the HandsOn5_3App class in the HandsOn5_3.h file:

```
Function: OnIdle()
```

9. Edit the OnIdle() function in the HandsOn5_3App class in the HandsOn5_3.cpp file as follows:

```
BOOL CHandsOn5_3App::OnIdle(LONG lCount)
{
BOOL bRet;

bRet = CWinApp::OnIdle(lCount);

if( m_pSplashScreen != NULL ){
 if( GetCurrentTime() - m_dwSplashTime >=
  m_pSplashScreen->m_dwSplashTime ){
  if( m_nCount > 20 ){
  m_pSplashScreen->DestroyWindow();
   delete m_pSplashScreen;
   m_pSplashScreen = NULL;
   }
  else{
  CImageAreaProcesses *pImageAreaProcess =
```

```
        new CImageAreaProcesses(
          m_pSplashScreen->GetImage() );
        m_dwSplashTime = GetCurrentTime();
        pImageAreaProcess->MedianFilter();
        delete pImageAreaProcess;
        m_pSplashScreen->Redraw();
        }
      }
    bRet = TRUE;
    }

    return( bRet );

  }
```

10. Compile and run the program.

When the program runs, you'll see a splash screen with a pickup truck. After about 10 seconds, it'll become blurry, as shown in Figure 5-4.

Figure 5-4: This splash screen uses image processing techniques to alter the splash screen's image.

ON THE WEB

There are several sites on the Web that you'll find helpful. Some have images that you can use for your splash screens, and some have suggestions for image types that you can use.

Nordensson Lynn Advertising

This site specializes in advertising. There are many examples of splash screen art for various enterprise types. Figure 5-5 shows the site's page that covers splash screens.

Figure 5-5: This site is interested in splash screens from an advertising perspective.

InstallShield

This site is dedicated to demonstrating features of InstallShield. This section is about splash screens, and a sample is shown in Figure 5-6.

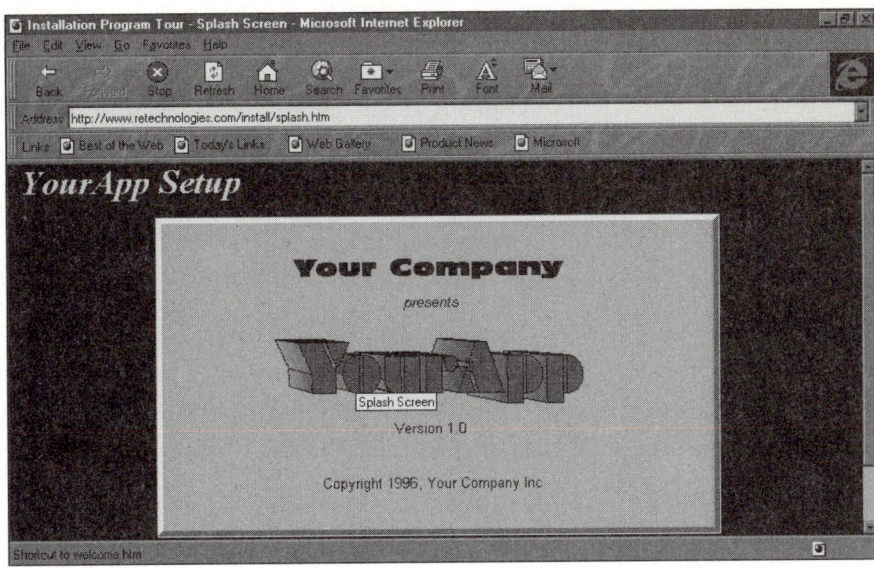

Figure 5-6: InstallShield makes use of splash screens for all of its installations.

Lorrex Inc.

This site promotes its promotion presentation software. Here, in Figure 5-7, it shows an example splash screen that was created with its software.

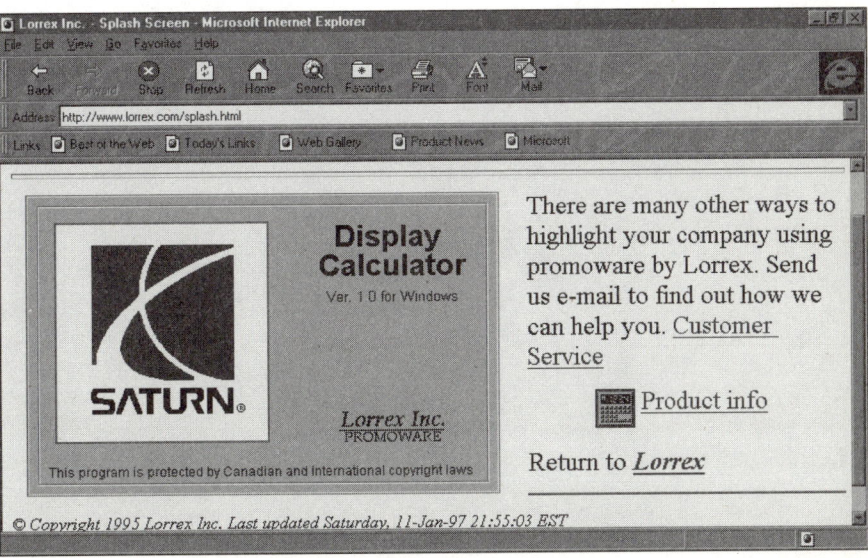

Figure 5-7: This presentation software allows you to create splash screens for your presentations.

MOVING ON

Now that you've learned how to use the CSplashScreen class, make sure all of your programs get off to a good start with a great-looking splash screen. See if you can be creative and think of new ways to use the image processing classes to enhance the CSplashScreen class.

The next chapter covers TWAIN data acquisition. It's a great way to obtain image files from pictures you have hanging on your wall or in photo albums. You can then use these images in some great splash screens.

Chapter 6

TWAIN Data Acquisition

*Look at the stars! Look, look up at the skies! scan all
the fire-folk sitting in the air.*
—Gerard Manley Hopkins

In this age of cost-cutting and economizing, everyone is looking for
ways to save money. One of the best ways to follow this trend in your
computing is to work more efficiently—by eliminating manual data entry.
This chapter takes a step in that direction by introducing you to TWAIN
and giving you a class library that lets you scan images and save them to
disk. TWAIN is the device-independent API for talking to scanners. Using
TWAIN and the scanner class library, you can develop entire applications
that read information from paper and incorporate it in many ways.

One application that's waiting to be developed is a form reader. It
would be useful in situations where customers go to a place of business,
fill out a multiple-choice form, have an employee scan it in, then update
the company's database and generate the appropriate transaction. If such
an application were available, it could save companies millions of dollars
in menial data entry costs.

After you complete the hands-on exercises in this chapter, you should
have little trouble adding scanner input to your programs.

TWAIN—WHAT IS IT?

With the introduction of scanners and other image-acquisition devices, eager computer users discovered the value of incorporating images into their work. However, supporting the display and manipulation of this raster data placed a high cost on application developers. They needed to create user interfaces and build in control for the wide assortment of available image devices. Once an application was prepared to support a given device, developers faced the discouraging reality of having to revise their products with new capabilities and features in order to stay current.

Developers of image-acquisition devices and software applications recognized the need for a standard communication method between the image devices and the applications. They believed that a standard would benefit both groups and the product's users as well. It would allow the device vendors' products to be accessed by more applications, and application vendors could access data from those devices regardless of device type. The TWAIN API was developed because of this need for consistency and simplification.

The Creation & Implementation of TWAIN

TWAIN is a device-independent API for talking to scanners and similar image acquisition devices. It removes the hardware-dependent variables so that applications can talk to a common API.

The goal of the small group of software and hardware companies that created TWAIN was to provide an open multiplatform solution to interconnect raster input devices with application software. The original Working Group comprised representatives from five companies: Aldus, Caere, Eastman Kodak, Hewlett-Packard, and Logitech. Three other companies, Adobe, Howtek, and Software Architects, also contributed significantly.

The design of TWAIN began in January 1991. Review of the original TWAIN Developer's Toolkit was completed in January 1992. The original Toolkit was reviewed by the TWAIN Coalition. The Coalition includes approximately 300 individuals representing 200 companies that continue to influence and guide the future direction of TWAIN.

The TWAIN Implementor's Matrix is a listing of applications and devices supporting TWAIN. Information included is company name, contact name, product, release, and platform. Also included are TWAIN developers. Additions are made by submitting the TWAIN Implementor's Matrix Application to the TWAIN Working Group. Both the matrix and the application are available via CompuServe in HP's GO HP PERIPH forum under TWAIN.

The matrix is also available on Logitech's FaxBack: you can call Logitech's FaxBack system at 800-245-0000 and request document number 4714 (TWAIN Implementors Matrix). The Matrix lists Mac and Windows applications and sources. (You may need to contact the individual companies to verify completion of product.)

THE ELEMENTS OF TWAIN

TWAIN defines a standard software protocol and API for communication between software applications and image acquisition devices. The three key elements of TWAIN are:

❑ **The application software**. An application must be modified to use TWAIN.

❑ **The Source Manager software**. This software manages the interactions between the application and the Source. The code is provided in the TWAIN Developer's Toolkit and should be shipped free with each TWAIN application and Source.

❑ **The Source software**. This software controls the image acquisition device and is written by the device developer to comply with TWAIN specifications. Traditional device drivers are now included with the Source software and do not need to be shipped by applications.

THE BENEFITS OF USING TWAIN

Three sets of people benefit from the TWAIN interface. Most important are the end users of software. They don't have to worry about telling each application which acquisition device they're using. That's already done when they install the hardware's drivers and the TWAIN API dlls. The software developers benefit because they don't have to worry about the complexities of thousands of different devices. There's just one common interface to learn and use. And of course the software publishers have far less technical support and related headaches because there's less chance that the software will have trouble communicating with the device.

I've seen scanner input routines for a lot of Windows software. Most fax software has built-in scanner support so that documents can be easily scanned and sent as faxes through a fax modem card. A number of word processors link to scanners by accepting scanned-in data that's converted to text using OCR (optical recognition) software. Art and desktop publishing programs use scanner input to obtain images that enhance documents or illustrate ideas.

As the number of applications accepting scanner input increases, it won't be long before the scanner becomes standard equipment at the desk or workstation. You should make an effort to provide for supporting scanner input if it makes sense for your programs. And to add further fuel to the fire, many people are buying multifunction machines that have print, fax, and scanning capabilities.

After scouring the online services and Internet sites, I found very little that helped me in the initial development phase of my work. The TWAIN Developer's Toolkit, which can be downloaded or purchased for a nominal charge, is hard to read and understand—even harder to make sense of and use in a program.

However, using TWAIN with the CScanner class library removes all of the complexities, and scanning images can be as simple as adding a few lines of code to a program.

The TWAIN API is provided by the TWAIN Working Group. The hardware drivers are provided by the hardware manufacturers. And the CScanner class library is provided on the Companion CD-ROM that comes with this book.

Benefits for the Application Developer

❐ Users have a simple way to incorporate images from any compatible raster device without leaving the application.

❐ It is no longer necessary to write, support, or ship device drivers for scanners. The TWAIN-compliant image acquisition devices provide Source software modules that eliminate the need to create and ship device drivers.

❐ The application can access data from any TWAIN-compliant image peripheral simply by modifying the application code once using the high-level TWAIN application programming interface. No customization by product is necessary. TWAIN image peripherals can include desktop scanners, hand scanners, digital cameras, frame grabbers, image databases, or any other raster image source that complies with the TWAIN protocol and API.

❐ The developer determines the features and capabilities an image-acquisition device can provide. The application can then restrict the Source to offer only those capabilities that are compatible with the application's needs and abilities.

❐ The application developer does not need to provide a user interface to control the image-acquisition process. A software user interface module is shipped with every TWAIN-compliant Source device to handle that process. Of course, the developer may provide a user interface for acquisition.

Benefits for the Source Developer

❑ Increased use and support of the product will result. More applications will become image consumers as a result of the ease of implementation and breadth of device integration that TWAIN provides.

❑ Developers can provide a proprietary user interface for their devices, which allows them to present the newest features to the user without waiting for the applications to incorporate them into their interfaces.

❑ Reduced implementation costs mean money saved. Rather than create and support various versions of device-control software to integrate with various applications, a single TWAIN-compliant Source can be created.

Benefit for the End User

❑ Users get a simple way to incorporate images into their documents. They can access the image in fewer steps because they never need to leave the applications.

HOW TO GET SUPPORT

For technical and marketing support for TWAIN, you can contact the TWAIN Working Group directly by e-mailing to **twain-wg@caere.com**. The Working Group discusses TWAIN-specific problems but not vendor-specific problems. If you have a vendor-specific issue, with either an application or raster acquisition device, you should contact that vendor directly.

Because the Working Group receives a fair number of HP questions, we are including the address for HP Developer Support: **peterd@gr.hp.com**.

Many TWAIN questions are answered by members of the TWAIN community at large. For this reason, you may want to send some types of questions to the whole community: **twain@caere.com**.

How to Get Information on TWAIN

HPFirst is a fax reply system at Hewlett-Packard; this system contains two TWAIN documents:

❑ 3130 TWAIN Toolkit order form

❑ 3129 TWAIN White Paper

To receive these documents, call from a touch-tone phone or fax machine and information will be faxed to you.

❏ **Inside the US or Canada:** 800-333-1917
❏ **Outside the US or Canada:** 208-344-4809

How to Order a Toolkit

The entire Toolkit minus the printed manual is included on the Companion CD-ROM that comes with this book. It can be found in the TWAIN\ TWAINKIT directory. You may want to order a Toolkit and get the printed manual, though.

❏ **U.S./Canada:** Call (800) 722-0379 and order the TWAIN Toolkit.

❏ **International:** Outside the U.S./Canada, use HPFirst (a fax reply system at Hewlett-Packard). Call from a touch-tone phone or fax machine: 208-344-4809. Request document number 3130.

THE TWAIN CLASS LIBRARY

The class library that's included on the Companion CD-ROM acts as a layer between your application and the TWAIN API. This makes it much easier to incorporate TWAIN support. If you want to explore the inner workings of the TWAIN interface, you can start by looking at the TWAIN Developer's Toolkit that's on the CD-ROM. It's going to be hard to fully exploit the function calls, though, without the printed documentation.

All source code and support files to rebuild the SCANNER.LIB file can be found in the TWAIN\TWAINLib directory on the CD-ROM.

THE TWAINDEMO

We've built a simple demonstration program that shows what the class library can do. The program can be found in the TWAIN\TWAINDemo directory on the CD-ROM. Using File Manager or Program Manager, run the program named TWAINDemo.exe. It's a multiple-document program. When it runs, all you'll see is an empty window.

To scan a document, select New from the File menu. You'll first see a dialog box, shown in Figure 6-1, asking you for your scan preference. Three choices allow you to scan in interactive mode, scan an 8 1/2 by 11 image, or scan an 8 1/2 by 14 image.

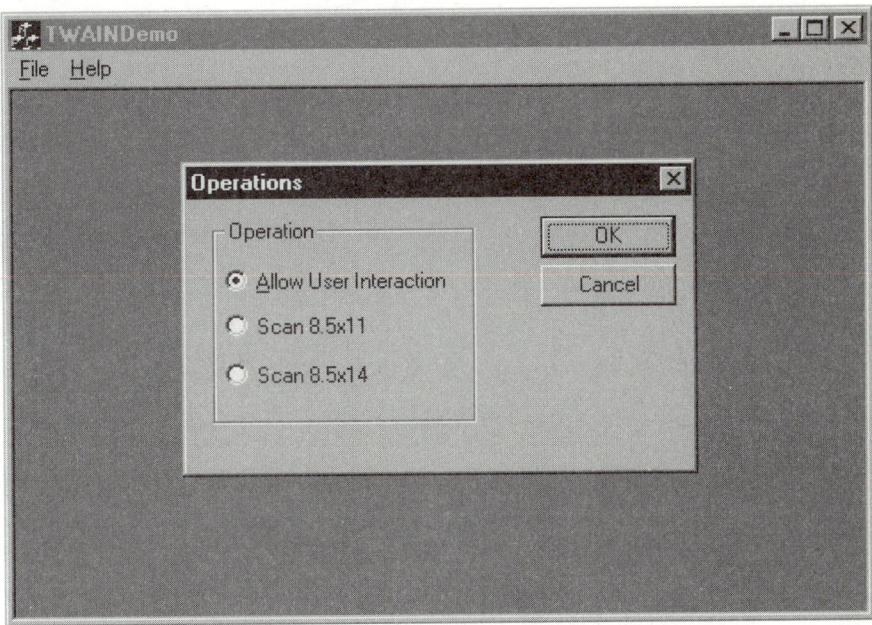

Figure 6-1: You can have the program allow complete user interaction or restrict the user to one of two preset document sizes.

Once you've made your selection, the program will display the TWAIN interface dialog, as shown in Figure 6-2, or begin a scan. It's important to note that the noninteractive mode, where the TWAIN interface dialog doesn't appear, is not guaranteed. Sometimes, especially with older drivers, the dialog box may appear, even if you request not to have it appear. My own scanner, which was purchased in March of 1994, wouldn't allow scans without the dialog box until I downloaded updated drivers. You may find yourself in the same situation; if you do, consider obtaining updated drivers.

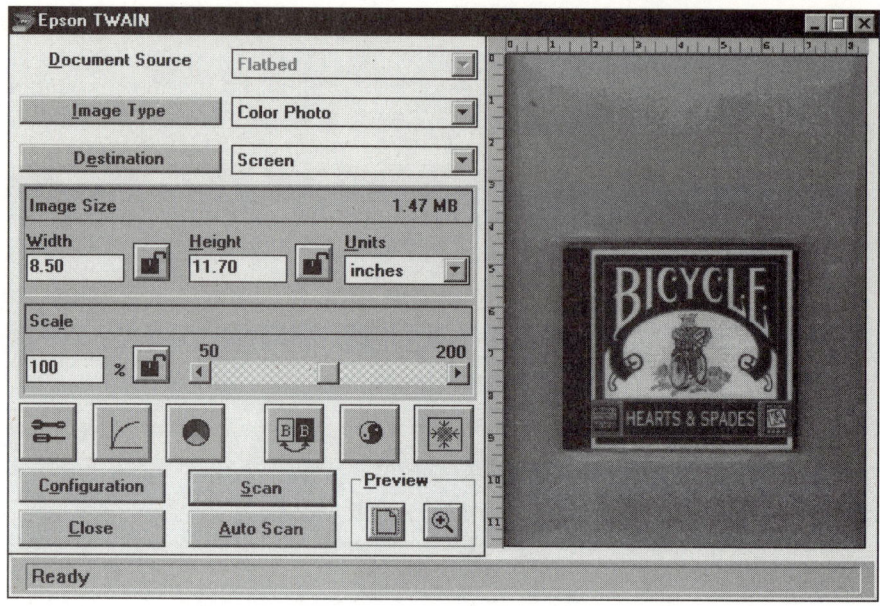

Figure 6-2: The TWAIN user interface gives you plenty of power to obtain the exact image you want.

After the image is scanned, it'll appear in the newly created MDI window. If you used the TWAIN dialog box, you'll notice that it disappears after the scan. You can change this in your own programs. The TWAIN API allows multiple scans with the TWAIN dialog box open as shown in Figure 6-3. The scanner class library allows you to set this, and as a matter of fact it defaults to allowing multiple scans. This means that users must close the TWAIN dialog box before it disappears.

The Scan demo allows you to save images to disk as BMP, GIF, JPEG, PCX, TGA (Targa) , or TIF files as shown in Figure 6-4. Once the image is scanned, it's transformed into a picture class using a CImageObject class from the image library (explained in Chapter 1).

Figure 6-3: The Scan demo allows you to scan a number of images.

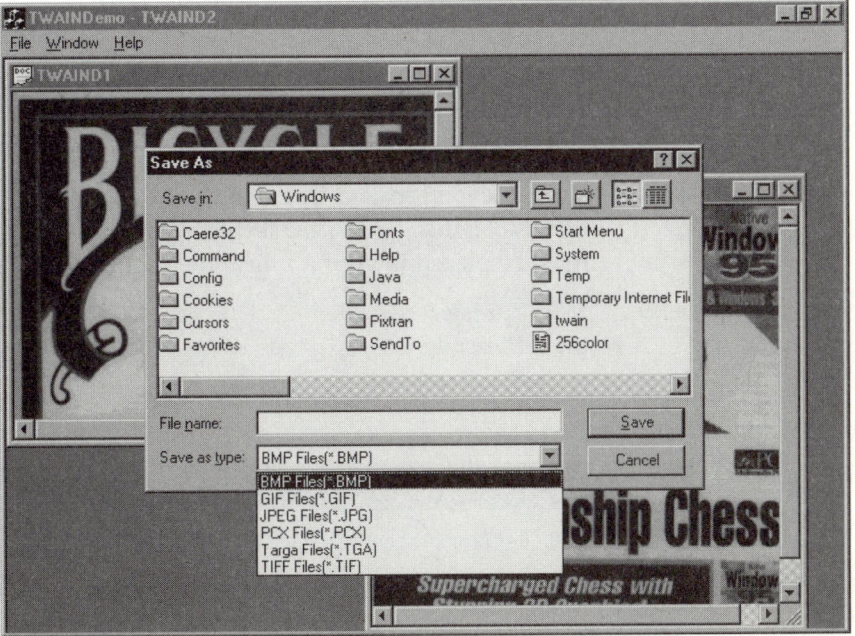

Figure 6-4: You can save the scanned images to disk.

CSCANNER CLASS LIBRARY FUNCTION CALLS

This section is provided as a reference to the public function calls the CScanner class library offers. As with the other class libraries, simplicity was a goal during the design of this class library. You don't want to spend hours or days learning how to use a class library. You want to be able to use it in less than an hour. As a result, it doesn't take much to acquire images—just a few lines of code.

You may want to skip over this section and read the section entitled "Behind TWAINDemo," which shows how the calls are used. For some people, it's better to look at the usage of function calls before actually studying the syntax.

StartPicture()

Prototype: `BOOL StartPicture( void );`

Purpose: This function gets the scan process started. It doesn't do the actual scanning, though. It simply opens the source and prepares it for scanning.

Arguments: None

Returns:: BOOL: TRUE for success, FALSE for FAIL

PreTranslateMessage()

Prototype: `BOOL PreTranslateMessage( MSG *pMsg, int *pMessage );`

Purpose: This function is called from your window's PreTranslateMessage( ) function. Note: this is not a substitute for a virtual PreTranslateMessage( ) that must be placed in your application's active window class.

Arguments: MSG *pMsg
int *pMessage

Returns: BOOL: TRUE for success, FALSE for FAIL.

GetTranslatedMessage()

Prototype: `BOOL GetTranslatedMessage( CDC *pDC, int Message );`

Purpose: This function is called when there's a TWAIN message waiting. If the message was a scanned image, it returns a CImageObject pointer.

Arguments: CDC *pDC
int Message

Returns: BOOL: TRUE for success, FALSE for FAIL

Kill()

Prototype: `void Kill( void );`

Purpose: This removes and closes the TWAIN sources and interface items.

Arguments: None

Returns: void

SetPixelParams()

Prototype: `void SetPixelParams( int flags = USER_SELECTION, int x1 = -1, int y1 = -1, int x2 = -1, int y2 = -1 );`

Purpose: This function sets the parameters with which the program will perform the next scan. The flags variable gives you two options. One, defined as USER_SELECTION, allows users to interact using the TWAIN dialog. Another, defined as MULTIPLE_SCANS, allows users to do multiple scans while the TWAIN dialog remains open. A value of zero prevents the TWAIN dialog from appearing (unless the driver doesn't support this option), and causes the class library to perform a single scan before the dialog disappears. The other four parameters specify the pixel coordinates of the image to be scanned. You can leave any or all of them as -1, and default values (set by the TWAIN driver) will be used.

Arguments: int flags
0, or a combination of USER_SELECTION and MULTIPLE_SCANS
int x1, y1, x2, y2

Returns: Nothing

SetInchParams( )

Prototype: `void SetInchParams( int flags = USER_SELECTION, int WidthInch = -1, int WidthFrac = -1, int HeightInch = -1, int HeightFrac = -1 );`

Purpose: This function sets the parameters with which the program will perform the next scan. The flags variable gives you the same two options described in SetPixelParams( ). The other four parameters specify the value of the right margin and the bottom margin in inches. For instance, if you want to scan a document that's 4 inches wide and 5 inches high, your values to this function will be 4, 0, 5, and 0. (Note that the document must originate at the upper left corner of the scanner.) The second and fourth parameters are percentage values. For instance, if you want to scan a document that's 4 1/2 inches wide and 6 3/4 inches high, your values to this function will be 4, 50, 6, 75.

Arguments: int flags
0, or a combination of USER_SELECTION and MULTIPLE_SCANS
int WidthInch int WidthFrac int HeightInch
int HeightFrac

Behind TWAINDemo

TWAIN Demo was created with the Visual C++ AppWizard. It has a multiple-document interface and no initial toolbar. The window class is a CScrollView class. After creating the program, the ImageObject, ImageLoad, and TWAINLib libraries were added to the linker. To do this, select Project from the Options menu. Choose the Linker button, and when the Linker Options dialog appears, add ImageObject, ImageLoad, and TWAINLib to the Libraries list. (Remember to add them to both the debug and release projects.)

Most of the code that has anything to do with the scanner library is in TWAINDemoView.cpp. First, though, we'll talk about the small number of functions that are found in other modules.

Note: As with many other demo programs that accompany this book, all Set Focus messages are used to set the child window's palette. The ClassWizard makes it easy to create the function.

The CMainFrame Class

The main frame constructor sets a single variable to 0. The variable's name is mOperation and is used to remember which choice the user made when the first dialog appears after selecting New from the File menu.

The CMainFrame( ) Code

```
CMainFrame::CMainFrame( )
{
    m_nOperation = 0;
}
```

Allowing Users to Select Operations

This function simply calls the operation selection dialog and records the user's choice.

The GetOperation( ) Code

```
void CMainFrame::GetOperation( void )
{
    COperationDialog OperationDlg;
    OperationDlg.m_Selection = m_nOperation;
    if( OperationDlg.DoModal() == IDOK )
        m_nOperation = OperationDlg.m_Selection;
}
```

Creating a New Document

In TWAINDemoDoc.cpp you'll find OnNewDocument( ). This function first looks at the CScanner class, which is a member of the CMainFrame class. Since there's only one scanner, there's only one scanner class. The scanner can't be invoked multiple times. We must check to see if it's already in use when users try to create new documents.

After the document is created, this function then asks which type of operation the user wants.

The OnNewDocument( ) Code

```
BOOL CTWAINDemoDoc::OnNewDocument()
{
    CMainFrame *pFrame =
        (CMainFrame *) AfxGetApp()->m_pMainWnd;
    if( pFrame->m_Scanner.mDSOpened ||
        pFrame->m_Scanner.mDSMOpened ||
        pFrame->m_Scanner.mAquiring ){
        AfxMessageBox( "The scanner is in use!");
        return( FALSE );
        }

    if (!CDocument::OnNewDocument())
        return FALSE;

    pFrame->GetOperation();

    return TRUE;
}
```

Saving Files

The only other function that was added to TWAINDemoDoc.cpp was an override for OnFileSaveAs( ). It simply gets a filename using the File Selector Common Dialog box, then lets the picture class do the saving.

The OnFileSaveAs( ) Code

```
void CTWAINDemoDoc::OnFileSaveAs()
{
    char szFilter[] = "BMP Files(*.BMP)|*.BMP|\
GIF Files(*.GIF)|*.GIF|\
JPEG Files(*.JPG)|*.JPG|\
PCX Files(*.PCX)|*.PCX|\
Targa Files(*.TGA)|*.TGA|\
TIFF Files(*.TIF)|*.TIF||";

    CFileDialog FileDlg( FALSE, NULL, NULL,
  OFN_HIDEREADONLY, szFilter );

    if( FileDlg.DoModal () == IDOK ){

        CMainFrame *pFrame =
      (CMainFrame *) AfxGetApp()->m_pMainWnd;
        BOOL max;
        CMDIChildWnd *pChild =
      pFrame->MDIGetActive( &max );

        if( pChild != NULL ){
         CTWAINDemoView *pView =
           (CTWAINDemoView *)
         pChild->GetActiveView();
            CString PathName =
           FileDlg.GetPathName();
         pView->SaveAs(PathName.GetBuffer(3));
            }
        }
    }
```

The View Constructor

The view class's constructor performs two variable initializations. It sets the CImageObject pointer named m_pImage to NULL, so that we don't try to use it before it's actually allocated, and sets the m_bScannerInvoked flag to FALSE so that we know later on if the scanner has been in action.

The CTWAINDemoView( ) Code

```
CTWAINDemoView::CTWAINDemoView( )
{
    m_pImage = NULL;
    m_bScannerInvoked = FALSE;
}
```

The View Destructor

The view class's destructor deletes the picture class if it's been allocated. It also makes sure the scanner is all closed by calling the CScanner.Kill( ) function.

The ~CScanView( ) Code

```
CScanView::~CScanView( )
{
    if( m_pImage ) delete m_pImage;

    CMainFrame *pFrame =
        (CMainFrame *) AfxGetApp( )->m_pMainWnd;
    pFrame->m_Scanner.Kill( );
}
```

Drawing the Acquired Image

If a picture has been scanned, it's drawn in the OnDraw function. Before it's drawn, the window is prepared with OnPrepareDC( ) so that the scroll bars correctly draw. StartPicture( ) is called at the end of OnDraw( ), but just once. Subsequent calls to OnDraw( ) don't make subsequent calls to StartPicture( ).

You might notice that the scanning parameters are set with calls to SetPixelParams( ) and SetInchParams( ). The call to SetPixelParams( ) doesn't specify the scan coordinates, since it's telling the CScanner class to allow full user interaction. The calls to SetInchParams( ) specify scanning 8 1/2 by 11 documents and 8 1/2 by 14 documents, respectively.

The OnDraw( ) Code

```
void CTWAINDemoView::OnDraw(CDC* pDC)
{
    CTWAINDemoDoc* pDoc = GetDocument();
    ASSERT_VALID(pDoc);

    if( m_pImage != NULL ){
        CSize SizeTotal;
        SizeTotal.cx = m_pImage->GetWidth();
        SizeTotal.cy = m_pImage->GetHeight();
        SetScrollSizes (MM_TEXT, SizeTotal);
        OnPrepareDC (pDC);
        m_pImage->Draw( pDC );
        }

    if( !m_bScannerInvoked ){
        m_bScannerInvoked = TRUE;
        CMainFrame *pFrame =
        (CMainFrame *) AfxGetApp()->m_pMainWnd;
        CTWAINDemoView *View = this;
        if( !pFrame->m_nOperation )
        pFrame->m_Scanner.SetPixelParams(
    USER_SELECTION );
        else if( pFrame->m_nOperation == 1 )
          pFrame->m_Scanner.SetInchParams( 0,
        8, 50, 11, 0 );
        else
          pFrame->m_Scanner.SetInchParams( 0,
        8, 50, 14, 0 );
        pFrame->m_Scanner.StartPicture(
    View->m_hWnd );
        }
}
```

Intercepting Scanner MessagesWithout adding this to your window class, there's no chance that the TWAIN API will work. It must maintain a message dialog with your window. Add a virtual prototype to your include and then add this function to the module code.

This function calls the scanner class's PreTranslateMessage( ) function (which I must emphasize is NOT a virtual function that's related to this one). The scanner's PreTranslateMessage( ) function decides if the message is a scanner message. If not, this PreTranslateMessage( ) function calls the base class PreTranslateMessage( ) function and returns the value.

If a scanner message is detected, the scanner class GetTranslatedMessage( ) function is called to either get a picture or close up shop (or both).

The PreTranslateMessage( ) Code

```
BOOL CTWAINDemoView::PreTranslateMessage(
 MSG *msg )
{
    int nMessage;
    CMainFrame *pFrame =
        (CMainFrame *) AfxGetApp()->m_pMainWnd;

if(!pFrame->m_Scanner.PreTranslateMessage(msg,
 &nMessage))
return(CScrollView::PreTranslateMessage(msg));

  if( nMessage ){
    if( pFrame->m_Scanner.GetTranslatedMessage(
    nMessage ) ){
        if( m_pImage != NULL ) delete m_pImage;
        m_pImage = new CImageObject( "TEMP.BMP" );
    InvalidateRect( NULL, FALSE );
        UpdateWindow();
        }
    else{
        CTWAINDemoDoc* pDoc = GetDocument ();
        pDoc->OnCloseDocument ();
        }
    }

    return( TRUE );
}
```

Setting the Palette When Receiving Focus

This function is added via the ClassWizard so that the application can set the palette when each child window receives the focus.

The OnSetFocus( ) Code

```
void CTWAINDemoView::OnSetFocus(CWnd* pOldWnd)
{
    CView::OnSetFocus(pOldWnd);

    if( m_pImage != NULL ){
        CClientDC ClientDC( this );
        m_pImage->SetPalette( &ClientDC );
        }
}
```

Saving Images

The last function needed was a SaveAs( ) routine that the OnSaveAs( ) function of the document class can call. This function does the actual picture-saving stuff necessary before the picture class can save to disk.

The SaveAs( ) Code

```
void CTWAINDemoView::SaveAs( const char *pszFilename )
{
    if( m_pImage == NULL ){
        AfxMessageBox( "No picture to save!" );
        return;
        }

    BeginWaitCursor ();
    if( m_pImage->Save( pszFilename ) )
        SetWindowText( pszFilename );
    EndWaitCursor ();
}
```

Acquiring TWAIN Images in a Nutshell

The first thing you'll need to do is declare a CScanner object somewhere so that it won't go out of scope. For now, we'll declare a global variable as follows:

```
CScanner g_Scanner;
```

Perform the following code only once before invoking the TWAIN user interface. (Make sure the pView is a valid pointer to the view class.)

```
m_Scanner.SetPixelParams( USER_SELECTION );
m_Scanner.StartPicture( pView->m_hWnd );
```

Add the following virtual function to the view class. If the CScanner class function GetTranslatedMessage() returns TRUE, a file named TEMP.BMP will contain the image.

```
BOOL CTWAINDemoView::PreTranslateMessage(
 MSG *msg )
{
 int nMessage;

 if( m_Scanner.PreTranslateMessage( msg,
  &nMessage))
  return(
   CScrollView::PreTranslateMessage( msg ) );

if( nMessage &&
 m_Scanner.GetTranslatedMessage( nMessage ) )
 // retrieve image file "TEMP.BMP"
 }

 return( TRUE );
}
```

Creating Programs That Use TWAIN Data Acquisition

The following three hands-on exercises will get you warmed up so that you can move on to create your own applications with TWAIN support. Going through them won't take very long, and the investment of time will be well worth it, since you'll then have mastered acquiring images with the CScanner class library.

You may be asking why you should type in the code for each exercise. Why not just load the project from disk? I've learned from experience that you get the most benefit from doing, rather than just reading.

Hands-On 1: Acquiring an Image to a Disk File

The first exercise invokes the TWAIN interface and allows the user to scan an image. To keep things simple, the image isn't displayed within the application but is saved to a file called TEMP.BMP.

If, when the program first runs, you scan an image, you'll be notified that the scan was successful. You'll see an alert box telling you that the image was saved to a file named TEMP.BMP as shown in Figure 6-5.

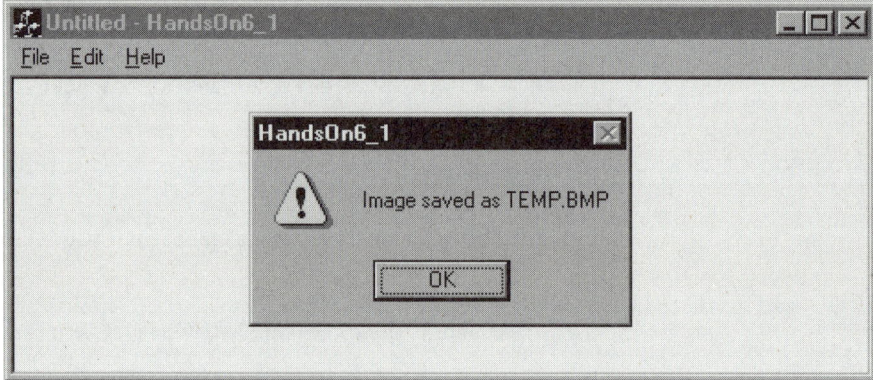

Figure 6-5: This first example doesn't display the scanned image in the application, so things can be kept as simple as possible.

The following steps take you through the process of creating your first TWAIN application.

1. Create a Visual C++ project named HandsOn6_1 with the following attributes:
   - ❐ Single-document interface
   - ❐ English language
   - ❐ No database support
   - ❐ No compound document support
   - ❐ No automation or ActiveX control support
   - ❐ 3D controls, but no other features
   - ❐ No source file comments
   - ❐ Link MFC as a shared DLL

2. Select Settings from the Project menu. Choose the Link tab. Add the following libraries to the Object/library modules field. The libraries for the release and debug versions are different; both are listed below.

Release Project Libraries	Debug Project Libraries
TWAIN_32.lib	TWAIN_32.lib
TWAINLib.lib	TWAINLibD.lib

3. Add the following include to the HandsOn6_1View.h file:

```
#include "scanner.h"
```

4. Add the following variable declarations to the CHandsOn6_1View class in the HandsOn6_1View.h file:

```
CScanner m_Scanner;
BOOL m_bScannerInvoked;
```

5. Add the following code to the CHandsOn6_1View constructor:

```
m_bScannerInvoked = FALSE;
```

6. Add the following code to the CHandsOn6_1View destructor:

```
m_Scanner.Kill();
```

7. Edit the OnDraw function in the CHandsOn6_1View class in the HandsOn6_1View.cpp file as follows:

```
void CHandsOn6_1View::OnDraw(CDC* pDC)
{
    CHandsOn6_1Doc* pDoc = GetDocument();
    ASSERT_VALID(pDoc);

    if( !m_bScannerInvoked ){
        m_bScannerInvoked = TRUE;
        CHandsOn6_1View *pView = this;
        m_Scanner.SetPixelParams(USER_SELECTION);
        m_Scanner.StartPicture( pView->m_hWnd );
        }
}
```

8. Add the following functions to the CHandsOn6_1View class in the HandsOn6_1View.h file:

```
virtual BOOL PreTranslateMessage( MSG * );
```

9. Add the PreTranslateMessage function in the CHandsOn6_1View class in the HandsOn6_1View.cpp file as follows:

```
BOOL CHandsOn6_1View::PreTranslateMessage( MSG *msg )
{
 int nMessage;

 if( !m_Scanner.PreTranslateMessage( msg,
  &nMessage ) )
  return( CView::PreTranslateMessage(msg));

 if( nMessage ){
  if(m_Scanner.GetTranslatedMessage(nMessage))
   AfxMessageBox( "Image saved as TEMP.BMP" );
  else{
   CHandsOn6_1Doc* pDoc = GetDocument();
   pDoc->OnCloseDocument();
   }
 }

 return( TRUE );
}
```

10. Compile and run the program.

When the program runs, you'll get the TWAIN user interface dialog. If you successfully scan an image, the program will alert you that the image was saved to a file named TEMP.BMP.

Hands-On 2: Displaying an Acquired Image

This exercise is just slightly more complicated that the last one. It uses a CImageObject class to load the TEMP.BMP file and display it in the application's view window, as shown in Figure 6-6.

While the last exercise simply scanned the image, this exercise loads the image temporary file (TEMP.BMP) into a CImageObject class. It then displays the image in the view class's OnDraw() function.

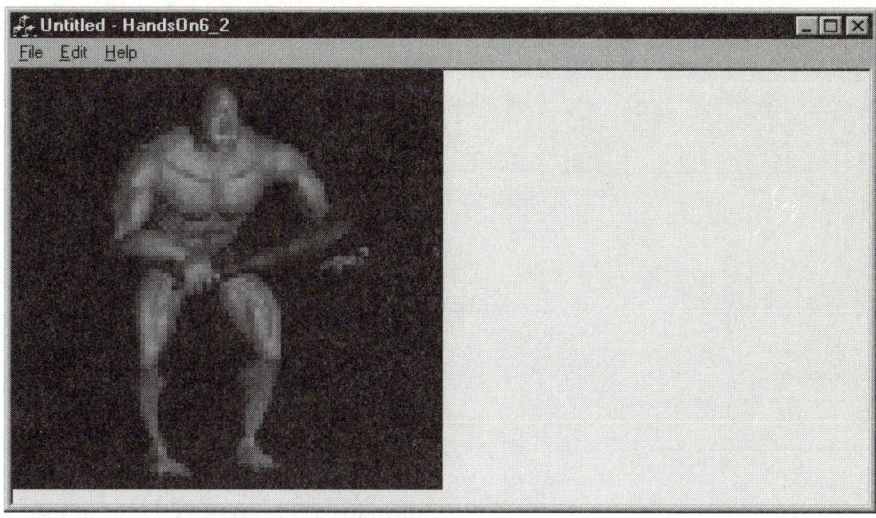

Figure 6-6: This application displays images that are successfully scanned.

The following steps will help you easily create this application.

1. Create a Visual C++ project named HandsOn6_2 with the following attributes:

   ❒ Single-document interface

   ❒ English language

   ❒ No database support

   ❒ No compound document support

   ❒ No automation or ActiveX control support

   ❒ 3D controls, but no other features

   ❒ No source file comments

   ❒ Link MFC as a shared DLL

2. Select Settings from the Project menu. Choose the Link tab. Add the following libraries to the Object/library modules field. The libraries for the release and debug versions are different; both are listed below.

Release Project Libraries	Debug Project Libraries
ImageLoad.lib	ImageLoad.lib
ImageObject.lib	ImageObjectD.lib
TWAIN_32.lib	TWAIN_32.lib
TWAINLib.lib	TWAINLibD.lib

3. Add the following includes to the HandsOn6_2View.h file:

```
#include "scanner.h"
#include "ImageObject.h"
```

4. Add the following variable declarations to the CHandsOn6_2View class in the HandsOn6_2View.h file:

```
CScanner m_Scanner;
BOOL m_bScannerInvoked;
CImageObject *m_pImage;
```

5. Add the following code to the CHandsOn6_2View constructor:

```
m_bScannerInvoked = FALSE;
m_pImage = NULL;
```

6. Add the following code to the CHandsOn6_2View destructor:

```
m_Scanner.Kill();
if( m_pImage != NULL )
    delete m_pImage;
```

7. Edit the OnDraw function in the CHandsOn6_2View class in the HandsOn6_2View.cpp file as follows:

```
void CHandsOn6_2View::OnDraw(CDC* pDC)
{
    CHandsOn6_2Doc* pDoc = GetDocument();
    ASSERT_VALID(pDoc);

    if( !m_bScannerInvoked ){
        m_bScannerInvoked = TRUE;
        CHandsOn6_1View *pView = this;
        m_Scanner.SetPixelParams(USER_SELECTION);
        m_Scanner.StartPicture( pView->m_hWnd );
        }

    if( m_pImage != NULL ){
        m_pImage->SetPalette( pDC );
        m_pImage->Draw( pDC );
        }
}
```

8. Add the following function to the CHandsOn6_2View class in the HandsOn6_2View.h file:

```
virtual BOOL PreTranslateMessage( MSG * );
```

9. Add the PreTranslateMessage function in the CHandsOn6_2View class in the HandsOn6_2View.cpp file as follows:

```
BOOL CHandsOn6_2View::PreTranslateMessage( MSG *msg )
{
 int nMessage;
 if( !m_Scanner.PreTranslateMessage( msg,
  &nMessage ) )
  return( CView::PreTranslateMessage( msg ) );

 if( nMessage ){
  CClientDC ClientDC( this );
  if( m_Scanner.GetTranslatedMessage(
   &ClientDC, nMessage ) ){
   m_pImage = new CImageObject( "TEMP.BMP" );
   InvalidateRect( NULL, TRUE );
   UpdateWindow();
   }
  else{
   CHandsOn6_2Doc* pDoc = GetDocument();
   pDoc->OnCloseDocument();
   }
  }

 return( TRUE );

}
```

10. Compile and run the program.

When the program runs, you'll get the chance to scan in an image. If you're successful in your scan, the image will be drawn in the application's view window.

Hands-On 3: Acquiring Multiple Images

This third exercise allows you to scan multiple images. The program supports multiple documents. Each document contains a scanned image. Of course, this program is more complex than the last two. It adds code to display all images that have been scanned the same as the second exercise added to this code. But supporting multiple documents makes it a much more usable program. You'll enjoy scanning in several images, then comparing them.

You can scan as many images as your computer has memory for. In Figure 6-7 you'll see the application with two images.

Figure 6-7: This application scans multiple images and keeps one in each of the multiple document interface child views.

If you follow these steps, you'll have no trouble creating this multiple-document application.

1. Create a Visual C++ project named HandsOn6_3 with the following attributes:

   ❏ Multiple-document interface
   ❏ English language
   ❏ No database support
   ❏ No compound document support
   ❏ No automation or ActiveX control support
   ❏ 3D controls, but no other features
   ❏ No source file comments
   ❏ Link MFC as a shared DLL

2. Select Settings from the Project menu. Choose the Link tab. Add the following libraries to the Object/library modules field. The libraries for the release and debug versions are different; both are listed below.

Release Project Libraries	Debug Project Libraries
ImageLoad.lib	ImageLoad.lib
ImageObject.lib	ImageObjectD.lib
TWAIN_32.lib	TWAIN_32.lib
TWAINLib.lib	TWAINLibD.lib

3. Add the following includes to the HandsOn6_3View.h file:

```
#include "scanner.h"
#include "ImageObject.h"
```

4. Add the following variable declarations to the CHandsOn6_3View class in the HandsOn6_3View.h file:

```
CScanner m_Scanner;
BOOL m_bScannerInvoked;
CImageObject *m_pImage;
```

5. Add the following code to the CHandsOn6_3View constructor:

```
m_bScannerInvoked = FALSE;
m_pImage = NULL;
```

6. Add the following code to the CHandsOn6_3View destructor:

```
m_Scanner.Kill();
if( m_pImage != NULL )
    delete m_pImage;
```

7. Edit the OnDraw function in the CHandsOn6_3View class in the HandsOn6_3View.cpp file as follows:

```
void CHandsOn6_3View::OnDraw(CDC* pDC)
{
    CHandsOn6_3Doc* pDoc = GetDocument();
    ASSERT_VALID(pDoc);

    if( !m_bScannerInvoked ){
        m_bScannerInvoked = TRUE;
        CHandsOn6_3View *pView = this;
        m_Scanner.SetPixelParams(USER_SELECTION);
        m_Scanner.StartPicture( pView->m_hWnd );
        }
```

```
            if( m_pImage != NULL ){
                m_pImage->SetPalette( pDC );
                m_pImage->Draw( pDC );
                }
        }
```

8. Add the following functions to the CHandsOn6_3View class in the HandsOn6_3View.h file:

```
virtual BOOL PreTranslateMessage( MSG * );
```

9. Add the PreTranslateMessage function in the CHandsOn6_3View class in the HandsOn6_3View.cpp file as follows:

```
BOOL CHandsOn6_3View::PreTranslateMessage( MSG *msg )
{
 int nMessage;
 if( !m_Scanner.PreTranslateMessage( msg,
  &nMessage ) )
  return( CView::PreTranslateMessage( msg ) );

 if( nMessage ){
  CClientDC ClientDC( this );
  if( m_Scanner.GetTranslatedMessage(
   &ClientDC, nMessage ) ){
   m_pImage = new CImageObject( "TEMP.BMP" );
   InvalidateRect( NULL, TRUE );
   UpdateWindow();
   }
  else{
   CHandsOn6_3Doc* pDoc = GetDocument();
   pDoc->OnCloseDocument();
   }
  }

 return( TRUE );

}
```

10. Compile and run the program.

When this application runs, you'll have the chance to scan as many images as you want.

On the Web

There are quite a few sites on the World Wide Web that you'll find useful. Here are a few to get you started.

The TWAIN Developer's Files

There's a site devoted to keeping the latest TWAIN developer's files at http://www.twain.org/www/toolkit.html. Here, you can download the latest developer's kit and any support files that have been made available. Figure 6-8 shows the site.

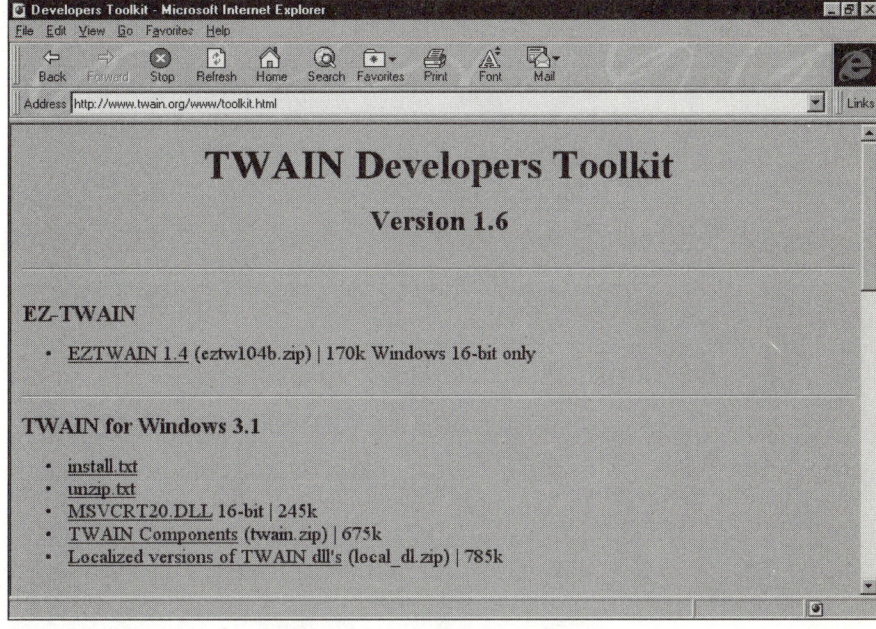

Figure 6-8: This is the best site for TWAIN developers.

A TWAIN Tutorial

Another site for TWAIN developers can be found at http://www.salug.org/~davidm/twain/chap3.html. It's more of a tutorial on developing TWAIN applications than a repository of files. This site is pictured in Figure 6-9.

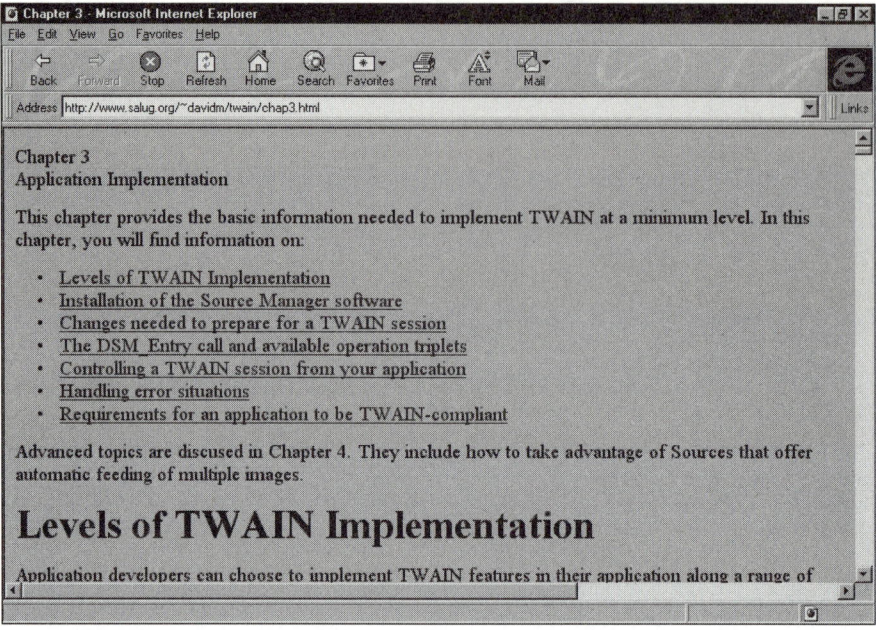

Figure 6-9: This site teaches about developing TWAIN-compliant applications.

SHAREWARE & COMMERCIAL DEMOS

Graphic Workshop is a fantastic shareware program you'll learn to rely on. Not only does it change file formats and modify image attributes but it also supports TWAIN-compliant devices such as scanners. Figure 6-10 shows the program when it first runs.

Figure 6-10: Graphic Workshop is a fine program that has TWAIN support.

Moving On

Now that you've learned how to use the TWAINLib class library that comes with this book, plan your strategy. Add TWAIN support to any application where it makes sense. Your customers will thank you.

The next chapter covers region maps. These allow you to make regions of the screen respond to mouse movements and clicks. It's a great class library that you'll find very useful.

Meanwhile, tell me of your TWAIN conquests—I'd love to hear. E-mail me at ivt-rcl@interpath.com. Tell me what you've done, or send me your entire application!

Chapter 7

Region Maps

*Regions are easily mapped, but
the residents are easily unmapped.*
—Frank Cosme

Regions have to do with geography, and geography reminds us of subjects we had in school. This chapter, however, is all about mapping regions of the computer screen and how you can display those regions and allow users to interact with them.

The class library provided in this chapter can be used for any application in which you want to designate sections of the screen to be used for particular items. For instance, you might want to create a product catalog. One section could be used for automotive products and another for athletic products. The second demo shows how to create a product catalog application with this CRgnMap class.

One thing each application that uses the CRgnMap class needs is data. The data tells the program what regions are on the screen and what labels will appear when they're selected. There are two data files: standard format and NCSA format. NCSA data files are one of the most common types of map data format. The other data file is specific to the CRgnMap class and contains information for display.

Besides the NCSA data file, there's another file the application loads. It's a comment file containing three important pieces of information. In the file is the text that will appear when the mouse is pointing to a region, the text that will appear when the mouse is pointing to a region and the button is pressed, and the color in which the region will be drawn.

The comment file is not part of the NCSA file, nor is it used by any commercial programs. The MakeMap program generates the NCSA file and a comment file for you. If you used another program to create the NCSA map data, you could create the comment data file with a text editor. There are NCSA data files available from third-party vendors. These can be used too, as long as a comment file is created.

THE RGNMAPLIB CLASS LIBRARY

The class library can be used for geographical data, or anything else for that matter. Creating regions on the screen isn't necessarily geography-specific. You may want to create a multimedia presentation where certain regions of the screen have different results when the mouse button is clicked. You might also want to create an electronic catalog of products in which the screen is sectioned off into product categories.

Regardless of your application for the CRgnMap class, you'll still need to use the MakeMap program to create data files. The class won't know whether you're presenting geographic regions or biological charts. Every region map is the same—it has an NCSA and a comment data file.

This section starts off by describing the file format for the two data files. It then goes on to describe the CRgnMap class.

NCSA Data File Format

NCSA data files are composed of ASCII text, each line ending with a carriage return/line feed pair.

Each line of text in the data files represents one region. There is no apparent limit to the length of each line.

The first five characters of each line of data are always *poly* . Note that the fifth character is a blank space.

The next text in the line of data is a URL specification. This is in case you want your program or application to associate a region with a URL. The URL always ends with a blank space.

The next text in the line of data is a list of coordinate points for the region. The coordinates are paired, each pair representing the X and Y coordinates of a single point.

Example 1

```
poly http://www.dade_county.com 124,80   400,80   400,120 124,120
```

This line of data can be associated with the URL at http://www.dade_county.com (if the application so desires) and will encompass a polygon with coordinates 124, 80; 400, 80; 400, 120; 124, 120. This is a rectangular region with an upper left coordinate of 124, 80 and a lower right coordinate of 400, 120.

Example 2

```
poly http://www.interpath.com 100,100 200,100 300,150 200,200
100,200
```

This line of data can be associated with the URL at http://www.interpath.com (if the application so desires) and will encompass a polygon with 100, 100; 200, 100; 300, 150; 200, 200; 100, 200. This is a pentagon shape of unequal sides.

Comment File Format

Comment data files are ASCII text, each line ending with a carriage return/line feed pair.

Each line of text in the data files represents one region. There is no limit to the length of each line.

The first text in the line of data is the text that will appear when the mouse points to a region when the mouse button is not pressed. At the end of this text, a semicolon character (;) indicates the end of this segment of text.

The next text in the line of data is the text that will appear when the mouse points to a region when the mouse button is pressed. At the end of this text, a semicolon character (;) indicates the end of this segment of text.

The next information is the color number in which the polygon will be drawn. Values range from 0 to 15. A list of what each value represents follows.

Color Name	Color Index
Black	0
Blue	1
Green	2
Cyan	3

➡

239

Color Name	Color Index
Red	4
Magenta	5
Brown	6
Light Gray	7
Dark Gray	8
Light Blue	9
Light Green	10
Light Cyan	11
Light Red	12
Light Magenta	13
Yellow	14
White	15

Example 1

```
Florida;The Capital is Tallahassee;3
```

This line will cause the string "Florida" to be displayed when the mouse points to the region this data line references. (Let's hope the region it references is Florida.) The string "The Capital is Tallahassee" will appear instead of the string "Florida" when the mouse points to the region this data line references and the mouse button is pressed. The region will be drawn in cyan since color 3 is cyan.

Example 2

```
North Carolina;The Capital is Raleigh;14
```

This line will cause the string "North Carolina" to be displayed when the mouse points to the region this data line references. The string "The Capital is Raleigh" will appear instead of the string "North Carolina" when the mouse points to the region this data line references and the mouse button is pressed. The region will be drawn in yellow, since color 14 is yellow.

The MakeMap Program

There's a program called MakeMap included with this applet in the RgnMap directory on the Companion CD-ROM. The program can be run by executing the MakeMap.exe program. The program's source code is not included since it was written some time ago with Visual C++ 1.52.

The purpose of the program is to create NCSA and comment data files for the CRgnMap class to load. With the MakeMap program, you can create maps of any geographical areas. Then, the Load() function can be given the filename so that it loads in the newly created data files.

When the MakeMap program first runs, you'll see a blank window. The program will have no image that's displayed in the view window, no map data that's loaded, and no polygon data that draws.

In short, the program lets you define polygonal regions by clicking the mouse on the screen. If you wanted, you could simply define the polygons in the blank window. That would require you to know exactly where the regions should be. Alternately, you could load in an image file and use it to help you define the regions.

Most sets of map data are made from some existing pictures. The map data that was created for the RegionMap demo application was based on an image file. This image file is named map.gif and can be found in the RgnMap\RegionMap directory on the Companion CD-ROM that comes with this book. Figure 7-1 shows the MakeMap program with the map.gif file loaded in.

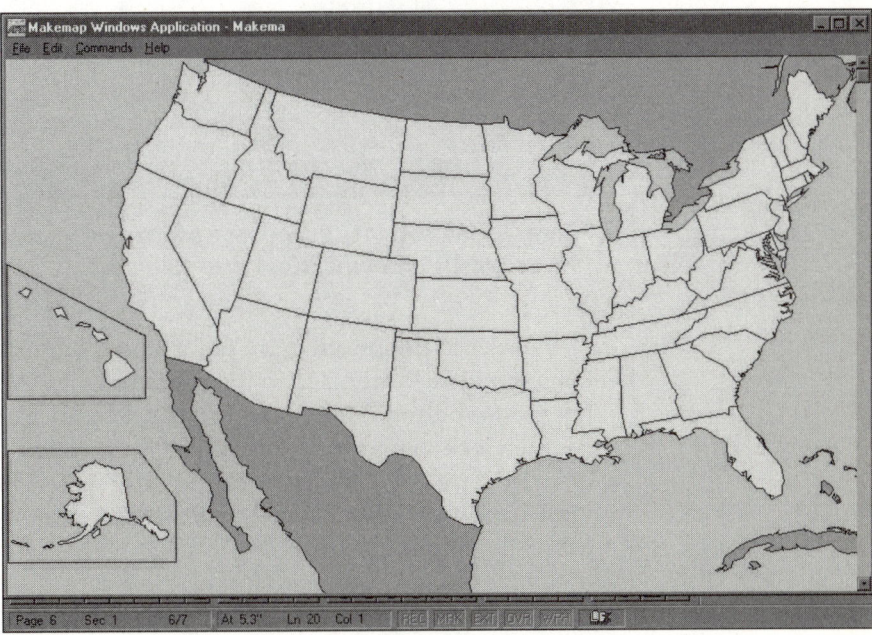

Figure 7-1: Here's the MakeMap program with the map.gif file loaded in. Loading an image file makes the map creation process much easier.

To begin the map creation process, select New State from the Commands menu. A dialog box such as the one shown in Figure 7-2 will appear. In the dialog box, you'll be able to specify a URL, a label for when the mouse is pointing to the region, a comment for when the mouse is pointing to the region and the mouse button is pressed, and a color.

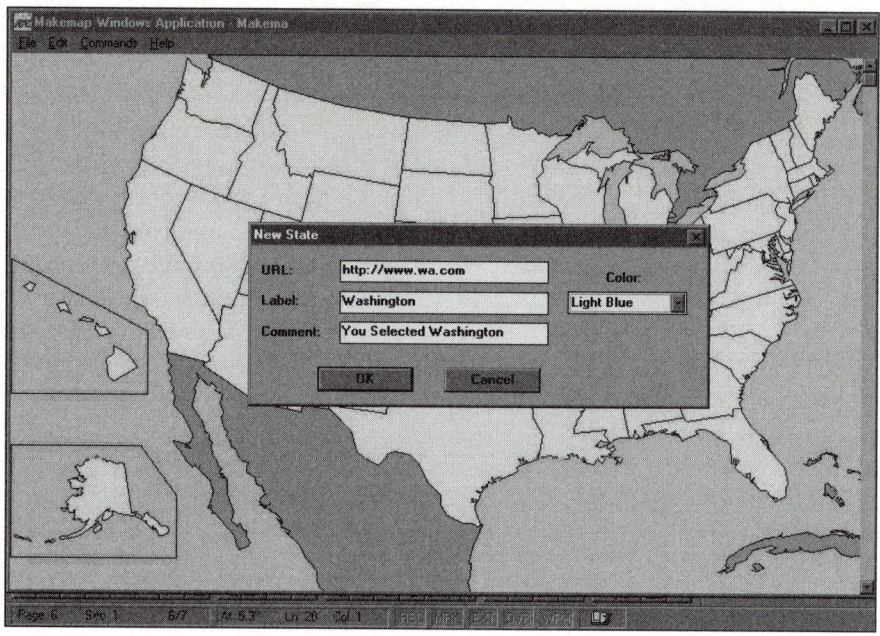

Figure 7-2: Most of this information becomes part of the comment file. Only the URL becomes part of the NCSA map data file.

In order to define a region, point to one vertex of the region and click the left mouse button. Go to the next vertex in the region and click the left mouse button. Make sure you consistently go either clockwise or counterclockwise around the vertices of the region. Once you've clicked on each vertex of a region, click the right mouse button anywhere in the view window. This will end the creation process for the region you're currently defining.

Notice in the Commands menu the Show Map and Show Polygons options. The image that's loaded in will be displayed if the Show Map option is checked. The polygons will be drawn if the Show Polygons option is checked. Figure 7-3 shows what you'll see after you've defined the state of Texas if you switch to the Show Polygons option.

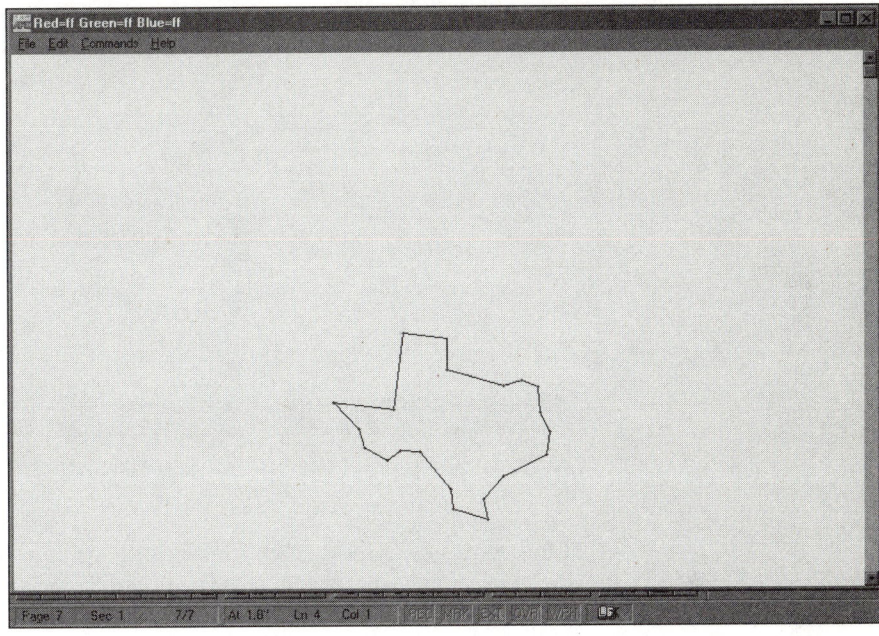

Figure 7-3: If you define Texas and switch to the Show Polygons option, this is what you'll see.

You might want to see the polygons filled in with the color you selected. There's an option in the Commands menu named Filled Polygons that causes the polygons to be drawn filled with the selected color. Figure 7-4 shows Texas filled in with light blue.

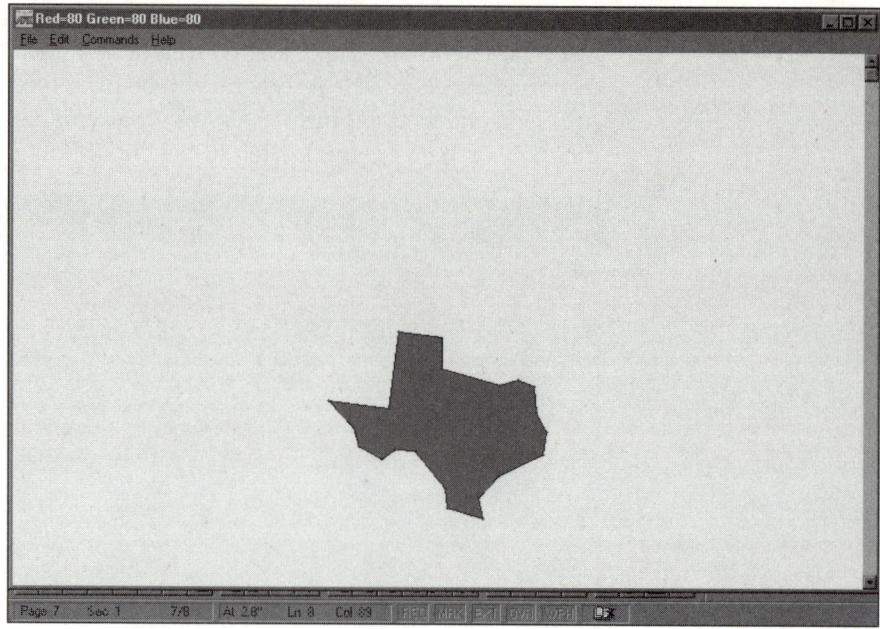

Figure 7-4: You may prefer to see the map filled with color. Here, Texas is light blue.

Once you've defined all of the regions, go to the File menu and select Save Raw State Data. A file selector will appear allowing you to save the raw data. The data is saved in a format that only the MakeMap program can load and understand. It's a good idea to save this data so that if you want to add regions later, you can simply load the raw data file and add the regions.

You also need to go to Save NCSA Data and Save Comment Data. Both of these can be found in the File menu.

Make sure that if you move the MakeMap.exe file from the RgnMap directory on the Companion CD-ROM, you also copy the DLL files in that RgnMap directory. These are the image-loading DLLs and must accompany the MakeMap program.

THE REGIONMAP DEMO

We've built a demonstration program that shows what the CRgnMap class library can do. It can be found in the RgnMap\RegionMap directory on the Companion CD-ROM. Run the Bubble.exe program, and you'll see a map of the United States drawn with GDI polygons, as shown in Figure 7-5.

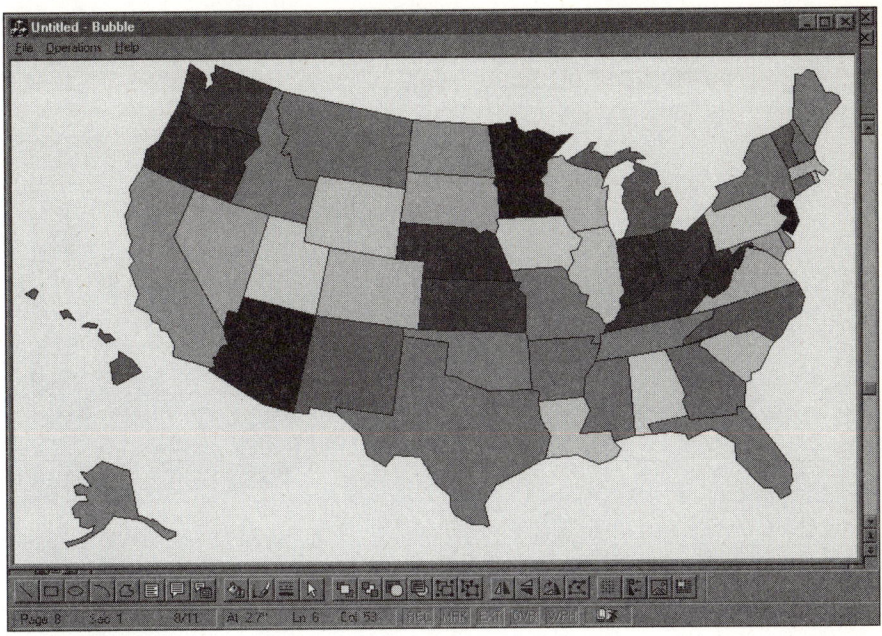

Figure 7-5: When the RegionMap program first runs, you'll see a map of the United States drawn with polygonal regions.

As you move the mouse over the states in the map you'll see the name of the state appear in a rectangle. In Figure 7-6 the mouse is pointing to Nebraska.

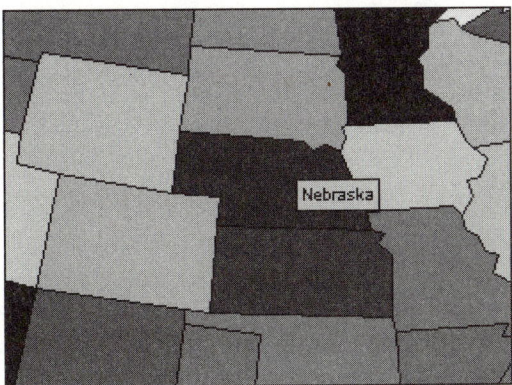

Figure 7-6: When the mouse points to a state, the name of the state appears in a rectangle.

Another popular state is California where 20 percent of the nation's population lives. Figure 7-7 shows the program when the mouse is pointing to California.

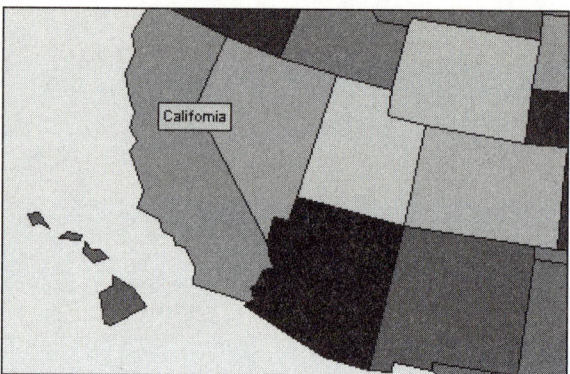

Figure 7-7: The state of California is where the mouse is pointing in this figure.

In the comment data file, there's a second text field. This is the text that's displayed when the mouse button is pressed and the mouse is pointing to the state. Figure 7-8 shows the program when the mouse is pointing to Florida and the left mouse button is pressed.

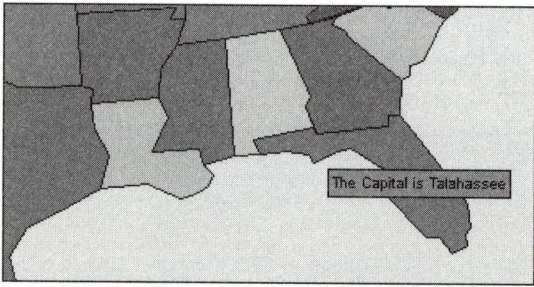

Figure 7-8: Here, the left mouse button is pressed and the state of Florida is under the mouse cursor.

There are only two states in the sample data file that have different text for both fields in the comment data file. North Carolina is the other one. In Figure 7-9 you can see that the capital of North Carolina is Raleigh when the mouse points to North Carolina and the left mouse button is pressed.

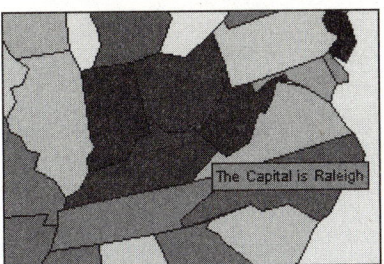

Figure 7-9: In this figure North Carolina is under the mouse cursor and the left mouse button is pressed.

You'll need a way to know which state is under the mouse cursor if your application is to interact with the CRgnMap class. In this RegionMap demo program, clicking the right mouse button on a state brings up a message box showing the name of the state that was selected. The message box is created in the application code, not the CRgnMap class. This is what makes it different than pressing the left mouse button. When the left mouse button is pressed, the CRgnMap class takes care of changing the text and the rectangle color. Figure 7-10 shows the application after the right mouse button has been clicked on South Dakota.

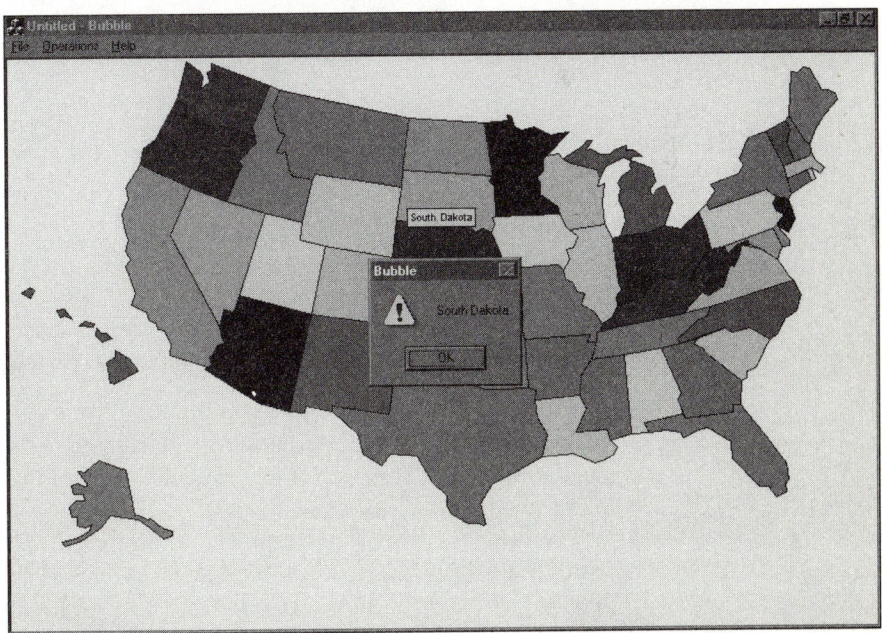

Figure 7-10: The application needs to know which region is being pointed to. This figure shows the application responding to the information after a right mouse button click.

You have one more option with the demo program: you can have it load an image file and draw it within your application instead of having the CRgnMap class draw the regions using GDI calls. Figure 7-11 shows the program with the map.gif file loaded in. Loading in images allows users to see more detail than if you simply let the class draw simple polygons.

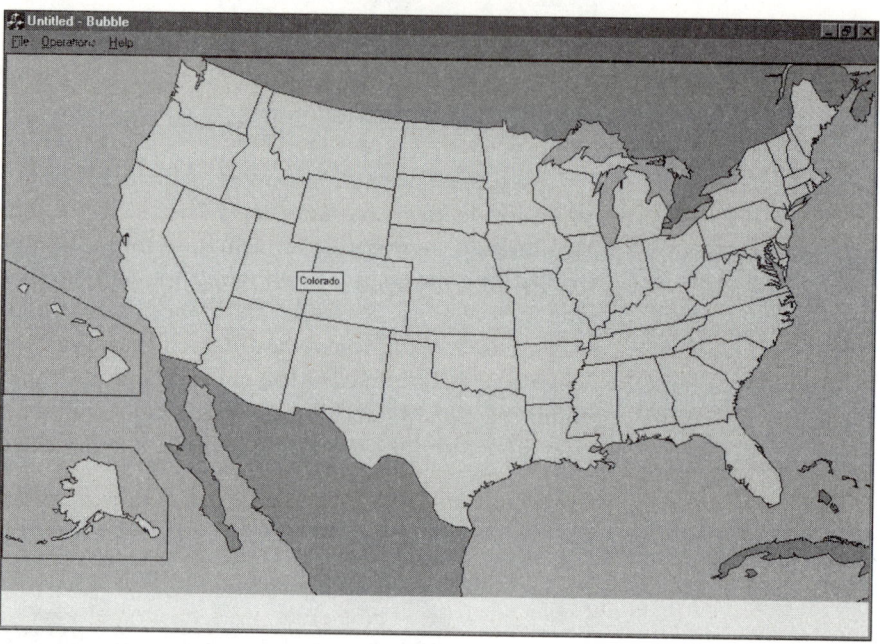

Figure 7-11: The same image used to create the map data files can be loaded and displayed in a program.

THE RGNMAPLIB CLASS LIBRARY FUNCTION CALLS

This section is provided as a reference to the public function calls the region map library offers. Since the library was designed with simplicity as a major goal, there aren't many calls. The region map library is simple—it just takes a few lines of code.

You may want to skip over this section and read the section entitled "Behind RegionMap," which shows how the calls are used. (For some people, it's better to look at the usage of function calls before actually studying their syntax.)

CRgnMap()

Prototype: `CRgnMap( BOOL bDraw, BOOL bBackgroundFlag, BOOL bForceFlag );`

Purpose: This is the constructor for the CRgnMap class. It takes as arguments a flag saying whether to draw the regions, a flag saying whether to redraw the background during undraw operations, and a flag saying whether to force the rectangular region to follow the mouse every time it moves. Each one of these options will be elaborated on with changes to the demo program.

Arguments: BOOL bDraw, Defaults to TRUE
BOOL bBackgroundFlag, Defaults to TRUE
BOOL bForceFlag, Defaults to FALSE

Returns: Nothing

Load()

Prototype: `BOOL Load( const char *pNCSAFile, const char *pCommentFile );`

Purpose: This function loads the NCSA data and the comment data.

Arguments: const char *pNCSAFile
const char *pCommentFile

Returns: BOOL: TRUE if successful, FALSE if not

DrawRgns()

Prototype: `void DrawRgns( CDC *pDC );`

Purpose: This function draws all of the map's regions.

Arguments: CDC *pDC

Returns: Nothing

CheckBubbles()

Prototype: `void CheckBubbles( int nX, int nY, BOOL bMouseButtonPressed, CDC *pDC );`

Purpose: This function checks to see if the mouse is in one of the map's regions. If it is, the rectangular region with the region's text will appear on the screen. If the mouse button is pressed, the color will be the selected color, and the text that appears in the rectangle will be the second text field from the comment data file.

249

Arguments: int nX
int nY
BOOL bMouseButtonPressed
CDC *pDC

Returns: Nothing

SetScaleFactor()

Prototype: `void SetScaleFactor( int nScaleFactorX, int nScaleFactorY );`

Purpose: This function sets the scale factor for the map regions. If you want the map regions to be drawn twice as wide as the NCSA data and three times as high as the NCSA data, you use SetScaleFactor(200, 300).

Arguments: int nScaleFactorX
int nScaleFactorY

Returns: Nothing

ReScale()

Prototype: `void ReScale( void );`

Purpose: This function rescales the regions of a map. This is different than the SetScaleFactor() function because this can be used even after the data has been loaded and the map regions created.

Arguments: None

Returns: Nothing

GetRegion()

Prototype: `BOOL GetRegion( BOOL *pbMouseState, char *pszText );`

Purpose: This function returns the mouse state and the text of a region. If no region is being pointed to, the function returns FALSE. If there is a valid region under the mouse cursor, the function returns TRUE.

Arguments: BOOL *pbMouseState
char *pszText

Returns: BOOL: TRUE if the mouse is pointing to a valid region, FALSE if not

CRegion()

Prototype: `CRegion( POI NT *pPoints, int nPoints );`

Purpose: The Cregion class is used by the CRgnMap class to keep track of the regions in the map. This is the constructor for the Cregion class and it takes as arguments a list of X/Y coordinates and the number of coordinate points in the list.

Arguments: POI NT *pPoints
int nPoints

Returns: Nothing

InRegion()

Prototype: `BOOL InRegion( int nX, int nY );`

Purpose: This function determines if the two points, nX and nY, are in the region. It's usually used to see if the mouse coordinates are in a given region.

Arguments: int nX
int nY

Returns: BOOL

DrawRegion()

Prototype: `void DrawRegion( CDC *pDC );`

Purpose: This function draws a region using the Windows GDI Polygon function.

Arguments: CDC *pDC

Returns: Nothing

ReScale()

Prototype: `void ReScale( int nScaleFactorX, int nScaleFactorY );`

Purpose: This function rescales the coordinates of a map region.

Arguments: int nScaleFactorX
int nScaleFactorY

Returns: Nothing

CMapBubble()

Prototype: `CMapBubble( CString &Text, CString &SelectedText, COLORREF NormalColor, COLORREF SelectedColor, BOOL bBackgroundFlag );`

Purpose: The CMapBubble class is used by the CRgnMap class to draw the rectangular regions containing the text that comes from the comment file. This constructor takes arguments that allow it to know how to draw the text in the rectangles.

Arguments: CString &Text
CString &SelectedText
COLORREF NormalColor
COLORREF SelectedColor
BOOL bBackgroundFlag, Defaults to TRUE

Returns: Nothing

Draw()

Prototype: `void Draw( int nX, int nY, CFont *pFont, CDC *pDC, BOOL bForce );`

Purpose: This function draws the rectangle with the region text.

Arguments: int nX
int nY
CFont *pFont
CDC *pDC
BOOL bForce, Defaults to FALSE

Returns: Nothing

UnDraw()

Prototype: `void UnDraw( CDC *pDC );`

Purpose: This function undraws the rectangle that previously contained the region's text.

Arguments: CDC *pDC

Returns: Nothing

SetState()

Prototype: `void SetState( BOOL bState );`

Purpose: This function sets the state of the region's text. It is true if the mouse button is down, false if the mouse button is not down.

Arguments: BOOL bState

Returns: Nothing

GetState()

Prototype: `BOOL GetState( void );`

Purpose: This function returns the state of the region's text rectangle. If the area is selected with a depressed mouse button, this function returns TRUE. Otherwise it returns FALSE.

Arguments: None

Returns: BOOL

BEHIND REGIONMAP

Complete source code for RegionMap can be found in the RgnMap\ RegionMap directory of the Companion CD-ROM. This section shows the highlights of the program's source code and gives explanations for each. You should take note that the final executable file is named Bubble.exe.

RegionMap was created with the Visual C++ AppWizard with the following settings:

- ❏ Single-document interface
- ❏ English language
- ❏ No database support
- ❏ No compound document support
- ❏ No automation or ActiveX control support
- ❏ 3D controls, but no other features
- ❏ Yes source file comments
- ❏ MFC linked as a static library

Creating & Loading the Object

All of the source code related to the region map is contained in the BubbleView.cpp file. The CBubbleView constructor is where the CRgnMap class is created and the data is loaded.

One other important thing is setting the CImageObject variable m_pImage to NULL. When this variable is NULL, the CRgnMap class draws the regions on its own. When the variable is not NULL, then it's assumed an image was loaded in. This image is drawn with the CImageObject Draw() function instead of letting the CRgnMap class draw the regions.

The CBubbleView() Constructor

```
CBubbleView::CBubbleView()
{

 m_pImage = NULL;
 m_pRgnMap = new CRgnMap();
 m_pRgnMap->Load( "US.MAP", "US.CMT" );

}
```

Deleting the Objects

When the program is ready to quit, you must delete the CRgnMap object, and the CImageObject object if it's loaded. This is done in the CBubbleView destructor.

The CBubbleView() Destructor

```
CBubbleView::~CBubbleView()
{

 if( m_pRgnMap != NULL )
  delete m_pRgnMap;

 if( m_pImage != NULL )
  delete m_pImage;

}
```

Drawing the Regions

The regions are drawn from the OnDraw() function of the CBubbleView class. This makes it easy since a device context pointer is passed in.

You should note here that the first thing that's done is examine the m_pImage pointer variable. If it's not NULL, it's pointing to an image that was loaded in. If an image was loaded in, we'll draw it instead of the plain polygonal regions. The image will most likely be more attractive than the plain polygons.

If there's no loaded image, we let the CRgnMap class do the drawing. The DrawRgns() function is called and passed the device context pointer.

The OnDraw() Function

```
void CBubbleView::OnDraw(CDC* pDC)
{
CBubbleDoc* pDoc = GetDocument();
ASSERT_VALID(pDoc);

if( m_pImage != NULL ){
 m_pImage->SetPalette( pDC );
 m_pImage->Draw( pDC );
 }
else m_pRgnMap->DrawRgns( pDC );

}
```

Checking the Mouse Position

When users move the mouse around, the mouse position must be checked to see if it's pointing to one of the map's regions. You don't actually have to do the dirty work—the CRgnMap class does it for you. All you have to do is call the CheckBubbles() function. The mouse X and Y-coordinates must be passed, as well as a flag indicating whether the mouse button is pressed and a device context pointer.

The CheckBubbles() function takes care of moving the rectangular region around on the screen. It decides what text to display and what color to draw in the background of the rectangular region.

255

The OnMouseMove() Function

```
void CBubbleView::OnMouseMove(UINT nFlags, CPoint point)
{

CClientDC ClientDC( this );
m_pRgnMap->CheckBubbles( point.x, point.y,
 ( nFlags & MK_LBUTTON ) != 0, &ClientDC );

CView::OnMouseMove(nFlags, point);
}
```

Mouse Button Clicks

Your program must let the CRgnMap class know when the mouse button has been pressed. By doing this, you allow the CRgnMap class to change the color of the rectangular region and the text that's drawn in the region.

The easiest way to do this is to use the Class Wizard and create an OnLButtonDown() function. From this function, you can call the CRgnMap's CheckBubbles() function.

The OnLButtonDown(), OnLButtonUp() & OnLButtonDblClk() Functions

```
void CBubbleView::OnLButtonDown(UINT nFlags, CPoint point)
{

CClientDC ClientDC( this );
m_pRgnMap->CheckBubbles( point.x,
 point.y,TRUE, &ClientDC );

CView::OnLButtonDown(nFlags, point);
}

void CBubbleView::OnLButtonUp(UINT nFlags, CPoint point)
{

CClientDC ClientDC( this );
m_pRgnMap->CheckBubbles( point.x,
 point.y, FALSE, &ClientDC );

CView::OnLButtonUp(nFlags, point);
}
```

```
void CBubbleView::OnLButtonDblClk(UINT nFlags, CPoint point)
{

CClientDC ClientDC( this );
m_pRgnMap->CheckBubbles( point.x,
 point.y, FALSE, &ClientDC );

CView::OnLButtonDblClk(nFlags, point);
}
```

Interacting With the CRgnMap Class

Your program will need at some point to know which region the mouse is pointing to. The demo program uses right mouse button clicks to ask the CRgnMap class which region is being pointed to.

You can interrogate the CRgnMap class from anywhere in your program, not just from a handler such as the OnRButtonDown() function.

The OnRButtonDown() Function

```
void CBubbleView::OnRButtonDown(UINT nFlags, CPoint point)
{

char szText[150];
BOOL bMouseState;
if( m_pRgnMap->GetRegion( &bMouseState,
 szText ) )
 AfxMessageBox( szText );


CView::OnRButtonDown(nFlags, point);
}
```

Stretching the Region Map

The demo program allows you to stretch the region map to 150, 200, 250, and 300 percent of its original size. Of course, you can go back and reset it to 100 percent if you want.

If you have an image loaded, it's not a good idea to stretch the region map. That's because the image itself won't be stretched, and what you see on the screen won't correctly correspond to the region map data that's been stretched.

The CImageObject class has the ability to stretch images. This is functionality that can be added to the program if you choose to do this.

The OnOperationsStretch() Functions

```
void CBubbleView::OnOperationsStretchto150()
{

 m_pRgnMap->SetScaleFactor( 150, 150 );
 m_pRgnMap->ReScale();
 InvalidateRect( NULL, TRUE );
 UpdateWindow();

}

void CBubbleView::OnOperationsStretchto200()
{

 m_pRgnMap->SetScaleFactor( 200, 200 );
 m_pRgnMap->ReScale();
 InvalidateRect( NULL, TRUE );
 UpdateWindow();

}

void CBubbleView::OnOperationsStretchto250()
{

 m_pRgnMap->SetScaleFactor( 250, 250 );
 m_pRgnMap->ReScale();
 InvalidateRect( NULL, TRUE );
 UpdateWindow();

}

void CBubbleView::OnOperationsStretchto300()
{

 m_pRgnMap->SetScaleFactor( 300, 300 );
 m_pRgnMap->ReScale();
 InvalidateRect( NULL, TRUE );
 UpdateWindow();

}

void CBubbleView::OnOperationsStretchto100()
{

 m_pRgnMap->SetScaleFactor( 100, 100 );
```

```
m_pRgnMap->ReScale();
InvalidateRect( NULL, TRUE );
UpdateWindow();

}
```

Loading an Image

Loading an image is a simple matter. The most complicated part is invoking a file selector dialog and getting the filename. The code to actually load the image is one line.

For more information about loading images, see Chapter 1. It has detailed explanations of how the CImageObject class works.

The OnFileOpen() Function

```
char szFilter[] = "BMP Files(*.BMP)|*.BMP|GIF
Files(*.GIF)|*.GIF|PCX Files(*.PCX)|*.PCX|Targa
Files(*.TGA)|*.TGA|Jpeg Files(*.JPG)|*.JPG|Tif
Files(*.TIF)|*.TIF||";

void CBubbleView::OnFileOpen()
{
 static int nIndex = 1;

 CFileDialog FileDlg( TRUE, NULL, NULL, OFN_HIDEREADONLY,
    szFilter );
 FileDlg.m_ofn.nFilterIndex = (DWORD) nIndex;

 if( FileDlg.DoModal() == IDOK ){
  if( m_pImage != NULL )
   delete m_pImage;
  CString PathName = FileDlg.GetPathName();
  PathName.MakeUpper();
  BeginWaitCursor();
  m_pImage = new CImageObject( PathName );
  EndWaitCursor();
  nIndex = (int) FileDlg.m_ofn.nFilterIndex;
  InvalidateRect( NULL, TRUE );
  UpdateWindow();
 }

}

void CBubbleView::OnOperationsImage()
{
```

259

```
     if( m_pImage != NULL ){
      delete m_pImage;
      m_pImage = NULL;
      InvalidateRect( NULL, TRUE );
      UpdateWindow();
      }
     else OnFileOpen();

  }

  void CBubbleView::OnUpdateOperationsImage(CCmdUI* pCmdUI)
  {

   if( m_pImage != NULL )
    pCmdUI->SetCheck( TRUE );
   else pCmdUI->SetCheck( FALSE );

  }
```

Loading & Displaying Region Maps in a Nutshell

The first thing you'll need to do is obtain an image by scanning one or creating one with a paint program. A simple one such as the one in Figure 7-12 is good for getting started.

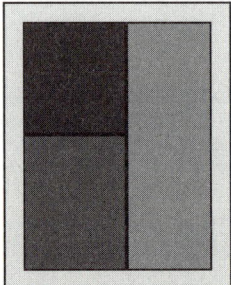

Figure 7-12: A simple image is the best way to get started.

The next thing you'll do is run the MakeMap program and load the image. Figure 7-13 shows the simple image loaded into the MakeMap program.

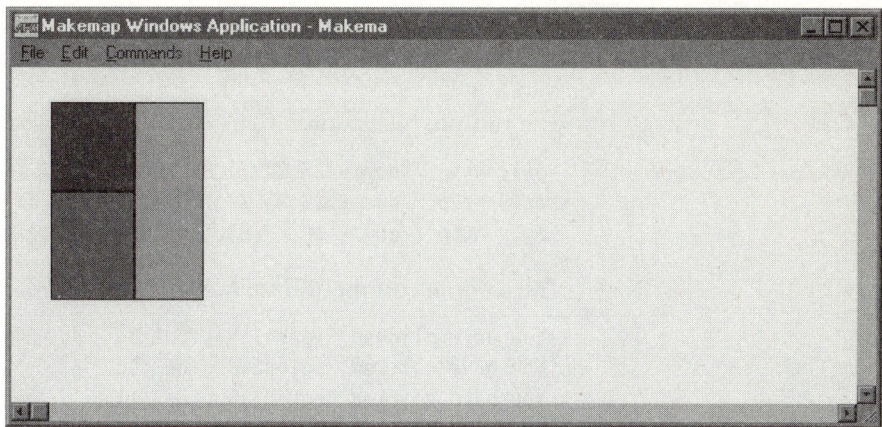

Figure 7-13: The simple image is loaded into the MakeMap program.

Begin by creating each region. Select New State from the Commands menu. Then fill in the fields in the dialog box so that the comment data will have what you want to appear in the rectangular boxes. Figure 7-14 shows the dialog box for this example.

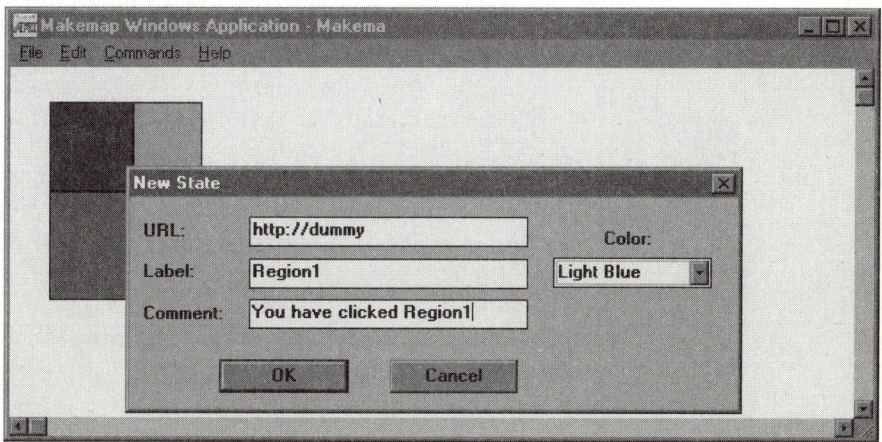

Figure 7-14: You'll need to fill in the fields in this dialog box so that the comment data file will have accurate information.

Finally, when all regions have been developed, save the raw data, the NCSA data, and the comment data files. The NCSA and comment data files follow.

The sample NCSA data file:

```
poly http://dummy 27,24 27,85 83,85 84,24
poly http://dummy 28,85 27,160 82,160 83,85
poly http://dummy 84,24 83,160 130,160 130,24
```

The sample comment data file:

```
You have clicked Region1;Region1;9
You have clicked Region2;Region2;10
You have clicked Region3;Region3;11
```

The next thing you'll need to do is create a program. In the program include RgnMapLib.h and declare a CRgnMap object that won't go out of scope. For instance, the following code can be in your view class include file:

```
#include "RgnMapLib.h"
CRgnMap *m_pRgnMap;
```

Allocate the region map object and then load the data. You can do this in your view class constructor as follows:

```
m_pRgnMap = new CRgnMap();
m_pRgnMap->Load( "NutShell.map", "NutShell.cmt" );
```

Now all you have to do is have the region map drawn from within your application's view class OnDraw() function. Figure 7-15 shows the program in action. Following is the code you should add:

```
m_pRgnMap->Draw( pDC );
```

Use the Class Wizard to add a [OnMouseMove()] function. Add the following code to it:

```
CClientDC ClientDC( this );
m_pRgnMap->CheckBubbles( point.x, point.y,
( nFlags & MK_LBUTTON ) != 0, &ClientDC );
```

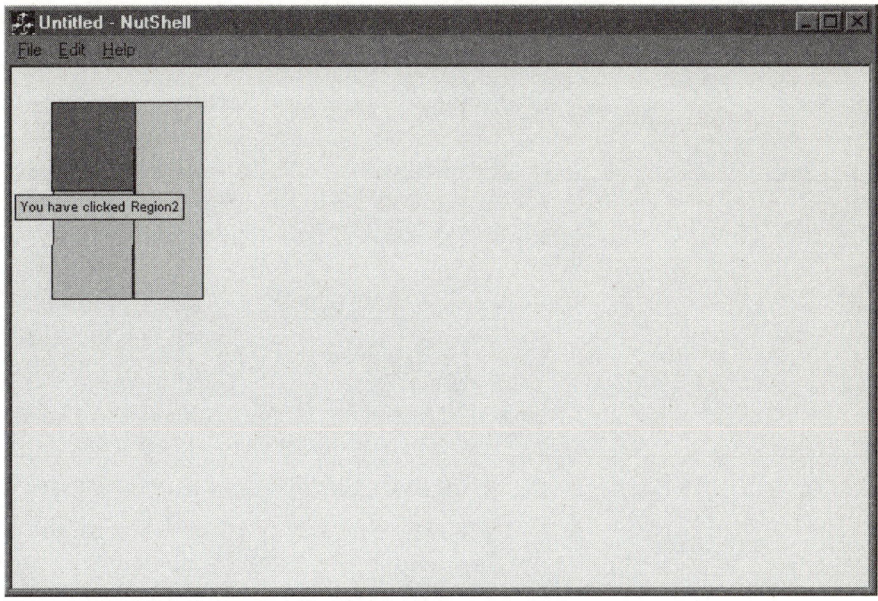

Figure 7-15: The simple nutshell program in action.

CREATING PROGRAMS THAT USE REGION MAPS

As usual, your training wouldn't be complete without some exercises to get you up to speed on using the CRgnMap class library. Two different exercises follow. They will transform you into CRgnMap class library experts.

Hands-On 1: Using a Map of Africa

In order to create this hands-on exercise, you'll have to use the MapMake program and create the region map data for the image of Africa that's provided. Once you're done, you'll be able to move the mouse over the African countries and have the country name appear as the mouse moves.

Follow the directions and you'll have no trouble with this exercise.

1. Create a Visual C++ project named HandsOn7_1 with the following attributes:

   ❒ Single-document interface

   ❒ English language

   ❒ No database support

   ❒ No compound document support

   ❒ No automation or ActiveX control support

❏ 3D controls, but no other features

❏ No source file comments

❏ Link MFC as a static library

2. Select Settings from the Project menu. Choose the Link tab. Add the following libraries to the Object/library modules field. The libraries for the release and debug versions are different. Both are listed below.

Release Project Libraries	Debug Project Libraries
RgnMapLib.lib	RgnMapLibD.lib
ImageLoad.lib	ImageLoad.lib
ImageObject.lib	ImageObjectD.lib

3. Set the Active Configuration to Win32 Release.

4. Copy the file Africa.bmp from the \rgnmap\samples directory on the Companion CD-ROM to the newly created project directory.

5. Run the MakeMap program and load the Africa.bmp file as shown in Figure 7-16. From the Commands menu, select New State and enter in the country information. For each country, outline the country's border by clicking the left mouse; then when the border is completed, click the right mouse button.

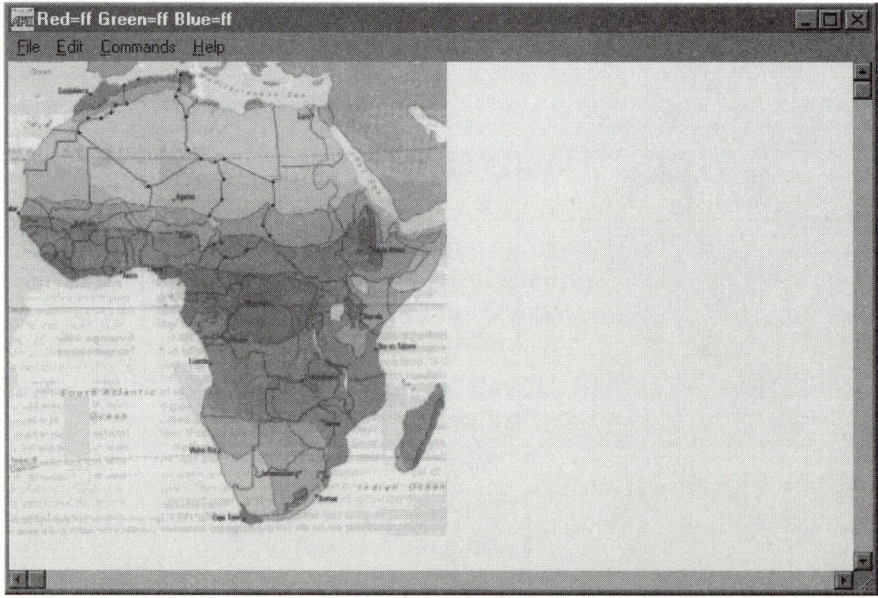

Figure 7-16: The Africa.bmp file loaded into the MakeMap program.

6. While creating the borders for the Africa region map data files, check to make sure the polygons are correct by selecting Show Polygons from the Commands menu in the MakeMap program. Figure 7-17 shows the program during the data creation process with filled polygons on the screen.

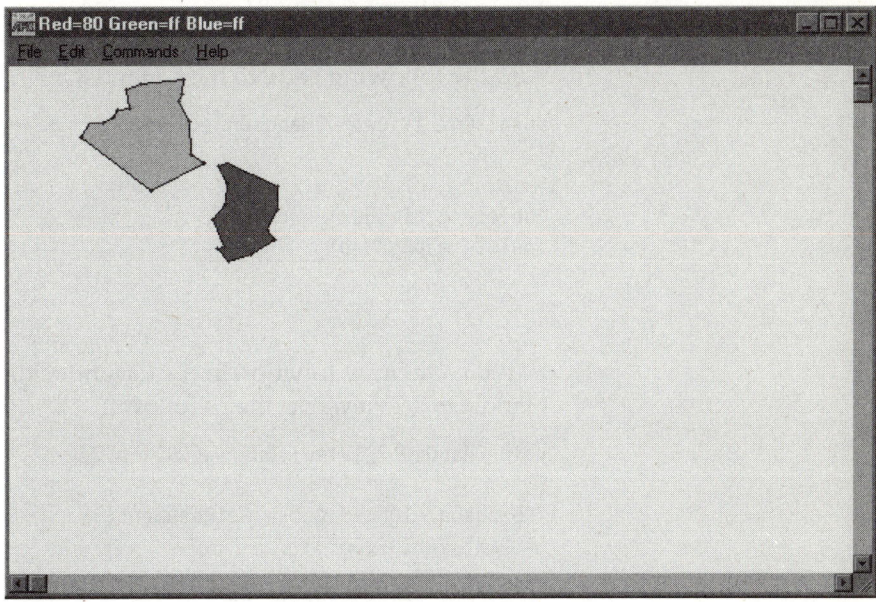

Figure 7-17: You should check the map data you're creating from time to time by selecting Show Polygons from the Commands menu.

7. Switch back to Visual C++ and add the following includes to the HandsOn7_1View.h file:

```
#include "ImageObject.h"
#include "RgnMapLib.h"
```

8. Add the following variable declarations to the CHandsOn7_1View class in the HandsOn7_1View.h file:

```
CImageObject *m_pImage;
CRgnMap *m_pRgnMap;
```

9. Add the following code to the CHandsOn7_1View constructor:

```
CHandsOn7_1View::CHandsOn7_1View()
{
```

```
m_pImage =
 new CImageObject( "Africa.bmp" );
m_pRgnMap = new CRgnMap();
m_pRgnMap->Load( "africa.map",
  "africa.cmt" );

}
```

10. Add the following code to the CHandsOn7_1View destructor:

```
CHandsOn7_1View::~CHandsOn7_1View()
{

delete m_pImage;
delete m_pRgnMap;

}
```

11. Edit the OnDraw function in the CHandsOn7_1View class in the HandsOn7_1View.cpp file as follows:

```
void CHandsOn7_1View::OnDraw(CDC* pDC)
{
CHandsOn7_1Doc* pDoc = GetDocument();
ASSERT_VALID(pDoc);

m_pImage->SetPalette( pDC );
m_pImage->Draw( pDC );

}
```

12. Add the following functions with the Class Wizard to the CHandsOn7_1View class in the HandsOn7_1View.h file:

```
Name:OnLButtonDown()  Message:WM_LBUTTONDOWN
Name:OnMouseMove()  Message:WM_MOUSEMOVE
```

13. Edit the OnLButtonDown function in the CHandsOn7_1View class in the HandsOn7_1View.cpp file as follows:

```
void CHandsOn7_1View::OnLButtonDown(UINT nFlags, CPoint point)
{
CClientDC ClientDC( this );
m_pRgnMap->CheckBubbles( point.x, point.y,
  TRUE, &ClientDC );

CView::OnLButtonDown(nFlags, point);
}
```

14. Edit the OnMouseMove function in the CHandsOn7_1View class in
    the HandsOn7_1View.cpp file as follows:

```
void CHandsOn7_1View::OnMouseMove(UINT nFlags, CPoint point)
{
 CClientDC ClientDC( this );
 m_pRgnMap->CheckBubbles( point.x, point.y,
  ( nFlags & MK_LBUTTON ) == 0, &ClientDC );

 CView::OnMouseMove(nFlags, point);
}
```

15. Compile and run the program.

When the program runs, you'll see the map of Africa appear. As you
move the mouse across a region, you'll see that region's name appear, as
in Figure 7-18.

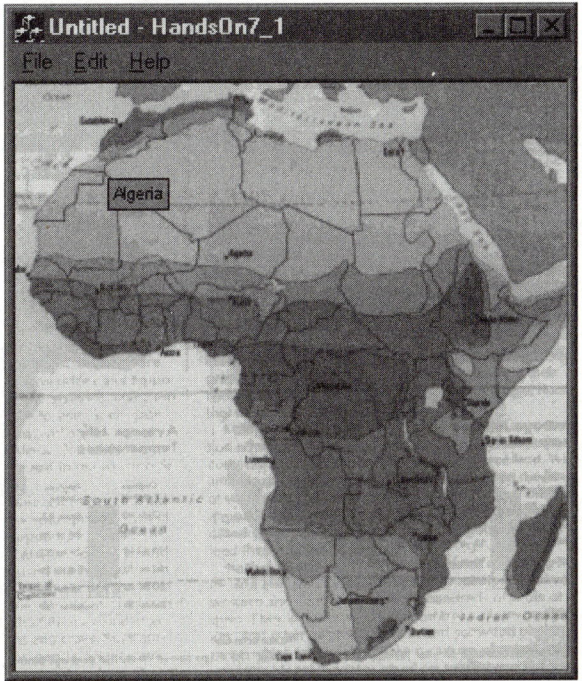

Figure 7-18: As you move the mouse, the name of each region will appear.

267

If you click on a region, you'll see the second text field appear as it does in Figure 7-19.

Figure 7-19: When you click the mouse on a region, the second text field will be displayed in the rectangular box.

Hands-On 2: Creating a Map of a Grasshopper

In order to create this hands-on exercise, you'll need to use the MakeMap program and create the region map data for the image of the grasshopper that's shown in Figure 7-20. Once you're done, you'll be able to move the mouse over the parts of the grasshopper and have each part name appear.

Follow these directions and you'll have that map of a grasshopper in no time at all.

1. Create a Visual C++ project named HandsOn7_2 with the following attributes:

    ❏ Single-document interface

    ❏ English language

    ❏ No database support

    ❏ No compound document support

❑ No automation or ActiveX control support

❑ 3D controls, but no other features

❑ No source file comments

❑ Link MFC as a static library

2. Select Settings from the Project menu. Choose the Link tab. Add the following libraries to the Object/library modules field. The libraries for the release and debug versions are different. Both are listed below.

Release Project Libraries	Debug Project Libraries
RgnMapLib.lib	RgnMapLibD.lib
ImageLoad.lib	ImageLoad.lib
ImageObject.lib	ImageObjectD.lib

3. Set the Active Configuration to Win32 Release.

4. Copy the file GrassHopper.bmp from the \rgnmap\samples directory on the Companion CD-ROM to the newly created project directory.

5. Run the MakeMap program and load the GrassHopper.bmp file as shown in Figure 7-20. From the Commands menu, select New State and enter in the anatomical part information. For each part, outline the part's border by clicking the left mouse button; then when the border is completed, click the right mouse button.

Figure 7-20: The GrassHopper.bmp file loaded into the MakeMap program.

6. While creating the borders for the grasshopper region map data files, check to make sure the polygons are correct by selecting Show Polygons from the Commands menu in the MakeMap program. Figure 7-21 shows the program during the data creation process with filled polygons on the screen.

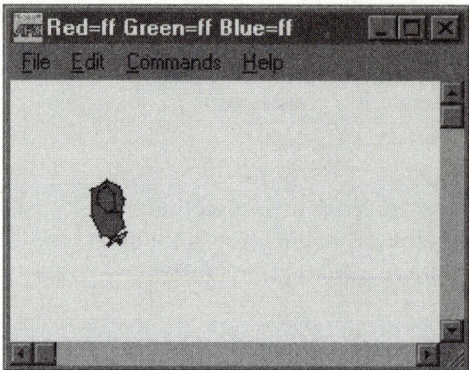

Figure 7-21: You should check the map data you're creating from time to time by selecting Show Polygons from the Commands menu.

7. Add the following includes to the HandsOn7_2View.h file:

```
#include "ImageObject.h"
#include "RgnMapLib.h"
```

8. Add the following variable declarations to the CHandsOn7_2View class in the HandsOn7_2View.h file:

```
CImageObject *m_pImage;
CRgnMap *m_pRgnMap;
```

9. Add the following code to the CHandsOn7_2View constructor:

```
CHandsOn7_2View::CHandsOn7_2View()
{
 m_pImage =
  new CImageObject( "GrassHopper.bmp" );
 m_pRgnMap = new CRgnMap( TRUE, TRUE, TRUE );
 m_pRgnMap->Load( "grass.map",
    "grass.cmt" );
}
```

10. Add the following code to the CHandsOn7_2View destructor:

```
CHandsOn7_2View::~CHandsOn7_2View()
{
 delete m_pImage;
 delete m_pRgnMap;
}
```

11. Edit the OnDraw function in the CHandsOn7_2View class in the
    HandsOn7_2View.cpp file as follows:

```
void CHandsOn7_2View::OnDraw(CDC* pDC)
{
 CHandsOn7_2Doc* pDoc = GetDocument();
 ASSERT_VALID(pDoc);

 m_pImage->SetPalette( pDC );
 m_pImage->Draw( pDC );

}
```

12. Add the following functions with the Class Wizard to the
    CHandsOn7_2View class in the HandsOn7_2View.h file:

```
Name:OnLButtonDown()  Message:WM_LBUTTONDOWN
Name:OnMouseMove()  Message:WM_MOUSEMOVE
```

13. Edit the OnLButtonDown function in the CHandsOn7_2View class
    in the HandsOn7_2View.cpp file as follows:

```
void CHandsOn7_2View::OnLButtonDown(UINT nFlags, CPoint point)
{
 CClientDC ClientDC( this );
 m_pRgnMap->CheckBubbles( point.x, point.y,
  TRUE, &ClientDC );

 CView::OnLButtonDown(nFlags, point);
}
```

14. Edit the OnMouseMove function in the CHandsOn7_2View class in
    the HandsOn7_2View.cpp file as follows:

```
void CHandsOn7_2View::OnMouseMove(UINT nFlags, CPoint point)
{
 CClientDC ClientDC( this );
 m_pRgnMap->CheckBubbles( point.x, point.y,
  ( nFlags & MK_LBUTTON ) == 0, &ClientDC );

 CView::OnMouseMove(nFlags, point);
}
```

15. Compile and run the program.

When the program runs, you'll see the image of a grasshopper appear. As you move the mouse across the grasshopper's parts, you'll see their part names appear, as in Figure 7-22.

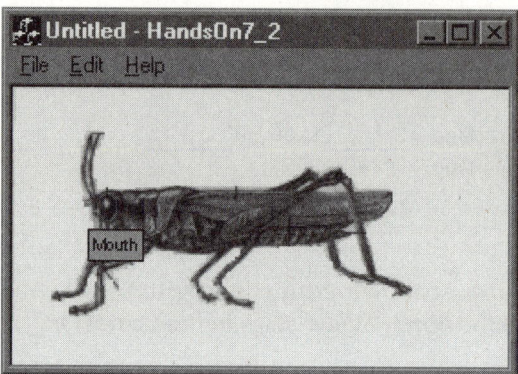

Figure 7-22: As you move the mouse, the name of each part will appear.

One thing to note about this hands-on exercise is the arguments passed to the CRgnMap constructor. The first two are the default values. But the third isn't the default value. By making the argument TRUE, the rectangular area with the region's text follows the mouse every time the mouse cursor moves. For some applications, this may be what you want rather than having the rectangular region with text stay in a single spot once a region has been activated.

SHAREWARE & COMMERCIAL DEMOS

One really nice demo program I found is called The MapUSA Program. It's similar to the RegionMap demo program that comes early in this chapter. But it offers much more detail about the state when you click on it. This feature could easily be added to the RegionMap demo program. Figure 7-23 shows the MapUSA Program.

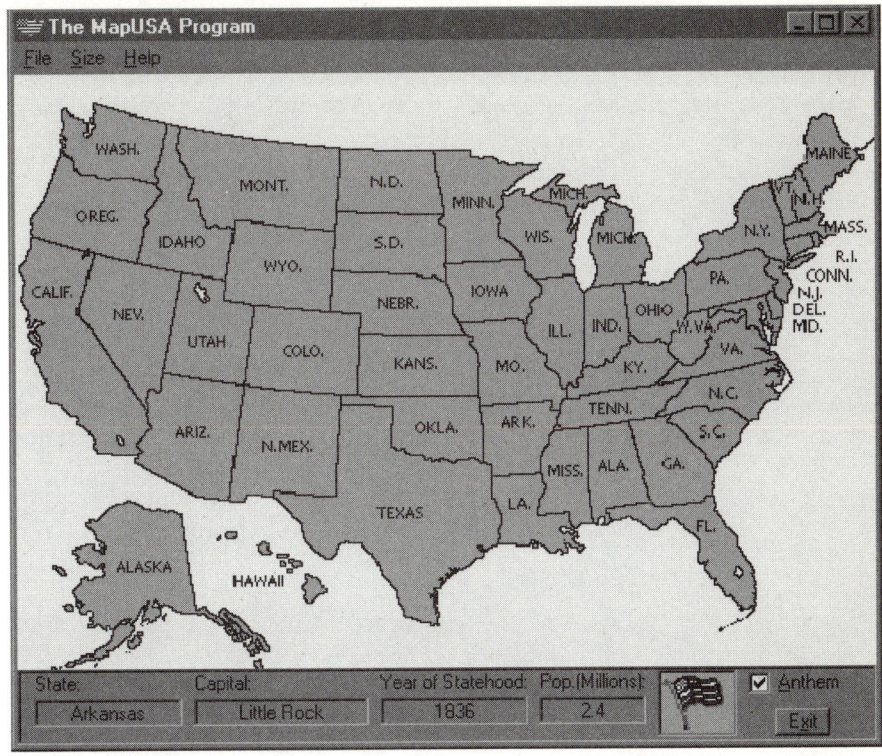

Figure 7-23: The MapUSA Program is a great way for kids to learn about the states in the USA.

MOVING ON

You've seen how to use the CRgnMap class library. You've learned how to use it with some hands-on exercises. Now it's up to you to use your newly acquired skills and create some great applications.

The next chapter in the book covers animation. Like graphical region maps, animation provides a good way to use graphics to communicate with users.

Chapter 8

Animation

*Pink algorithms merrily compute
paintings elongated sprites.*
—My Computer

Pictures enhance a program's appearance and increase communication potential immensely. The Images chapter (Chapter 1) emphasizes this point and provides the tools for you to add pictures to your applications. The next step is to add animations to your programs. While quite a few applications display images, very few utilize animation techniques. That's a shame because animations aren't much more difficult to implement than simple images. Small images can be used if developers are worried about disk space and load time. Even animations with small images are effective.

Of the hundreds of pieces of software I've seen, I usually recall the ones that have animations in the About dialog box. This simple touch says someone took the time to really polish this application.

Many tutorial and training programs benefit from animation. Showing a student several frames that illustrate changing a tire, for instance, can be more effective than showing three still pictures. Depicting algebraic formulas that change dynamically as they're solved is a technique used by many educational companies. It makes a far greater impact than simply describing the steps in words.

Animation is almost a requirement for games. If you have aspirations to develop games—whether your target is public domain, shareware, or commercial—this chapter will be a great starting point. You may even find that the routines presented here can serve all of your needs!

THE ANIMATION CLASS LIBRARY

The animation library utilizes the picture library to load the pictures from disk. Once the pictures are loaded from a list, parameters for their movement and placement are stored. After that, a timer calls the animation class to update the animation. The entire process is easy and straightforward. The hardest part is making the lists of positions, delay values, and other information the library needs.

Several functions make using the class library easy. Among these are the Pause(), Restart(), and Redraw() functions. With only a few lines, you can get an animation started and let it perform in the background with absolutely no worry on your part.

All of the source code to rebuild the Animation.lib file is in the ANIMATION\Animation directory on the Companion CD-ROM that accompanies this book.

The AnimationDemo

This simple demonstration program found in the ANIMATIO\ AnimationDemo directory on the Companion CD-ROM shows what the class library can do. Using File Manager or Program Manager, run the program named AnimationDemo.exe. It's a multiple-document program. When it first runs, you'll see three different windows open, one at a time. It takes a few seconds for each one to load its animation images and initialize.

To view any of the three animation windows, click the left mouse button on it, or use the Window menu to select the window you want to appear in the foreground. The first animation we'll talk about is the one called Static Animation. Go ahead and select the Static Animation window, and make sure you can see the entire window.

Notice that five sets of bubbles rise up to the top of the screen. Each set of bubbles is a separate animation but each is loaded, initialized, and updated in the same way.

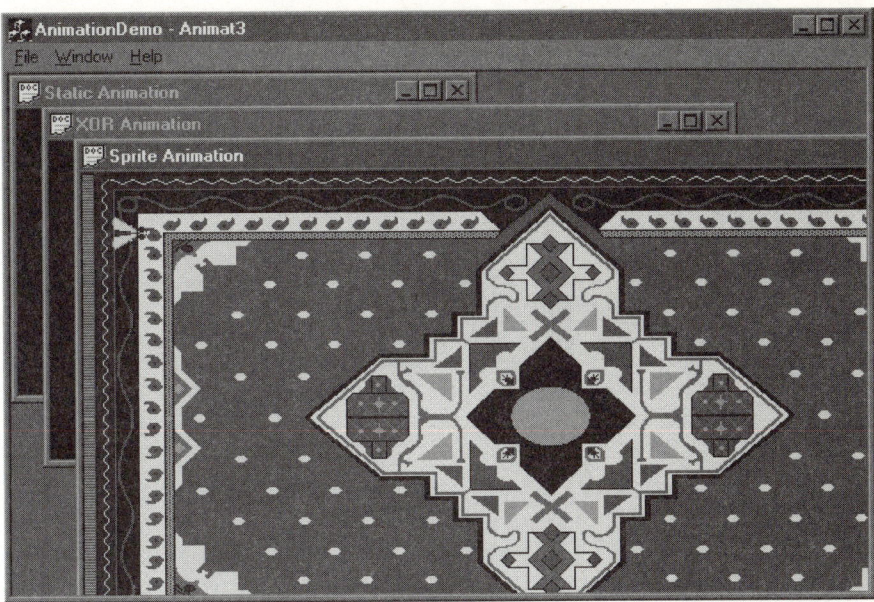

Figure 8-1: When AnimationDemo first runs, you'll see its three windows open and wait while their animation images are being loaded.

Static Animations such as these bubbles are accomplished with a series of bitmap images. The images are drawn on the screen in a sequence that gives the illusion of motion. For our bubble example, the second and third images are drawn with the bubbles at higher altitudes. By drawing image 1, then image 2, then image 3, and then repeating, the bubbles appear to be continuously rising to the surface. Figure 8-2 shows our three animation bitmaps.

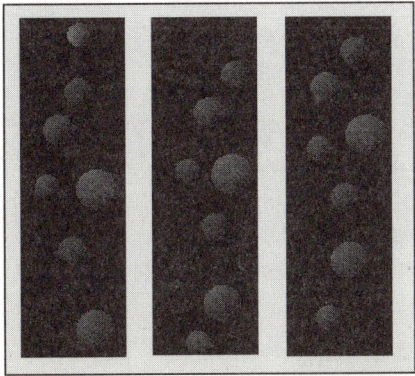

Figure 8-2: Looking at the three bubble images will give you an idea of what it takes to create multiple-stage bitmaps for animations.

Select the XOR Animation window next. You'll see three different creatures that resemble the original Space Invaders characters from the early 1980s. There's a section entitled "XOR Blits Explained" that gets into the nitty gritty of XOR animation. These three creatures are each made of two different images. To produce the animation effect, each image is alternately drawn to the screen. This gives the illusion that the invaders are walking (Figure 8-3).

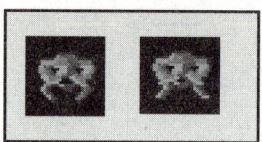

Figure 8-3: A two-stage animation gives the illusion that the creatures are walking.

The window of the third type of animation is labeled Sprite Animation. That's because this animation type takes all of the steps necessary to move over a bitmap without permanently destroying the bitmap on the screen. Sprites save the region of the screen to which they will draw, mask the destination screen according to the shape of the source bitmap, then draw the source bitmap on the screen. Before moving the sprite to a different location, the rectangular region is restored. A complete explanation of this technique comes later in this chapter.

If you select the Sprite Animation window, you'll see a fly going back and forth across the window over a carpet. The important thing to notice here is that even though the fly has an irregular shape, it draws so that the background bitmaps look normal. You can see the carpet between the fly's wings. There are 16 fly animation frames loaded, but only four are used for this example, shown in Figure 8-4.

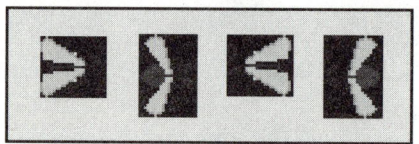

Figure 8-4: Only 4 of the 16 fly images are used for this example.

The last animation example you'll find in the program is a Static Animation in the About dialog box. This type of animation in dialog boxes is something many programmers will want to add to their application. If you select About AnimationView from the Help menu, you'll see a three-stage animation, shown in Figure 8-5.

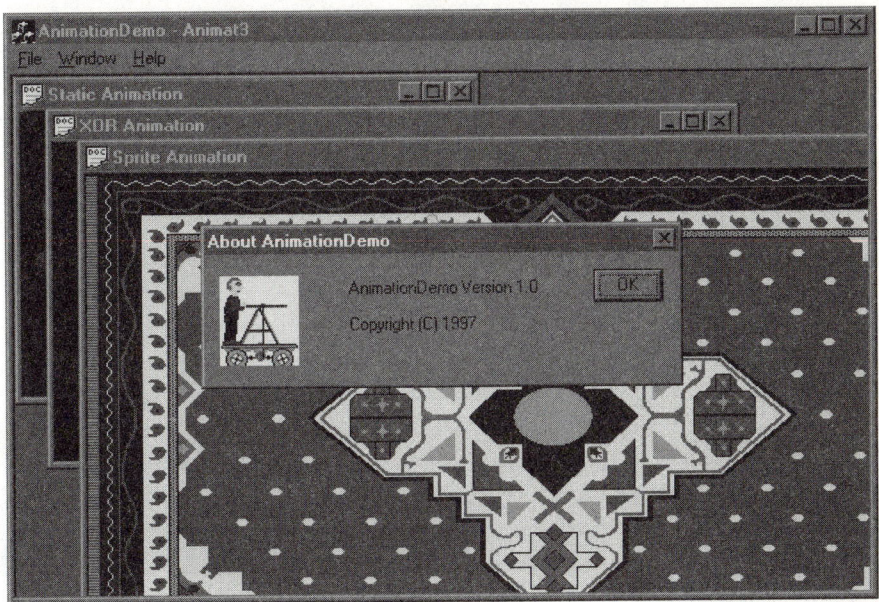

Figure 8-5: A three-stage animation appears in the About dialog.

CANIMATION CLASS LIBRARY FUNCTION CALLS

This section is provided as a reference to the public function calls the animation library offers. Since the library was designed with simplicity as a major goal, there aren't many calls. That's good, because using animations is easy—it just takes a few lines of code.

You may want to skip over this section and read the section entitled "Behind AnimationDemo," which shows how the calls are used. (For some people, it's helpful to look at how the call is used before studying its syntax.)

CAnimation()

Prototype:
```
CAnimation( CDC *pDC, char **Filename, int nNumberOfBitmaps,
    int *nCoordinates, int *nFrameOrder, DWORD *dwPeriod, int nFrames,
    int nType, BOOL bReplay, int nCurrentFrame );
```

Purpose: This is the animation class constructor. It takes all of the information necessary to create the animation as arguments. Once the animation class is constructed, no other information needs to be provided in order for it to perform its functions.

Arguments: CDC *pDC
char **Filename
int nNumberOfBitmaps
int *nCoordinates
int *nFrameOrder
DWORD *dwPeriod
int nFrames
int nType, Defaults to STATIC_ANIMATION
BOOL bReplay, Defaults to TRUE
int nCurrentFrame, Defaults to 0

Service()

Prototype: `void Service( CDC *pDC );`

Purpose: This function must be called in order to advance the animation. If this function was never called, the animation images would never move positions. This function should be called from a timer that's started in one of the application classes. The frame or view classes are usually the easiest. The timer delay should be any value that updates the animation regularly enough to give you the effect you desire.

Arguments: CDC *pDC

Returns: Nothing

Draw()

Prototype: `void Draw( CDC *pDC );`

Purpose: This function draws an animation in its current state.

Arguments: CDC *pDC

Returns: Nothing

Redraw()

Prototype: `void Redraw( CDC *pDC );`

Purpose: This function draws an animation. Its main use is to update the animation in response to a redraw message. For this reason, this function should be called from the view class's OnDraw() function.

Arguments: CDC *pDC

Returns: Nothing

SetPal()

Prototype: `void SetPal( CDC *pDC );`

Purpose: This function sets the system palette with the animation images' palette. You don't need to use this call when the animation is first created, since the palette gets set at that time. This call will be used most often from the OnQueryNewPalette() function or the SetFocus() function.

Arguments: CDC *pDC

Returns: Nothing

Pause()

Prototype: `void Pause( void );`

Purpose: This function toggles the state of the animation class pause variable. To pause an animation, call this function. To unpause an animation, make this call again.

Arguments: None

Returns: Nothing

Restart()

Prototype: `void Restart( CDC *pDC );`

Purpose: This function starts an animation back to its first frame.

Arguments: CDC *pDC

Returns: Nothing

APutImage()

Prototype: `void APutImage( CDC *pDC, int x, int y );`

Purpose: This function blits a bitmap to the screen in replace mode. The difference between doing this and making a standard BitBlt call is that this function masks the image. It uses the RGB color values that are passed in to create a mask for the screen. The animation library expects RGB values of 0 for all mask values.

Arguments: CDC *pDC
int x
int y

Returns: Nothing

BLIT OPERATIONS USED IN THE ANIMATION CLASS

This section will help you understand the differences between the BitBlt operations the animation library uses. The BitBlt function performs what's commonly known as a *blit*. This is programmer jargon for "drawing an image to the screen." The static animations use the most common version, the SRCCOPY BitBlt. The XOR animations use a less common version, the SRCINVERT BitBlt. And the sprite animations use a combination of SRCAND and SRCPAINT BitBlts.

Replace Blits Explained

I've spent about 20 hours trying to explain image-blitting to a friend. (Not all at once, thank goodness.) This person is a capable programmer and very intelligent. But because he grew up writing DOS text-based software, he had never been forced to think about image blits. I have the feeling that the longer you go without thinking about what's happening during image-blitting operations, the harder it is to finally learn.

With that in mind, I'd like to do my part to make absolutely sure that you understand the basic principles. That's why for the first three hands-on sections in this chapter, I'm going to end with explanations of these three common blit operations from a theoretical standpoint. Then I can send a copy of this book to my friend!

Static Animations use the SRCCOPY raster operation. Sometimes these kinds of blits are referred to as replace blits. This is the easiest type of blit to understand. We'll be talking about an image that has a width of 14 and a height of 9. Our theoretical screen has a width of 21 and a height of 25.

Let's say we wanted to blit the image to the screen beginning at screen coordinate 2, 2 (assuming a base of 0). One by one, each pixel would be placed into screen memory so that when the blit operation was done, the screen's data would be overwritten by an exact copy of the image data. (I told you this type of blit operation would be easy to understand.)

Figures 8-6 and 8-7 show an image and a white screen before a blit operation, then the image and screen after the blit operation. Values for the four different pixel types are given. While these aren't important right now, get used to seeing them because the other blit operations will require us to use them.

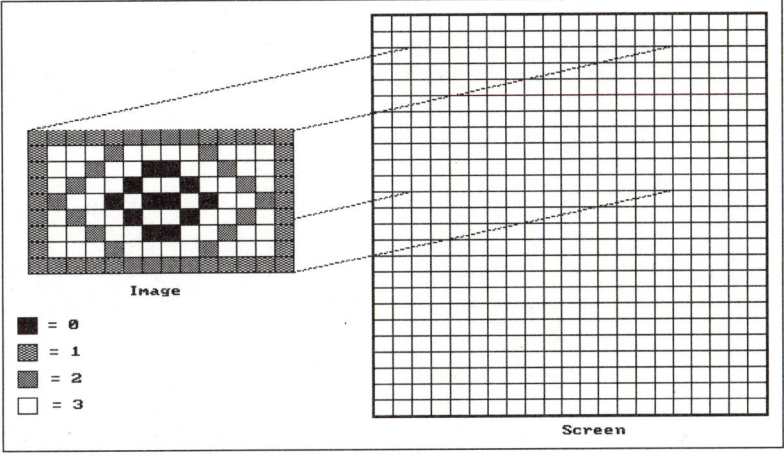

Figure 8-6: An image and a white screen before a blit operation.

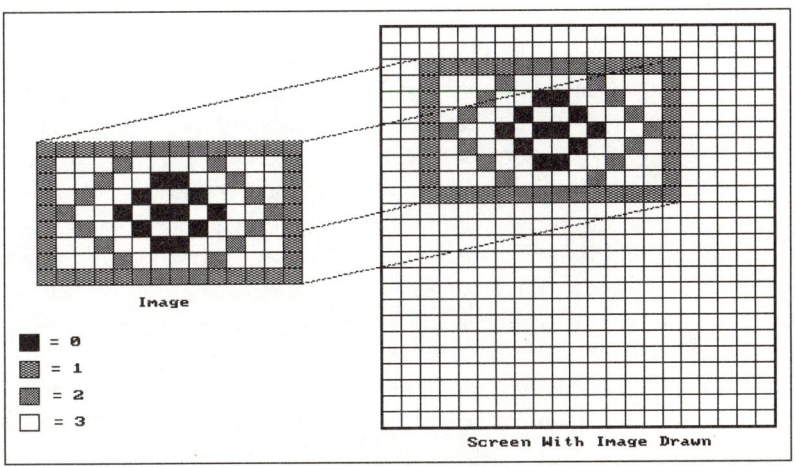

Figure 8-7: An image and a screen after a SRCCOPY blit.

XOR Blits Explained

Most programmers can handle replace blits (SRCCOPY). It gets more difficult to understand when a blit uses the XOR operation. An image's bits are XORed to the screen when an image is drawn when the SRCINVERT raster operation is specified in the BitBlt function. Almost everyone knows how to use the trick that toggles the value of a variable between 0 and 1. You just type the line Variable ^= 1 and the Variable toggles between 0 and 1 every time you encounter this code. Combining two rectangular regions of bits, however, is an operation of a different color.

The XOR operation takes two values and performs a bitwise operation on them. If both bits are 0, the result is 0; if both bits are 1, the result is 0; if one bit is 1 and one bit is 0, the result is 1; and if one bit is 0 and one bit is 1, the result is 1. Here's a chart.

Input Bits	A	B	Output Bit
	0	0	0
	1	1	0
	0	1	1
	1	0	1

Once again, our example will depict an image that has a width of 14 and a height of 9. Our theoretical screen has a width of 21 and a height of 25.

Imagine that we wanted to blit the image to the screen beginning at screen coordinate 2, 2 (assuming a base of 0). One by one, each pixel would be XORed with the data in screen memory, so that when the blit operation was done the screen's data would represent both images XORed together. (This one's not so easy!)

The next seven illustrations, Figures 8-8 through 8-14, show (1) all possible combinations (numerical and graphical) of the illustration values (Figure 8-8), (2) an image and a blank screen before a blit operation (Figure 8-9), (3) the image and the screen after the blit operation to the blank screen (Figure 8-10), (4) an image and a white screen before a blit operation (Figure 8-11), (5) the image and screen after the blit operation to the white screen (Figure 8-12), (6) an image and a patterned screen before a blit operation (Figure 8-13), and (7) the image and the screen after the blit operation (Figure 8-14). Values for the four different pixel types are given. While these aren't important right now, get used to seeing them because the other blit operations will require us to use them.

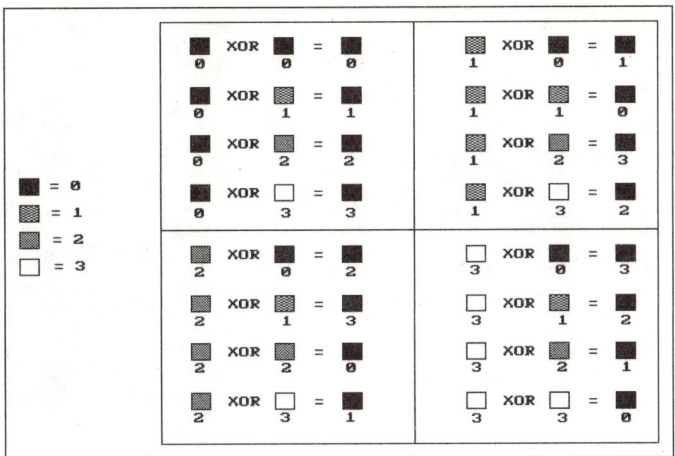

Figure 8-8: All values calculated from XOR operations on all combinations of values from 0 to 3.

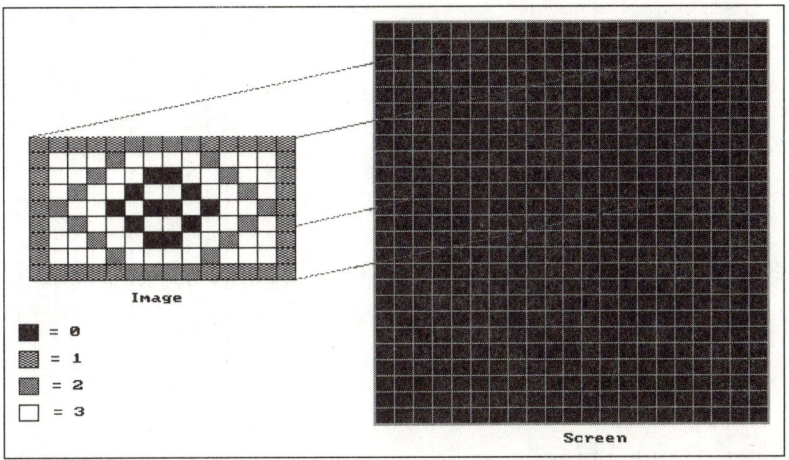

Figure 8-9: An image and a blank screen before a blit operation.

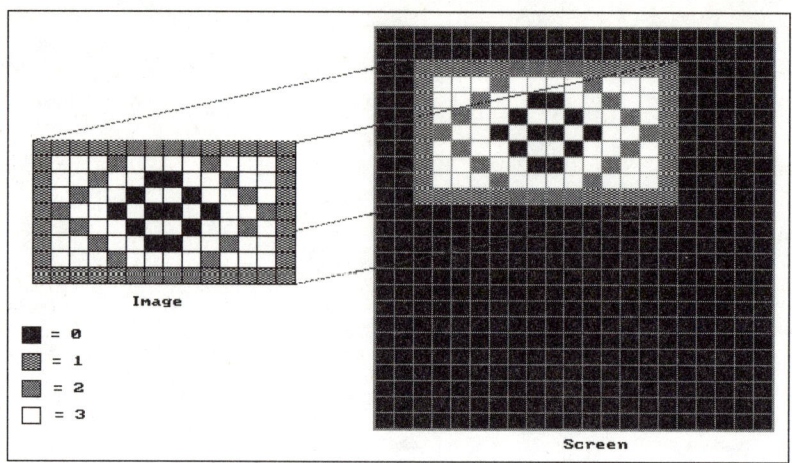

Figure 8-10: A figure and the resulting screen after the image was XORed with a blank screen.

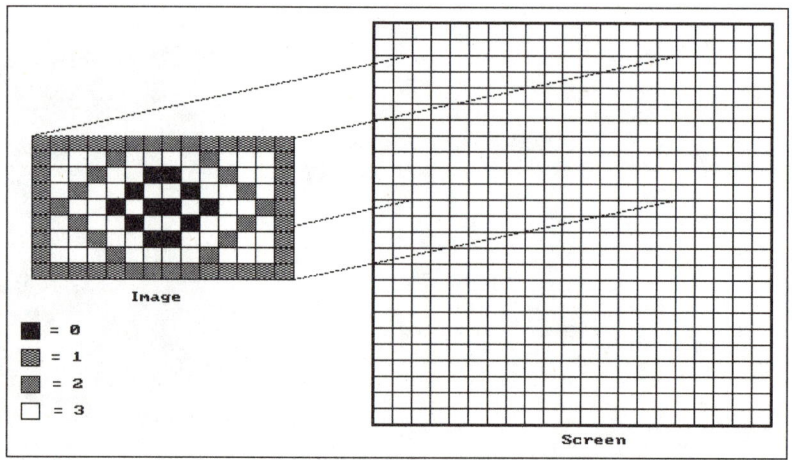

Figure 8-11: An image and a white screen before a blit operation.

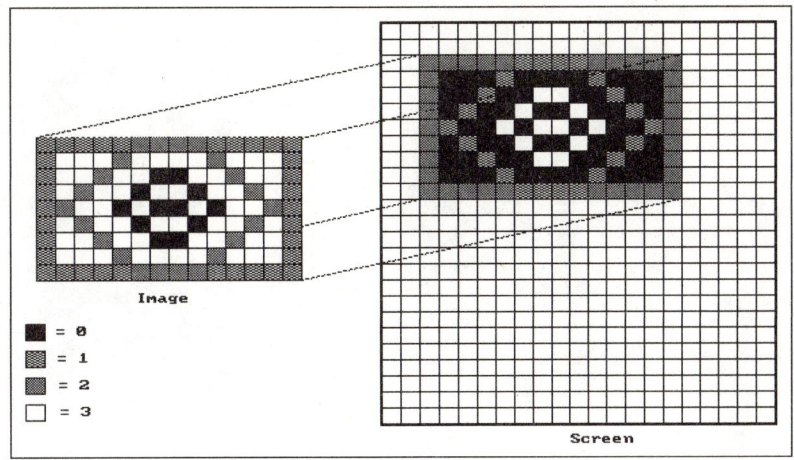

Figure 8-12: An image and a resulting screen after the image was XORed to the screen.

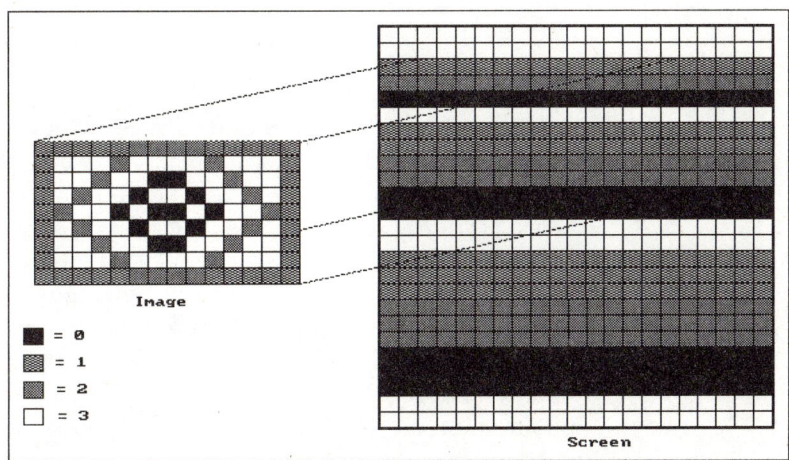

Figure 8-13: An image and a patterned screen before a blit operation.

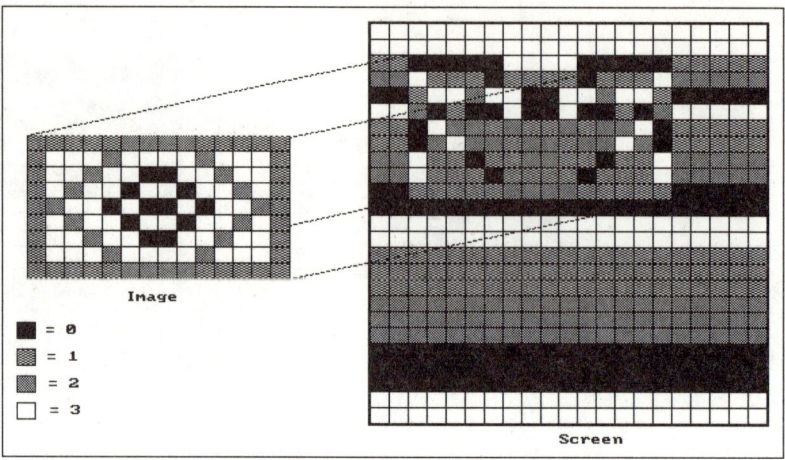

Figure 8-14: An image and the resulting screen after the image was XORed to a patterned screen.

Sprite Blits Explained

The hardest of the three animation types to understand is the Sprite type. There are three steps that happen each time a Sprite animation image is drawn. Any time one moves, there are four operations.

We start off by saving the rectangular region to which the image will be drawn. Our example has an image that's 14 pixels wide and 9 pixels high. The example screen is 21 pixels wide and 25 pixels high. The rectangular region to which the image will be drawn is 14 pixels by 9 pixels. We need a bitmap buffer big enough to hold the background image. The animation library automatically allocates this when you create a Sprite animation. Before the image is drawn, the bits are copied from the screen into the save/restore bitmap buffer. Later, this data will be used to restore the background before we move the image to another location.

Once we've saved the destination rectangular region, we can begin drawing. There's one problem you must realize before we go on. Most Sprite-type images will not be perfect rectangles. They may have rounded corners or portions that should be transparent. The fly in the AnimationDemo program is a perfect example of this. Between its wings are areas through which you expect to see the carpet.

Let's consider a simpler example where the corners of an image are rounded. If we simply copied the bits to the screen, we'd see the black space of the rounded corners on the screen too. The next two figures (Figures 8-15 and 8-16) illustrate this.

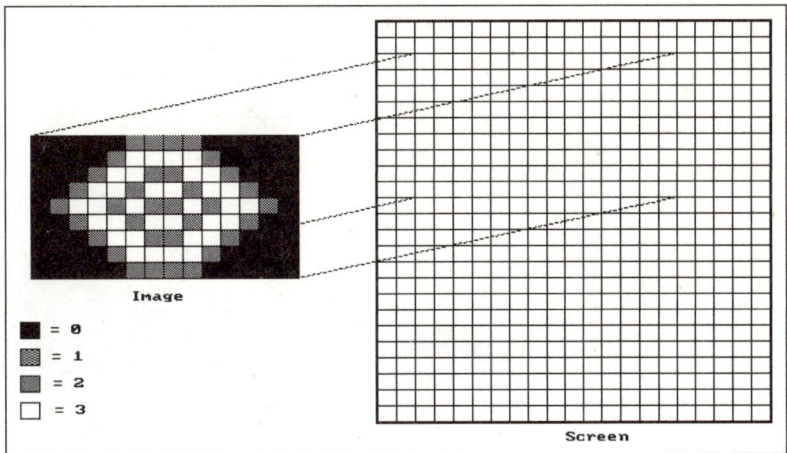

Figure 8-15: Many images have rounded corners that should not be drawn on the screen.

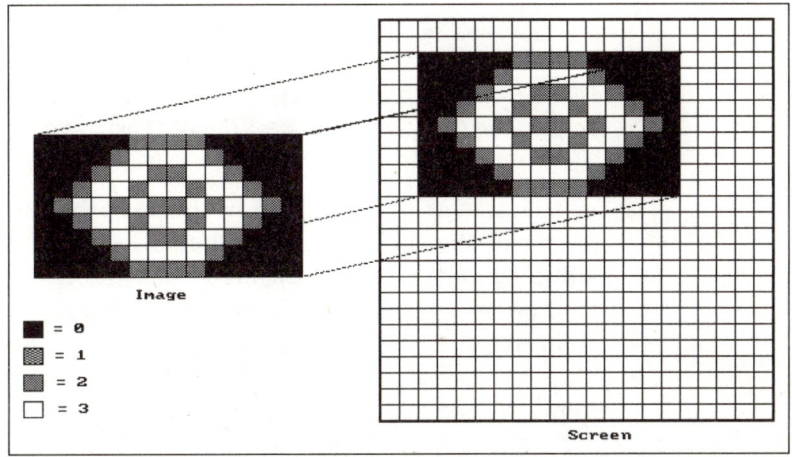

Figure 8-16: The black space of the rounded corners becomes part of the screen if we simply copy the image into the screen.

Two steps must be taken to correctly draw the image without the rounded corners showing. It's important to note that the animation class library uses black (RGB(0,0,0)) exclusively for its mask color. That could be changed, but we felt this would be the most common color choice for masking, and we wanted to make things as easy as possible.

The first thing we must do is develop a mask. The mask will be used to remove all bits that are on the screen where the desired image will be drawn. In other words, we'll develop a mask so that when it's combined with the screen using the AND bitwise operator, all of the screen to which the image will be drawn, except the rounded corners, will become empty (or black). It's like taking a cookie cutter and stamping a part of the screen out. Figure 8-17 illustrates this.

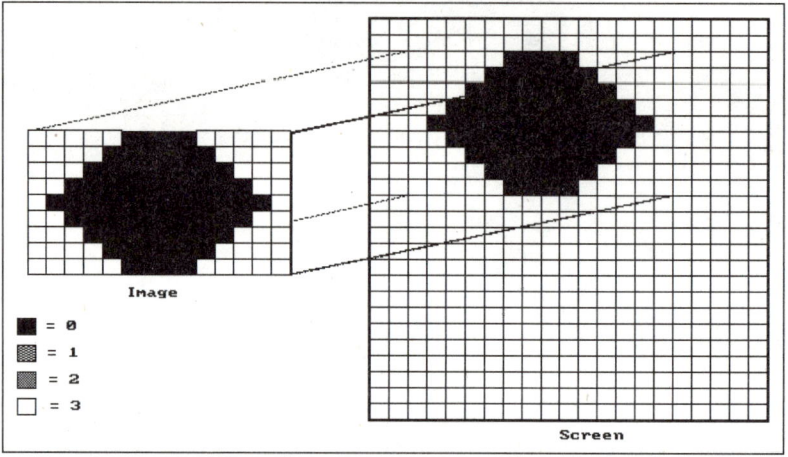

Figure 8-17: The correct mask can make even an irregular screen area empty in preparation for drawing the bits. The AND bitwise operation is used.

The last step to correctly draw the image bits on the screen is to blit them with the OR bitwise operation. That way, the empty screen memory will combine with any of the image bits in such a way that they'll retain their original value. That's because the empty screen has values of zero, and zeros don't affect other values when performing OR bitwise operations. The rounded corners will leave the screen unaffected, since the rounded corners of the image have values of zero and, once again, these don't alter other values when performing bitwise OR operations. Figure 8-18 shows the resultant screen image

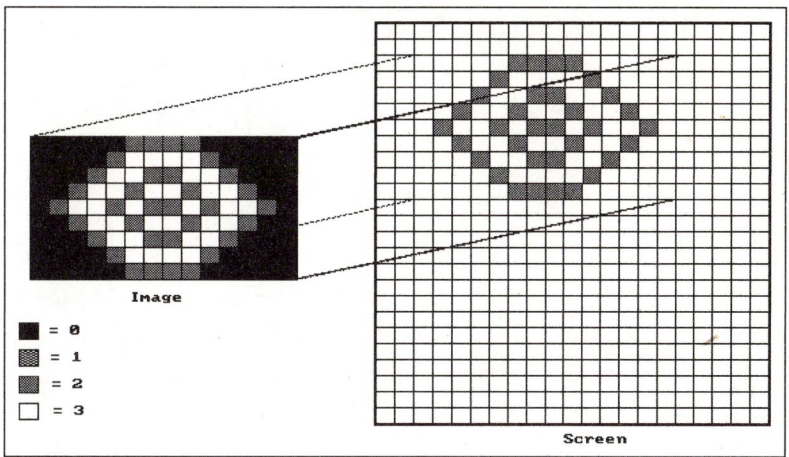

Figure 8-18: Once the screen has been masked, the image data is ORed to the screen.

Before moving the Sprite to a different location, the rectangular region that was stored must be put back on the screen. The entire process of saving, masking, and drawing is repeated.

BEHIND ANIMATIONDEMO

AnimationDemo was created with the Visual C++ AppWizard. It has a multiple document interface and no initial toolbar. After creating the program, the ImageObject and Animation library files were added to the linker. To do this, select Project from the Options menu. Choose the Linker button, and when the Linker Options dialog appears, add ImageObject and Animation to the Libraries list.

The code that creates the three main animations can be found in the CMainFrame class in the MainFrm.cpp file. A variable named m_nChildrenCreated is initialized to zero in the CMainFrame constructor. This variable is used to keep track of how many animations have been created.

Rather than create all three animations at the same time, they're created one second apart. This way, anyone watching the program can see them appear one at a time.

Starting the Timer

A timer is started in the CMainFrame class with a delay of 1000 milliseconds, or one second. The timer is used to create the animations.

The OnCreate() Code

```
int CMainFrame::OnCreate(LPCREATESTRUCT lpCreateStruct)
{
 if (CMDIFrameWnd::OnCreate(lpCreateStruct)
  == -1)
  return -1;

 SetTimer( 1, 1000, NULL );

 return 0;
}
```

Performing the Timer Code

The timer code is called once every second. Each time through the timer, another animation is created. A function in the CAnimationDemo class named FileNew() is called when an animation is to be created. The FileNew() function in the CAnimationDemo class simply calls the OnFileNew() function. The reason the OnFileNew() function can't be called from the CMainFrame class is that it's a protected member and can only be called from the CAnimationDemo class.

The OnTimer() Code

```
void CMainFrame::OnTimer(UINT nIDEvent)
{

 if( m_nChildrenCreated < 2 ){
  CAnimationDemoApp *pApp =
   CAnimationDemoApp *) AfxGetApp();
  pApp->FileNew();
  m_nChildrenCreated++;
  }

 CMDIFrameWnd::OnTimer(nIDEvent);
}
```

Creating the Animations

The animations are actually created in the CAnimationDemoView class in the AnimationDemoView.cpp file. The function that does the creation is the OnDraw() function. A variable named m_nAnimationLoaded determines if the animation has been loaded. If it hasn't, it performs the animation loading code in the OnDraw() function. This code follows.

The First Section of the OnDraw() Code

```
int i;
int *Coordinates1;
int *FrameOrder1;
DWORD *Period1;

if( !m_nAnimationLoaded ){
 BOOL bMaximized;
 CMainFrame *pFrame =(CMainFrame *)
  AfxGetApp()->m_pMainWnd;
 CChildFrame *pActiveChild = CChildFrame *)
  pFrame->MDIGetActive( &bMaximized );

 BeginWaitCursor();
 switch( m_nAnimationType ){

  case 0:
   for( i=0; i<5; i++ ){
    m_pAnimation[i] = new CAnimation( pDC,
    Filename0, 3, Coordinates0, FrameOrder0,
    Period0, 3, STATIC_ANIMATION, TRUE, i%3);
    m_pAnimation[i]->Draw( pDC );
    Coordinates0[0] += 64;
    Coordinates0[2] += 64;
    Coordinates0[4] += 64;
    }
   pActiveChild->SetWindowPos( NULL, 0, 0,
    m_pAnimation[0]->m_pImage[0]->m_nWidth*5,
  m_pAnimation[0]->m_pImage[0]->m_nHeight+20,
    SWP_NOZORDER | SWP_NOMOVE );
   break;

  case 1:
   Coordinates1 = new int [16*4*2];
   FrameOrder1 = new int [16*4];
   Period1 = new DWORD [16*4];
   for( i=0; i<16*4; i++ ){
```

```
      Period1[i] = 1000L;
      FrameOrder1[i] = ( i & 1 );
      if( i < 16 ) Coordinates1[i*2] =
       20 + ( i & 15 ) * 20;
      else if( i < 32 ) Coordinates1[i*2] =
       20 + 15 * 20 - ( i & 15 ) * 20;
      else if( i < 48 ) Coordinates1[i*2] =
       20 + ( i & 15 ) * 20;
      else Coordinates1[i*2] =
       20 + 15 * 20 - ( i & 15 ) * 20;
      Coordinates1[i*2+1] =
       40 + ( i / 16 ) * 30;
       }

    for( i=0; i<3; i++ ){
     m_pAnimation[i] = new CAnimation( pDC,
      Filename1, 2, Coordinates1, FrameOrder1,
      Period1, 16 * 4, XOR_ANIMATION, TRUE,
      i * 24 );
     m_pAnimation[i]->Draw( pDC );
      }

    delete [] Period1;
    delete [] FrameOrder1;
    delete [] Coordinates1;
    break;

  case 2:
   m_pImage =
    new CImage( "PICTURES\\CARPET.GIF" );

   pActiveChild->SetWindowPos( NULL, 0, 0,
    m_pImage->m_nWidth,
    m_pImage->m_nHeight + 20,
    SWP_NOZORDER | SWP_NOMOVE );

   Coordinates1 = new int [32*2];
   FrameOrder1 = new int [32*2];
   Period1 = new DWORD [32];
   for( i=0; i<16; i++ ){
    Coordinates1[i*2] = 20 + i * 30;
    Coordinates1[i*2+1] = 30 - ( i & 1 ) * 2;
    Period1[i] = 1000L;
    FrameOrder1[i] = 4 + ( i & 1 );
     }
   for( i=16; i<32; i++ ){
```

```
          Coordinates1[i*2] =
            20 + 16 * 30 - ( i - 16 ) * 30;
          Coordinates1[i*2+1] =
            80 - ( i & 1 ) * 2;
          Period1[i] = 1000L;
          FrameOrder1[i] = 12 + ( i & 1 );
                        }

    m_pAnimation[0] = new CAnimation( pDC,
      Filename2, 16, Coordinates1, FrameOrder1,
      Period1, 16 * 2, SPRITE_ANIMATION );
    m_pImage->Draw( pDC );
    m_pAnimation[0]->Draw( pDC );

    delete [] Coordinates1;
    delete [] FrameOrder1;
    delete [] Period1;
    break;
  }
EndWaitCursor();
m_nAnimationLoaded = TRUE;
}
```

Redrawing Animations

Your application's view windows will get redraw messages that cause
the OnDraw() function to be called. As shown in the previous section, if
the animation hasn't already been loaded, it's loaded in the first part of
the OnDraw() function. After all of that's done, the animation must be
redrawn. This is so that when something moves across the view window
or the view window is moved, the animations are refreshed.

The following code is very simple. It decides what kind of animation
this view class is, then it loops through each animation of the class and
calls the animation class Redraw() method.

The Last Part of the OnDraw() Code

```
    int i;

    switch( m_nAnimationType ){
     case 0:
      for( i=0; i<5; i++ )
       m_pAnimation[i]->Redraw( pDC, NULL );
      break;
```

295

```
case 1:
 for( i=0; i<3; i++ )
  m_pAnimation[i]->Redraw( pDC, NULL );
 break;
case 2:
 m_pImage->Draw( pDC );
 m_pAnimation[0]->Redraw( pDC,
  &m_pImage->m_DisplayBitmap );
 break;
}
```

Servicing the Animation

The animation must move through its list of coordinates. Once it reaches the end of the list, it begins over again at the beginning. In order for this to happen, the animation class Service() function must be called. So that it happens in a periodic manner, the Service() function is called from the view class timer. The timer code follows.

The OnTimer() Code

```
void CAnimationDemoView::OnTimer(UINT nIDEvent)
{
 if( m_nAnimationLoaded ){
  CClientDC dc( this );
  for( int i=0; i<6; i++ ){
   if( m_pAnimation[i] != NULL )
    m_pAnimation[i]->Service( &dc );
  }
 }
    CView::OnTimer(nIDEvent);
}
```

Setting the Focus

Each animation window may receive a Set Focus message. When this happens, the palette must be set for 256-color images. The following code is the OnSetFocus() function that's part of the view class. It sets the animation palette every time a message is sent indicating that the view window got the focus. For images that don't have a palette, nothing will happen inside of the image class.

The OnSetFocus() Code

```
void CAnimationDemoView::OnSetFocus(CWnd* pOldWnd)
{
 CView::OnSetFocus(pOldWnd);

 if( m_nAnimationLoaded ){
  CClientDC dc( this );
  if( m_pAnimation[0] != NULL )
   m_pAnimation[0]->SetPal( &dc );
  }
}
```

USING ANIMATIONS IN A NUTSHELL

This section will simplify animations as much as possible so that you can completely understand them. In order to create a three-frame static animation, the following instructions are all you need.

Three different images will be loaded into the animation. They are PIC1.BMP, PIC2.BMP, and PIC3.BMP. The CAnimation class needs to know the destination coordinates to which it will draw the upper left corner of the images. This example uses an array to let the CAnimation class know that all of the images will be drawn to the X/Y coordinate, 10, 14.

The frame order is 0, 1, 2. The frame order will almost always be consecutive numbers such as this. Allowing you to specify a frame order that's not consecutive is a convenience that the CAnimation class provides.

The delay time for each animation frame is 1000 milliseconds. This translates into one second.

```
static char *szFilename[] = { "PIC1.BMP", "PIC2.BMP", "PIC3.BMP" };
static int nCoordinates[] = { 10, 14, 10, 14, 10, 14 };
static int nFrameOrder[] = { 0, 1, 2 };
static DWORD dwPeriod[] = { 1000, 1000, 1000 };

m_pAnimation =
 new CAnimation( &dc, szFilename, 3,
  nCoordinates, nFrameOrder, dwPeriod, 3,
  STATIC_ANIMATION, TRUE, 0 );
```

To draw the animation requires only the two lines of code that follow:

```
m_pAnimation->SetPal( &dc );
m_pAnimation->Draw( &dc );
```

To redraw the animation in response to a redraw message requires only the following two lines of code:

```
m_pAnimation->SetPal( &dc );
m_pAnimation->Redraw( &dc );
```

To service the animation and move it through its frames and positions requires only the following line of code:

```
m_pAnimation->Service( &dc );
```

CREATING PROGRAMS THAT USE ANIMATIONS

The following five hands-on exercises will get you warmed up so that you can move on to create your own applications with animations. Going through them won't take very long, and the investment of time will be well worth it since you'll then have mastered creating and using animations.

Hands-On 1: Creating a Static Animation

This exercise will start with the simplest type of animation, a static animation. As described earlier, these animations use simple SRCCOPY BitBlts. Follow the steps that come next, and you'll have no trouble implementing your first animation in a program.

1. Create a Visual C++ project named HandsOn8_1 with the following attributes:

   ❏ Single-document interface
   ❏ English language
   ❏ No database support
   ❏ No compound document support
   ❏ No automation or ActiveX control support
   ❏ 3D controls, but no other features
   ❏ No source file comments
   ❏ Link MFC as a static library

2. Select Settings from the Project menu. Choose the Link tab. Add the following libraries to the Object/library modules field. The libraries for the release and debug versions are different; both are listed below.

Release Project Libraries	Debug Project Libraries
ImageLoad.lib	ImageLoad.lib
ImageObject.lib	ImageObjectD.lib
Animation.lib	AnimationD.lib

3. Set the Active Configuration to Win32 Release.

4. Copy the following files from the \ANIMATIO\SAMPLES directory on the Companion CD-ROM to the newly created project directory.

```
PIC1.BMP
PIC2.BMP
PIC3.BMP
```

5. Add the following include to the HandsOn8_1View.h file:

```
#include "Animation.h"
```

6. Add the following variable declaration to the CHandsOn8_1View class in the HandsOn8_1View.h file:

```
CAnimation *m_pAnimation;
```

7. Add the following code to the CHandsOn8_1View constructor:

```
CHandsOn8_1View::CHandsOn8_1View()
{
 m_pAnimation = NULL;
}
```

8. Add the following code to the CHandsOn8_1View destructor:

```
CHandsOn8_1View::~CHandsOn8_1View()
{
 if( m_pAnimation != NULL )
  delete m_pAnimation;
}
```

9. Edit the OnDraw function in the CHandsOn8_1View class in the HandsOn8_1View.cpp file as follows:

```
void CHandsOn8_1View::OnDraw(CDC* pDC)
{
 CHandsOn8_1Doc* pDoc = GetDocument();
 ASSERT_VALID(pDoc);
```

```
    if( m_pAnimation == NULL ){
     static char *szFilename[] = { "PIC1.BMP",
      "PIC2.BMP", "PIC3.BMP" };
     static int nCoordinates[] = { 10, 14, 10,
      14, 10, 14 };
     static int nFrameOrder[] = { 0, 1, 2 };
     static DWORD dwPeriod[] = { 1000, 1000, 1000 };

     m_pAnimation =
      new CAnimation( pDC, szFilename, 3,
      nCoordinates, nFrameOrder, dwPeriod, 3,
      STATIC_ANIMATION, TRUE, 0 );
     }

   if( m_pAnimation != NULL ){
    m_pAnimation->SetPal( pDC );
    m_pAnimation->Redraw( pDC, NULL );
    }
   }
```

10. Add the following functions with the Class Wizard to the CHandsOn8_1View class in the HandsOn8_1View.h file:

```
Name:OnCreate()  Message:WM_CREATE
Name:OnSetFocus()  Message:WM_SETFOCUS
Name:OnTimer()  Message:WM_TIMER
```

11. Edit the OnCreate function in the CHandsOn8_1View class in the HandsOn8_1View.cpp file as follows:

```
int CHandsOn8_1View::OnCreate(LPCREATESTRUCT lpCreateStruct)
{
  return -1;

 SetTimer( 1, 1000, NULL );

  return 0;
}
```

12. Edit the OnSetFocus function in the CHandsOn8_1View class in the HandsOn8_1View.cpp file as follows:

```
void CHandsOn8_1View::OnSetFocus(CWnd* pOldWnd)
{
 if( m_pAnimation != NULL ){
  CClientDC ClientDC( this );
  m_pAnimation->SetPal( &ClientDC );
  }
}
```

13. Edit the OnTimer function in the CHandsOn8_1View class in the HandsOn8_1View.cpp file as follows:

```
void CHandsOn8_1View::OnTimer(UINT nIDEvent)
{
 if( m_pAnimation != NULL ){
  CClientDC ClientDC( this );
  m_pAnimation->Service( &ClientDC );
  }

 CView::OnTimer(nIDEvent);
}
```

14. Compile and run the program.

What you'll see when you run the program is a three-frame animation of a man on a railroad cart. He's moving the handle up and down so that he can get where he's going. Figure 8-19 shows the program running.

Figure 8-19: This first exercise implements a simple three-frame animation.

Hands-On 2: Creating a Four-Frame Static Animation

The next hands-on exercise is similar to the first, except that it is a four-frame animation. Once again, a static animation is used.

1. Create a Visual C++ project named HandsOn8_2 with the following attributes:

   ❑ Single-document interface

   ❑ English language

   ❑ No database support

   ❑ No compound document support

   ❑ No automation or ActiveX control support

   ❑ 3D controls, but no other features

   ❑ No source file comments

   ❑ Link MFC as a static library

2. Select Settings from the Project menu. Choose the Link tab. Add the following libraries to the Object/library modules field. The libraries for the release and debug versions are different; both are listed below.

Release Project Libraries	Debug Project Libraries
ImageLoad.lib	ImageLoad.lib
ImageObject.lib	ImageObjectD.lib
Animation.lib	AnimationD.lib

3. Set the Active Configuration to Win32 Release.

4. Copy the following files from the \ANIMATIO\SAMPLES directory on the Companion CD-ROM to the newly created project directory.

   ```
   SHOWANM1.BMP
   SHOWANM2.BMP
   SHOWANM3.BMP
   SHOWANM4.BMP
   ```

5. Add the following include to the HandsOn8_2View.h file:

   ```
   #include "Animation.h"
   ```

6. Add the following variable declaration to the CHandsOn8_2View class in the HandsOn8_2View.h file:

   ```
   CAnimation *m_pAnimation;
   ```

7. Add the following code to the CHandsOn8_2View constructor:

```
CHandsOn8_2View::CHandsOn8_2View()
{
 m_pAnimation = NULL;
}
```

8. Add the following code to the CHandsOn8_2View destructor:

```
CHandsOn8_2View::~CHandsOn8_2View()
{
 if( m_pAnimation != NULL )
  delete m_pAnimation;
}
```

9. Edit the OnDraw function in the CHandsOn8_2View class in the HandsOn8_2View.cpp file as follows:

```
void CHandsOn8_2View::OnDraw(CDC* pDC)
{
 CHandsOn8_2Doc* pDoc = GetDocument();
 ASSERT_VALID(pDoc);

 if( m_pAnimation == NULL ){
  static char *szFilename[] = {
   "SHOWANM1.BMP", "SHOWANM2.BMP",
   "SHOWANM3.BMP", "SHOWANM4.BMP" };
  static int nCoordinate[] = {
   20, 20, 20, 20, 20, 20, 20, 20 };
  static int nFrameOrder[] = { 0, 1, 2, 3 };
  static DWORD dwPeriod[] = { 1000, 1000,
   1000, 1000 };
  BeginWaitCursor();
  m_pAnimation = new CAnimation( pDC,
   szFilename, 4, nCoordinate,
   nFrameOrder, dwPeriod, 4,
   STATIC_ANIMATION, TRUE, 0 );
  m_pAnimation->Draw( pDC );
  EndWaitCursor();
  }
 else{
  m_pAnimation->SetPal( pDC );
  m_pAnimation->Redraw( pDC, NULL );
  }
}
```

10. Add the following functions with the Class Wizard to the CHandsOn8_2View class in the HandsOn8_2View.h file:

```
Name:OnSetFocus()  Message:WM_SETFOCUS
Name:OnCreate()  Message:WM_CREATE
Name:OnTimer()  Message:WM_TIMER
```

11. Edit the OnSetFocus function in the CHandsOn8_2View class in the HandsOn8_2View.cpp file as follows:

```
void CHandsOn8_2View::OnSetFocus(CWnd* pOldWnd)
{

  if( m_pAnimation != NULL ){
  CClientDC ClientDC( this );
  m_pAnimation->SetPal( &ClientDC );
   }


}
```

12. Edit the OnCreate function in the CHandsOn8_2View class in the HandsOn8_2View.cpp file as follows:

```
int CHandsOn8_2View::OnCreate(LPCREATESTRUCT lpCreateStruct)
{
   return -1;

  SetTimer( 1, 100, NULL );

   return 0;
}
```

13. Edit the OnTimer function in the CHandsOn8_2View class in the HandsOn8_2View.cpp file as follows:

```
void CHandsOn8_2View::OnTimer(UINT nIDEvent)
{
 if( m_pAnimation != NULL ){
  CClientDC ClientDC( this );
  m_pAnimation->Service( &ClientDC );
   }

 CView::OnTimer(nIDEvent);
}
```

14. Compile and run the program.

When the program runs, you'll see a small image appear in the upper left corner of the view window. The image will then change to the second frame's image, the third frame's image, then the fourth frame's image. It will then restart the animation sequence back to the first frame's image. Figure 8-20 shows the application.

Figure 8-20: This hands-on exercise shows a simple four-frame static animation.

Hands-On 3: Creating an XOR Animation

The third hands-on exercise has you creating an XOR animation. This is slightly more difficult to understand than the static animations. Work through this exercise so you have a good grasp on simple XOR animations.

Unlike the last two hands-on exercises, the images in this one change coordinates as the animation progresses.

1. Create a Visual C++ project named HandsOn8_3 with the following attributes:

   ❏ Single-document interface

   ❏ English language

   ❏ No database support

❑ No compound document support

❑ No automation or ActiveX control support

❑ 3D controls, but no other features

❑ No source file comments

❑ Link MFC as a static library

2. Select Settings from the Project menu. Choose the Link tab. Add the following libraries to the Object/library modules field. The libraries for the release and debug versions are different; both are listed below.

Release Project Libraries	Debug Project Libraries
ImageLoad.lib	ImageLoad.lib
ImageObject.lib	ImageObjectD.lib
Animation.lib	AnimationD.lib

3. Set the Active Configuration to Win32 Release.

4. Copy the file BALL.BMP from the \ANIMATIO\SAMPLES directory on the Companion CD-ROM to the newly created project directory.

5. Add the following include to the HandsOn8_3View.h file:

```
#include "Animation.h"
```

6. Add the following variable declarations to the CHandsOn8_3View class in the HandsOn8_3View.h file:

```
CAnimation *m_pAnimation[6];
int m_nCoordinate[50];
int m_nFrameOrder[25];
DWORD m_dwPeriod[25];
BOOL m_bAnimationLoaded;
```

7. Add the following code to the CHandsOn8_3View constructor:

```
CHandsOn8_3View::CHandsOn8_3View()
{

m_bAnimationLoaded = FALSE;
for( int i=0; i<6; i++ )
```

```
    m_pAnimation[i] = NULL;

    }
```

8. Add the following code to the CHandsOn8_3View destructor:

```
CHandsOn8_3View::~CHandsOn8_3View()
{
  for( int i=0; i<6; i++ )
    if( m_pAnimation[i] !=NULL )
      delete m_pAnimation[i];
}
```

9. Edit the OnDraw function in the CHandsOn8_3View class in the HandsOn8_3View.cpp file as follows:

```
void CHandsOn8_3View::OnDraw(CDC* pDC)
{
  CHandsOn8_3Doc* pDoc = GetDocument();
  ASSERT_VALID(pDoc);

  CRect Rect;
  pDC->SelectStockObject( BLACK_BRUSH );
  pDC->SelectStockObject( BLACK_PEN );
  GetClientRect( &Rect );
  pDC->Rectangle( Rect );

  if( !m_bAnimationLoaded ){
    static char *szFilename[] = { "BALL.BMP" };
    BeginWaitCursor ();

    Rect.right -= 25;
    Rect.bottom -= 25;
    int x = 0;
    int y = Rect.bottom >> 1;
    int XStep = Rect.right / 12;
    int YStep = -( Rect.bottom / 12 );

    for( int frame=0; frame<24; frame++ ){

      m_nCoordinate[frame*2] = x;
      x += XStep;
      if( x >= Rect.right ){
        x -= ( x - Rect.right + 1 );
        XStep = -XStep;
      }
```

```
    else if( x < 0 ){
     x += ( -x + 1 );
     XStep = -XStep;
     }

    m_nCoordinate[frame*2+1] = y;
    y += YStep;
    if (y >= Rect.bottom){
     y -= ( y - Rect.bottom + 1 );
     YStep = -YStep;
     }
    else if( y < 0 ){
     y += ( -y + 1 );
     YStep = -YStep;
     }
    m_nFrameOrder[frame] = 0;
    m_dwPeriod[frame] = 100;
     }

   for( int i=0; i<6; i++ ){
   m_pAnimation[i] =
    new CAnimation( pDC, szFilename, 1,
     m_nCoordinate,
     m_nFrameOrder, m_dwPeriod, 24,
     XOR_ANIMATION,
     TRUE, i * 4 );
   m_pAnimation[i]->Draw( pDC );
    }

   EndWaitCursor ();
   m_bAnimationLoaded = TRUE;
    }
   else{
    for( int a=0; a<6; a++ ){
     if( m_pAnimation[a] != NULL )
      m_pAnimation[a]->Redraw( pDC, NULL );
     }
    }
   }
```

10. Add the following functions with the Class Wizard to the
    CHandsOn8_3View class in the HandsOn8_3View.h file:

```
Name:OnSetFocus()  Message:WM_SETFOCUS
Name:OnCreate()  Message:WM_CREATE
Name:OnTimer()  Message:WM_TIMER
```

11. Edit the OnSetFocus function in the CHandsOn8_3View class in the HandsOn8_3View.cpp file as follows:

```
void CHandsOn8_3View::OnSetFocus(CWnd* pOldWnd)
{
 if( m_pAnimation[0] != NULL ){
  CClientDC ClientDC( this );
  m_pAnimation[0]->SetPal( &ClientDC );
  }
}
```

12. Edit the OnCreate function in the CHandsOn8_3View class in the HandsOn8_3View.cpp file as follows:

```
int CHandsOn8_3View::OnCreate(LPCREATESTRUCT lpCreateStruct)
{
  return -1;

 SetTimer( 1, 100, NULL );

  return 0;
}
```

13. Edit the OnTimer function in the CHandsOn8_3View class in the HandsOn8_3View.cpp file as follows:

```
void CHandsOn8_3View::OnTimer(UINT nIDEvent)
{
 if( m_bAnimationLoaded ){
  CClientDC ClientDC( this );
  for( int i=0; i<6; i++ ){
   m_pAnimation[i]->Service( &ClientDC );
   m_pAnimation[i]->m_dwLastEventServiced =
    m_pAnimation[i]->m_dwLastEventServiced;
   }
  }

  CView::OnTimer(nIDEvent);
}
```

14. Compile and run the program.

When the program runs, you'll see six balls appear on the screen. They'll all be in a hexagonal formation when they start. Once everything is initialized, the balls move in a clockwise direction. Figure 8-21 shows the program screen.

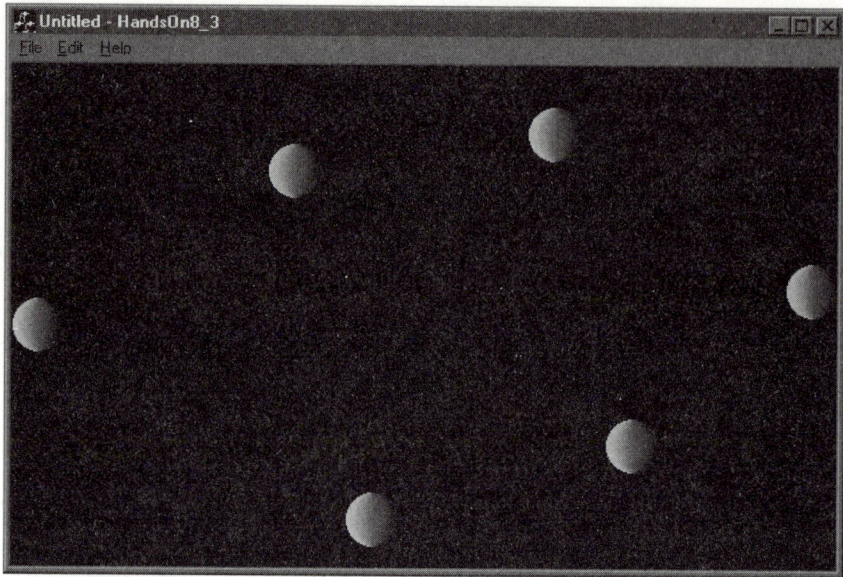

Figure 8-21: The six balls in this program move in a clockwise direction.

Hands-On 4: Creating a Sprite Animation

It's time to create an application that displays a Sprite animation. You'll find it slightly more involved than the last three exercises, but if you worked through them, you've already gotten the basics of animation under your belt.

Follow the next steps and you'll have an application with Sprite animation working in no time flat. This application is different than the last three because it uses sprite animation and has a background bitmap.

1. Create a Visual C++ project named HandsOn8_4 with the following attributes:

   ❏ Single-document interface

   ❏ English language

   ❏ No database support

   ❏ No compound document support

   ❏ No automation or ActiveX control support

   ❏ 3D controls, but no other features

     ❏ No source file comments

     ❏ Link MFC as a static library

2. Select Settings from the Project menu. Choose the Link tab. Add the following libraries to the Object/library modules field. The libraries for the release and debug versions are different; both are listed below.

Release Project Libraries	Debug Project Libraries
ImageLoad.lib	ImageLoad.lib
ImageObject.lib	ImageObjectD.lib
Animation.lib	AnimationD.lib

3. Set the Active Configuration to Win32 Release.

4. Copy the file following files from the \ANIMATIO\SAMPLES directory on the Companion CD-ROM to the newly created project directory.

```
R1.BMP
R2.BMP
R3.BMP
R4.BMP
XINA.GIF
```

5. Add the following includes to the HandsOn8_4View.h file:

```
#include "Animation.h"
#include "ImageObject.h"
```

6. Add the following variable declarations to the CHandsOn8_4View class in the HandsOn8_4View.h file:

```
CAnimation *m_pAnimation;
CImageObject *m_pImage;
CBitmap m_Background;
```

7. Add the following code to the CHandsOn8_4View constructor:

```
CHandsOn8_4View::CHandsOn8_4View()
{

  m_pAnimation = NULL;
  m_pImage = NULL;

}
```

311

8. Add the following code to the CHandsOn8_4View destructor:

```
CHandsOn8_4View::~CHandsOn8_4View()
{

 if( m_pImage != NULL )
  delete m_pImage;
 if( m_pAnimation != NULL )
  delete m_pAnimation;

}
```

9. Edit the OnDraw function in the CHandsOn8_4View class in the HandsOn8_4View.cpp file as follows:

```
void CHandsOn8_4View::OnDraw(CDC* pDC)
{
 CHandsOn8_4Doc* pDoc = GetDocument();
 ASSERT_VALID(pDoc);

 if( m_pAnimation == NULL ){
  static char *szFilename[] = { "R1.BMP",
   "R2.BMP", "R3.BMP", "R4.BMP" };
  BeginWaitCursor();
  int *pnCoordinate = new int[50];
  int *pnFrameOrder = new int[25];
  DWORD *pdwPeriod = new DWORD[25];

  for( int i=0; i<25; i++ ){
   pnCoordinate[i*2] = 200;
   pnCoordinate[i*2+1] = 390 - i * 15;
   pnFrameOrder[i] = i & 3;
   pdwPeriod[i] = 300;
   }

  m_pAnimation =
   new CAnimation( pDC, szFilename, 4,
   pnCoordinate, pnFrameOrder, pdwPeriod, 25,
   SPRITE_ANIMATION, TRUE, 0 );

  delete [] pnCoordinate;
  delete [] pnFrameOrder;
  delete [] pdwPeriod;

  m_pImage = new CImageObject( "XINA.GIF" );
  m_Background.CreateCompatibleBitmap( pDC,
   m_pImage->GetWidth(),
```

```
   m_pImage->GetHeight() );
  CDC WorkDC;
  WorkDC.CreateCompatibleDC( pDC );
  CBitmap *pOldBitmap;
  pOldBitmap = (CBitmap *)
   WorkDC.SelectObject( &m_Background );
  m_pImage->Draw( &WorkDC );
  WorkDC.SelectObject( pOldBitmap );

  EndWaitCursor();
  }

 if( m_pImage != NULL ){
  m_pImage->SetPalette( pDC );
  m_pImage->Draw( pDC );
  }
 if( m_pAnimation != NULL )
  m_pAnimation->Redraw( pDC, &m_Background );

}
```

10. Add the following functions with the Class Wizard to the CHandsOn8_4View class in the HandsOn8_4View.h file:

```
Name:OnSetFocus()  Message:WM_SETFOCUS
Name:OnCreate()  Message:WM_CREATE
Name:OnTimer()  Message:WM_TIMER
```

11. Edit the OnSetFocus function in the CHandsOn8_4View class in the HandsOn8_4View.cpp file as follows:

```
void CHandsOn8_4View::OnSetFocus(CWnd* pOldWnd)
{
 if( m_pImage != NULL ){
  CClientDC ClientDC( this );
  m_pImage->SetPalette( &ClientDC );
  }
}
```

12. Edit the OnCreate function in the CHandsOn8_4View class in the HandsOn8_4View.cpp file as follows:

```
int CHandsOn8_4View::OnCreate(LPCREATESTRUCT lpCreateStruct)
{
  return -1;
```

313

```
SetTimer( 1, 100, NULL );

return 0;
}
```

13. Edit the OnTimer function in the CHandsOn8_4View class in the HandsOn8_4View.cpp file as follows:

```
void CHandsOn8_4View::OnTimer(UINT nIDEvent)
{
  if( m_pAnimation != NULL ){
   CClientDC ClientDC( this );
   m_pAnimation->Service( &ClientDC );
   }

  CView::OnTimer(nIDEvent);
}
```

14. Compile and run the program.

When the program runs, you'll see the cursor change to an hourglass shape as the images load. Then a picture of Xina will appear. On top of that, a rocket ship will move vertically. Figure 8-22 shows the application window.

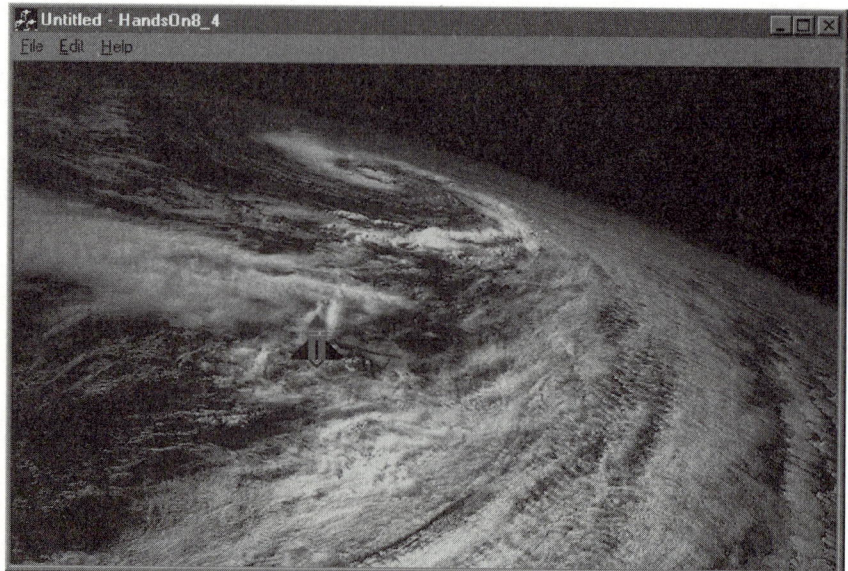

Figure 8-22: This hands-on exercise features a rocket that moves across an image of Xina.

On the Web

Animation is big at many Web sites. Just to give you a sampling, several are mentioned here. If you get the chance, visit them.

3D Animation

If you consider moving into the realm of 3D animation, the site shown in Figure 8-23 is for you. It's located at http://www.sbtech.com/model.htm. As you can see from the illustration, it specializes in 3D animation.

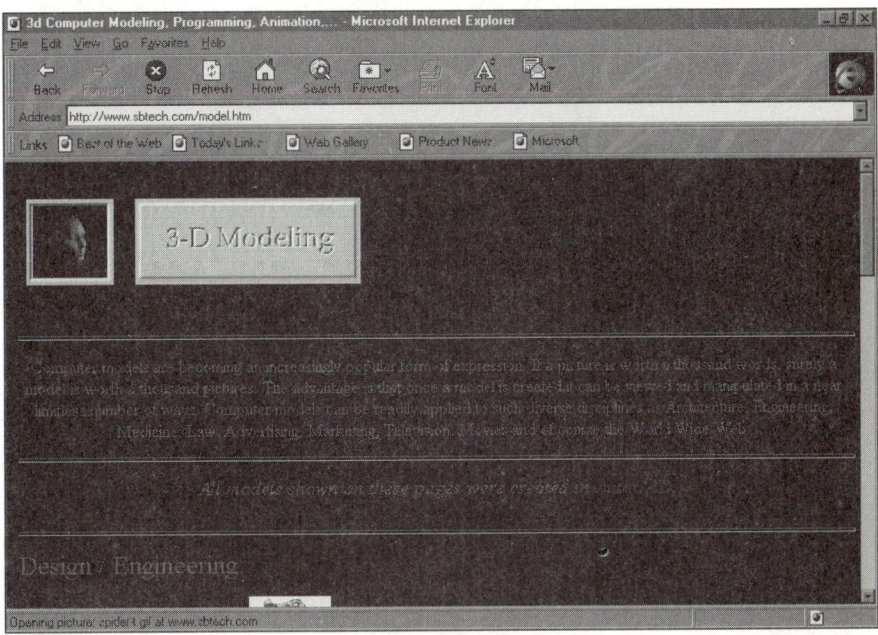

Figure 8-23: This site's specialty is 3D animation.

Animation Books

There's an extensive collection of books on the subject of computer animation located at http://intertain.com/store/new-browse/ Computers__Programming-Computer_animation.html (see Figure 8-24).

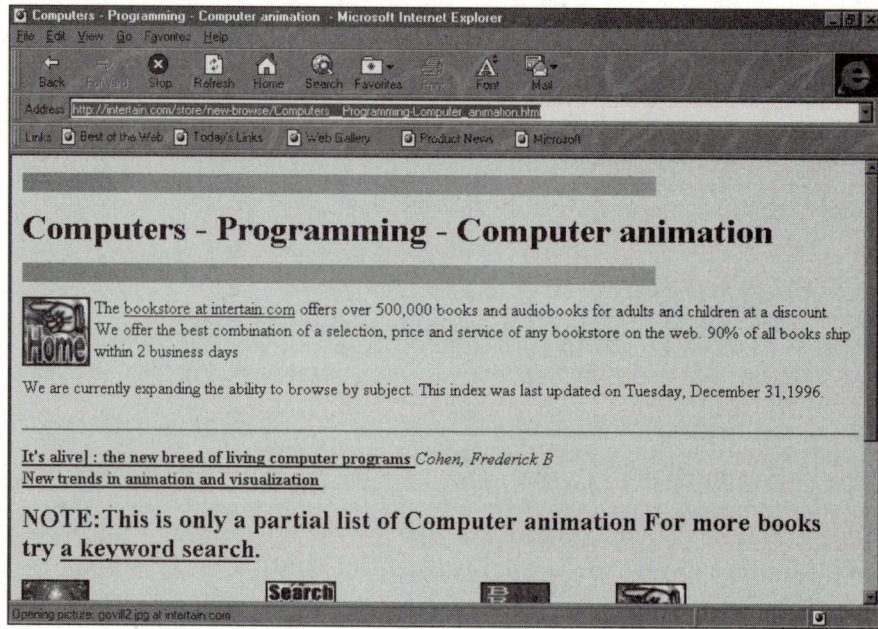

Figure 8-24: This site contains references to many books on computer animation.

SHAREWARE & COMMERCIAL DEMOS

There's a fast-animation library available for Windows programs. The company that publishes it, Ted Gruber Software, originally offered a DOS-only animation library. Now they've expanded to a Windows version.

As you can see from their demo version of Tetris in Figure 8-25, it's a complete package that enables fast graphics and animation.

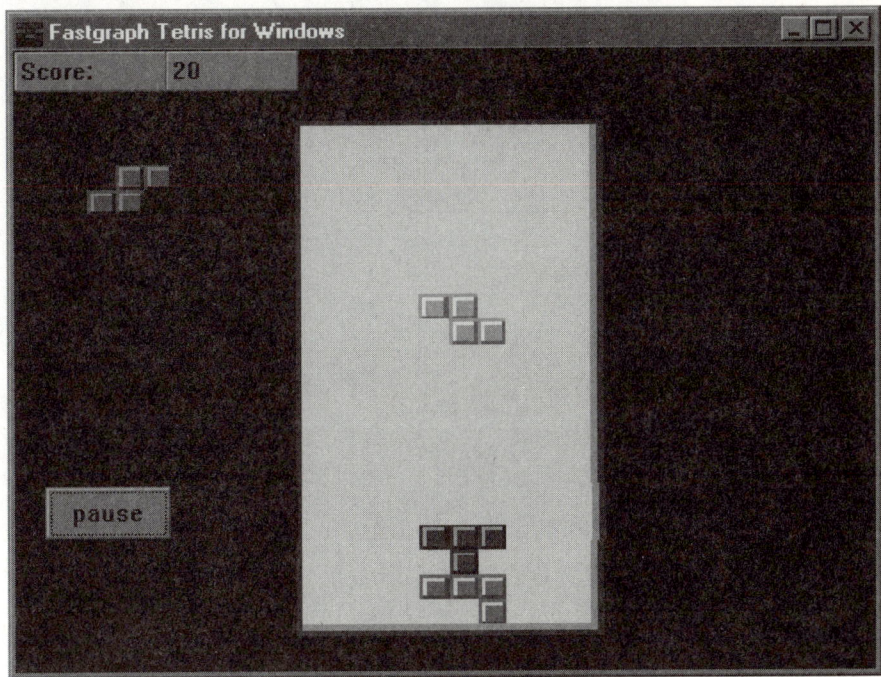

Figure 8-25: This demo of Tetris shows the capabilities of the Ted Gruber graphics and animation library.

The Media!Lab animation library may be the best there is. The demo shown in Figure 8-26 displays five animated objects in varying sizes. It's smooth and convincing, showing that the performance is very high.

Figure 8-26: This demo has five animations going simultaneously.

MOVING ON

In this chapter you've learned the basics of animation. You've seen the demo program that comes on the Companion CD-ROM, and you've learned about the animation class library. Use what you know to add animations to your applications. You'll communicate ideas and concepts much better, and you'll have a more attractive application.

Working through the five hands-on exercises will get you used to using the animation class library to the point where you can strike out on your own. Now get busy and create some great applications that have animations.

Chapter 9

Video

Never confuse motion with action.
–Ben Franklin

In previous chapters we covered Windows graphics and the basics of computer animation. Now we are ready to step it up a notch and enter the world of digitized video. We'll get to the heart of multimedia and provide you with the tools to add live action video and stunning graphics to your Visual C++ applications.

With the growing popularity of CD-ROM and increasingly faster processors, video is practically a requirement for acceptable multimedia applications. Video offers many advantages over traditional animation techniques. Digitized video animations can be much more detailed, even feature live footage—and without much loss in quality. With constantly improving compression ratios, video is improving in quality at the same time it's shrinking in file size.

When you are considering digitized video as an option for your applications, ask yourself what your users would prefer: a video of the President's inaugural address or the text from the speech, an actual clip from a movie or a page from the screenplay. I think the benefits speak for themselves.

Visual C++ 5 and the MFC have provided the developer with a control to easily play AVI files in your applications. Unfortunately, this control is severely limited and does not provide all of the functionality we need to create real multimedia. Luckily, though, Microsoft does provide support for playing AVI files in the Win32 SDK. We have taken advantage of this support to create a class library that is much easier for you to use and fits in with the MFC class structure. The Video class library that comes with this book along with the Windows multimedia library (WINMM.LIB) provided with Visual C++ 5 provide a quick and easy method for adding video to any Windows 95 or Windows NT application. Get ready to make your applications come alive with multimedia.

VIDEO FOR WINDOWS

Video for Windows utilizes digitized video in the Audio-Visual Interleaved (AVI) format. An AVI file interleaves waveform audio (in WAVE file format) and video data (in device-independent bitmap or DIB format).

An AVI file can be played in Windows with no additional hardware (of course, it will be smoother and faster with a video accelerator). Windows provides support for AVI files through the combination of the Video for Windows libraries and the Media Control Interface (MCI). The MCI will be revisited later in this book in the chapters on playing sound, MIDI, and CD audio.

Video for Windows Run Time

To play AVI files, your computer must have the Video for Windows run-time libraries installed on your system. Nearly every system shipped with Windows 95 already has this support. In case for some reason your computer does not have Video for Windows or AVI support, we have included them on the Companion CD-ROM in the VIDEO\VFW11D directory. Just unzip the file VFW.ZIP to your hard drive then run SETUP.EXE.

THE VIDEO CLASS LIBRARY

The Video class library can be linked with any Visual C++ 5 project (you must also link WINMM.LIB). Once you're all set up, you are ready to add digitized video to your multimedia applications. You don't need to know what's going on behind the scene—the class library will do all the work for you.

CD-ROM

The library offers much more than just the ability to play back digitized video. You can pause the playback, skip frame by frame through the video, change the speed of the playback, and play the video full-screen. If you want to examine the class library in detail or make changes to the member functions, the source code is included on the Companion CD-ROM.

All source code and support files to rebuild Video.lib can be found in the VIDEO\Video directory on the Companion CD-ROM that comes with this book.

THE VIDEOPLAYER DEMO

We've built a simple demonstration program that shows what the class library can do. The program can be found in the VIDEO\VideoPlayer directory on the Companion CD-ROM. Using File Manager or Program Manager, run the program named VideoPlayer.exe. It's a MDI program that loads and plays AVI files. When it first runs, you'll see an empty application. To get started, open the SAMPLE.AVI file included on the Companion CD-ROM.

Once the file is opened, the first frame of the video displays (see Figure 9-1). You can now play, pause, and stop the video, or even step through it frame by frame.

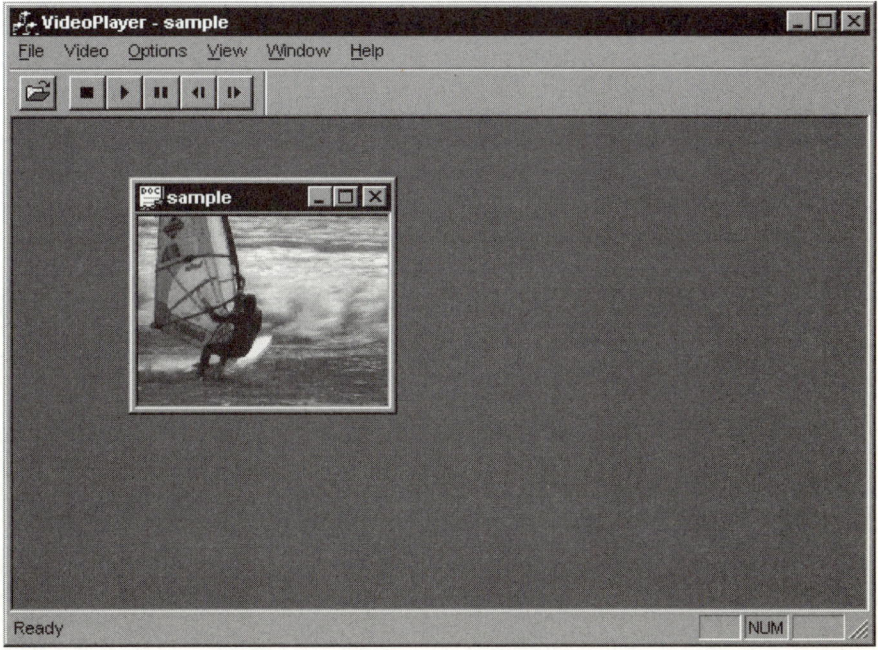

Figure 9-1: VideoPlayer playing an AVI file.

In addition to the standard playback features, VideoPlayer lets you modify the playback characteristics of the video. The Options menu allows you to loop the playback, toggle the audio on and off, and adjust the speed of playback. The normal playback speed is 1000. Speed values of 500 will play the video at half-speed and 2000 will play at double-speed (See Figure 9-2).

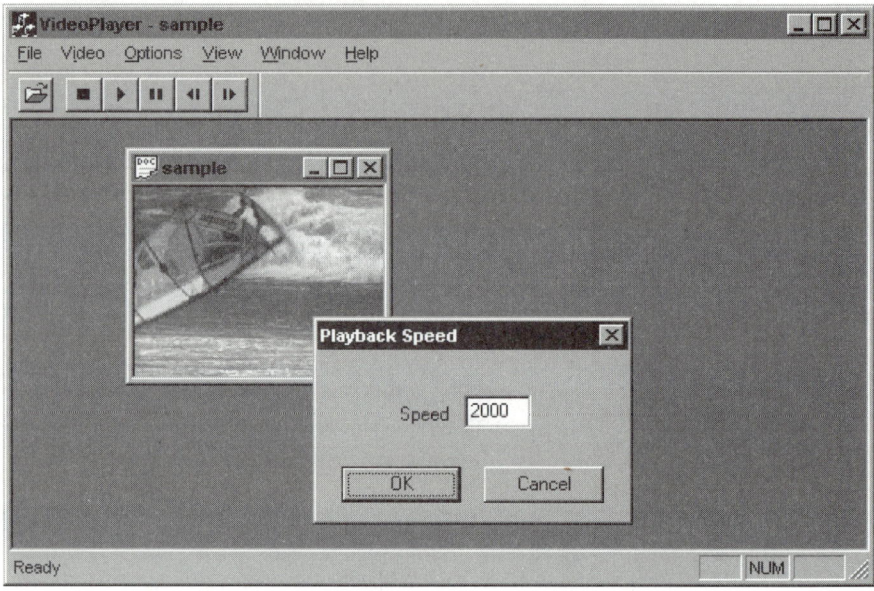

Figure 9-2: VideoPlayer lets you adjust the speed of video playback.

You will also find Full Screen playback under the Options menu. This selection plays the video in full-screen mode. The video mode returns to normal when the playback is complete (unless looping is activated) or when a mouse button or key is pressed.

PLAYING AVI FILES

The Microsoft API provides two different ways for playing AVI files. The MFC class CAnimateCtrl allows for very basic playback of AVI files with some strict limitations. This control can be used in some simple situations and will be covered in the next section. The second way to play an AVI file is through the Media Control Interface (MCI). This method has much better support for AVI playback and will be the backbone of our Video class library. We will also describe this method in more detail in the following sections.

CAnimateCtrl

The CAnimateCtrl class provides the functionality of the Windows common animation control. An animation control is a rectangular window that displays a clip in AVI format. Animation controls can play only simple AVI clips and are limited by the following requirements:

❏ There must be exactly one video stream and it must have at least one frame.

❏ There can be at most two streams in the file. The second stream is usually an audio stream, although CAnimateCtrl cannot play audio.

❏ The clip must either be uncompressed or compressed with RLE8 compression.

❏ No palette changes are allowed in the video stream.

The CAnimateCtrl is very simple to use and is especially useful for adding animations to dialog boxes. Once you create the control, it's as easy as calling the Open, Play, and Stop member functions. Windows 95 makes extensive use of this control within the operating system. For example, the Windows Explorer displays a moving magnifying glass as the system searches for a file and animates files as they are sent to the recycle bin.

The Media Control Interface

Using the functionality of the Media Control Interface, we have created the Video class library that makes playing AVI files as easy as using the CAnimateCtrl, without the restricted requirements. The MCI works directly with the Video for Windows drivers and allows for much greater control over the video playback. You can skip this section if you just want to use the Video library and are not concerned with how it works.

The MCI can be implemented with one of two functions: mciSendCommand() or mciSendString(). Although they both serve the same purpose and both produce the same result, they have different syntax. One uses a command-based interface and the other uses a string-based interface. We will only use mciSendCommand because the command-based interface should seem more logical to programmers accustomed to the Windows command-based API.

The mciSendCommand() function is used to communicate with the MCI device, either to send command messages (MCI_OPEN, MCI_PLAY) or to query for information (MCI_STATUS) on the device. The MCI command-based messaging interface allows for a lot of flexibility through the use of MCI parameter blocks. The parameter blocks are structures defined in MMSYSTEM.H that allow large amounts of information to be passed to and returned from the mciSendCommand() function.

323

mciSendCommand()

Prototype:
```
DWORD mciSendCommand (UINT wDeviceID, UINT wMessage, DWORD dwParam1,
    DWORD dwParam2);
```

Purpose: This function is the core of the MCI. It is used to do all communication with the MCI device.

Arguments: UINT wDeviceID, the device that receives the message
UINT wMessage, the MCI command message
DWORD dwParam1: specifies flags for the command
DWORD dwParam2: specifies a pointer to the parameter block to be used

Returns: Zero if successful, otherwise the low-order word contains an error

The MCI device ID identifies which device has been opened. This value is returned in the parameter block when you send the MCI_OPEN command and should be saved for later use. The ID is used to identify this device when sending subsequent commands. The following is a brief overview of the MCI commands that are relevant to AVI playback.

MCI Commands

MCI_OPEN	Opens the device.
MCI_CLOSE	Closes the device.
MCI_PLAY	Starts the video playback.
MCI_STOP	Stops the video playback.
MCI_PAUSE	Pauses the video playback.
MCI_SEEK	Seeks to a specific frame within the AVI file.
MCI_STEP	Steps through the video by a specific number of frames.
MCI_PUT	Positions the playback window within its parent.
MCI_WHERE	Determines the size and position of the playback window.
MCI_SET	Used with other flags described below.
MCI_STATUS	Used with other flags described below.

MCI_SET Flags

MCI_SET_TIME_FORMAT	Changes the time format: in this case we use frames to determine length and position.
MCI_SET_AUDIO	Toggles audio channels on and off.
MCI_DGV_SET_SPEED	Changes the speed of the playback. 1000 is the normal value. Therefore, 500 is half-speed and 2000 is double-speed.

MCI_STATUS Flags	
MCI_STATUS_LENGTH	Gets the length of the video in frames.
MCI_STATUS_MODE	Gets the current status of the video playback.
MCI_STATUS_POSITION	Gets the current frame of the video.
MCI_DGV_STATUS_AUDIO	Determines if the audio channels are on or off.
MCI_DGV_STATUS_SPEED	Gets the current speed of video playback.

Other File Formats

Many third-party developers offer MCI drivers that allow you to play files of different formats with the MCI commands.

 For example, Autodesk offers a driver and DLLs that allow you to play FLC and FLI files with the MCI functions. A flic player, the associated files, and instructions for using the driver are included on the Companion CD-ROM. The self-expanding file is called WINPLA.EXE and is in the VIDEO\Autodesk directory.

CVIDEO CLASS LIBRARY FUNCTION CALLS

This section is provided as a reference to the public function calls the CVideo class library offers. The calls are simple and should be easy to implement in your own programs.

You may want to skip over this section and read the section entitled "Behind VideoPlayer," which shows how the calls are used (for some people, it's better to look at the usage of function calls before actually studying the syntax).

CVideo()

Prototype: `CVideo (void);`

Purpose: This is the constructor. It simply creates a CVideo object and initializes its internal variables.

Arguments: None

Returns: Nothing

~CVideo()

Prototype: `~CVideo (void);`

Purpose: This is the destructor. It closes the MCI device if it has been opened.

Arguments: None

Returns: Nothing

Open()

Prototype: `BOOL Open (CString Filename, CWnd *pWnd, int nX = 0, int nY = 0);`

Purpose: This function opens the MCI device, sets the time format, seeks to the beginning of the video, and positions the playback window within the parent window.

Arguments: CString Filename
CWnd *pWnd, the parent window
int nX, Defaults to 0
int nY, Defaults to 0

Returns: BOOL: TRUE for success, FALSE for failure

Close()

Prototype: `void Close (void);`

Purpose: This function stops the playback and closes the MCI device.

Arguments: None

Returns: Nothing

Play()

Prototype: `BOOL Play (BOOL bLoop = FALSE, BOOL bFullScreen = FALSE);`

Purpose: This function plays the file from the current position. It can also loop the playback and play full-screen.

Arguments: BOOL bLoop, Defaults to FALSE
BOOL bFullScreen, Defaults to FALSE

Returns: BOOL: TRUE for success, FALSE for failure

Stop()

Prototype: `void Stop (void);`

Purpose: This function stops the playback and seeks back to the beginning of the file.

Arguments: None

Returns: Nothing

Pause()

Prototype: `void Pause (void);`

Purpose: This function pauses the file.

Arguments: None

Returns: Nothing

GetWidth()

Prototype: `int GetWidth (void)`

Purpose: This function returns the width of the video.

Arguments: None

Returns: int nWidth

GetHeight()

Prototype: `int GetHeight (void)`

Purpose: This function returns the height of the video.

Arguments: None

Returns: int nHeight

GetTotalFrames()

Prototype: `int GetTotalFrames (void);`

Purpose: This function returns the number of frames in the video.

Arguments: None

Returns: int nFrames

327

GetCurrentFrame()

Prototype: `int GetCurrentFrame (void);`

Purpose: This function returns the current frame of the video playback.

Arguments: None

Returns: int nFrame

IsPlaying()

Prototype: `BOOL IsPlaying (BOOL *bPaused);`

Purpose: This function returns the playing status and supplies the paused status in the first parameter. If the file is paused, IsPlaying() will still return TRUE.

Arguments: BOOL *bPaused

Returns: BOOL: TRUE if playing or paused, otherwise FALSE

SeekTo()

Prototype: `BOOL SeekTo (int nFrame);`

Purpose: This function seeks to a specific frame in the video. If the file was playing, it will automatically resume.

Arguments: int nFrame

Returns: BOOL: TRUE for success, FALSE for failure

SkipForward()

Prototype: `void SkipForward (int nFrames);`

Purpose: This function skips forward a specific number of frames. If the file was playing, it will be paused.

Arguments: int nFrames

Returns: Nothing

SkipBack()

Prototype: `void SkipBack (int nFrames);`

Purpose: This function skips back a specific number of frames. If the file was playing, it will be paused.

Arguments: int nFrames

Returns: Nothing

GetSpeed()

Prototype: `int GetSpeed (void);`

Purpose: This function returns the speed of the video playback. 1000 is the normal value.

Arguments: None

Returns: int nSpeed

SetSpeed()

Prototype: `void SetSpeed (int nSpeed);`

Purpose: This function changes the current speed of the video playback. A value of 500 is half-speed and 2000 is double-speed.

Arguments: int nSpeed

Returns: Nothing

GetSound()

Prototype: `BOOL GetSound (void);`

Purpose: This function returns the status of the audio channel.

Arguments: None

Returns: BOOL bSound, TRUE if on, otherwise FALSE

SetSound()

Prototype:	`void SetSound (BOOL bSound);`
Purpose:	This function sets the status of the audio channel.
Arguments:	BOOL bSound
Returns:	None

Behind VideoPlayer

VideoPlayer was created with the Visual C++ AppWizard with the following settings:

- ❏ Multiple-document interface
- ❏ English language
- ❏ No database support
- ❏ No compound document support
- ❏ No automation or ActiveX control support
- ❏ Docking toolbar, Initial status bar, and 3D controls
- ❏ Added "avi" as the File extension under Advanced Options
- ❏ Yes source file comments
- ❏ MFC linked as a static library

The basic functions for playing an AVI file are very easy to use. You must open the device before you use it and close it when you are done. In between, you can call any of the member functions you need. In this demo program, we will do this from within the functionality of a Multiple Document Interface (MDI) application.

Opening the File

Since this is an MDI application, opening a file is automatically handled by the framework of the program. We store our CVideo object in the CView class and name it m_Video. This way a CVideo object will automatically be created every time a new file (and Cview class) is opened. We use the CView::OnInitialUpdate() function to get the filename of the AVI file from the CDocument class and initialize our class object. We also use this opportunity to size the MDIChildFrame window to the size of the video.

```
void CVideoPlayerView::OnInitialUpdate()
{
 CView::OnInitialUpdate();

 CVideoPlayerDoc* pDoc = GetDocument();

 CString Filename = pDoc->GetPathName ();
 if (!Filename.IsEmpty ()){
  if (m_Video.Open(pDoc->GetPathName(),this)){
   int Width, Height, Border, Caption;
   Border = GetSystemMetrics (SM_CXSIZEFRAME);
   Caption = GetSystemMetrics (SM_CYCAPTION);
   Width = m_Video.GetWidth ();
   Height = m_Video.GetHeight ();
   CWnd *pWnd = GetParentFrame ();
   pWnd->SetWindowPos (NULL, 0, 0, Width +
    Border * 2, Height + Caption + Border * 2,
    SWP_NOZORDER | SWP_NOMOVE);
   }
  else{
   MessageBox ("Could not open the video.",
    "Error", MB_OK | MB_ICONSTOP);
   }
  }
 }
```

Member Functions

The rest of the functionality for the application takes place within the
CMainFrame class. All menu and toolbar commands are routed through
the CMainFrame message handler. The functions for each command
must obtain a pointer to the current CVideo class object. Once we get the
active MDIChildFrame window and its corresponding CView, we have
access to the m_Video object. (Believe it or not, that's the hard part.) Then
all we have to do is call the member functions for the command we want
to execute.

```
void CMainFrame::OnVideoStop()
{
 CMDIChildWnd *pChild =
  (CMDIChildWnd *) GetActiveFrame ();
 CVideoPlayerView *pView =
  (CVideoPlayerView *)pChild->GetActiveView();
```

```
   if (pView != NULL)
    pView->m_Video.Stop ();
  }

void CMainFrame::OnVideoPlay()
{
 CMDIChildWnd *pChild =
  (CMDIChildWnd *) GetActiveFrame ();
 CVideoPlayerView *pView =
  (CVideoPlayerView *)pChild->GetActiveView();

 if (pView != NULL)
  pView->m_Video.Play(m_bLoop, m_bFullScreen);
}

void CMainFrame::OnVideoPause()
{
 CMDIChildWnd *pChild =
  (CMDIChildWnd *) GetActiveFrame ();
 CVideoPlayerView *pView =
  (CVideoPlayerView *)pChild->GetActiveView();

 if (pView != NULL)
  pView->m_Video.Pause ();
}

void CMainFrame::OnVideoFrameback()
{
 CMDIChildWnd *pChild =
  (CMDIChildWnd *) GetActiveFrame ();
 CVideoPlayerView *pView =
  (CVideoPlayerView *)pChild->GetActiveView();

 if (pView != NULL)
  pView->m_Video.SkipBack (1);
}

void CMainFrame::OnVideoFrameforward()
{
 CMDIChildWnd *pChild =
  (CMDIChildWnd *) GetActiveFrame ();
 CVideoPlayerView *pView =
  (CVideoPlayerView *)pChild->GetActiveView();

 if (pView != NULL)
  pView->m_Video.SkipForward (1);
}
```

Playback Options

We also handle the additional playback options from within the CMainFrame class. Some of the commands, such as Loop and Full Screen, simply toggle a member variable that is used when the Play() function is called. While others, such as Speed and Sound, call member functions that adjust the playback characteristics.

```cpp
void CMainFrame::OnOptionsLoop()
{
    m_bLoop ^= 1;
}


void CMainFrame::OnOptionsFullscreen()
{
    m_bFullScreen ^= 1;
}

void CMainFrame::OnOptionsSpeed()
{
 CMDIChildWnd *pChild =
  (CMDIChildWnd *) GetActiveFrame ();
 CVideoPlayerView *pView =
  (CVideoPlayerView *)pChild->GetActiveView();

 CSpeed SpeedDlg;
 SpeedDlg.m_nSpeed= pView->m_Video.GetSpeed();

 if (SpeedDlg.DoModal () == IDOK)
  pView->m_Video.SetSpeed (SpeedDlg.m_nSpeed);
}

void CMainFrame::OnOptionsSound()
{
 CMDIChildWnd *pChild =
  (CMDIChildWnd *) GetActiveFrame ();
 CVideoPlayerView *pView =
  (CVideoPlayerView *)pChild->GetActiveView();

 if (pView != NULL){
  BOOL bSound = pView->m_Video.GetSound ();
  bSound ^= 1;
  pView->m_Video.SetSound (bSound);
  }
}
```

```
void CMainFrame::OnUpdateOptionsSound(CCmdUI* pCmdUI)
{
CMDIChildWnd *pChild =
 (CMDIChildWnd *) GetActiveFrame ();
CVideoPlayerView *pView =
 (CVideoPlayerView *)pChild->GetActiveView();

if (pView != NULL){
 BOOL bSound = pView->m_Video.GetSound ();
 pCmdUI->Enable (1);
 pCmdUI->SetCheck (bSound);
 }
else{
 pCmdUI->Enable (0);
 }
}
```

CREATING PROGRAMS THAT USE VIDEO

The following two hands-on exercises will get you started creating applications with the Video class library. Going through them won't take very long, and the investment of time will be well worth it.

You may be wondering why you should type in the code for each exercise—why not just load the project from disk? In my experience, you learn more by doing than just reading.

Each of these exercises is designed to be as simple as possible, so there is a limit to the amount of error-checking that is done. Under normal circumstances, the application should check to see if the functions succeed and provide feedback to the user.

 ## Hands-On 1: Playing an AVI File

In this first example, we demonstrate the absolute minimum amount of code needed to play an AVI file with the Video class library.

To play an AVI file we need a parent window in which to play the video. In this case we simply use the CView class created by the application framework as the parent and play the video in the upper left corner.

1. Create a Visual C++ project named HandsOn9_1 with the following attributes:

   ❏ Single-document interface

   ❏ English language

   ❏ No database support

   ❏ No compound document support

   ❏ No automation or ActiveX control support

   ❏ 3D controls, but no other features

   ❏ No source file comments

   ❏ Link MFC as a static library

2. Select Settings from the Project menu. Choose the Link tab. Add to the Object/library modules field the following libraries. The libraries for the release and debug versions are defferent. Both are listed below.

Release Project Libraries	Debug Project Libraries
Video.lib	VideoD.lib
winmm.lib	winmm.lib

3. Set the Active Configuration to Win32 Release.

4. Copy the file SAMPLE.AVI from the \VIDEO\Samples directory on the Companion CD-ROM to the newly created project directory.

5. Add the following include to the HandsOn9_1View.h file:

   ```
   #include "Video.h"
   ```

6. Add the following variable declaration to the CHandsOn9_1View class in the HandsOn9_1View.h file:

   ```
   public:
    CVideo m_Video;
   ```

7. Add a Video menu item with a Play submenu to the IDR_MAINFRAME menu resource as shown in Figure 9-3.

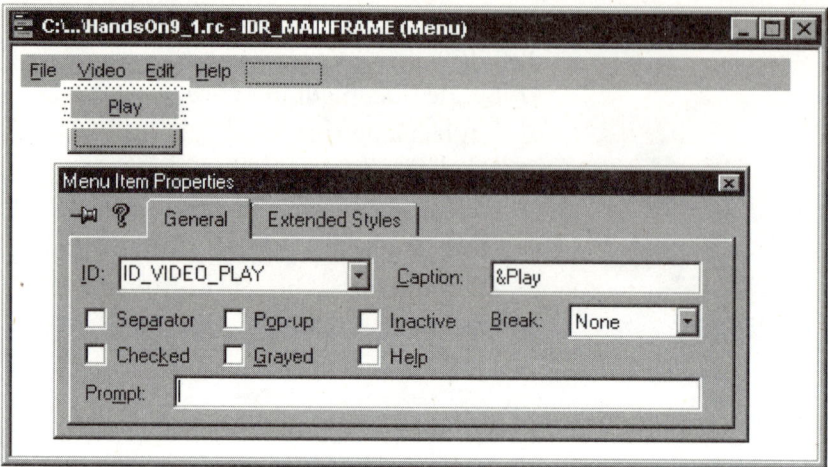

Figure 9-3: Edit the menu resource for the Hands-On 1 example.

8. Add the following functions with the Class Wizard to the CHandsOn9_1View class:

```
Name: OnInitialUpdate() Message: OnInitialUpdate
Name: OnVideoPlay() Message: WM_COMMAND
Menu ID: ID_VIDEO_PLAY
```

9. Edit the OnInitialUpdate() function in the CHandsOn9_1View class in the HandsOn9_1View.cpp file as follows:

```
void CHandsOn9_1View::OnInitialUpdate()
{
 CView::OnInitialUpdate();

 m_Video.Open ("sample.avi", this);
}
```

10. Edit the OnVideoPlay() function in the CHandsOn9_1View class in the HandsOn9_1View.cpp file as follows:

```
void CHandsOn9_1View::OnVideoPlay()
{
 m_Video.Play ();
}
```

11. Compile and run the program.

When the program runs, the first frame of the video is displayed in the view windows as shown in Figure 9-4. Select Play from the Video menu and watch the AVI file in action. It's as simple as that.

Figure 9-4: When the program runs, the first frame of the video is displayed.

There is a lot more you could do to improve this program. You could resize the view window to fit the video, or even center the video within the window. Also, you would probably want to take advantage of the built-in file structure to let you open different AVI files. As a good exercise, you could make the necessary additions to bring this simple hands-on example up to the level of the VideoPlayer demo discussed earlier in this chapter.

Hands-On 2: Video in an About Box

In this exercise, we add an AVI file to our About box. This gives your application a very nice touch and is extremely easy to do. This would be the ideal situation in which to use the CAnimateCtrl, but since we need to take advantage of an AVI with sound and a full color palette, we use the Video class library.

1. Create a Visual C++ project named HandsOn9_2 with the following attributes:
   - ❑ Single-document interface
   - ❑ English language
   - ❑ No database support
   - ❑ No compound document support
   - ❑ No automation or ActiveX control support
   - ❑ 3D controls, but no other features
   - ❑ No source file comments
   - ❑ Link MFC as a static library

2. Select Settings from the Project menu. Choose the Link tab. Add to the Object/library modules field the following libraries. The libraries for the release and debug versions are defferent. Both are listed below.

Release Project Libraries	Debug Project Libraries
Video.lib	VideoD.lib
winmm.lib	winmm.lib

3. Set the Active Configuration to Win32 Release.

4. Copy the file SAMPLE.AVI from the \VIDEO\Samples directory on the Companion CD-ROM to the newly created project directory.

5. Add the following include to the HandsOn9_2App.cpp file:

```
#include "Video.h"
```

6. Add the following variable declaration to the CAboutDlg class in the HandsOn9_2App.cpp file:

```
public:
 CVideo m_Video;
```

7. Edit the IDD_ABOUTBOX dialog resource to make room for the video, as shown in Figure 9-5.

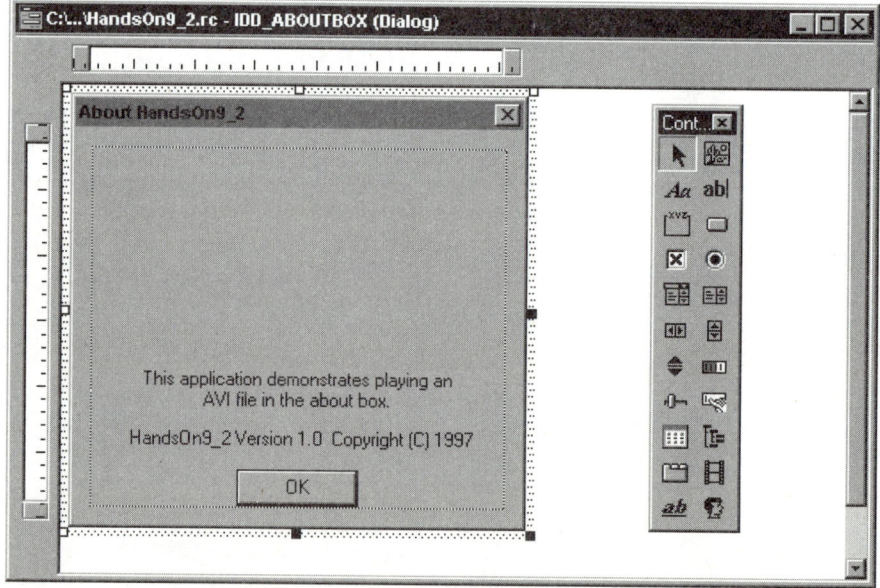

Figure 9-5: Edit the About dialog resource for the Hands-On 2 example.

8. Add the following functions with the Class Wizard to the CAboutDlg class:

   ```
   Name: OnInitDialog()  Message: WM_INITDIALOG
   ```

9. Edit the OnInitDialog() function in the CAboutDlg class in the CHandsOn9_2App.cpp file as follows:

   ```
   BOOL CAboutDlg::OnInitDialog()
   {
   CDialog::OnInitDialog();

   m_Video.Open ("sample.avi", this, 60, 15);
   m_Video.Play (TRUE);

   return TRUE;
   }
   ```

10. Compile and run the program.

Once the program runs, select About HandsOn9_2 from the Help menu. The About dialog will be displayed with the AVI file playing, as shown in Figure 9-6.

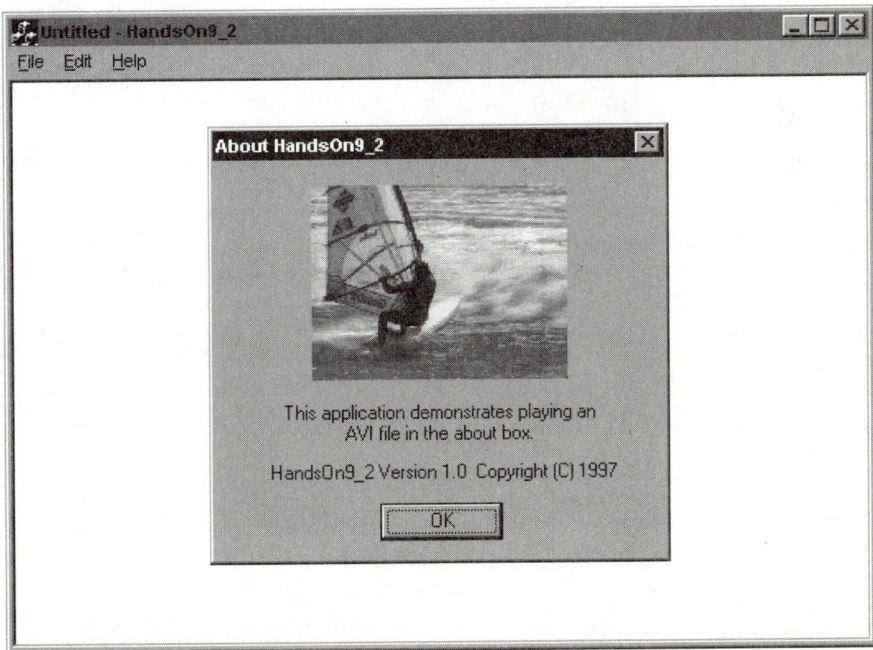

Figure 9-6: The About dialog will continuously loop the video playback.

ON THE WEB

If you searched the World Wide Web you could probably find anything you wanted pertaining to video and AVI files. To save you some time, though, we have picked out a few sites that you might find helpful. Have fun surfing.

CineWeb

www.digigami.com/cineweb

Digigami CineWeb lets users and developers play video over the Web (see Figure 9-7). The technology features streaming video, to relieve you of having to wait to see the results. CineWeb supports Video for Windows and other file formats.

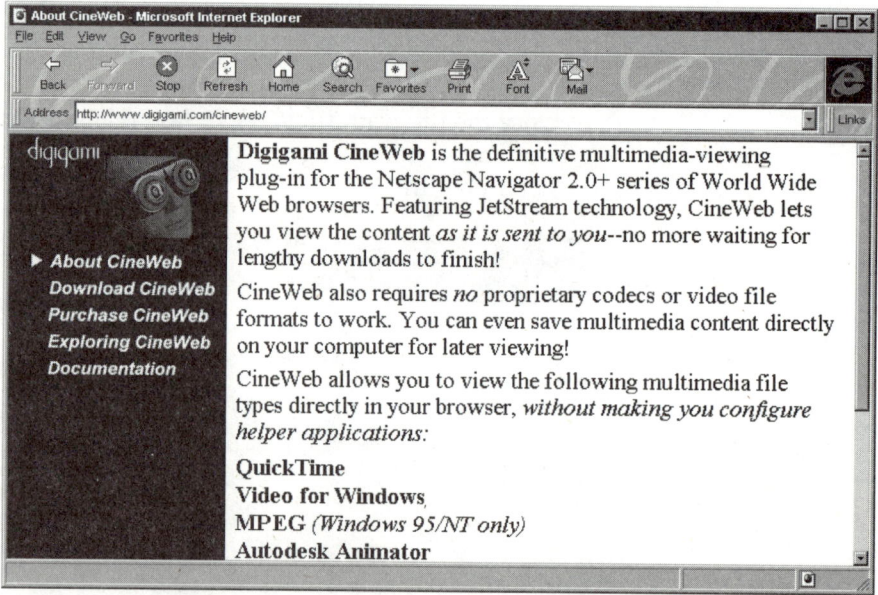

Figure 9-7: CineWeb lets you play video over the Internet.

Lenel

www.lenel.com/lenel

Lenel Systems International develops and markets advanced multimedia OCXs, VBXs, and development toolkits for Microsoft Visual Basic, Visual C++, Visual FoxPro, Access, Borland Delphi, Powerbuilder, and virtually any Microsoft Windows, Windows 95, and Windows NT development environment.

Metagraphics

www.metagraphics.com

Metagraphics offers the MEDIA!LAB multimedia animation graphics programming toolkits for Windows from their Web site. If you're looking for high-performance graphics programming tools, this is the spot.

Hyperionics

www.hyperionics.com

HyperCam, by Hyperionics, captures the action from Win 95 or NT screens in any graphics mode, including cursor movements and sound, and saves it to standard AVI movie files. This is a great application for creating demonstrations, presentations, and tutorials (see Figure 9-8).

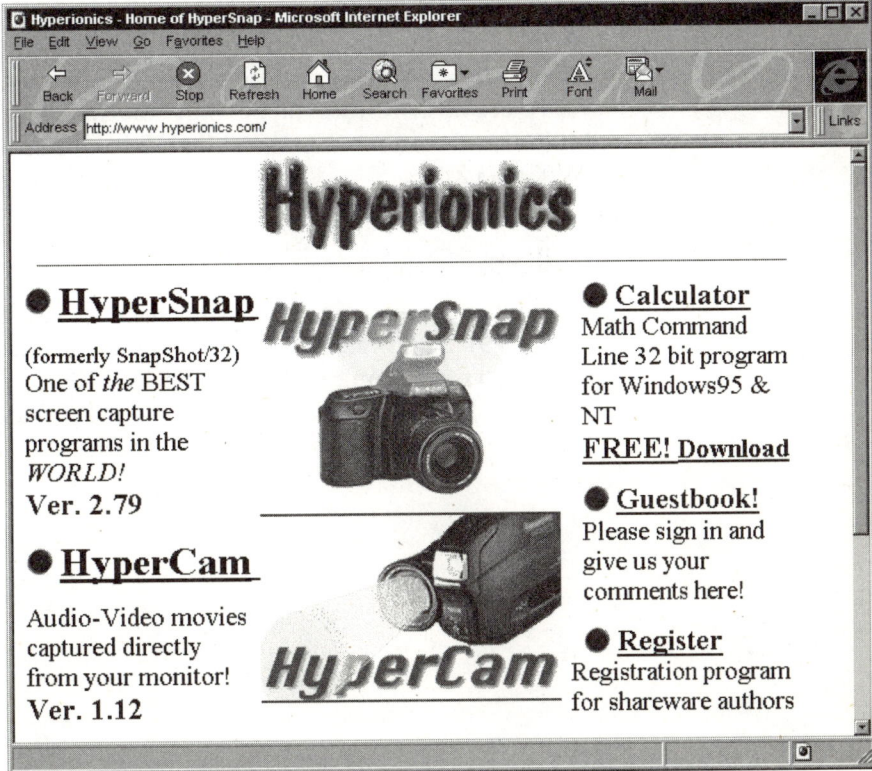

Figure 9-8: The Hyperionics home page.

Video & Animation Tools

www.windows95.com/apps/video.html

This site has a great list of shareware, freeware, demos, and Web sites devoted to video and animation. This page offers many useful utilities and tools.

SHAREWARE & COMMERCIAL DEMOS

If you don't have access to the World Wide Web but can log on to CompuServe or America Online, we have included a few locations where you can find files that may be helpful. Here are some examples of what we found.

AVI Constructor

AVI Constructor allows you to create an AVI file from a series of bitmaps. This is a great way to create your own AVI files for your own applications. This piece of shareware can be found on CompuServe in the Windows Multimedia Forum's (GO WINMM) Video for Windows library. The file is AVIC1495.ZIP.

AviLxp

AviLxp is a shareware video player that offers a lot of functionality (see Figure 9-9). It allows you to zoom AVI files, change the playback attributes, and much more. You can find the file AVILXP.ZIP on CompuServe in the Windows Multimedia Forum's (GO WINMM) Video for Windows library.

Figure 9-9: AviLxp is a shareware video player with many features.

WinHelp

This is a demo of a WinHelp extension library that lets you play video and audio in your Windows Help files. The file is called WHDEMO.ZIP and can be found on America Online. To find the file and others that may interest you, go to the PC Development Forum, enter Software Libraries, and select Windows Development.

MOVING ON

This chapter is just the beginning of the long road toward creating great multimedia applications. In later chapters we will add sound, MIDI, and CD audio to our multimedia arsenal. Pretty soon, you will be creating great-looking and great-sounding professional programs. You can use video to add a nice touch to any program, or you can base whole applications on digital video—either way, we have provided you with an easy way to add that functionality to your own work.

I'm always interested in seeing what other developers do using these libraries as a starting point. If you come up with a great application, some useful modifications to the library, or even just a couple of questions you want to ask, feel free to contact me at ivt-rcl@interpath.com.

Chapter 10

Using the Class Library in Applications

Some programmers have class, but C++
programmers always use their class.
—*Mike Martin*

This chapter is different than every other chapter in the book. It takes class libraries that we've covered in previous chapters and shows you how to use them in other ways than the examples already given. This chapter is no less important than earlier chapters. As a matter of fact, you might find yourself coming back to this chapter more often than the others because it shows you how to use the class libraries in combination with each other and in combination with many of the features that Visual C++ 5 has to offer.

We start things off with printing images on the printer. Application backgrounds are a great place to use images. You can tile or center an image in a view window or an MDI application's frame window. Two programs show you how.

Putting images into the clipboard and retrieving images from the clipboard are the next subjects. This can be important if you're writing a paint program or an image manipulation program. Many times it is convenient to capture the screen (by pressing the PrintScrn key, which sends the image into the clipboard) then use it as an image.

PRINTING IMAGES

This section on printing images to the printer starts out slow. The first thing you'll do is print "Hello Printer World!" This simple program is modified to print a single image. You'll then make changes that scale the image to fit the entire page. Finally, you'll print four images on one piece of paper.

Hands-On 1: Printing Simple Text to the Printer

This is the warmup exercise. In it you'll simply send the text "Hello Printer World" to the printer. It's the easiest way of showing you how to print without getting bogged down in details.

If you want to review image loading, consult Chapter 1. It teaches you how to use the CImageObject class to load, display, and manipulate images.

1. Create a Visual C++ project named HelloPrinter with the following attributes:

   ❒ Single-document interface
   ❒ English language
   ❒ No database support
   ❒ No compound document support
   ❒ No automation or ActiveX control support
   ❒ Printing and Print Preview, and 3D controls, but no other features
   ❒ No source file comments
   ❒ Link MFC as a shared DLL

2. Add an OnPrint() function to the CHelloPrinterView class with the Class Wizard.

3. Edit the OnPrint() function in the HelloPrinterView.cpp file as follows:

```
void CHelloPrinterView::OnPrint(CDC* pDC, CPrintInfo* pInfo)
{

pDC->TextOut( 0, 0, "Hello Printer World!",
 20 );

CView::OnPrint(pDC, pInfo);
}
```

4. Compile and run the program.

When the program first runs, you'll see just a blank view window. Go to the File menu and select Print. Your printer's setup dialog box will appear and allow you to make changes to the printer settings. Click OK and then a sheet of paper will be printed. On the paper will be the text "Hello Printer World!"

Hands-On 2: Loading, Displaying & Printing an Image

This exercise loads an image then allows you to print it. It relies on the ImageObject class library for the imaging functions. The image will appear in the view window letting you know that it's been loaded.

Instead of creating a new project, you'll use the project from the HandsOn10_1 exercise and modify it. The instructions for making the changes follow.

1. Select Settings from the Project menu. Choose the Link tab. Add the following libraries to the Object/library modules field. The libraries for the release and debug versions are different; both are listed below.

Release Project Libraries	Debug Project Libraries
ImageLoad.lib	ImageLoad.lib
ImageObject.lib	ImageObjectD.lib

2. Copy the file PIC1.BMP from the \images\samples directory on the Companion CD-ROM to the HelloPrinter project directory.

3. Add the following include to the HelloPrinterView.h file:

    ```
    #include "ImageObject.h"
    ```

4. Add the following variable declaration to the CHelloPrinterView class in the HelloPrinterView.h file:

    ```
    CImageObject *m_pImage;
    ```

5. Add the following code to the CHelloPrinterView constructor:

    ```
    m_pImage = NULL;
    ```

6. Add the following code to the CHelloPrinterView destructor:

    ```
    if( m_pImage != NULL )
      delete m_pImage;
    ```

7. Edit the OnDraw function in the CHelloPrinterView class in the HelloPrinterView.cpp file as follows:

```
void CHelloPrinterView::OnDraw(CDC* pDC)
{
CHelloPrinterDoc* pDoc = GetDocument();
ASSERT_VALID(pDoc);

if( m_pImage == NULL )
 m_pImage = new CImageObject( "PIC1.BMP" );

if( m_pImage != NULL ){
 m_pImage->SetPalette( pDC );
 m_pImage->Draw( pDC );
 }

}
```

8. Edit the OnPrint() function in the HelloPrinterView.cpp file as follows:

```
void CHelloPrinterView::OnPrint(CDC* pDC, CPrintInfo* pInfo)
{

pDC->TextOut( 0, 0, "Hello Printer World!",
 20 );

CView::OnPrint(pDC, pInfo);
}
```

9. Compile and run the program.

When the program runs, you'll see the image appear in the view window, as shown in Figure 10-1.

When you print, the image is sent to the printer. If your printer has a fairly high density such as 300 dots per inch (dpi) or greater, the image will be very small on the screen. Figure 10-2 shows you what you might see if you printer to a laser printer with a high density.

Figure 10-1: The image is displayed in the view window.

Figure 10-2: The image will be small on the paper if your printer has a high resolution, as most laser printers have.

Hands-On 3: Expanding the Image

The ImageObject library has a function built in that can resize an image. This exercise takes the small image from the previous exercise and stretches it to a size that's four times larger. This image is then sent to the printer, and the resulting image on the piece of paper is much larger.

As with the second exercise, this exercise uses the same HelloPrinter code. Use the same project you ended up with in the second exercise and modify the OnPrint function as follows:

```
void CHelloPrinterView::OnPrint(CDC* pDC, CPrintInfo* pInfo)
{

CImageObject *pImage = new CImageObject();
*pImage = *m_pImage;
pImage->Stretch( m_pImage->GetWidth() * 4,
 m_pImage->GetHeight() * 4 );
pImage->Draw( pDC );
delete pImage;

CView::OnPrint(pDC, pInfo);
}
```

When the program first runs, it'll look the same as it did in the second exercise. But when you print, the image will be much larger, as shown in Figure 10-3. If your printer doesn't have enough memory and you get a buffer overrun error, reduce the multiplication factor from four to three.

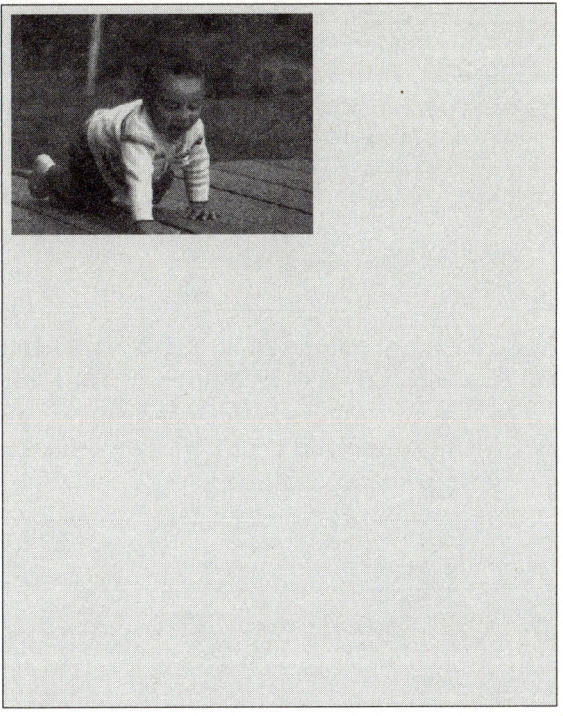

Figure 10-3: You can make an image larger with the built-in Stretch() function of the ImageObject library.

Hands-On 4: Centering the Expanded Image

Centering the expanded image on the paper may be something you'd like to do. This exercise is exactly the same as the last one except that it centers the image on the paper.

As with the third exercise, this exercise uses the same HelloPrinter code. Use the same project you ended up with in the second exercise and modify the OnPrint function as follows:

```
void CHelloPrinterView::OnPrint(CDC* pDC, CPrintInfo* pInfo)
{

CImageObject *pImage = new CImageObject();
*pImage = *m_pImage;
pImage->Stretch( m_pImage->GetWidth() * 4,
 m_pImage->GetHeight() * 4 );
int nX = ( pInfo->m_rectDraw.right -
```

```
    pInfo->m_rectDraw.left ) / 2;
  int nY = ( pInfo->m_rectDraw.bottom -
  pInfo->m_rectDraw.top ) / 2;
  pImage->Draw( pDC,
    nX - ( pImage->GetWidth() / 2 ),
    nY - ( pImage->GetHeight() / 2 ) );
  delete pImage;

  CView::OnPrint(pDC, pInfo);
}
```

When the program first runs, it'll look the same as it did in the third hands-on exercise. This time, though, it'll be centered on the sheet of paper, as shown in Figure 10-4. Once again, if your printer doesn't have enough memory and you get a buffer overrun error, reduce the multiplication factor from four to three.

Figure 10-4: You can make an image larger with the built-in Stretch() function of the ImageObject library, and then center it using some simple math.

Hands-On 5: Loading, Displaying & Printing Multiple Images

It's unlikely that applications you write will print a single image on one sheet of paper. Most programs need the capability to send multiple images to a single sheet of paper.

This exercise loads four images and displays them in the view window. They're not displayed so that each one can be seen distinctly. Instead, they overlap each other. They're only displayed so you can tell that all four images have been loaded, as shown in Figure 10-5.

Figure 10-5: The only reason the program displays all four images is so that you know they've all been loaded.

As with the previous exercises, modify the existing HelloPrinter program code to produce this version of the program. The steps to modify the program follow:

1. Copy the following files from the \images\samples directory on the Companion CD-ROM to the HelloPrinter project directory:

   ❏ PIC2.BMP

   ❏ PIC3.BMP

   ❏ PIC4.BMP

2. Change the variable declarations to the following in the CHelloPrinterView class in the HelloPrinterView.h file:

```
CImageObject *m_pImage[4];
```

3. Edit the following code in the CHelloPrinterView constructor:

```
for( int i=0; i<4; i++ )
 m_pImage[i] = NULL;
```

4. Edit the following code in the CHelloPrinterView destructor:

```
for( int i=0; i<4; i++ )
 if( m_pImage[i] != NULL )
  delete m_pImage[i];
```

5. Edit the OnDraw function in the CHelloPrinterView class in the HelloPrinterView.cpp file as follows:

```
void CHelloPrinterView::OnDraw(CDC* pDC)
{
CHelloPrinterDoc* pDoc = GetDocument();
ASSERT_VALID(pDoc);

char *szFilename[] = { "PIC1.BMP",
 "PIC2.BMP", "PIC3.BMP", "PIC4.BMP" };

int i;
for( i=0; i<4; i++ )
 if( m_pImage[i] == NULL )
  m_pImage[i] =
   new CImageObject( szFilename[i] );

for( i=0; i<4; i++ ){
 if( m_pImage[i] != NULL ){
  m_pImage[i]->SetPalette( pDC );
  m_pImage[i]->Draw( pDC, i * 20, i * 20 );
  }
 }

}
```

6. Edit the OnPrint() function in the HelloPrinterView.cpp file as follows:

```
void CHelloPrinterView::OnPrint(CDC* pDC, CPrintInfo* pInfo)
{

 for( int i=0; i<4; i++ ){
  if( m_pImage[i] != NULL ){
   CImageObject *pImage = new CImageObject();
   *pImage = *m_pImage[i];
   pImage->Stretch( m_pImage[i]->GetWidth()*2,
    m_pImage[i]->GetHeight() * 2 );
   int nWidth = ( pInfo->m_rectDraw.right -
    pInfo->m_rectDraw.left ) / 2;
   int nX = ( i % 2 ) * nWidth + (nWidth / 2);
   int nHeight = ( pInfo->m_rectDraw.bottom -
    pInfo->m_rectDraw.top ) / 2;
   int nY = ( i / 2 ) * nHeight + (nHeight/2);
   pImage->Draw( pDC,
    nX - ( pImage->GetWidth() / 2 ),
    nY - ( pImage->GetHeight() / 2 ) );
   delete pImage;
   }
  }

 CView::OnPrint(pDC, pInfo);
}
```

7. Compile and run the program.

When the program runs, you'll see the overlapped images as you saw in Figure 10-5. When you print, all four images will be sent to the printer. Before they're sent, they're all doubled in size vertically and horizontally. The images are then centered inside of each quadrant of the sheet of paper. Figure 10-6 shows what you'll see when you run this program and print.

Figure 10-6: All four images will be sent to the printer.

Using Images for Application Backgrounds

The next two exercises use images for application backgrounds. The first uses an image for a single-document interface program's view window. The second uses an image for a multiple-document interface program's frame window. Both are techniques that you'll find handy for enhancing the appearance of your programs.

Hands-On 6: Using an Image for a View Window's Background

This application loads in a single image. Inside of the OnDraw() function, the program looks to determine the size of the view window's client rectangle (that's the area inside of the window's borders).

If the size of the image is different from the size of the client rectangle, a new image is created and the size is changed so that it fits the view window exactly. The image will rarely have its original aspect ratio because users will resize the view window without regard for the aspect ratio of the background image. Figure 10-7 shows the background image in a view window that's fairly wide but very short.

Figure 10-7: This view window makes the background image become flattened.

If you make the window width very narrow and the window height somewhat high, you'll get a skinny image. Figure 10-8 shows the view window with a tall, skinny image.

Figure 10-8: The image can be tall and skinny instead of short and wide.

357

The steps for creating the ViewBackground project follow:

1. Create a Visual C++ project named ViewBackground with the following attributes:

   ❏ Single-document interface
   ❏ English language
   ❏ No database support
   ❏ No compound document support
   ❏ No automation or ActiveX control support
   ❏ 3D controls, but no other features
   ❏ No source file comments
   ❏ Link MFC as a shared DLL

2. Select Settings from the Project menu. Choose the Link tab. Add the following libraries to the Object/library modules field. The libraries for the release and debug versions are different; both are listed below.

Release Project Libraries	Debug Project Libraries
ImageLoad.lib	ImageLoad.lib
ImageObject.lib	ImageObjectD.lib

3. Copy the file PIC5.BMP from the \images\samples directory on the Companion CD-ROM to the newly created project directory.

4. Add the following include to the ViewBackgroundView.h file:

```
#include "ImageObject.h"
```

5. Add the following variable declarations to the CViewBackgroundView class in the ViewBackgroundView.h file:

```
CImageObject *m_pImage;
CImageObject *m_pDisplayImage;
```

6. Add the following code to the CViewBackgroundView constructor:

```
m_pImage = NULL;
m_pDisplayImage = NULL;
```

7. Add the following code to the CViewBackgroundView destructor:

```
if( m_pImage != NULL )
 delete m_pImage;

if( m_pDisplayImage != NULL )
 delete m_pDisplayImage;
```

8. Edit the OnDraw function in the CViewBackgroundView class in the ViewBackgroundView.cpp file as follows:

```
void CViewBackgroundView::OnDraw(CDC* pDC)
{
 CViewBackgroundDoc* pDoc = GetDocument();
 ASSERT_VALID(pDoc);

 if( m_pImage == NULL ){
  m_pImage = new CImageObject( "PIC5.BMP" );
  m_pDisplayImage = new CImageObject();
  if( m_pDisplayImage != NULL )
   *m_pDisplayImage = *m_pImage;
  }

 if( m_pDisplayImage != NULL ){
  RECT Rect;
  GetClientRect( &Rect );
  int nWidth = Rect.right - Rect.left;
  int nHeight = Rect.bottom - Rect.top;
  if( nWidth != m_pDisplayImage->GetWidth() ||
   nHeight != m_pDisplayImage->GetHeight() ){
   delete m_pDisplayImage;
   m_pDisplayImage = new CImageObject();
   if( m_pDisplayImage != NULL ){
    *m_pDisplayImage = *m_pImage;
    m_pDisplayImage->Stretch(nWidth, nHeight);
    }
   pDC->SelectClipRgn( NULL );
   }
  if( m_pDisplayImage != NULL ){
   m_pDisplayImage->SetPalette( pDC );
   m_pDisplayImage->Draw( pDC );
   }
  }

 }
```

9. Compile and run the program.

When the program runs, you'll see the sunset image appear in the view window. As you resize the view window, you'll see the width and height of the image change.

Hands-On 7: Using an Image to Tile a Frame Window's Background

This exercise takes an image and uses it to tile the background of a CMainFrame window. The image is resized before it's used because you won't want to tile a large image.

This program has a multiple-document interface. You can open as many windows as you have memory for. Under the windows, the tiled image will be drawn as shown in Figure 10-9.

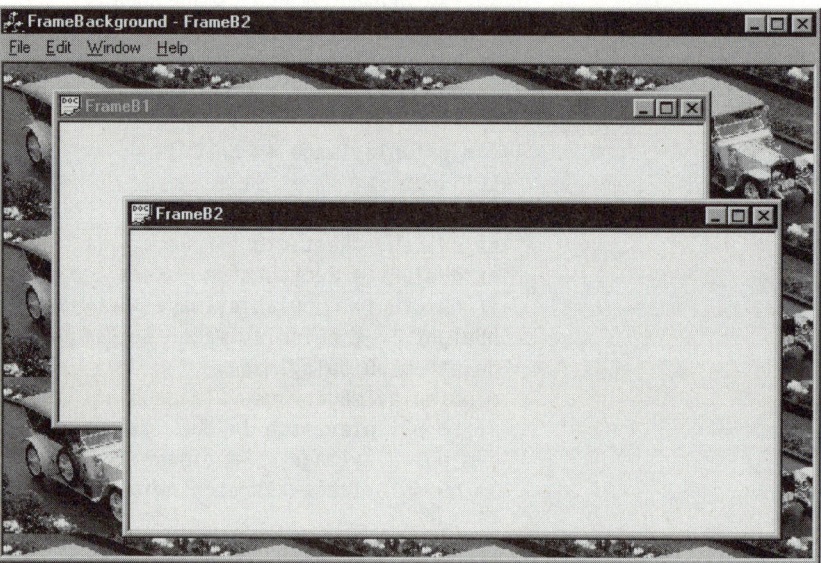

Figure 10-9: This program has an image that's used to tile the CMainFrame window.

The steps to create the program follow:

1. Create a Visual C++ project named FrameBackground with the following attributes:
   - ❏ Multiple-document interface
   - ❏ English language
   - ❏ No database support
   - ❏ No compound document support
   - ❏ No automation or ActiveX control support
   - ❏ 3D controls, but no other features
   - ❏ No source file comments
   - ❏ Link MFC as a shared DLL

2. Select Settings from the Project menu. Choose the Link tab. Add the following libraries to the Object/library modules field. The libraries for the release and debug versions are different. Both are listed below.

Release Project Libraries	Debug Project Libraries
ImageLoad.lib	ImageLoad.lib
ImageObject.lib	ImageObjectD.lib

3. Copy the file PIC9.BMP from the \image\samples directory on the Companion CD-ROM to the newly created project directory.

4. With the Class Wizard, add a class named CFrameClient that's derived from CWnd. Save the code to client.cpp and the include to client.h.

5. Add the following include to client.h:

```
#include "ImageObject.h"
```

6. Add the following variable and function declarations to client.h:

```
virtual WNDPROC* GetSuperWndProcAddr (void);
CImageObject *m_pImage;
```

7. Edit the CFrameClient constructor in the client.cpp file to the following:

```
m_pImage =
 new CImageObject( "PIC9.BMP" );
if( m_pImage != NULL )
 m_pImage->Stretch( 153, 115 );
```

8. Edit the CFrameClient destructor in the client.cpp file to the following:

```
if( m_pImage != NULL )
 delete m_pImage;
```

9. Add the following function to the CFrameClient class in the client.cpp file:

```
WNDPROC *CFrameClient::GetSuperWndProcAddr()
{

 static WNDPROC NEAR pfnSuper = NULL;

 return( &pfnSuper );

}
```

361

10. Add the following function with the Class Wizard to the CFrameClient class:

   Name: OnEraseBkgnd() Message: WM_ERASEBKGND

11. Edit the OnEraseBkgnd() function in the CFrameClient class in the client.cpp file as follows:

```
BOOL CFrameClient::OnEraseBkgnd(CDC* pDC)
{

 if( m_pImage == NULL )
  return( CWnd::OnEraseBkgnd( pDC ) );

 int nWidth, nHeight;
 int x, y = 0;
 RECT Rect;
 GetClientRect( &Rect );

 nWidth = m_pImage->GetWidth();
 nHeight = m_pImage->GetHeight();

 while( y < Rect.bottom ){
  x = 0;
  while( x < Rect.right ){
   m_pImage->Draw( pDC, x, y );
   x += nWidth;
   }
  y += nHeight;
  }

 return TRUE;

}
```

12. Add the following include to MainFrm.h:

   ```
   #include "client.h"
   ```

13. Add the following variable to MainFrm.h:

   ```
   CFrameClient mFrameClient;
   ```

14. Add the following function with the Class Wizard to the CMainFrame class:

   Name: OnCreate() Message: WM_CREATE

15. Edit the OnCreate function in the CMainFrame class in the MAINFRM.CPP file as follows:

```
int CMainFrame::OnCreate(LPCREATESTRUCT lpCreateStruct)
{
  return -1;

  mFrameClient.SubclassWindow(m_hWndMDIClient);

  return 0;
}
```

16. Compile and run the program.

When the application runs, you'll see the image drawn in the CMainFrame window. You can open additional child windows and move them around. The background image will be drawn automatically.

GETTING AN IMAGE FROM THE CLIPBOARD

This exercise takes the bitmap data from the clipboard and loads it into a CImageObject class. When the program runs, there won't be any child windows visible. If you select New from the File menu, a new child window will be created with any bitmap data that's in the clipboard.

Figure 10-10 shows the program when it's running. You can open as many child windows as your computer has memory for.

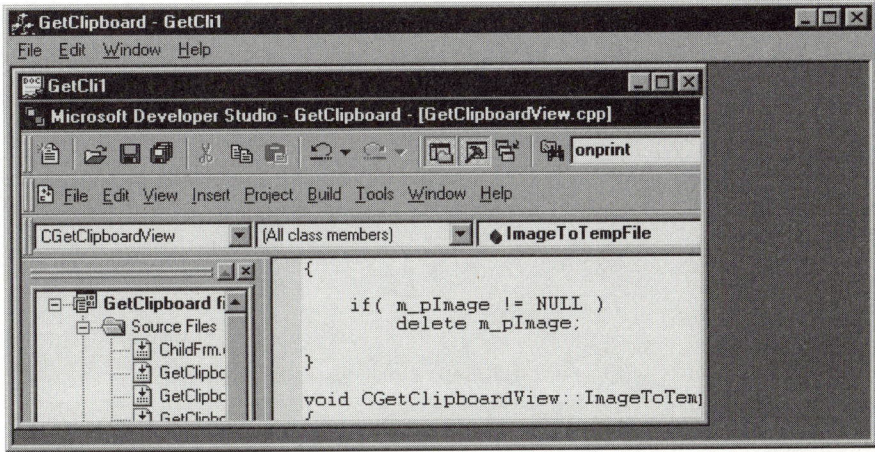

Figure 10-10: When you create a new child window, the bitmap data in the clipboard is loaded into the child window.

Hands-On 8: Copying an Image From the Clipboard

All of the steps to create this application follow.

1. Create a Visual C++ project named GetClipboard with the following attributes:

   ❒ Multiple-document interface

   ❒ English language

   ❒ No database support

   ❒ No compound document support

   ❒ No automation or ActiveX control support

   ❒ 3D controls, but no other features

   ❒ No source file comments

   ❒ Link MFC as a shared DLL

2. Select Settings from the Project menu. Choose the Link tab. Add the following libraries to the Object/library modules field. The libraries for the release and debug versions are different; both are listed below.

Release Project Libraries	Debug Project Libraries
ImageLoad.lib	ImageLoad.lib
ImageObject.lib	ImageObjectD.lib

3. Comment the following code out in the GetClipboard.cpp file:

```
// Parse command line for standard shell
// commands, DDE, file open
//  CCommandLineInfo cmdInfo;
//  ParseCommandLine(cmdInfo);

// Dispatch commands specified on the command
// line
//  if (!ProcessShellCommand(cmdInfo))
//    return FALSE;
```

4. Add the following include to the GetClipboardView.h file:

```
#include "ImageObject.h"
```

5. Add the following variable declaration to the CGetClipboardView class in the GetClipboardView.h file:

```
CImageObject *m_pImage;
```

6. Add the following code to the CGetClipboardView constructor:

```
ImageToTempFile();

m_pImage =
 new CImageObject( "TEMP.BMP" );
```

7. Add the following code to the CGetClipboardView destructor:

```
if( m_pImage != NULL )
  delete m_pImage;
```

8. Edit the OnDraw function in the CGetClipboardView class in the GetClipboardView.cpp file as follows:

```
void CGetClipboardView::OnDraw(CDC* pDC)
{
CGetClipboardDoc* pDoc = GetDocument();
ASSERT_VALID(pDoc);

 if( m_pImage != NULL ){
  m_pImage->SetPalette( pDC );
  m_pImage->Draw( pDC );
  }

}
```

9. Add the following function to the CGetClipboardView class in the GetClipboardView.h file:

```
void ImageToTempFile( void );
```

10. Add the ImageToTempFile function in the CGetClipboardView class in the GetClipboardView.cpp file as follows:

```cpp
void CGetClipboardView::
ImageToTempFile( void )
{
 if( ::OpenClipboard( NULL ) ){
  HBITMAP hBitmap;
  hBitmap =
  (HBITMAP) ::GetClipboardData( CF_BITMAP );

  if( hBitmap != NULL ){

   HANDLE hPalette;
   hPalette = ::GetClipboardData( CF_PALETTE );
   DWORD dwPaletteSize = 0;
   if( hPalette != NULL )
    dwPaletteSize = ::GlobalSize( hPalette );

   BITMAP bm;
   ::GetObject(hBitmap, sizeof( BITMAP ),&bm);
   BITMAPFILEHEADER bfh;
   BITMAPINFOHEADER bih;
   memset(&bfh, 0, sizeof( BITMAPFILEHEADER));
   memset(&bih, 0, sizeof( BITMAPINFOHEADER));

   DWORD dwImageSize =
    bm.bmHeight * bm.bmWidthBytes;

   bfh.bfType = 'MB';
   bfh.bfSize = sizeof( BITMAPFILEHEADER ) +
    sizeof( BITMAPINFOHEADER ) +
    dwPaletteSize +
    dwImageSize;

   bfh.bfOffBits =
    sizeof( BITMAPFILEHEADER ) +
    sizeof( BITMAPINFOHEADER ) +
    dwPaletteSize;

   bih.biSize = sizeof( BITMAPINFOHEADER );
   bih.biWidth = bm.bmWidth;
   bih.biHeight = bm.bmHeight;
   bih.biPlanes = bm.bmPlanes;
   bih.biBitCount = bm.bmBitsPixel;
   bih.biSizeImage = ::GlobalSize( hBitmap );
```

```
        CFile cf;
        if( cf.Open( "TEMP.BMP",
         CFile::modeCreate | CFile::modeWrite ) ){
         cf.Write(&bfh, sizeof( BITMAPFILEHEADER));
         cf.Write(&bih, sizeof( BITMAPINFOHEADER));
         if( hPalette != NULL ){
          char *pBuffer =
           (char *) ::GlobalLock( hPalette );
          cf.Write( pBuffer, dwPaletteSize );
          ::GlobalUnlock( hPalette );
         }
         char *pDataBuffer =
          new char [dwImageSize];
         if( pDataBuffer != NULL ){
          ::GetBitmapBits( hBitmap,
           dwImageSize, pDataBuffer );
          for( int i=0; i<bm.bmHeight; i++ ){
           int nOffset;
           nOffset = bm.bmHeight - i - 1;
           nOffset *= bm.bmWidthBytes;
           cf.Write(
            &pDataBuffer[nOffset],
            bm.bmWidthBytes );
          }
          delete [] pDataBuffer;
         }
        }
       }

       ::CloseClipboard();
      }

    }
```

11. Compile and run the program.

When it runs, you'll see an empty frame window with no child windows. Make sure you press the PrintScrn button so that the screen is captured into the clipboard. Then press Ctrl+N to create a new child window. The image will be loaded into the child window and displayed.

On the Web

There are quite a few sites on the Web that you'll find useful in your imaging pursuits. This section has a sampling of sites that we found helpful.

VT ImageBase

There's a nice collection of images that can be viewed and downloaded at http://scholar2.lib.vt.edu. If you find yourself short of images to use in your programs, check out this site, shown in Figure 10-11.

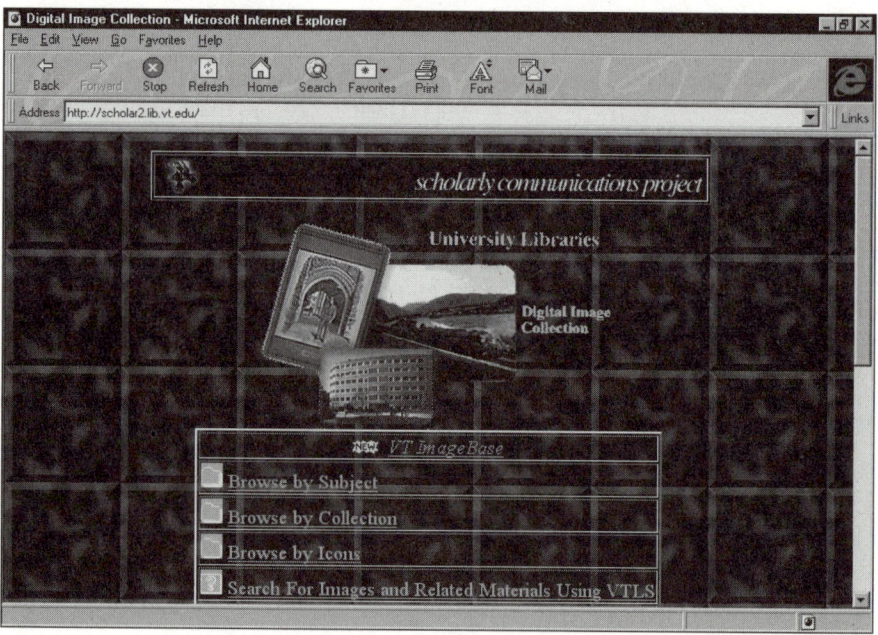

Figure 10-11: This site contains a nice assortment of images.

Primate Image Collection

Many specialized image collections can be found, such as those you'll find at the http://night.primate.wisc.edu/pin/images/gorillas.html site. This one specializes in primates. As you can see in Figure 10-12, gorillas are everywhere.

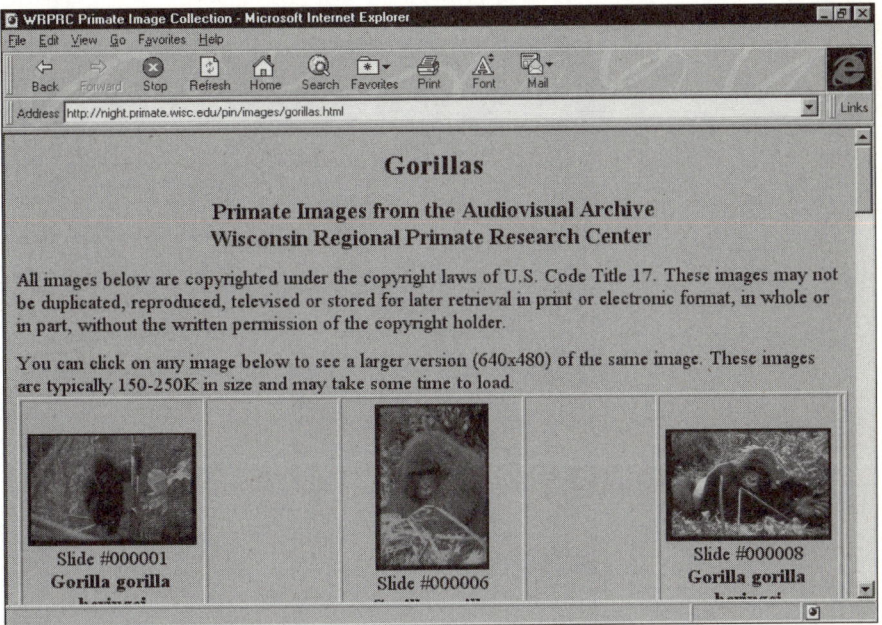

Figure 10-12: Gorillas anyone? This site has just about every gorilla I ever imagined.

Garbo Astronomy Image Collection

Astronomy images are a favorite for most computer owners. Computer users have a natural affinity for space and astronomy. Thumbnails give you a small peek before you spend time downloading the entire image, as shown in Figure 10-13. The site can be found at http://garbo.uwasa.fi/pc/gifcraft.html.

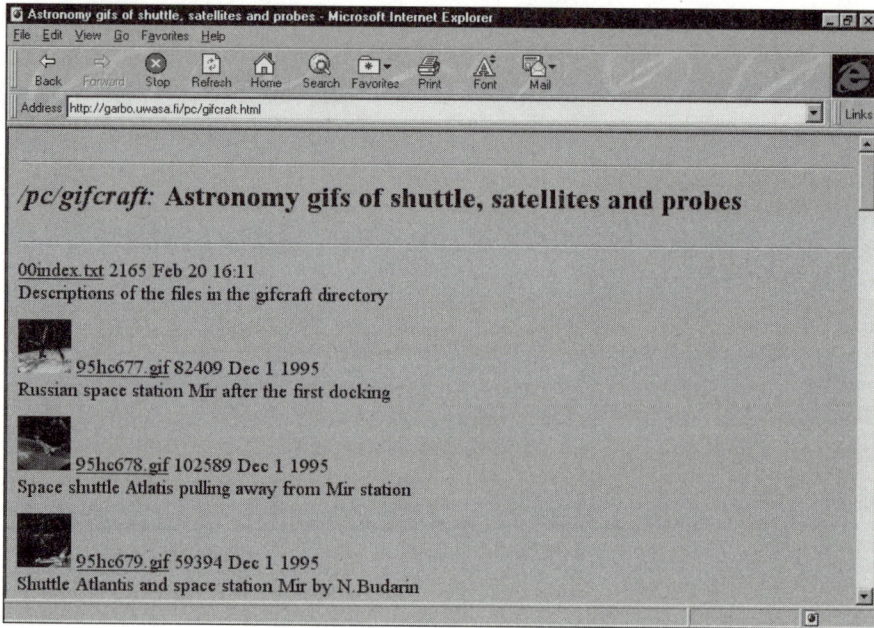

Figure 10-13: Thumbnail images let you see what's available before you have to spend large amounts of time downloading images.

Moving On

In this chapter, you've learned how to use the ImageObject class library in practical ways. Among the things you've learned is how to print images and how to get images from the clipboard. These are two valuable lessons that you'll find helpful when you write your own graphics applications.

The next few chapters deal with sound, another important component for today's multimedia applications. In Chapter 11, coming up next, you'll learn how to play MIDI files.

Chapter 11

MIDI

I don't know anything about music.
In my line you don't have to.
–Elvis Presley

That's a fitting quote for this chapter. Believe it or not, you don't need to know anything about music or MIDI to add music to your Visual C++ applications. We will cover the basics of MIDI and the Windows MIDI interface, but you could still easily use the classes presented here to add music to your programs without a lot of instruction.

Adding music is one of the easiest ways to enhance your multimedia applications. Nearly every popular computer game or multimedia title features some sort of background music, either MIDI or CD audio (which we cover in Chapter 13). Music is very effective for putting the user in a specific mood or evoking certain feelings. The right music at the right time can work wonders for you and your Visual C++ programs.

WHAT IS MIDI?

The Musical Instrument Digital Interface (MIDI) is a protocol originally developed within the music industry by several large companies involved in the production of electronic music synthesizers. It has since been adopted by the computer industry and is the standard format for multimedia music files. A MIDI file is a set of commands for storing and transmitting information about music. MIDI devices on your computer, such as sound cards, interpret this information and use it to create music. In simpler terms, a MIDI file is the electronic equivalent of sheet music.

Windows 95 supports the General MIDI Specification, which is the industry standard on how MIDI is developed and used. This standard defines the particular sounds and instruments that are supported, as well as the commands that control them. Microsoft and most MIDI sound card manufacturers support this standard.

You may wonder why you need to learn about MIDI when you can skip to Chapter 13 and add CD audio to your applications. Although CD audio is the current trend and is of a much higher quality, MIDI music does still have its advantages. For instance, your applications may not be CD-based, or you may not want to require your user to have a CD-ROM drive. MIDI is cheaper to produce than CD audio, and there is a huge library of MIDI music available on the Internet and through freeware and shareware. Finally, using a high-end CD-ROM product, it is necessary to pause the CD audio every time your program accesses the disc, whereas MIDI music can continue to play without interruption.

Although Microsoft provides support for playing MIDI files, there is nothing built in to Visual C++ or the Microsoft Foundation Classes (MFC) to help you implement this support. MFC is the set of class libraries that are supposed to take the complexities out of Windows programming. The Midi class library that comes with this book and the Windows multimedia library (WINMM.LIB) provided with Visual C++ provide a quick and easy method for adding MIDI music to any Windows 95 or Windows NT application. Good luck making your programs come alive with MIDI music!

THE MIDI CLASS LIBRARY

The Midi class library can be linked with any Visual C++ project (you must also link WINMM.LIB). Before you know it, you will be playing MIDI files in your own applications. You don't need to know what's going on behind the scenes—the class library will do all the work for you.

The library offers much more than just the ability to play MIDI files. You can pause the playback, skip around to different positions within the file, and even change the tempo of the playback. Of course, if you want to examine the class library in detail or make changes to the member functions, the source code is included on the Companion CD-ROM.

All source code and support files to rebuild Midi.lib can be found in the MIDI\Midi directory on the Companion CD-ROM that comes with this book.

The MidiPlayer Demo

We've built a simple demonstration program that shows what the class library can do. The program can be found in the MIDI\MidiPlayer directory on the Companion CD-ROM. Using File Manager or Program Manager, run the program named MidiPlayer.exe. It's a dialog-based program that loads and plays MIDI files. When the program first runs, all you'll see is the interface, as pictured in Figure 11-1. Notice that most of the buttons are grayed out since no MIDI file has been opened.

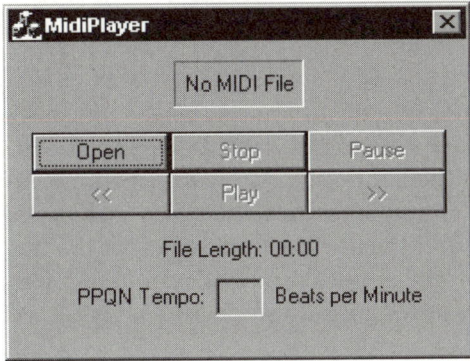

Figure 11-1: When MidiPlayer first runs, you'll see this interface for playing MIDI files.

You must first open a MIDI file by pressing the Open button. Go ahead and open one of the samples provided on the Companion CD-ROM in the MIDI\Samples directory. Once the file is opened the buttons become active, and information about the file is displayed in the dialog as shown in Figure 11-2.

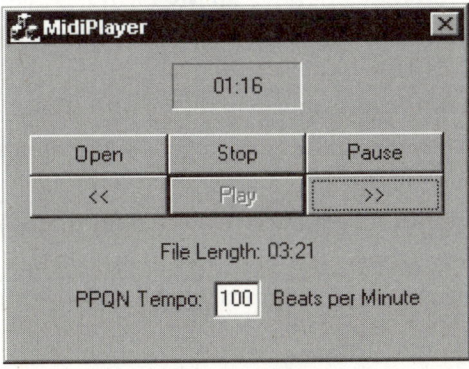

Figure 11-2: After you load a MIDI file, the relevant buttons become active.

MARKMIDI

When attempting to play some MIDI files, you may get a dialog box informing you that the file is not authored for Windows.

The DOS-based utility MARKMIDI, which comes on the Visual C++ CD, can be used to mark such MIDI files and avoid this warning in the future. The program does not verify that the file is authored correctly—it only marks the file as authored for Windows. The utility has the following syntax:

```
MARKMIDI SrcFilename DestFilename
```

Using the MidiPlayer you can play, stop, and pause the MIDI file. You can also use the control buttons to skip positions within the file. You can even adjust the tempo setting for the playback. It works best if you only change the tempo when the MIDI playback is stopped. The current position within the file, the total length of the file, and the tempo are all displayed in the application. Finally, when you exit the program, the class library automatically stops the playback and closes the device.

Troubleshooting

If you're not hearing sound from the MidiPlayer demo application, there may be something wrong with your MIDI sound setup.

First, make sure your sound card is installed properly. If your sound card can play WAV files, such as the standard Windows event sounds, then it is working correctly. Otherwise, use the Add New Hardware option from the Control Panel to access your hardware controls and set up the sound card.

Second, you may not have an MCI MIDI driver installed on your system. To verify that a MIDI driver is enabled, follow these steps and refer to Figure 11-3:

1. In the Multimedia option in the Control Panel, click the Advanced tab.

2. In the Multimedia Devices list, click the plus sign next to Media Control Devices.

3. Click the MIDI Sequencer Device, and then click the Properties button.

4. In the properties dialog box, click Use This Media Control Device.

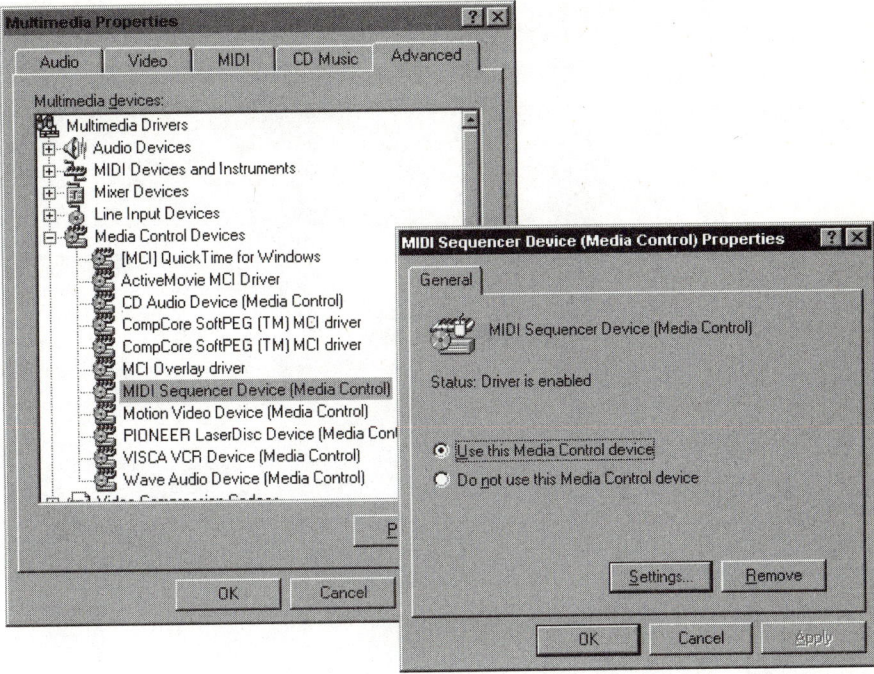

Figure 11-3: Verify that a MIDI driver is enabled.

If the MIDI Sequencer Device does not appear in the Multimedia Device list, the driver is not installed. To install the MCI MIDI driver, follow these steps and refer to Figure 11-4:

1. In the Add New Hardware option in the Control Panel, click No, when prompted, to have Windows 95 search for your Hardware.

2. In the Hardware Types list, click Sound, Video, and Game Controllers.

3. Click Microsoft MCI in the Manufacturers list, and then click MIDI Sequencer Device in the Models list.

4. Click the Finish button.

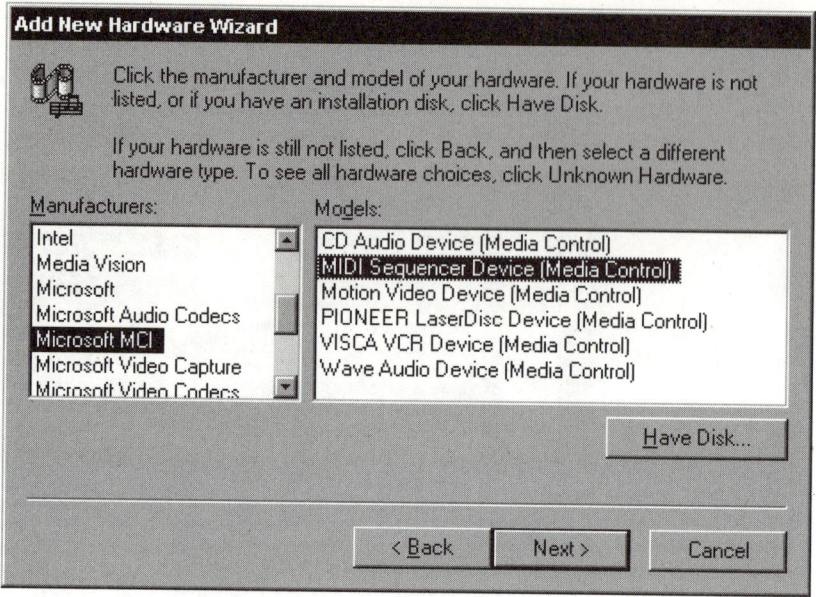

Figure 11-4: Installing the MCI MIDI driver.

PLAYING MIDI FILES WITH THE MEDIA CONTROL INTERFACE

The Microsoft API provides three different ways for applications to work with MIDI files.

❏ The Media Control Interface (MCI). This is the most basic method and is the one used to develop the Midi class library. It is described in detail in the next section.

❏ Stream buffers. This format allows an application to manipulate buffers of MIDI data. Stream buffers are useful if an application requires precise control over MIDI playback.

❏ Low-level MIDI services. Applications that require complete control over the MIDI data can use these services.

The Media Control Interface

All the work at the heart of the MIDI class library is done by the Media Control Interface. The MCI allows for control of the Windows MIDI sequencer. The MCI supports MIDI output only, so we will not be doing any MIDI input in this chapter. If you need these services, you have to use the low-level MIDI functions. You can skip this section if you just want to use the Midi library and are not concerned with how it works.

The MCI can be implemented with one of two functions: mciSendCommand() or mciSendString(). Although they both serve the same purpose and both produce the same result, they have different syntax. One uses a command-based interface and the other uses a string-based interface. We will only use the mciSendCommand because the command-based interface should seem more logical to programmers accustomed to the Windows command-based API.

The mciSendCommand() function is used to communicate with the MCI device, to either send command messages (MCI_OPEN, MCI_PLAY) or query for information (MCI_STATUS) on the device. The MCI command-based messaging interface allows for a lot of flexibility through the use of MCI parameter blocks. The parameter blocks are structures defined in MMSYSTEM.H that allow large amounts of information to be passed to and returned from the mciSendCommand() function.

mciSendCommand()

Prototype: `DWORD mciSendCommand (UINT wDeviceID, UINT wMessage, DWORD dwParam1, DWORD dwParam2);`

Purpose: The core function of MCI, used to do all communication with the MCI device.

Arguments: UINT wDeviceID, the device that receives the message.
UINT wMessage, the MCI command message.
DWORD dwParam1: specifies flags for the command.
DWORD dwParam2: specifies a pointer to the parameter block to be used.

Returns: Zero if successful, otherwise the low-order word contains an error.

The MCI device ID identifies which device has been opened. This value is returned in the parameter block when you send the MCI_OPEN command—it should be saved for later use. The ID is used to identify this device when sending subsequent commands. The following is a brief overview of the MCI commands that are relevant to MIDI playback.

MCI Commands

MCI_OPEN	Opens the device.
MCI_CLOSE	Closes the device.
MCI_PLAY	Starts the file playback.
MCI_STOP	Stops the file playback.
MCI_PAUSE	Pauses the file playback.
MCI_SEEK	Seeks to a specific position within the file.
MCI_SET	Used with other flags described below.
MCI_STATUS	Used with other flags described below.

MCI_SET Flags

MCI_SET_TIME_FORMAT	Changes the time format.
MCI_SEQ_SET_TEMPO	Changes the tempo for playback. If the MIDI file is type PPQN, this value is in beats per minute. If the file is type SMPTE, this value is in frames per second.

MCI_STATUS Flags

MCI_STATUS_LENGTH	Gets the length of the file.
MCI_STATUS_MODE	Gets the current status of the file playback.
MCI_STATUS_POSITION	Gets the file position in the current time format.
MCI_STATUS_TIME_FORMAT	Gets the current time format.
MCI_SEQ_STATUS_DIVTYPE	Determines if the file is a PPQN or SMPTE type of file.
MCI_SEQ_STATUS_TEMPO	Gets the current tempo of the playback. If the MIDI file is type PPQN, this value is in beats per minute. If the file is type SMPTE, this value is in frames per second.

CMIDI CLASS LIBRARY FUNCTION CALLS

This section is provided as a reference to the public function calls the CMidi class library offers. The calls are simple and should be easy to implement in your own programs.

You may want to skip over this section and read the section entitled "Behind MidiPlayer," which shows how the calls are used. For some people, it's better to look at the usage of function calls before actually studying the syntax.

CMidi()

Prototype: `CMidi (void);`

Purpose: This is the constructor. It simply creates a CMidi object and initializes its internal variables.

Arguments: None

Returns: Nothing

~CMidi()

Prototype: `~CMidi (void);`

Purpose: This is the destructor. It closes the MCI device if it has been opened.

Arguments: None

Returns: Nothing

GetDevices()

Prototype: `int GetDevices (void);`

Purpose: This function returns the number of devices installed on the system that support MIDI output.

Arguments: None

Returns: int: nDevices

Open()

Prototype: `BOOL Open (CString Filename);`

Purpose: This function opens the MCI device, sets the time format, and seeks to the beginning of the MIDI file.

Arguments: None

Returns: BOOL: TRUE for success, FALSE for failure

Close()

Prototype: `void Close (void);`

Purpose: This function stops the file and closes the MCI device.

Arguments: None

Returns: Nothing

Play()

Prototype: `BOOL Play (void);`

Purpose: This function plays the file from the current position.

Arguments: None

Returns: BOOL: TRUE for success, FALSE for failure

Stop()

Prototype: `void Stop (void);`

Purpose: This function stops the file from playing and seeks back to the beginning of the file.

Arguments: None

Returns: Nothing

Pause()

Prototype: `void Pause (void);`

Purpose: This function pauses the file.

Arguments: None

Returns: Nothing

GetTotalLength()

Prototype: `void GetTotalLength (int *pnMinutes, int *pnSeconds);`

Purpose: This function supplies the total length of the MIDI file.

Arguments: int *pnMinutes, -1 if function fails
int *pnSeconds, -1 if function fails

Returns: Nothing

GetMinutes()

Prototype: `int GetMinutes (void);`

Purpose: This function returns the minutes value of the current file position.

Arguments: None

Returns: int: nMinutes, -1 if function fails

GetSeconds()

Prototype: `int GetSeconds (void);`

Purpose: This function returns the seconds value of the current file position.

Arguments: None

Returns: int: nSeconds, -1 if function fails

IsPlaying()

Prototype: `BOOL IsPlaying (BOOL *bPaused);`

Purpose: This function returns the playing status and supplies the paused status in the first parameter. If the file is paused, IsPlaying() will still return TRUE.

Arguments: BOOL *bPaused

Returns: BOOL: TRUE if playing or paused, otherwise FALSE

SeekTo()

Prototype:	`BOOL SeekTo (int nMinute, int nSecond);`
Purpose:	This function seeks to a specific position in the MIDI file. If the file was playing, it will automatically resume.
Arguments:	int nMinute int nSecond
Returns:	BOOL: TRUE for success, FALSE for failure

SkipForward()

Prototype:	`void SkipForward (int nSeconds);`
Purpose:	This function skips forward a specific number of seconds. If the file was playing, it will automatically resume.
Arguments:	int nSeconds
Returns:	Nothing

SkipBack()

Prototype:	`void SkipBack (int nSeconds);`
Purpose:	This function skips back a specific number of seconds. If the file was playing, it will automatically resume.
Arguments:	int nSeconds
Returns:	Nothing

GetDivisionType()

Prototype:	`int GetDivisionType (void);`
Purpose:	This function determines the division type format of the MIDI file.
Arguments:	None
Returns:	int: 0 if the division type is PPQN, 1 if it is SMPTE

GetTempo()

Prototype: `int GetTempo (void);`

Purpose: This function returns the tempo of the MIDI file. For PPQN files, the return value is in beats per minute. For SMPTE files, the return value is in frames per second.

Arguments: None

Returns: int nTempo

SetTempo()

Prototype: `void SetTempo (int nTempo);`

Purpose: This function changes the current tempo of the MIDI file. For PPQN files, nTempo is in beats per minute. For SMPTE files, nTempo is in frames per second.

Arguments: int nTempo

Returns: Nothing

BEHIND MIDIPLAYER

MidiPlayer was created with the Visual C++ AppWizard with the following settings:

- ❏ Dialog-based application
- ❏ English language
- ❏ About box and 3D controls
- ❏ No automation, ActiveX, or WOSA support
- ❏ Yes source file comments
- ❏ MFC linked as a static library

MIDI Basics

The basic functions for playing a MIDI file are very easy to use. You must open the device before you use it and close it when you are done. In between, you can call any of the MIDI functions you need. We open the device in the OnOpen() function. The device will automatically be closed by the m_Midi destructor, but the device must be closed if the user opens another MIDI file.

The OnOpen() Code

In this function we open the device and prepare the applications for playback. First, we display a file selector and allow the user to open any MIDI file on their system. If they select a valid file, we close any open device, then attempt to open the new file. Next, the total length of the MIDI file, in minutes and seconds, will be displayed. Finally, we determine if the file is of type PPQN or SMPTE and display the current tempo.

```
void CMidiPlayerDlg::OnOpen()
{
CString Filter;
Filter = "MIDI Files (*.MID)|*.MID||";

CFileDialog FileDlg (TRUE, NULL, NULL,
 OFN_HIDEREADONLY, Filter);
if (FileDlg.DoModal () == IDOK){
 // Close the device if already open
 m_Midi.Close ();
 // Attempt to open the device
 if (!m_Midi.Open (FileDlg.GetPathName ())){
  MessageBox ("Cannot play this file.",
    "Error", MB_OK | MB_ICONSTOP);
  return;
  }
 }
else{
 return;
 }

// Display the total file length
CString Length;
int nMinutes, nSeconds;
m_Midi.GetTotalLength (&nMinutes, &nSeconds);
Length.Format ("File Length: %02d:%02d",
 nMinutes, nSeconds);
if (nMinutes == -1)
 Length = "File Length: 00:00";
SetDlgItemText (IDC_LENGTH, Length);

// Display the midi file tempo
CString DivType, TempoType;
if (m_Midi.GetDivisionType ()){
 DivType = "SMPTE Tempo:";
 TempoType = "Frames per Second";
 }
```

```
else{
 DivType = "PPQN Tempo:";
 TempoType = "Beats per Minute";
 }

SetDlgItemText (IDC_DIVTYPE, DivType);
SetDlgItemText (IDC_TEMPOTYPE, TempoType);
SetDlgItemInt (IDC_TEMPO, m_Midi.GetTempo());
}
```

Play, Stop & Pause

These functions are very simple and, along with the Open() function, are the only functions you really need to play MIDI audio. Each function handler contains just a one-line call to the corresponding class library function.

```
void CMidiPlayerDlg::OnStop()
{
 m_Midi.Stop ();
}

void CMidiPlayerDlg::OnPlay()
{
 m_Midi.Play ();
}

void CMidiPlayerDlg::OnPause()
{
 m_Midi.Pause ();
}
```

Changing Position & Tempo

The class library functions can also be used to change the playback of the MIDI file. The SkipForward() and SkipBack() library functions allow the program to scan the current playback, and the SetTempo() library function changes the current tempo.

The OnTimer() Code

The SkipForward() and SkipBack() functions are called from the OnTimer() function if the corresponding button is pressed. These functions skip a number of seconds specified by the function argument. In this example, we skip five seconds every time the OnTimer() function detects that the button has been pressed.

We are also using the OnTimer() function to update the current position of the file playback (in minutes and seconds) and update the status of the control buttons.

```
void CMidiPlayerDlg::OnTimer(UINT nIDEvent)
{
// Skip forward or back if skip buttons
// pressed
CButton *pButton;
pButton = (CButton *) GetDlgItem(
 IDC_SKIPFORWARD);
if (pButton->GetState () & 0x0004)
 m_Midi.SkipForward (5);
pButton = (CButton *) GetDlgItem(
 IDC_SKIPBACK);
if (pButton->GetState () & 0x0004)
 m_Midi.SkipBack (5);

// Display the current time
CString Status;
BOOL bFileReady = TRUE;
Status.Format ("%02d:%02d",
 m_Midi.GetMinutes(),
 m_Midi.GetSeconds ());
if (m_Midi.GetMinutes () == -1){
 Status = "No MIDI File";
 bFileReady = FALSE;
 }
SetDlgItemText (IDC_STATUS, Status);

// Update all the buttons
CWnd *pWnd;
pWnd = GetDlgItem (IDC_SKIPBACK);
pWnd->EnableWindow (bFileReady);
pWnd = GetDlgItem (IDC_SKIPFORWARD);
pWnd->EnableWindow (bFileReady);
pWnd = GetDlgItem (IDC_TEMPO);
pWnd->EnableWindow (bFileReady);

BOOL bPaused;
if (m_Midi.IsPlaying (&bPaused)){
 pWnd = GetDlgItem (IDC_PLAY);
 pWnd->EnableWindow (bPaused);
 pWnd = GetDlgItem (IDC_STOP);
```

```
pWnd->EnableWindow (bFileReady);
pWnd = GetDlgItem (IDC_PAUSE);
pWnd->EnableWindow (bFileReady && !bPaused);
 }
else{
 pWnd = GetDlgItem (IDC_PLAY);
 pWnd->EnableWindow (bFileReady);
 pWnd = GetDlgItem (IDC_STOP);
 pWnd->EnableWindow (FALSE);
 pWnd = GetDlgItem (IDC_PAUSE);
 pWnd->EnableWindow (FALSE);
 }

 CDialog::OnTimer(nIDEvent);
}
```

The OnChangeTempo() Code

When the user adjusts the tempo by changing the number in the tempo
edit control, the program will change the MIDI playback tempo. Simply
call the library function SetTempo() to do this. Keep in mind that this
value will be in beats per minute for PPQN files and frames per second
for SMPTE files. For proper results, the playback should be stopped
when you call the SetTempo() function.

```
void CMidiPlayerDlg::OnChangeTempo()
{
 int nTempo;
 nTempo = GetDlgItemInt (IDC_TEMPO);

 m_Midi.SetTempo (nTempo);
}
```

CREATING PROGRAMS THAT USE MIDI

The following two hands-on exercises will get you started on your jour-
ney to mastering the Midi class library. Going through them won't take
very long, and the investment of time will be well worth it.

You may be asking why you should type in the code for each exercise.
Why not just load the project from disk? In my experience, you always
learn more by doing.

Each of these exercises is designed to be as simple as possible, so there
is a limit to the amount of error checking that is done. Under normal
circumstances, the application should check to see if the functions succeed and provide feedback to the user.

387

Finding MIDI Files

All of these examples require a MIDI file for playback. We have pro-vided four sample files on the Companion CD-ROM in the MIDI\Samples directory.

However, when you are writing your own applications, you will also need your own MIDI files. If you happen to have a good understanding of music theory, you may be able to author your own files using a MIDI authoring program such as Cakewalk Pro. More likely, you will need to acquire files that have been written by others. Luckily, there is a large library of files on the Internet, CompuServe, and other online services. Most of these files are available free or for a small fee, and you can usually find every song you could possibly imagine. Check out the "On the Web" section at the end of this chapter for more information.

Hands-On 1: Playing a MIDI File in the Background

In this example, we will simply play MIDI music in the background of an application.

We will open the MIDI sequencer device in the CMainFrame construc-tor, then do all of the work in the OnTimer() function. Follow the steps correctly and you'll be amazed at how easy it is to add MIDI music to your application.

1. Create a Visual C++ project named HandsOn11_1 with the following attributes:

   ❒ Single-document interface

   ❒ English language

   ❒ No database support

   ❒ No compound document support

   ❒ No automation or ActiveX control support

   ❒ 3D controls, but no other features

   ❒ No source file comments

   ❒ Link MFC as a static library

2. Select Settings from the Project menu. Choose the Link tab. Add the following libraries to the Object/library modules field. The libraries for the release and debug versions are different. Both are listed below.

Release Project Libraries	Debug Project Libraries
Midi.lib	MidiD.lib
winmm.lib	winmm.lib

3. Set the Active Configuration to Win32 Release.

4. Copy the file SAMPLE1.MID from the \MIDI\Samples directory on the Companion CD-ROM to the newly created project directory.

5. Add the following include to the MainFrm.h file:

```
#include "Midi.h"
```

6. Add the following variable declaration to the CMainFrame class in the MainFrm.h file:

```
public:
 CMidi m_Midi;
```

7. Add the following code to the CMainFrame constructor:

```
CMainFrame::CMainFrame()
{
 m_Midi.Open ("Sample1.mid");
}
```

8. Add the following functions with the Class Wizard to the CMainFrame class:

```
Name: OnCreate()  Message: WM_CREATE
Name: OnTimer()   Message: WM_TIMER
```

9. Edit the OnCreate() function in the CMainFrame class in the MainFrm.cpp file as follows:

```
int CMainFrame::OnCreate(LPCREATESTRUCT
 lpCreateStruct)
{
 if (CFrameWnd::OnCreate(lpCreateStruct)== -1)
  return -1;

 SetTimer (1, 500, NULL);

 return 0;
}
```

10. Edit the OnTimer() function in the CMainFrame class in the MainFrm.cpp file as follows:

```
void CMainFrame::OnTimer(UINT nIDEvent)
{
// See if audio is already playing
BOOL bPaused;
if (!m_Midi.IsPlaying (&bPaused)){
  m_Midi.SeekTo (0, 0);
  m_Midi.Play ();
  }

CFrameWnd::OnTimer(nIDEvent);
}
```

11. Compile and run the program.

When the program runs, the MIDI file should automatically start playing in the background. After the end of the file is reached, the file will seek to the beginning and start playing again.

Hands-On 2: Advanced MIDI Playback

In this example, things get a little more advanced. This application allows you to play a MIDI file and skip around to different parts. It is a dialog-based application that uses a slider bar for controlling the file position. The slider will also automatically update to show the current position as the MIDI file plays.

1. Create a Visual C++ project named HandsOn11_2 with the following attributes:

   ❏ Dialog-based application
   ❏ English language
   ❏ About box and 3D controls
   ❏ No automation, ActiveX, or WOSA support
   ❏ Yes source file comments
   ❏ MFC linked as a static library

2. Select Settings from the Project menu. Choose the Link tab. Add the following libraries to the Object/library modules field. The libraries for the release and debug versions are different. Both are listed below.

Release Project Libraries	Debug Project Libraries
Midi.lib	MidiD.lib
winmm.lib	winmm.lib

3. Set the Active Configuration to Win32 Release.

4. Copy the file SAMPLE4.MID from the \MIDI\Samples directory on the Companion CD-ROM to the newly created project directory.

5. Add the following includes to the HandsOn11_2Dlg.h file:

```
#include "Midi.h"
```

6. Add the following variable declaration to the CHandsOn11_2Dlg class in the HandsOn11_2Dlg.h file:

```
public:
 CMidi m_Midi;
```

7. Add Stop and Play buttons and a slider bar to the IDD_HANDSON11_2_DIALOG resource as shown in Figure 11-5.

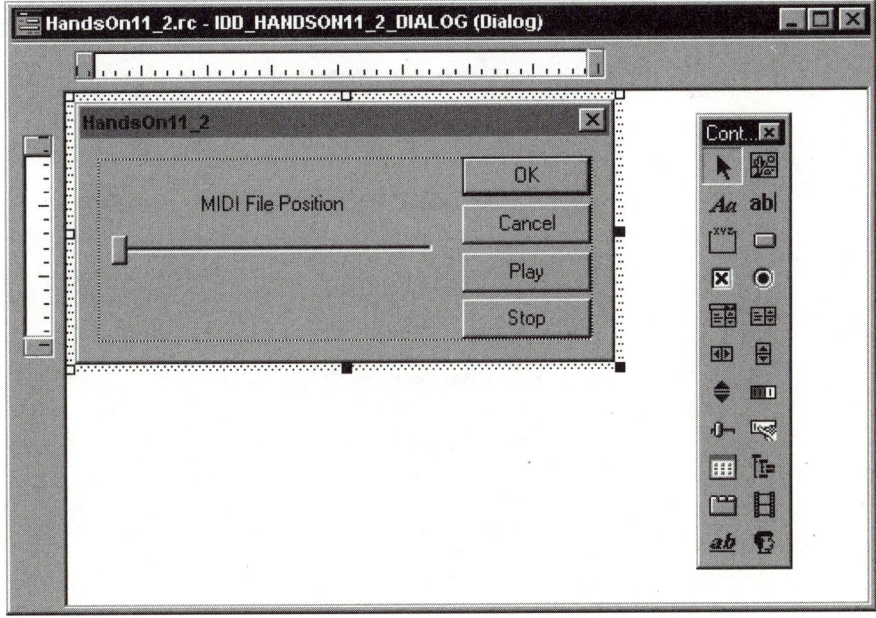

Figure 11-5: Edit the dialog resource for the Hands-On 2 example.

8. Add the following functions with the Class Wizard to the CHandsOn11_2Dlg class:

```
Name: OnTimer() Message: WM_TIMER
Name: OnPlay()  Message: BN_CLICKED
  Control: IDC_PLAY
Name: OnStop() Message: BN_CLICKED
    Control: IDC_STOP
```

9. Add the following variable with the Class Wizard to the CHandsOn11_2Dlg class:

```
Name: m_MIDISlider Type: CSliderCtrl
```

10. Edit the OnInitDialog() function in the CHandsOn11_2Dlg class in the CHandsOn11_2Dlg.cpp file as follows:

```
BOOL CHandsOn11_2Dlg::OnInitDialog()
{
CDialog::OnInitDialog();
    .

    .
    .

m_Midi.Open ("Sample4.mid");

SetTimer (1, 2000, NULL);

m_MIDISlider.SetRange (0, 100);

return TRUE;
}
```

11. Edit the OnPlay() function in the CHandsOn11_2Dlg class in the CHandsOn11_2Dlg.cpp file as follows:

```
void CHandsOn11_2Dlg::OnPlay()
{
int nSliderPos, nSliderSecs;
int nMinutes, nSeconds, nTotalSecs;

// Get the current slider position
nSliderPos = m_MIDISlider.GetPos ();

//Get the total length of the file in seconds
m_Midi.GetTotalLength (&nMinutes, &nSeconds);
nTotalSecs = (nMinutes * 60) + nSeconds;
```

```
// Figure out the slider position in seconds
nSliderSecs = (nTotalSecs/100) * nSliderPos;

// Calculate the minute and second
nMinutes = nSliderSecs / 60;
nSeconds = nSliderSecs % 60;

// Seek to that position and play
m_Midi.SeekTo (nMinutes, nSeconds);
m_Midi.Play ();
}
```

12. Edit the OnStop() function in the CHandsOn11_2Dlg class in the CHandsOn11_2Dlg.cpp file as follows:

```
void CHandsOn13_3Dlg::OnStop()
{
 m_Midi.Stop ();

 m_MIDISlider.SetPos (0);
}
```

13. Edit the OnTimer() function in the CHandsOn11_2Dlg class in the CHandsOn11_2Dlg.cpp file as follows:

```
void CHandsOn11_2Dlg::OnTimer(UINT nIDEvent)
{
 // Only update the slider position if the
 // file is playing
 BOOL bPaused;
 if (m_Midi.IsPlaying (&bPaused)){
  int nSliderPos;
  int nMinutes, nSeconds;
  DWORD dwCurrentSecs, dwTotalSecs;

  // Get the total length of the file in
  // seconds
  m_Midi.GetTotalLength (&nMinutes,
   &nSeconds);
  dwTotalSecs = (nMinutes * 60) + nSeconds;

  // Get the current position of the file in
  // seconds
  nMinutes = m_Midi.GetMinutes ();
  nSeconds = m_Midi.GetSeconds ();
  dwCurrentSecs = (nMinutes * 60) + nSeconds;
```

```
      // Figure out the new slider position
      nSliderPos = (dwCurrentSecs * 100) /
       dwTotalSecs;

      // Update the slider position
      m_MIDISlider.SetPos (nSliderPos);
       }

   CDialog::OnTimer(nIDEvent);
   }
```

14. Compile and run the program.

You are now ready to play the file. Simply use the Play and Stop buttons to play the audio. Adjusting the slider bar will skip you to different positions within the MIDI file.

ON THE WEB

There are many Web sites devoted entirely to MIDI music. You can find MIDI players, MIDI authoring tools, and libraries of MIDI files for nearly every type of music. Here are a few sites to get you started.

Cakewalk

www.cakewalk.com

Cakewalk offers excellent products for authoring MIDI and digital audio for your Windows computer. This Web page, shown in Figure ll-6, offers downloadable demos as well as information on commercial and professional packages. Keep in mind that you'll need a basic knowledge of music to author your own MIDI files.

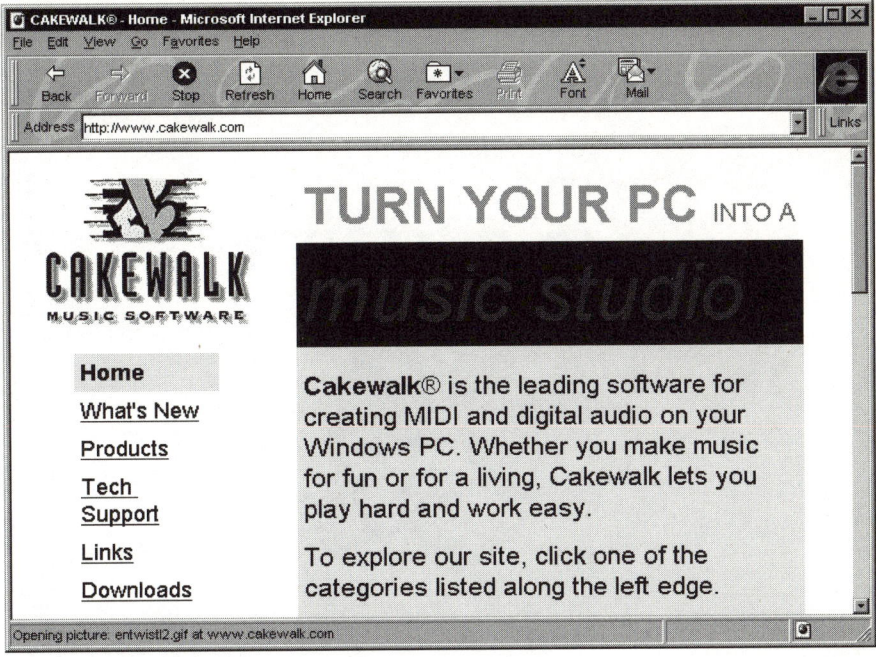

Figure 11-6: The Cakewalk Music Software home page.

Voyetra Technologies

www.voyetra.com

Voyetra Technologies provides a wide variety of innovative software for learning music, creating music, and controlling MIDI and audio on personal computers. Information on their products is available at this site.

Mabry Software

www.mabry.com

Mabry software sells VBX and OCX controls for playing and controlling MIDI devices. The MIDI Pack is made up of five controls that give you MIDI device and file access as well as interface indicators for user feedback and input. The source code is also available for an additional fee.

MidiWeb

www.midiweb.com

MidiWeb is a user-supported Web site that contains a huge collection of information on MIDI-related subjects. You will find many interesting projects and some shareware and freeware programs. (See Figure 11-7.)

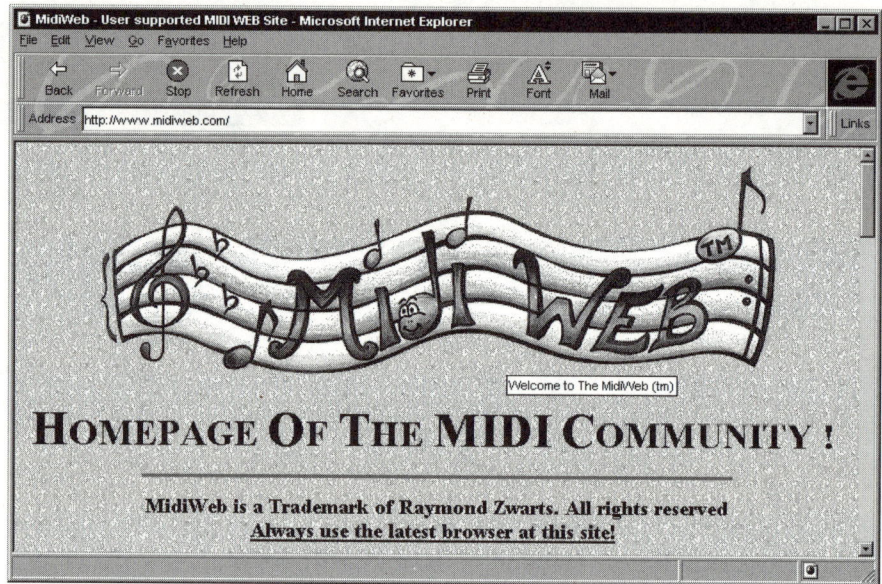

Figure 11-7: The MidiWeb homepage.

Crescendo

www.liveupdate.com

Crescendo is a MIDI music player for the Web that allows you to add MIDI background music to your own Web pages.

Files on the Web

If you are looking for MIDI files for your program, here are two great places to look:

❏ Standard MIDI Files on the Net, at www.aitech.ac.jp/~ckelly/ SMF.html, is an extensive list of sites that have standard MIDI files.

❏ The Complete MIDI File Directory, at www.flexfx.com, is an excellent library of MIDI files listed by musical category.

Shareware & Commercial Demos

For those of you who don't have access to the World Wide Web, there are plenty of shareware and commercial products available. We've included a few on the Companion CD-ROM, so feel free to take a look.

Wind Chimes

Wind Chimes is a cool little program developed by Syntrillium Software Corporation that uses MIDI audio to play wind chimes in the background on your Windows desktop. The shareware version can be found in the MIDI\Demos directory with the filename WC1SETUP.EXE (see Figure 11-8).

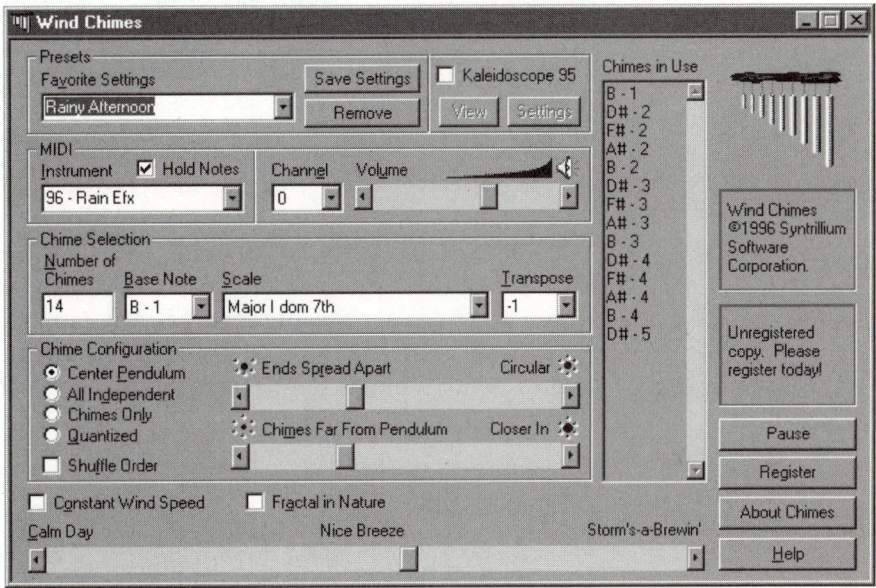

Figure 11-8: Wind Chimes by the Syntrillium Software Corporation.

MIDIART

MIDIART is a very neat Windows program that graphically displays a MIDI file by drawing art that corresponds to the changing music. This is a shareware application developed by AJF Consulting, Inc., that can be found in the MIDI\Demos directory with the filename MART30.ZIP.

MIDI Tool

MIDI Tool is another shareware application that was created by Sound Software Solutions (see Figure 11-9). It allows you to audition and play the standard MIDI sounds on your Windows system. The file MIDITOOL.ZIP can also be found in the MIDI\Demos directory.

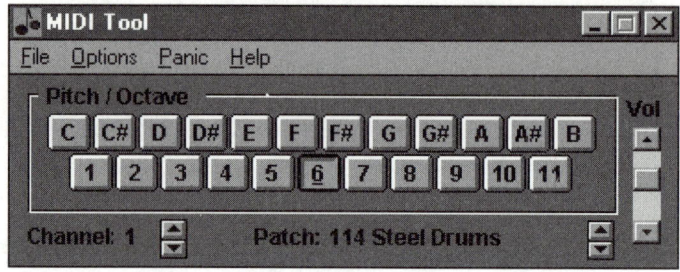

Figure 11-9: MIDI Tool is great for testing the different sounds your sound card is capable of producing.

PCALL

This is a free DLL and source code to read, play, modify, and save MIDI files. This code uses the low-level MIDI commands and would be useful if you want more control over your MIDI files than the Midi class library allows. All of the files can be found in PCALL.ZIP in the MIDI\Demos directory.

MOVING ON

Now that you understand how to add MIDI music to your applications, you are ready to move on. The next chapter, featuring support for sound and WAV files, explains how to add digitized audio and sound effects to your programs that already feature MIDI background music. These two chapters give you the basics you need to create a professional multimedia application.

As you experiment with adding MIDI music to your applications, I would like to see what you come up with. If you have any questions or some cool ideas you would like to share, feel free to contact me at ivt-rcl@interpath.com.

Chapter 12

Sound

> *My friend has a baby. I'm recording all the noises he*
> *makes so later I can ask him what he meant.*
> *—Steven Wright*

If Steven Wright was using the class library from this chapter, he could write his own Visual C++ application to record the sounds, save them to disk, and play them back many years later. That's just a small example of what you could do with the routines from this chapter. We will cover the basics of playing waveform audio (.WAV files) in addition to recording, saving, and playing multiple sounds at the same time. We will also examine how the functions behind the class library work, although you can still easily use the classes presented here to add sound to your programs without learning this functionality.

Adding sound to your application can truly enhance the user experience. Sound effects, digital audio, and music (discussed in Chapters 11 and 13) can take your multimedia application to the next level. By adding the dimension of sound, you are involving users on another level and bringing them closer to the world you are trying to create for them. Sound is also a great way to give users the ability to be more interactive with your application. If you use your imagination, the possibilities for sound in your Visual C++ programs are almost endless.

Visual C++ does include support for playing waveform audio. In this chapter, we will expand on that support and provide you with a class library that makes it much easier to add sound to your Windows applications. The Wave class library that comes with this book, along with the Windows multimedia library (WINMM.LIB) provided with Visual C++, provides a quick and easy method for adding sound effects to any Windows 95 or Windows NT application. We have also created a class library that takes advantage of the DirectSound technology built into Visual C++ to play multiple WAV files at the same time.

THE WAVE CLASS LIBRARY

The Wave class library can be linked with any Visual C++ project (you must also link WINMM.LIB). Now, you are ready to add sound to your own applications. You don't need to know what's happening within the class library—it will do all the work for you.

The library offers more than just the ability to play WAV files. The class library has a big advantage over the Windows sound routines, in that it loads the sound data into memory and can repeatedly play the sounds without a delay for loading. The library also provides the ability to record and save your own WAV files. If you want to examine the class library in detail or make changes to the member functions, the source code is included on the Companion CD-ROM.

TIP

All source code and support files to rebuild Wave.lib can be found in the SOUND\Wave directory on the Companion CD-ROM that comes with this book.

THE WAVESTUDIO DEMO

We've built a simple demonstration program that shows what the Wave class library can do. The program can be found in the SOUND\WaveStudio directory on the Companion CD-ROM. Using File Manager or Program Manager, run the program named WaveStudio.exe. It's a dialog-based program that loads and plays WAV files from disk or from the application's resource file. When it first runs, you'll see the interface as pictured in Figure 12-1.

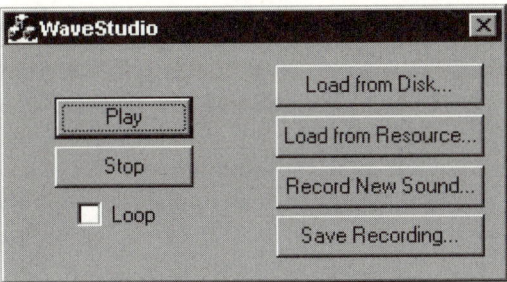

Figure 12-1: The WaveStudio interface.

You can open a WAV file by two different methods with WaveStudio. You can load a file from disk or from the WaveStudio resource file. To open a WAV from an applications resource file, the application must be compiled with the WAV files in the resource segment. The WaveStudio program was compiled with three sample WAV files in the resource. Go ahead and open one of the samples of either type. Once the file is opened, you can play the sound from memory and continuously loop the sound.

The WaveStudio program also allows you to record and save your own WAV files (you must have a microphone hooked up to your sound card). Once you are finished recording a sound, you can use the Play button to test out the recording. After you are satisfied, go ahead and save the file to disk (see Figure 12-2). Once the file is saved to disk, it behaves exactly like a sound file loaded from disk and can be played from memory and looped continuously.

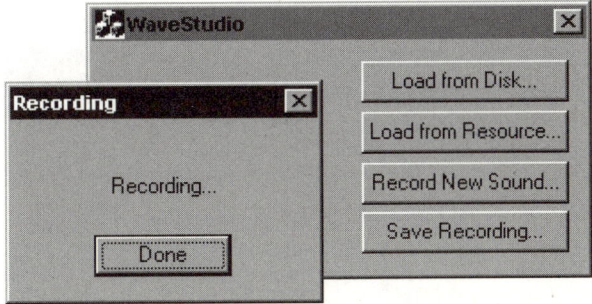

Figure 12-2: The WaveStudio demo program allows you to record your own WAV files.

CWave Class Library Function Calls

This section is provided as a reference to the public function calls of the CWave class library. The calls should be easy to use and easy to implement in your own programs.

You may want to skip over this section and read the section entitled "Behind WaveStudio." This section shows how the calls are used (for some people, it's better to look at the usage of function calls before actually studying the syntax).

CWave()

Prototype: `CWave (void);`

Purpose: This is the constructor. It simply creates a CWave object and initializes its internal variables.

Arguments: None

Returns: Nothing

~CWave()

Prototype: `~CWave (void);`

Purpose: This is the destructor. It calls the Close() member function.

Arguments: None

Returns: Nothing

GetDevices()

Prototype: `int GetDevices (void);`

Purpose: This function returns the number of devices installed on the system that support wave audio output.

Arguments: None

Returns: int: nDevices

LoadFromDisk()

Prototype: `BOOL LoadFromDisk (CString Filename);`

Purpose: This function opens the file and reads the waveform data into memory.

Arguments: CString Filename

Returns: BOOL: TRUE for success, FALSE for failure

LoadFromRes()

Prototype: `void LoadFromRes (CString ResID, HINSTANCE hInstance);`

Purpose: This function finds the waveform data in memory from the application's resource file.

Arguments: CString ResID; HINSTANCE hInstance

Returns: BOOL: TRUE for success, FALSE on failure

Close()

Prototype: `void Close (void);`

Purpose: This function stops the file from playing and releases memory that is storing the waveform data. You should not need to call this function, since it will automatically get called by the destructor. However, you can call it if you want to free up memory sooner.

Arguments: None

Returns: Nothing

Play()

Prototype: `BOOL Play (BOOL bLoop = FALSE);`

Purpose: This function plays the WAV file.

Arguments: BOOL bLoop, Defaults to FALSE

Returns: BOOL: TRUE for success, FALSE for failure

Stop()

Prototype: `void Stop (void);`

Purpose: This function stops the file from playing or recording.

Arguments: None

Returns: Nothing

Record()

Prototype: `BOOL Record (void);`

Purpose: This function records new waveform data. Recording will continue until the Stop() function is called.

Arguments: None

Returns: BOOL: TRUE for success, FALSE for failure

Save()

Prototype: `BOOL Save (CString Filename);`

Purpose: This function saves recorded waveform data to disk.

Arguments: CString Filename

Returns: BOOL: TRUE for success, FALSE for failure

PlayFromDisk()

Prototype: `static BOOL PlayFromDisk (CString Filename);`

Purpose: This static function synchronously plays a sound from disk.

Arguments: CString Filename

Returns: BOOL: TRUE for success, FALSE for failure

PlayFromRes()

Prototype: `static BOOL PlayFromRes (CString ResID, HINSTANCE hInstance);`

Purpose: This static function synchronously plays a sound from the application's resource file.

Arguments: CString ResID HINSTANCE hInstance

Returns: BOOL: TRUE for success, FALSE for failure

PLAYING WAV FILES

The Microsoft Windows Multimedia API provides three different ways for applications to work with WAV files:

- ❐ **The PlaySound() function.** This is a powerful function that allows playback of waveform audio with one line of code. We will use this as the basis for the Wave class library but we'll enhance it by preloading the sound data into memory.
- ❐ **The Media Control Interface (MCI).** This is similar to the method used in Chapter 11 to play MIDI files. The Wave class library uses this method for the recording and saving of WAV files.
- ❐ **Low-level waveform audio services.** Applications that require complete control over the waveform data can use these services.

The PlaySound() Function

The Windows API includes a function called PlaySound() that is used to play waveform audio. The function has two minor limitations: the entire sound must fit into available physical memory, and the sound must be in a data format supported by one of the installed audio drivers. A good rule of thumb is to use PlaySound() for files under 100K and MCI for files larger than that. The PlaySound() function offers the programmer a lot of flexibility for digitized sound playback. It will play disk-based WAV files, WAV resources, or specific system event sounds. It can loop sounds, play them asynchronously, and play them from memory. The Wave class library uses this function extensively. One of the main advantages of the class library is that it loads the waveform data into memory, then uses the PlaySound() function to play the sound. This allows the application to load the sound only once and eliminates any delay at the start of sound playback.

PlaySound()

Prototype: `BOOL PlaySound (LPCSTR pszSound, HMODULE hmod, DWORD fdwSound);`

Purpose: This function plays a sound specified by the given filename.

Arguments: LPCSTR pszSound, the filename, resource identifier, or system event, if NULL playback is stopped
HMODULE hmod, handle of the resource, if not playing a WAV resource it is NULL
DWORD fdwSound, specifies flags for the command

Returns: BOOL: TRUE for success, FALSE for failure

The Media Control Interface

The Media Control Interface (MCI) allows for control of the Windows waveform audio devices. The Wave class library uses the MCI to record and save WAV files.

The MCI can be implemented with one of two functions: mciSendCommand() or mciSendString(). Although they both serve the same purpose and both produce the same result, they have different syntax. One uses a command-based interface and the other uses a string-based interface. We will only use mciSendCommand because the command-based interface should seem more logical to programmers accustomed to the Windows command-based API.

The mciSendCommand() function is used to communicate with the MCI device by sending command messages such as MCI_OPEN and MCI_PLAY. The MCI command-based messaging interface allows for a lot of flexibility through the use of MCI parameter blocks. The parameter blocks are structures defined in MMSYSTEM.H that allow large amounts of information to be passed to and returned from the mciSendCommand() function.

mciSendCommand()

Prototype: `DWORD mciSendCommand (UINT wDeviceID, UINT wMessage, DWORD dwParam1, DWORD dwParam2);`

Purpose: This function is the core of MCI. It is used to do all communication with the MCI device.

Arguments: UINT wDeviceID, the device that receives the message
UINT wMessage, the MCI command message
DWORD dwParam1, specifies flags for the command
DWORD dwParam2, specifies a pointer to the parameter block to be used

Returns: Zero if successful, otherwise the low-order word contains an error.

The MCI device ID identifies which device has been opened. This value is returned in the parameter block when you send the MCI_OPEN command and should be saved for later use. The ID is used to identify this device when sending subsequent commands. The following is a brief overview of the MCI commands that we use and that are relevant to waveform audio.

MCI Commands	
MCI_OPEN	Opens the device.
MCI_CLOSE	Closes the device.
MCI_PLAY	Starts the file playback.
MCI_STOP	Stops the file playback.
MCI_SEEK	Seeks to a specific position within the file.
MCI_RECORD	Begins recording of waveform audio.
MCI_SAVE	Saves recorded audio to disk.

THE DIRECTWAVE CLASS LIBRARY

We have also built a simple class library based on Microsoft's DirectSound technology. The DirectWave class can be linked with any Windows 95 Visual C++ project (you must also link DSOUND.LIB).

The DirectWave library provides your application with the ability to play more than one sound at the same time. This is a huge advantage and can give your programs the appearance of much more activity. This library is more basic than the Wave library and does not support recording or saving of WAV files. However, the sound data is still preloaded into memory and provides more efficient playback than the standard Windows routines.

All source code and support files to rebuild the DirectWave.lib can be found in the SOUND\DirectWave directory on the Companion CD-ROM that comes with this book.

WAVEMIX.DLL

Unfortunately, the DirectSound technology is only available for programs designed specifically for Windows 95. If you are developing an application that needs to run under Win32s, don't fret. The WAVEMIX.DLL supports playback of up to eight WAV files simultaneously. You can find the WAVEMIX.DLL and samples on how to use it on the Microsoft Internet FTP site.

CDirectWave Class Library Function Calls

The CDirectWave class library is used exactly the same way as the CWave class library, except that it does not support resource files or recording. The only functions that need to be called are LoadFromDisk(), Play(), Stop(), and Close(). Except for LoadFromDisk(), all the functions share the same syntax as their CWave counterparts. The LoadFromDisk() prototype is listed below:

LoadFromDisk()

Prototype: `BOOL LoadFromDisk (CString Filename LPDIRECTSOUND pDSoundObject);`

Purpose: This function opens the file and reads the waveform data into memory.

Arguments: CString Filename
LPDIRECTSOUND pDSoundObject

Returns: BOOL: TRUE for success, FALSE for failure

Behind WaveStudio

WaveStudio was created with the Visual C++ AppWizard with the following settings:

- ❏ Dialog-based application
- ❏ English language
- ❏ About box and 3D controls
- ❏ No automation, ActiveX, or WOSA support
- ❏ Yes source file comments
- ❏ MFC linked as a static library

WAVE Basics

The basic functions for loading and playing a WAV file are very easy to use.

Loading the Sound

The Wave sound can be loaded as a disk-based file or from the application's resource. These two functions demonstrate this process. Once the Wave is loaded, it can be played repeatedly, since the waveform data has been loaded into memory.

```
void CWaveStudioDlg::OnLoaddisk()
{
 CString Filter;
 Filter = "Wave Files (*.WAV)|*.WAV||";

 CFileDialog FileDlg (TRUE, NULL, NULL,
  OFN_HIDEREADONLY, Filter);
 if (FileDlg.DoModal () == IDOK){
  if (!m_Wave.LoadFromDisk (
    FileDlg.GetPathName ())){
   MessageBox ("Sorry, could not open this
    file.", "Error", MB_OK | MB_ICONSTOP);
    }
  else{
   CWnd *pWnd;
   pWnd = GetDlgItem (IDC_PLAY);
   pWnd->EnableWindow (1);
   pWnd = GetDlgItem (IDC_STOP);
   pWnd->EnableWindow (1);
   pWnd = GetDlgItem (IDC_LOOP);
   pWnd->EnableWindow (1);
    }
   }
}

void CWaveStudioDlg::OnLoadres()
{
 CResSound SoundsDlg;
 SoundsDlg.m_nSound = 0;

 if (SoundsDlg.DoModal () == IDOK){
  CString ResName;
  ResName.Format ("IDR_WAVE%d",
   SoundsDlg.m_nSound + 1);
   if (!m_Wave.LoadFromRes (ResName,
```

```
    AfxGetResourceHandle ())){
    MessageBox ("Sorry, could not open this
     file.", "Error", MB_OK | MB_ICONSTOP);
    }
  else{
  CWnd *pWnd;
  pWnd = GetDlgItem (IDC_PLAY);
  pWnd->EnableWindow (1);
  pWnd = GetDlgItem (IDC_STOP);
  pWnd->EnableWindow (1);
  pWnd = GetDlgItem (IDC_LOOP);
  pWnd->EnableWindow (1);
  }
 }
}
```

Resource WAV Files

If you wish to use the Wave class library to play WAV files from resource memory, you must add the files to your application's resource file. Fortunately, Visual C++ has a predefined WAV resource type. To add a WAV file to your application from Visual C++, follow these steps:

1. Select Resource... from the Insert menu item.
2. Press the Import... button.
3. Change the file type selector to WAV Files.
4. Select your file and press Import.
5. Change the resource identifier from a constant value to a string, so it can be located by the class library—for example, IDR_WAVE1 to "IDR_WAVE1".

Play, Stop & Close

These functions are very simple and, along with the loading functions, are the only functions you really need to play waveform audio. You should not need to call the Close() function, since it is called in the destructor. However, you can call the function if you want to free the memory sooner than that.

```
void CWaveStudioDlg::OnPlay()
{
 m_Wave.Play (IsDlgButtonChecked (IDC_LOOP));
}
void CWaveStudioDlg::OnStop()
```

```
    {
 m_Wave.Stop ();
    }
```

Recording & Saving

You can also use the WaveStudio program to record and save your own WAV files. It's as simple as calling the Record() function to start and the Stop() function to finish. Once you have a sound you want to save, just call the Save() function with the filename you want.

```
void CWaveStudioDlg::OnRecord()
{
 m_Wave.Record ();

 CRecording RecordingDlg;
 RecordingDlg.DoModal ();

 m_Wave.Stop ();

 CWnd *pWnd;
 pWnd = GetDlgItem (IDC_PLAY);
 pWnd->EnableWindow (1);
 pWnd = GetDlgItem (IDC_STOP);
 pWnd->EnableWindow (1);
 pWnd = GetDlgItem (IDC_LOOP);
 pWnd->EnableWindow (1);
}

void CWaveStudioDlg::OnSave()
{
 CString Filter;
 Filter = "Wave Files (*.WAV)|*.WAV||";

 CFileDialog FileDlg (FALSE, NULL, NULL,
  OFN_OVERWRITEPROMPT, Filter);
 FileDlg.m_ofn.lpstrDefExt = "wav";
 if (FileDlg.DoModal () == IDOK){
  if (!m_Wave.Save (FileDlg.GetPathName ()))
   MessageBox ("Sorry, could not save this
    file.", "Error", MB_OK | MB_ICONSTOP);
  }
}
```

CREATING PROGRAMS THAT USE SOUND

The following three hands-on exercises will get you started on your way to making great multimedia applications. Going through them won't take very long, and the investment of time will be well worth it.

You may be asking why you should type in the code for each exercise. Why not just load the project from disk? In my experience, you'll learn more by doing than by just reading.

Each of these exercises is designed to be as simple as possible, so there is a limit to the amount of error checking that is done. Under normal circumstances, the application should check to see if the functions succeed and provide feedback to the user.

Finding WAV Files

All of these examples require WAV files for playback. We have provided some sample files on the Companion CD-ROM in the SOUND\Samples directory.

However, when you are writing your own applications, you may need your own WAV files. If you don't have the capability to create your own sound effects and digitized sound, there is a large library of files on the Internet, CompuServe, and other online services. Most of these files are available for free or a small fee, and you can usually find whatever you want. Check out the "On the Web" section at the end of this chapter for more information.

Hands-On 1: Playing Sound Files

In this example, we will create a program that plays a sound on a regular timed interval. The program's interface will look like a digital clock and will include a method for selecting the time interval. We will load the sound on startup and play it every time our interval elapses.

1. Create a Visual C++ project named HandsOn12_1 with the following attributes:
   - ❑ Dialog-based application
   - ❑ English language
   - ❑ About box and 3D controls
   - ❑ No automation, ActiveX, or WOSA support
   - ❑ Yes source file comments
   - ❑ MFC linked as a static library

2. Select Settings from the Project menu. Choose the Link tab. Add the following libraries to the Object/library modules field. The libraries for the release and debug versions are different. Both are listed below.

Release Project Libraries	Debug Project Libraries
Wave.lib	WaveD.lib
winmm.lib	winmm.lib

3. Set the Active Configuration to Win32 Release.

4. Copy the file RES3.WAV from the \SOUND\Samples directory on the Companion CD-ROM to the newly created project directory.

5. Add the following include to the HandsOn12_1Dlg.h file:

```
#include "Wave.h"
```

6. Add the following variable declaration to the CHandsOn12_1Dlg class in the HandsOn12_1Dlg.h file:

```
public:
 CWave m_Wave;
 int m_nMinute;
 int m_nInterval;
```

7. Edit the dialog resource IDD_HANDSON12_1_DIALOG to resemble the dialog shown in Figure 12-3.

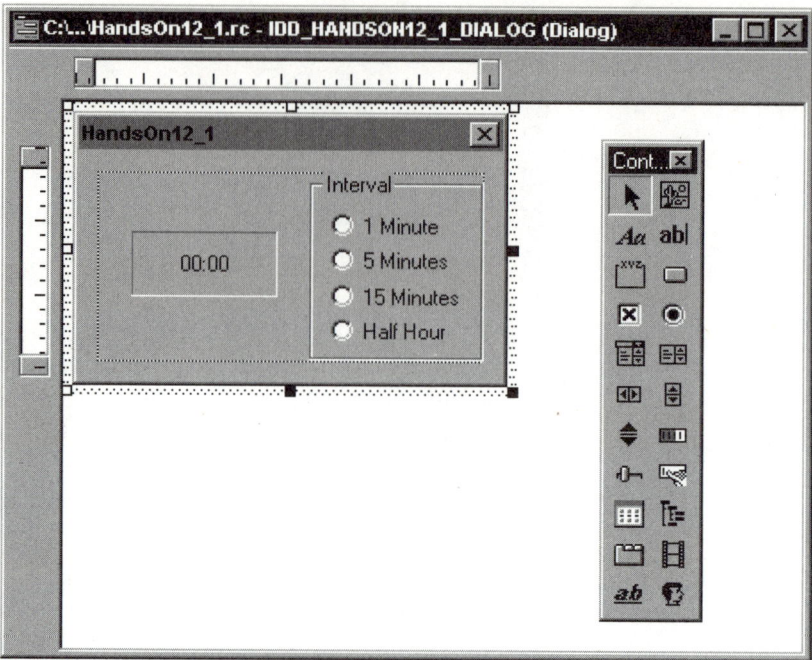

Figure 12-3: The dialog resource for the Hands-On 1 example.

8. Add the following functions with the Class Wizard to the CHandsOn12_1Dlg class:

```
Name: OnTimer()  Message: WM_TIMER
Name: OnInt1()   Message: BN_CLICKED
    Control: IDC_INT1
Name: OnInt2()   Message: BN_CLICKED
    Control: IDC_INT2
Name: OnInt3()   Message: BN_CLICKED
    Control: IDC_INT3
Name: OnInt3()   Message: BN_CLICKED
    Control: IDC_INT3
```

9. Edit the OnInitDialog() function in the CHandsOn12_1Dlg class in the CHandsOn12_1Dlg.cpp file as follows:

```
BOOL CHandsOn12_1Dlg::OnInitDialog()
{
 CDialog::OnInitDialog();
  .
  .
  .
```

```
m_Wave.LoadFromDisk ("res3.wav");

SetTimer (1, 5000, NULL);

m_nInterval = 0;
CheckRadioButton (IDC_INT1, IDC_INT4,
 IDC_INT1);

// Get the current time
CTime Time = CTime::GetCurrentTime ();
// Save the current minute for future use
m_nMinute = Time.GetMinute ();
int nHour = Time.GetHour ();
if (nHour == 0)
 nHour = 12;
if (nHour > 12)
 nHour -= 12;
// Display the time
CString TimeString;
TimeString.Format ("%02d:%02d", nHour,
 m_nMinute);
SetDlgItemText (IDC_TIME, TimeString);

return TRUE;
}
```

10. Edit the OnTimer() function in the CHandsOn12_1Dlg class in the CHandsOn12_1Dlg.cpp file as follows:

```
void CHandsOn12_1Dlg::OnTimer(UINT nIDEvent)
{
 // Get and display the current time
 CTime Time = CTime::GetCurrentTime ();
 int nHour = Time.GetHour ();
 int nMinute = Time.GetMinute ();
 if (nHour == 0)
  nHour = 12;
 if (nHour > 12)
  nHour -= 12;
 CString TimeString;
 TimeString.Format ("%02d:%02d", nHour,
  nMinute);
 SetDlgItemText (IDC_TIME, TimeString);

 // If the minute has changed see if we should
 // play the sound.
```

```
if (nMinute != m_nMinute){
 m_nMinute = nMinute;
 switch (m_nInterval){
  case 0:
   m_Wave.Play ();
   break;
  case 1:
   if (m_nMinute % 5 == 0)
    m_Wave.Play ();
   break;
  case 2:
   if (m_nMinute % 15 == 0)
    m_Wave.Play ();
   break;
  case 3:
   if (m_nMinute % 30 == 0)
    m_Wave.Play ();
   break;
  }
 }

CDialog::OnTimer(nIDEvent);
}
```

11. Edit the OnInt() functions in the CHandsOn12_1Dlg class in the
    CHandsOn12_1Dlg.cpp file as follows:

```
void CHandsOn12_1Dlg::OnInt1()
{
 m_nInterval = 0;
}


void CHandsOn12_1Dlg::OnInt2()
{
 m_nInterval = 1;
}


void CHandsOn12_1Dlg::OnInt3()
{
 m_nInterval = 2;
}


void CHandsOn12_1Dlg::OnInt4()
{
 m_nInterval = 3;
}
```

12. Compile and run the program.

Once you run the program, the current time will be displayed. Every time the specified interval elapses, the alarm will sound. It's as simple as that. You can leave the program running in the background while you perform other tasks and it will remind you when the next interval elapses. You could also modify this program to create your own little alarm clock by letting the user set the time they would like the alarm to sound.

Hands-On 2: Recording & Saving

This program serves as a very simple method for recording and saving your own WAV files. It is also a dialog-based application and contains four buttons for controlling the recording process.

1. Create a Visual C++ project named HandsOn12_2 with the following attributes:

   ❑ Dialog-based application

   ❑ English language

   ❑ About box and 3D controls

   ❑ No automation, ActiveX, or WOSA support

   ❑ Yes source file comments

   ❑ MFC linked as a static library

2. Select Settings from the Project menu. Choose the Link tab. Add the following libraries to the Object/library modules field. The libraries for the release and debug versions are different. Both are listed below.

Release Project Libraries	Debug Project Libraries
Wave.lib	WaveD.lib
winmm.lib	winmm.lib

3. Set the Active Configuration to Win32 Release.

4. Add the following include to the HandsOn12_2Dlg.h file:

```
#include "Wave.h"
```

5. Add the following variable declaration to the CHandsOn12_2Dlg class in the HandsOn12_2Dlg.h file:

```
public:
 CWave m_Wave;
```

6. Add Record, Stop, Play, and Save buttons to the
IDD_HANDSON12_2_DIALOG resource as shown in Figure 12-4.

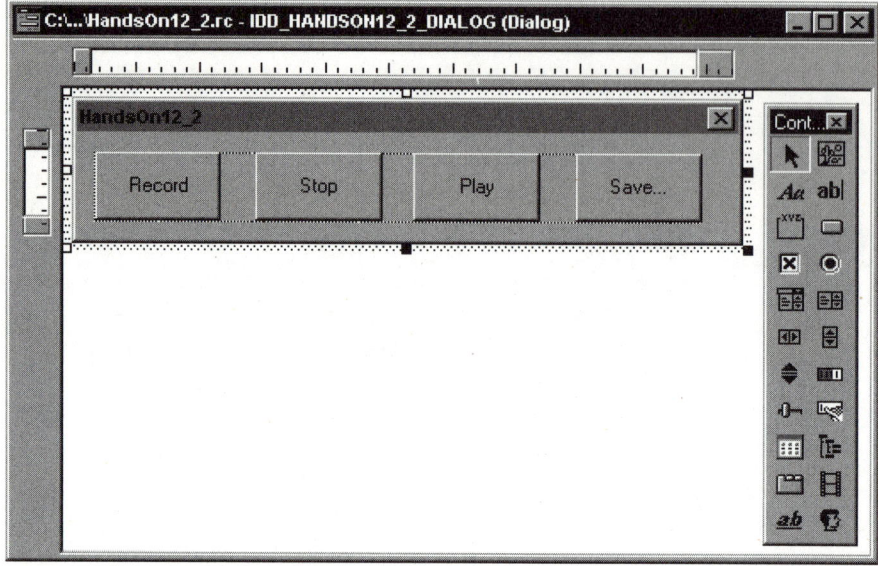

Figure 12-4: Edit the dialog resource for the Hands-On 2 example.

7. Add the following functions with the Class Wizard to the
CHandsOn12_2Dlg class:

```
Name: OnRecord()  Message: BN_CLICKED
  Control: IDC_RECORD
Name: OnStop() Message: BN_CLICKED
  Control: IDC_STOP
Name: OnPlay() Message: BN_CLICKED
  Control: IDC_PLAY
Name: OnSave() Message: BN_CLICKED
  Control: IDC_SAVE
```

8. Edit the OnInitDialog() function in the CHandsOn12_2Dlg class in
the CHandsOn12_2Dlg.cpp file as follows:

```
BOOL CHandsOn12_2Dlg::OnInitDialog()
{
 CDialog::OnInitDialog();
  .
  .
  .
```

```
CWnd *pWnd;
pWnd = GetDlgItem (IDC_STOP);
pWnd->EnableWindow (0);
pWnd = GetDlgItem (IDC_PLAY);
pWnd->EnableWindow (0);
pWnd = GetDlgItem (IDC_SAVE);
pWnd->EnableWindow (0);

return TRUE;
}
```

9. Edit the functions for the corresponding buttons of the CHandsOn12_2Dlg class in the CHandsOn12_2Dlg.cpp file as follows:

```
void CHandsOn12_2Dlg::OnRecord()
{
CWnd *pWnd;
pWnd = GetDlgItem (IDC_STOP);
pWnd->EnableWindow (1);
pWnd = GetDlgItem (IDC_PLAY);
pWnd->EnableWindow (0);
pWnd = GetDlgItem (IDC_SAVE);
pWnd->EnableWindow (0);

m_Wave.Record ();
}

void CHandsOn12_2Dlg::OnStop()
{
m_Wave.Stop ();

CWnd *pWnd;
pWnd = GetDlgItem (IDC_STOP);
pWnd->EnableWindow (0);
pWnd = GetDlgItem (IDC_PLAY);
pWnd->EnableWindow (1);
pWnd = GetDlgItem (IDC_SAVE);
pWnd->EnableWindow (1);
}

void CHandsOn12_2Dlg::OnPlay()
{
m_Wave.Play ();
}
```

```
void CHandsOn12_2Dlg::OnSave()
{
 CString Filter;
 Filter = "Wave Files (*.WAV)|*.WAV||";

 CFileDialog FileDlg (FALSE, NULL, NULL,
  OFN_OVERWRITEPROMPT, Filter);
 FileDlg.m_ofn.lpstrDefExt = "wav";
 if (FileDlg.DoModal () == IDOK)
  m_Wave.Save (FileDlg.GetPathName ());
}
```

10. Compile and run the program.

You are now ready to record your own sounds. Simply press the Record button to begin, the Stop button to stop recording, the Play button to test out your sound, and the Save button to save it to disk.

 ## Hands-On 3: Using DirectSound

In this example, we will take advantage of the DirectWave class library provided with this book. This application can play multiple WAV files simultaneously. It is a dialog-based application that loads three sounds for playback.

1. Create a Visual C++ project named HandsOn12_3 with the following attributes:

   ❏ Dialog-based application

   ❏ English language

   ❏ About box and 3D controls

   ❏ No automation, ActiveX, or WOSA support

   ❏ Yes source file comments

   ❏ MFC linked as a static library

2. Select Settings from the Project menu. Choose the Link tab. Add the following libraries to the Object/library modules field. The libraries for the release and debug versions are different. Both are listed below.

Release Project Libraries	Debug Project Libraries
DirectWave.lib	DirectWaveD.lib
DSound.lib	DSound.lib

3. Set the Active Configuration to Win32 Release.

4. Copy the files RES1.WAV, RES2.WAV, and RES3.WAV from the \SOUND\Samples directory on the Companion CD-ROM to the newly created project directory.

5. Add the following includes to the HandsOn12_3Dlg.h file:

```
#include <mmsystem.h>
#include <dsound.h>
#include "DirectWave.h"
```

6. Add the following variable declaration to the CHandsOn12_3Dlg class in the HandsOn12_3Dlg.h file:

```
public:
    LPDIRECTSOUND m_pDSoundObject;
    CDirectWave m_Wave[3];
```

7. Add buttons and controls to Stop and Play and Loop the sounds to the IDD_HANDSON12_3_DIALOG resource as shown in Figure 12-5.

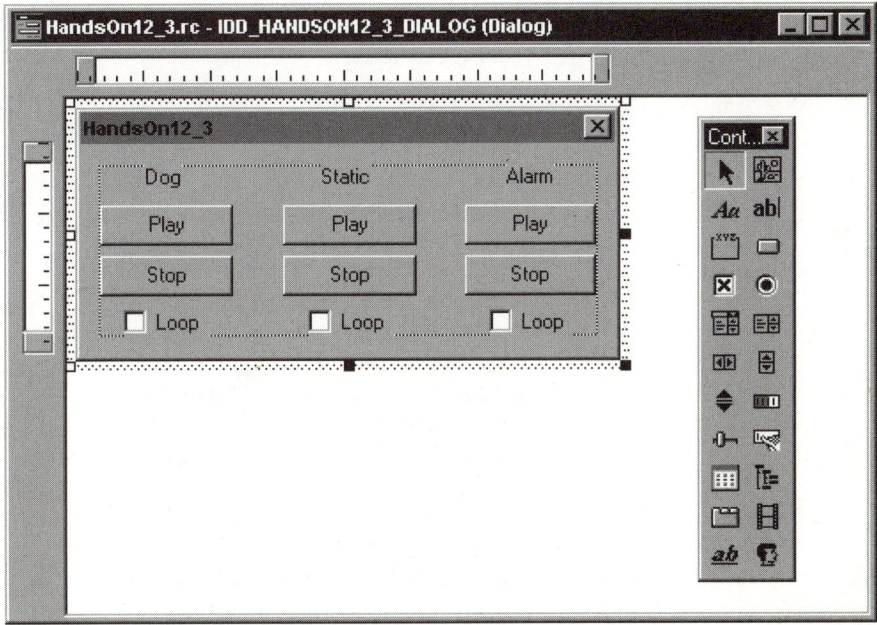

Figure 12-5: Edit the dialog resource for the Hands-On 3 example.

8. Add the following functions with the Class Wizard to the CHandsOn12_3Dlg class:

```
Name: OnCreate()   Message: WM_CREATE
Name: OnClose()    Message: WM_CLOSE
Name: OnPlay1()    Message: BN_CLICKED
  Control: IDC_PLAY1
Name: OnStop1()    Message: BN_CLICKED
  Control: IDC_STOP1
Name: OnPlay2()    Message: BN_CLICKED
  Control: IDC_PLAY2
Name: OnStop2()    Message: BN_CLICKED
  Control: IDC_STOP2
Name: OnPlay3()    Message: BN_CLICKED
  Control: IDC_PLAY3
Name: OnStop3()    Message: BN_CLICKED
  Control: IDC_STOP3
```

9. Edit the OnCreate() and OnClose() functions in the CHandsOn12_3Dlg class in the CHandsOn12_3Dlg.cpp file as follows:

```cpp
int CHandsOn12_3Dlg::OnCreate(LPCREATESTRUCT
lpCreateStruct)
{
 if (CDialog::OnCreate(lpCreateStruct) == -1)
  return -1;

 if (DirectSoundCreate (NULL,
   &m_pDSoundObject, NULL) == DS_OK){
  m_pDSoundObject->SetCooperativeLevel(
   this->m_hWnd, DSSCL_NORMAL);
  m_Wave[0].LoadFromDisk ("res1.wav",
   m_pDSoundObject);
  m_Wave[1].LoadFromDisk ("res2.wav",
   m_pDSoundObject);
  m_Wave[2].LoadFromDisk ("res3.wav",
   m_pDSoundObject);
  }
 else{
  AfxMessageBox ("Direct sound create
   failed.");
  }

 return 0;
}
```

```
void CHandsOn12_3Dlg::OnClose()
{
 m_Wave[0].Close ();
 m_Wave[1].Close ();
 m_Wave[2].Close ();
 m_pDSoundObject->Release ();

 CDialog::OnClose();
}
```

10. Edit the OnPlay() and OnStop() functions for each sound in the CHandsOn12_3Dlg class in the CHandsOn12_3Dlg.cpp file as follows:

```
void CHandsOn12_3Dlg::OnPlay1()
{
 m_Wave[0].Play (IsDlgButtonChecked(
   IDC_LOOP1));
}

void CHandsOn12_3Dlg::OnPlay2()
{
 m_Wave[1].Play (IsDlgButtonChecked(
   IDC_LOOP2));
}

void CHandsOn12_3Dlg::OnPlay3()
{
 m_Wave[2].Play (IsDlgButtonChecked(
   IDC_LOOP3));
}

void CHandsOn12_3Dlg::OnStop1()
{
 m_Wave[0].Stop ();
}

void CHandsOn12_3Dlg::OnStop2()
{
 m_Wave[1].Stop ();
}

void CHandsOn12_3Dlg::OnStop3()
{
 m_Wave[2].Stop ();
}
```

423

11. Compile and run the program.

Once the application starts up, simply use the Play and Stop buttons to start and stop each sound. You can also check the Loop box to make the sound play continuously.

ON THE WEB

There are many great Web sites devoted to waveform audio. You can find everything from WAV file players to libraries of WAV. Here are a few sites to get you started:

Yahoo!

www.yahoo.com/Computers_and_Internet/Multimedia/Sound/ Archives/WAV/

Yahoo! has a great list of Web sites that feature sound effects and sound clips in the WAV file format. You could spend hours searching through all of these sites and have a great time doing it.

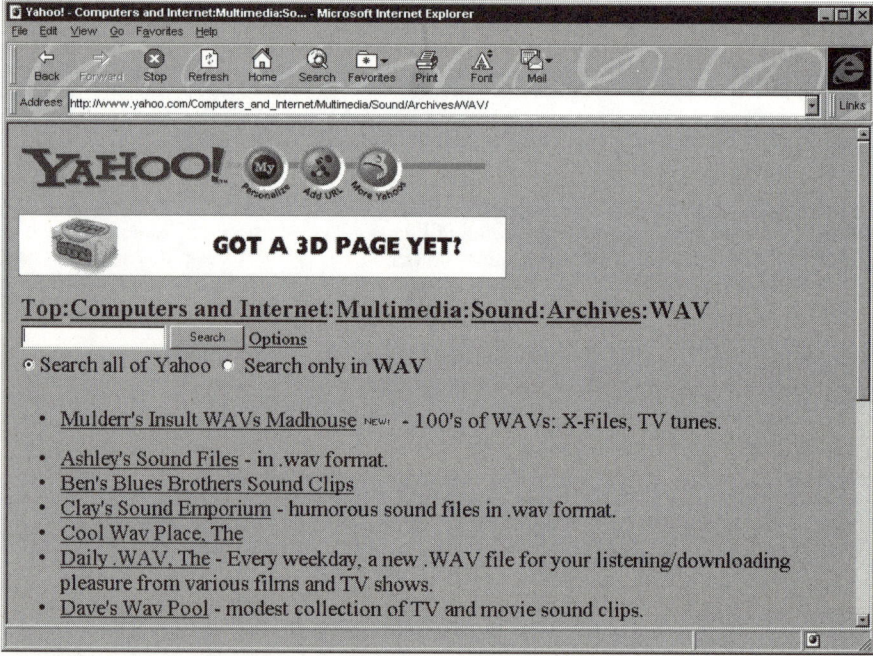

Figure 12-6: A Yahoo! search turns up a long list of sites devoted to WAV files.

Play Now

www.sr.se/rd/playnow/eindex.htm

The Swedish Broadcasting Corporation provides a technology called Play Now. Play Now will play WAV files over the Internet in real time instead of downloading them to your hard drive first.

DiamondWare, Ltd.

www.dw.com

DiamondWare's Sound ToolKit (STK) is a programmer's library that lets you quickly and easily add high-quality interactive audio to your game or multimedia application. It's available for Windows and supports every C/C++ compiler, Visual Basic, and Delphi.

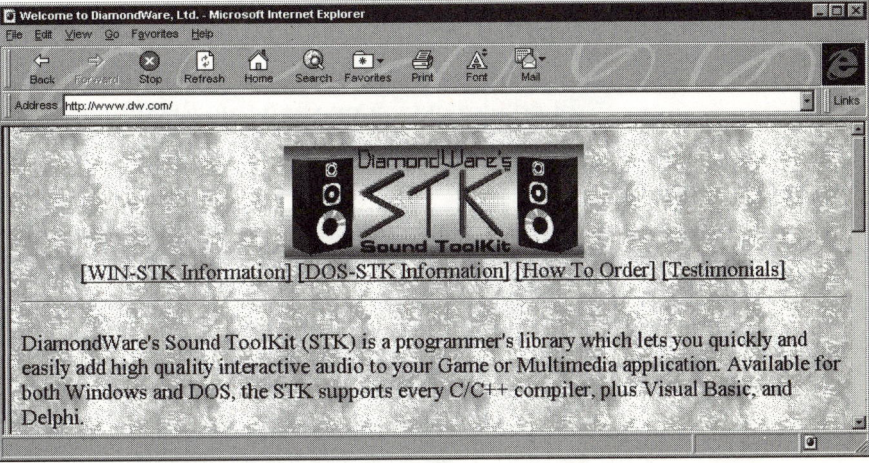

Figure 12-7: DiamondWare offers a library for playing audio in Windows applications.

Cool Edit

www.syntrillium.com/cool96.htm

Cool Edit is a digital sound editor for Windows created by Syntrillium Software Corporation. Cool Edit enables you to "paint" with sound: tones, pieces of songs, voices and miscellaneous noises, sine waves and sawtooth waves, noise, or just pure silence. Cool Edit also gives you a wide variety of special effects to "touch up" your sounds: reverberation, noise reduction, echo and delay, flanging, filtering, and many others.

RSX 3D

www.intel.com/ial/rsx/index.htm

If you're looking for something a little more advanced, you may be interested in Intel's RSX 3D technology. This latest version of the Realistic Sound Experience is a truly interactive positional 3D sound solution for the PC; it runs completely in software and is available for third-party developers.

SHAREWARE & COMMERCIAL DEMOS

For those of you who don't have access to the World Wide Web, there are plenty of shareware and commercial products available. We've included a few on the Companion CD-ROM, so feel free to take a look.

Awave

Awave is a shareware program by FMJ-Software that converts and plays sound files in over one hundred file formats from different platforms, synthesizers, and trackers. The file AWAVE30.ZIP can be found in the SOUND\Demos directory.

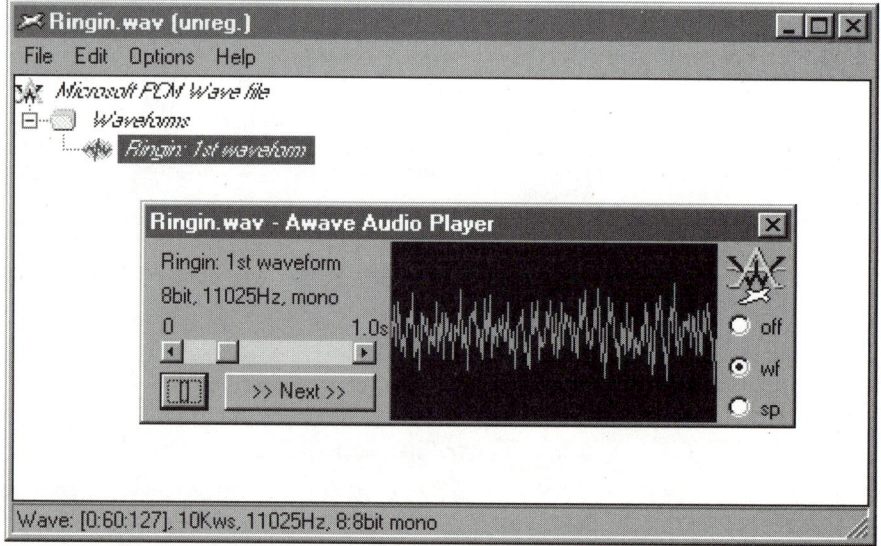

Figure 12-8: Awave can convert sound files from over 100 formats.

Speak

If you wish to play WAV files on a computer with no sound card, there is still hope. Microsoft provides instructions along with the required driver to do just that. The driver and instructional text are in the SPEAK.ZIP file in the SOUND\Demos directory.

Quack

The Quack Sound Effects Studio is a piece of shareware designed to help you create your own sound effects from scratch. It has a built-in library of predefined components and also lets you work from an existing WAV file. The QUACK.ZIP file can be found in the SOUND\Demos directory on the Companion CD-ROM.

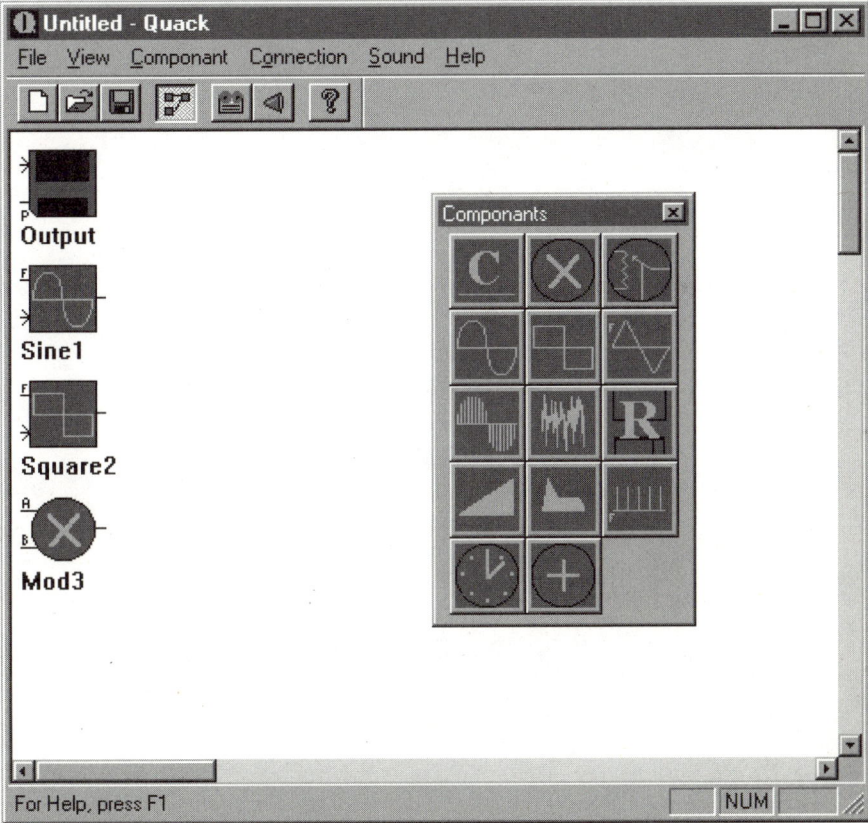

Figure 12-9: Quack allows you to create your own sounds from predefined components.

Moving On

By now, your multimedia applications should really be cooking. Now that you have learned how to add sound and music to your applications, you're ready to move on to CD audio. All you need to do is take a look at the shelves in your local computer store and you will see the endless possibilities of multimedia. Now that you have the know-how, you should be ready to implement your own ideas and join the competition.

This chapter covered only the tip of the iceberg as far as Windows sound capabilites are concerned. If you have the ambition and decide to take your applications to the next level, I would love to hear about them. So if you have any questions, suggestions, or ideas, please feel free to contact me at ivt-rcl@interpath.com.

Chapter 13

CD Audio

Without music life would be a mistake.
–Freidrich Nietzsche

CD audio. Sounds cool, doesn't it? Just having sound and music in your application is not enough anymore. Publishers want high-quality CD audio to compete with the top-of-the-line multimedia products.

What makes CD audio so great? First, and probably most important, is sound quality. CD audio has the unique advantage of sounding exactly the way the composer designed it and the musicians produced it. While a MIDI file playing on one person's computer could sound completely different than on another, CD audio will always sound exactly the same. Along with this improved sound quality comes the ability to completely immerse the user in the musical experience. You might be surprised at the effects high-quality audio can have on a computer user.

Another advantage of using CD audio is that it's very easy to skip to different tracks on a CD or to different positions within a track—CDs are organized in a format that most people are already familiar with.

Are there any disadvantages to CD audio? Unfortunately, CD audio, like everything else, is not perfect. The main disadvantage involves disc access. You can't play CD audio while you are accessing the CD for other purposes. So when your application accesses the CD to read data, you must pause the CD audio until the process is complete. Also, unless you happen to run your own music studio, CD quality audio may be expensive and hard to produce.

When making the decision to use CD audio in your applications, you must take all of these factors into account. But if you have the resources and the know-how to use CD audio, no other one feature can add more to the user experience. The CDAudio class library that comes with this book, along with the Windows multimedia library (WINMM.LIB) provided with Visual C++, can provide a quick and easy method for adding CD audio to any Windows 95 or Windows NT application. You can now make your programs sound like the ones the pros offer.

THE CDAudio CLASS LIBRARY

The CDAudio class library can be linked with any Visual C++ project (you must also link WINMM.LIB). With just a few additions to your application you can have all the features of a CD player in your own program. You don't have to learn the programming required to play CD audio. The class library will do all the work for you.

In addition to playing audio from the CD, you're provided with a set of functions that allow you to do much more: skip around on the CD, get information on the different tracks, and even open and close the CD drive. All of this is handled in a way that's transparent to the program. Of course, if you want to examine the class library in detail or make changes to the member functions, the source code is included on the Companion CD-ROM.

All source code and support files to rebuild CDAudio.lib can be found in the CDAUDIO\CDAudio directory on the Companion CD-ROM that comes with this book.

THE CDAudioPLAYER DEMO

We've built a simple demonstration program that shows what the class library can do. The program can be found in the CDAUDIO\CDAudio-Player directory on the Companion CD-ROM. Using File Manager or Program Manager, run the program named CDAudioPlayer.exe. It's a dialog-based program that looks like a CD player. When it first runs, all you'll see is the CD interface as pictured in Figure 13-1.

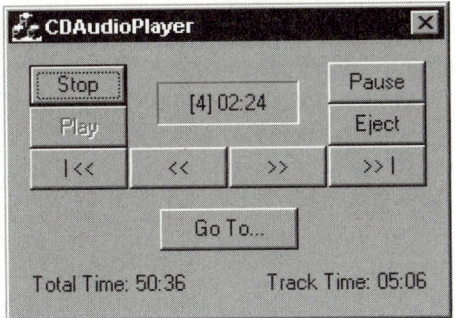

Figure 13-1: When CDAudioPlayer first runs, you'll see an interface similar to a CD player.

Using the CDAudioPlayer you can play, stop, and pause the CD audio. You can also use the control buttons to skip tracks and scan the current track. You can even open and close the CD drive by using the Eject button. Finally, you can jump to any point on the CD by using the Go To button (see Figure 13-2).

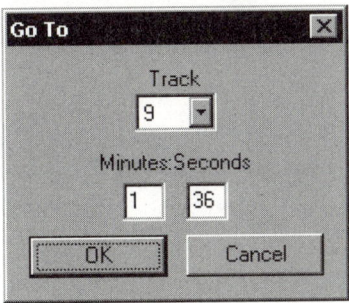

Figure 13-2: You can skip to any spot on a CD using the Go To dialog.

The current position on the CD, the total length of the CD, and the length of the current track are all displayed in the application. And to clean things up, the program will automatically stop the CD and close the device when you exit the program.

The Media Control Interface

The brains behind the CDAudio class library is the Media Control Interface (MCI). This is how Microsoft Windows interfaces with such devices as VCRs, video-disc players, and of course CD audio. You can skip this section if you just want to use the CDAudio library and are not concerned with how it works.

The MCI can be implemented with one of two functions: mciSendCommand() or mciSendString(). Although they both serve the same purpose and both produce the same result, they have different syntax. One uses a command-based interface and the other uses a string-based interface. We will only use the mciSendCommand because the command-based interface should seem more logical to programmers accustomed to the Windows command-based API.

The mciSendCommand() function is used to communicate with the MCI device, to either send command messages (MCI_OPEN, MCI_PLAY) or query for information (MCI_STATUS) on the device. The MCI command-based messaging interface allows for a lot of flexibility through the use of MCI parameter blocks. The parameter blocks are structures defined in MMSYSTEM.H that allow large amounts of information to be passed to and returned from the mciSendCommand() function.

mciSendCommand()

Prototype:
```
DWORD mciSendCommand (UINT wDeviceID, UINT wMessage, DWORD  dwParam1,
    DWORD dwParam2);
```

Purpose: The core function of MCI, used to do all communication with the MCI device.

Arguments: UINT wDeviceID, the device that receives the message
UINT wMessage, the MCI command message
DWORD dwParam1: specifies flags for the command
DWORD dwParam2: specifies a pointer to the parameter block to be used

Returns: Zero if successful, otherwise the low-order word contains an error

The MCI device ID identifies which audio device has been opened. This value is returned in the parameter block when you send the MCI_OPEN command—it should be saved for later use. The ID is used to identify this device when sending subsequent commands. The following is a brief overview of the MCI commands that are relevant to CD audio.

MCI Commands

MCI_OPEN	Opens the device.
MCI_CLOSE	Closes the device.
MCI_PLAY	Starts the audio playing.
MCI_STOP	Stops the audio playing.
MCI_PAUSE	Pauses the audio playing.
MCI_SEEK	Seeks to a specific position on the CD.
MCI_SET	Used with other flags described below.
MCI_STATUS	Used with other flags described below.

MCI_SET Flags

MCI_SET_TIME_FORMAT	Changes the time format.
MCI_SET_DOOR_OPEN	Opens the CD drive.
MCI_SET_DOOR_CLOSED	Closes the CD drive.

MCI_STATUS Flags

MCI_STATUS_CURRENT_TRACK	Gets the current track.
MCI_STATUS_LENGTH	Gets the length of the CD or a specific track.
MCI_STATUS_MODE	Gets the current status of the drive.
MCI_STATUS_NUMBER_OF_TRACKS	Gets the number of tracks on the CD.
MCI_STATUS_POSITION	Gets the current position in the current time format.
MCI_STATUS_READY	Checks to see if the device is ready.
MCI_STATUS_TIME_FORMAT	Gets the current time format.
MCI_CDA_STATUS_TYPE_TRACK	Checks to make sure the track is an audio track.
MCI_STATUS_MEDIA_PRESENT	Checks to make sure a CD is in the drive.

CCDAudio Class Library Function Calls

This section is provided as a reference to the public function calls the CDAudio class library offers. The calls are easy to use and should be pretty straightforward.

You may want to skip over this section and read the section entitled "Behind CDAudioPlayer," which shows how the calls are used. For some people, it's better to look at the usage of function calls before actually studying the syntax.

CCDAudio()

Prototype: `CCDAudio (void);`

Purpose: This is the constructor. It simply creates a CCDAudio object and initializes its internal variables.

Arguments: None

Returns: Nothing

~CCDAudio()

Prototype: `~CCDAudio (void);`

Purpose: This is the destructor. It closes the MCI device if it has been opened.

Arguments: None

Returns: Nothing

Open()

Prototype: `BOOL Open (void);`

Purpose: This function opens the MCI device, sets the time format, and seeks to the beginning of the CD.

Arguments: None

Returns: BOOL: TRUE for success, FALSE for failure

Close()

Prototype: `void Close (void);`

Purpose: This function stops the audio and closes the MCI device.

Arguments: None

Returns: Nothing

Play()

Prototype: `BOOL Play (void);`

Purpose: This function plays the audio from the current position. It will attempt to open the device if it is not already open.

Arguments: None

Returns: BOOL: TRUE for success, FALSE for failure

Stop()

Prototype: `void Stop (void);`

Purpose: This function stops the audio and seeks to the beginning of the CD.

Arguments: None

Returns: Nothing

Pause()

Prototype: `void Pause (void);`

Purpose: This function pauses the audio.

Arguments: None

Returns: Nothing

GetTotalTracks()

Prototype: `int GetTotalTracks (void);`

Purpose: This function returns the number of tracks on the CD.

Arguments: None

Returns: int: nTotalTracks, -1 if function fails

GetTotalLength()

Prototype: `void GetTotalLength (int *pnMinutes, int *pnSeconds);`

Purpose: This function supplies the total length of the audio CD.

Arguments: int *pnMinutes, -1 if function fails
int *pnSeconds, -1 if function fails

Returns: Nothing

GetTrackLength()

Prototype: `void GetTrackLength (int nTrack, int *pnMinutes, int *pnSeconds);`

Purpose: This function supplies the total length of an individual track.

Arguments: int nTrack
int *pnMinutes, -1 if function fails
int *pnSeconds, -1 if function fails

Returns: Nothing

GetCurrentTrack()

Prototype: `int GetCurrentTrack (void);`

Purpose: This function returns the current track of the audio CD.

Arguments: None

Returns: int: nCurrentTrack, -1 if function fails

GetMinutes()

Prototype: `int GetMinutes (void);`

Purpose: This function returns the minutes value of the current track position.

Arguments: None

Returns: int: nMinutes, -1 if function fails

GetSeconds()

Prototype: `int GetSeconds (void);`

Purpose: This function returns the seconds value of the current track position.

Arguments: None

Returns: int: nSeconds, -1 if function fails

GetFrames()

Prototype: `int GetFrames (void);`

Purpose: This function returns the frames value of the current track position.

Arguments: None

Returns: int: nFrames, -1 if function fails

IsDriveReady()

Prototype: `BOOL IsDriveReady (void);`

Purpose: This function determines if the drive is ready to play CD Audio. It will fail if the drive is open, if there is no CD in the drive, or if the drive is not ready.

Arguments: None

Returns: BOOL: TRUE if ready, otherwise FALSE

IsPlaying()

Prototype: `BOOL IsPlaying (BOOL *bPaused);`

Purpose: This function returns the playing status and supplies the paused status in the first parameter. If the track is paused, IsPlaying() will still return TRUE.

Arguments: BOOL *bPaused

Returns: BOOL: TRUE if playing or paused, otherwise FALSE

IsAudioTrack()

Prototype: `BOOL IsAudioTrack (int nTrack);`

Purpose: This function determines if a specific track is an audio or a data track.

Arguments: int nTrack

Returns: BOOL: TRUE if audio, otherwise FALSE

SeekTo()

Prototype: `BOOL SeekTo (int nTrack, int nMinute, int nSecond, int nFrame);`

Purpose: This function seeks to a specific position on the audio CD. If the audio was playing, it will automatically resume.

Arguments: int nTrack
int nMinute
int nSecond
int nFrame

Returns: BOOL: TRUE for success, FALSE for failure

SkipForward()

Prototype: `void SkipForward (int nSeconds);`

Purpose: This function skips forward a specific number of seconds. If the audio was playing, it will automatically resume.

Arguments: int nSeconds

Returns: Nothing

SkipBack()

Prototype: `void SkipBack (int nSeconds);`

Purpose: This function skips back a specific number of seconds. If the audio was playing, it will automatically resume.

Arguments: int nSeconds

Returns: Nothing

OpenDrive()

Prototype: `void OpenDrive (void);`

Purpose: This function opens the door on the CD drive.

Arguments: None

Returns: Nothing

CloseDrive()

Prototype: `void CloseDrive (void);`

Purpose: This function closes the door on the CD drive.

Arguments: None

Returns: Nothing

BEHIND CDAUDIOPLAYER

CDAudioPlayer was created with the Visual C++ AppWizard with the following settings:

- ☐ Dialog-based application
- ☐ English language
- ☐ About box and 3D controls
- ☐ No automation, ActiveX, or WOSA support
- ☐ Yes source file comments
- ☐ MFC linked as a static library

CD Audio Basics

The basic functions for playing CD audio are extremely easy to use. You must open the device before you use it and close it when you are done. In between, you can call any of the CD audio functions you need. The device gets opened in the OnInitDialog() function and gets closed automatically in the m_CDAudio destructor. A timer was also created to constantly display the CD information.

The OnInitDialog() Code

In the OnInitDialog() function we create a timer for later use and open the CD audio device.

```
BOOL CCDAudioPlayerDlg::OnInitDialog()
{
 CDialog::OnInitDialog();
    .

    .

    .

 SetTimer (1, 100, NULL);
 m_CDAudio.Open ();
 return TRUE;
}
```

Play, Stop, Pause & Eject

These functions are very straightfoward and are the heart of the application. Most simply contain one call to the library to perform the specified task. The OnPlay() function also contains some checking to make sure the CD is ready.

```
void CCDAudioPlayerDlg::OnPlay()
{
 // Make sure the drive is ready
 if (m_CDAudio.IsDriveReady ()){
  // Attempt to play the CD
  if (!m_CDAudio.Play ())
   MessageBox ("This CD cannot be played.",
    "Error", MB_OK | MB_ICONSTOP);
  }
 else{
  MessageBox ("The CD drive or audio CD is not
   ready.", "Error", MB_OK | MB_ICONSTOP);
  }
}
```

```
void CCDAudioPlayerDlg::OnStop()
{
 m_CDAudio.Stop ();
}

void CCDAudioPlayerDlg::OnPause()
{
     m_CDAudio.Pause ();
}

void CCDAudioPlayerDlg::OnEject()
{
 if (!m_CDAudio.IsDriveReady ())
  m_CDAudio.CloseDrive ();
 else
  m_CDAudio.OpenDrive ();
}
```

Changing Position

The SeekTo() function can be used to skip to a specific position on the CD. The CDAudioPlayer program uses the SeekTo() function to skip tracks and to jump to a position using the Go To dialog.

Track Back, Track Forward & Go To

Here we simply calculate where we want to go on the CD and then call the SeekTo() function with the specified parameters.

```
void CCDAudioPlayerDlg::OnTrackback()
{
 int nTrack;

 // Get the current track
 nTrack = m_CDAudio.GetCurrentTrack ();

 // If the track is just starting, skip to the
 // previous track
 if (m_CDAudio.GetMinutes () == 0 &&
  m_CDAudio.GetSeconds () < 2)
  nTrack--;

 // If it's the first track go to the last
 // track
 if (nTrack < 1)
  nTrack = m_CDAudio.GetTotalTracks ();
```

441

```
   // Skip to the track
   m_CDAudio.SeekTo (nTrack, 0, 0, 0);
   }

void CCDAudioPlayerDlg::OnTrackforward()
{
 int nTrack;

   // Get the current track
   nTrack = m_CDAudio.GetCurrentTrack ();

   // Skip to the next track
   nTrack++;

   // If it's the last track go to the first
   // track
   if (nTrack > m_CDAudio.GetTotalTracks ())
    nTrack = 1;

   // Skip to the track
   m_CDAudio.SeekTo (nTrack, 0, 0, 0);
   }

void CCDAudioPlayerDlg::OnGoto()
{
 CGotoDlg GotoDlg;

 GotoDlg.m_nTrack = 0;
 GotoDlg.m_nMinutes = 0;
 GotoDlg.m_nSeconds = 0;
 GotoDlg.m_nTotalTracks =
  mCDAudio.GetTotalTracks ();

   // Skip to the position
   if (GotoDlg.DoModal () == IDOK)
    m_CDAudio.SeekTo (GotoDlg.m_nTrack + 1,
     GotoDlg.m_nMinutes, GotoDlg.m_nSeconds, 0);
   }
```

The OnTimer() Code

The SkipForward() and SkipBack() functions are called from the OnTimer() function if the corresponding button is pressed. These functions skip a number of seconds specified by the function argument. In this example, we skip two seconds every time the OnTimer() function detects that the button has been pressed.

```
void CCDAudioPlayerDlg::OnTimer(UINT nIDEvent)
{
 // Skip forward or back if skip buttons
 // pressed
 CButton *pButton;
 pButton = (CButton *) GetDlgItem(
  IDC_SKIPFORWARD);
 if (pButton->GetState () & 0x0004)
  m_CDAudio.SkipForward (2);
 pButton = (CButton *) GetDlgItem(
  IDC_SKIPBACK);
 if (pButton->GetState () & 0x0004)
  m_CDAudio.SkipBack (2);

  .

  .

  .

 CDialog::OnTimer(nIDEvent);
}
```

CD Information

The current track, minutes, and seconds are displayed by
CDAudioPlayer. The total CD length and current track length are also
displayed. These values get updated in the OnTimer() function. The
inactive and active buttons are also updated in this function.

The OnTimer() Code

The rest of the OnTimer() function is used to get information from the
CD. Each section uses the basic CDAudio library functions to get the
information, formats the text string, and displays it in the corresponding
text control.

```
void CCDAudioPlayerDlg::OnTimer(UINT nIDEvent)
{

  .

  .

  .

 // Display the current track time
 CString Status;
 BOOL bDriveReady = TRUE;
 Status.Format ("[%d] %02d:%02d",
  m_CDAudio.GetCurrentTrack (),
  m_CDAudio.GetMinutes (),
  m_CDAudio.GetSeconds ());
```

```
if (m_CDAudio.GetCurrentTrack () == -1){
 Status = "No Audio CD";
 bDriveReady = FALSE;
 }
SetDlgItemText (IDC_STATUS, Status);

// Display the total CD time
CString Length;
int nMinutes, nSeconds;
m_CDAudio.GetTotalLength (&nMinutes,
 &nSeconds);
if (nMinutes != -1){
 Length.Format ("Total Time: %02d:%02d",
  nMinutes, nSeconds);
 SetDlgItemText (IDC_TOTALTIME, Length);
 }

// Display the total track time
m_CDAudio.GetTrackLength(
 m_CDAudio.GetCurrentTrack (), &nMinutes,
 &nSeconds);
if (nMinutes != -1){
 Length.Format ("Track Time: %02d:%02d",
  nMinutes, nSeconds);
 SetDlgItemText (IDC_CURRENTTIME, Length);
 }

CWnd *pWnd;
pWnd = GetDlgItem (IDC_GOTO);
pWnd->EnableWindow (bDriveReady);
pWnd = GetDlgItem (IDC_TRACKBACK);
pWnd->EnableWindow (bDriveReady);
pWnd = GetDlgItem (IDC_SKIPBACK);
pWnd->EnableWindow (bDriveReady);
pWnd = GetDlgItem (IDC_SKIPFORWARD);
pWnd->EnableWindow (bDriveReady);
pWnd = GetDlgItem (IDC_TRACKFORWARD);
pWnd->EnableWindow (bDriveReady);

BOOL bPaused;
if (m_CDAudio.IsPlaying (&bPaused)){
 pWnd = GetDlgItem (IDC_PLAY);
 pWnd->EnableWindow (bPaused);
 pWnd = GetDlgItem (IDC_STOP);
 pWnd->EnableWindow (bDriveReady);
 pWnd = GetDlgItem (IDC_PAUSE);
```

```
    pWnd->EnableWindow (bDriveReady &&
     !bPaused);
    }
  else{
   pWnd = GetDlgItem (IDC_PLAY);
   pWnd->EnableWindow (bDriveReady);
   pWnd = GetDlgItem (IDC_STOP);
   pWnd->EnableWindow (FALSE);
   pWnd = GetDlgItem (IDC_PAUSE);
   pWnd->EnableWindow (FALSE);
   }

   CDialog::OnTimer(nIDEvent);
}
```

CREATING PROGRAMS THAT USE CD AUDIO

Try the following three hands-on exercises to get warmed up so that you can move on to create your own masterpieces. Going through them won't take very long, and the investment of time will be well worth it, since you'll have mastered playing CD audio.

You may be asking why you should type in the code for each exercise. Why not just load the project from disk? In my experience, you always learn more by doing.

Each of these exercises is designed to be as simple as possible, so there is a limit to the amount of error checking that is done. For best results, make sure you have an audio CD in your drive before testing the following examples. Under normal circumstances, the application should check to make sure there is a CD in the drive and the drive is ready before attempting to play the audio or get CD information. If the CD is not ready, the application should give some sort of feedback to let the user know that the problem needs to be corrected.

■ ■

Writing CD Audio

This section is for those who wish to write their own CD-ROM and have access to a recordable CD drive.

When you want to write audio and application data to a CD you will need to follow the Red Book standards for a mixed-mode CD. Each CD can contain up to 99 tracks of information. Under the Red Book standards, the first track will contain your application and any additional data, and the remaining 98 tracks are free for use as CD audio tracks.

➡

Before you write the data to the CD, all of your audio must be stored as WAV files and converted to the 44.1 kHz 16-bit standard. Once you have all of your data and audio files ready, consult the manual for your recordable CD drive to find out how to write the data to the CD.

Keep in mind when playing audio from your application that the first audio track will be at track 2, since your application and data are on track 1. You can also use the CDAudio library function IsAudioTrack() to determine whether a track is audio or data.

■ ■

Hands-On 1: Playing CDAudio in the Background

In this example, we will simply play CD audio in the background of an application.

We will open the CD audio device in the CMainFrame constructor, then do all of the work in the OnTimer() function. Follow the steps correctly and you'll be amazed at how easy it is to add CD audio to your application.

1. Create a Visual C++ project named HandsOn13_1 with the following attributes:

   ❏ Single-document interface

   ❏ English language

   ❏ No database support

   ❏ No compound document support

   ❏ No automation or ActiveX control support

   ❏ 3D controls, but no other features

   ❏ No source file comments

   ❏ Link MFC as a static library

2. Select Settings from the Project menu. Choose the Link tab. Add the following libraries to the Object/library modules field. The libraries for the release and debug versions are different; both are listed below.

Release Project Libraries	Debug Project Libraries
CDAudio.lib	CDAudioD.lib
winmm.lib	winmm.lib

3. Set the Active Configuration to Win32 Release.

4. Add the following include to the MainFrm.h file:

```
#include "CDAudio.h"
```

5. Add the following variable declaration to the CMainFrame class in the MainFrm.h file:

```
public:
 CCDAudio m_CDAudio;
```

6. Add the following code to the CMainFrame constructor:

```
CMainFrame::CMainFrame()
{
 m_CDAudio.Open ();
}
```

7. Add the following functions with the Class Wizard to the CMainFrame class:

```
Name: OnCreate() Message: WM_CREATE
Name: OnTimer()  Message: WM_TIMER
```

8. Edit the OnCreate() function in the CMainFrame class in the MainFrm.cpp file as follows:

```
int CMainFrame::OnCreate(LPCREATESTRUCT
 lpCreateStruct)
{
 if (CFrameWnd::OnCreate(lpCreateStruct)== -1)
  return -1;

 SetTimer (1, 500, NULL);

 return 0;
}
```

9. Edit the OnTimer() function in the CMainFrame class in the MainFrm.cpp file as follows:

```
void CMainFrame::OnTimer(UINT nIDEvent)
{
 // See if audio is already playing
 BOOL bPaused;
 if (!m_CDAudio.IsPlaying (&bPaused)){
  // Cycle through tracks until an audio
  // track is found
```

```
    for (int i=1; i< m_CDAudio.GetTotalTracks();
      i++){
    if (m_CDAudio.IsAudioTrack (i)){
    // Seek to and play the audio track
    m_CDAudio.SeekTo (i, 0, 0, 0);
    m_CDAudio.Play ();
    break;
    }
   }
  }

  CFrameWnd::OnTimer(nIDEvent);
 }
```

10. Compile and run the program.

When the program runs, the CD audio should automatically start playing in the background. Keep in mind, you must have an audio CD in your CD drive for the program to work correctly.

Hands-On 2: Getting CD Audio Information

In this exercise you will get information from a CD. After inserting an audio CD in the drive, press the Get Info button and the information will be displayed. The finished application is shown in Figure 13-3.

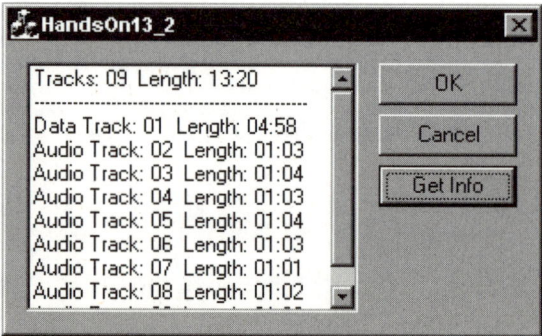

Figure 13-3: The completed application from the Hands-On 2 exercise.

For both Hands-On 2 and Hands-On 3 we will be creating dialog-based applications. These applications are easier to work with—they have no frame, view, or document classes. Dialog-based applications are especially well suited for the things we are doing in this chapter, such as a CD audio player.

1. Create a Visual C++ project named HandsOn13_2 with the following attributes:

   ❏ Dialog-based application

   ❏ English language

   ❏ About box and 3D controls

   ❏ No automation, ActiveX, or WOSA support

   ❏ Yes source file comments

   ❏ MFC linked as a static library

2. Select Settings from the Project menu. Choose the Link tab. Add the following libraries to the Object/library modules field. The libraries for the release and debug versions are different; both are listed below.

Release Project Libraries	Debug Project Libraries
CDAudio.lib	CDAudioD.lib
winmm.lib	winmm.lib

3. Set the Active Configuration to Win32 Release.

4. Add the following includes to the HandsOn13_2Dlg.cpp file:

   ```
   #include "CDAudio.h"
   ```

5. Add a Get Info button and a list box to the IDD_HANDSON13_2_DIALOG resource as shown in Figure 13-4.

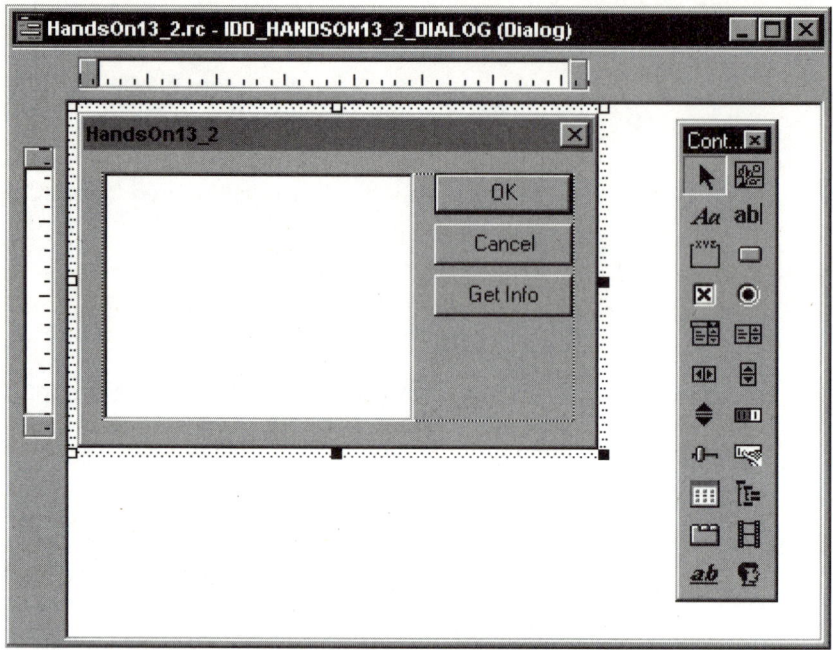

Figure 13-4: Edit the dialog resource for the Hands-On 2 example.

6. Add the following function with the Class Wizard to the CHandsOn13_2Dlg class:

```
Name: OnGetinfo()
  Control: IDC_GETINFO Message: BN_CLICKED
```

7. Add the following variable with the Class Wizard to the CHandsOn13_2Dlg class:

```
Name: m_CDList   Type: CListBox
```

8. Edit the OnGetinfo() function in the CHandsOn13_2Dlg class in the HandsOn13_2Dlg.cpp file as follows:

```
void CHandsOn13_2Dlg::OnGetinfo()
{
CCDAudio CDAudio;

// Attempt to open the CD device
if (CDAudio.Open ()){
```

```
// Clear out the list box
m_CDList.ResetContent ();

// Get the CD information
int nTracks, nMinutes, nSeconds;
nTracks = CDAudio.GetTotalTracks ();
CDAudio.GetTotalLength (&nMinutes,
 &nSeconds);

// Display the CD information
CString TrackString;
TrackString.Format ("Tracks: %02d  Length:
 %02d:%02d", nTracks, nMinutes, nSeconds);
m_CDList.AddString (TrackString);
TrackString = ("-----------------------------------------------");
m_CDList.AddString (TrackString);

// Display the individual track information
for (int i = 1; i <= nTracks; i++){
 CDAudio.GetTrackLength (i, &nMinutes,
  &nSeconds);
 if (CDAudio.IsAudioTrack (i))
  TrackString.Format ("Audio Track: %02d
   Length: %02d:%02d", i, nMinutes,
   nSeconds);
 else
  TrackString.Format ("Data Track: %02d
   Length: %02d:%02d", i, nMinutes,
   nSeconds);
 m_CDList.AddString (TrackString);
 }

// Close the device
CDAudio.Close ();
 }
}
```

9. Compile and run the program.

Put a CD in the drive, run the application, press the Get Info button, and the program will display the information as seen in Figure 13-3. The program will detect data tracks as well as audio tracks, so you can put mixed-mode CDs or even data CDs in the CD-ROM drive.

Hands-On 3: Advanced CD Audio

In this example, things get a little more advanced. This application allows you to play a CD and skip around to different parts. It is a dialog-based application that uses a slider bar for controlling the CD position. The slider will also automatically update to show the current position as the CD plays.

1. Create a Visual C++ project named HandsOn13_3 with the following attributes:

   ❒ Dialog-based application

   ❒ English language

   ❒ About box and 3D controls

   ❒ No automation, ActiveX, or WOSA support

   ❒ Yes source file comments

   ❒ MFC linked as a static library

2. Select Settings from the Project menu. Choose the Link tab. Add the following libraries to the Object/library modules field. The libraries for the release and debug versions are different; both are listed below.

Release Project Libraries	Debug Project Libraries
CDAudio.lib	CDAudioD.lib
winmm.lib	winmm.lib

3. Set the Active Configuration to Win32 Release.

4. Add the following include to the HandsOn13_3Dlg.h file:

```
#include "CDAudio.h"
```

5. Add the following variable declaration to the CHandsOn13_3Dlg class in the HandsOn13_3Dlg.h file:

```
public:
 CCDAudio m_CDAudio;
```

6. Add Stop and Play buttons and a slider bar to the IDD_HANDSON13_3_DIALOG resource as shown in Figure 13-5.

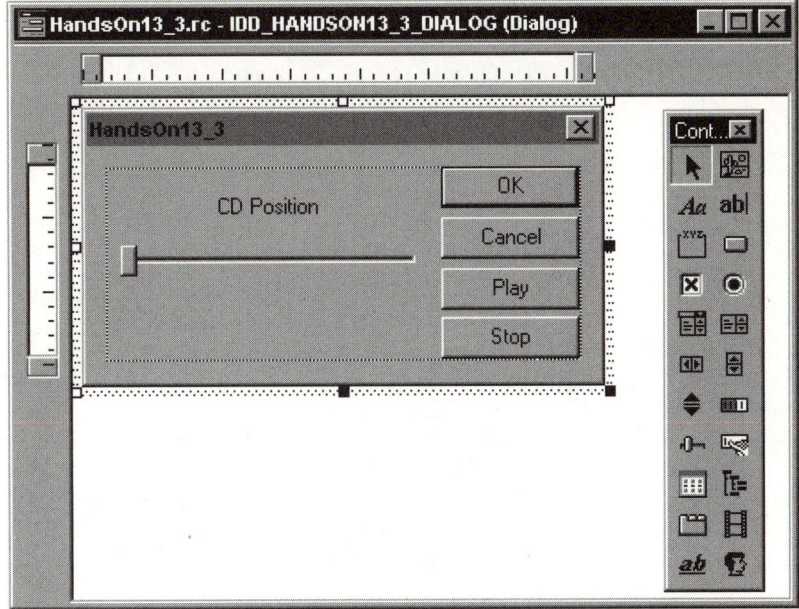

Figure 13-5: Edit the dialog resource for the Hands-On 3 example.

7. Add the following functions with the Class Wizard to the CHandsOn13_3Dlg class:

```
Name: OnTimer()   Message: WM_TIMER
Name: OnPlay()Message: BN_CLICKED
  Control: IDC_PLAY
Name: OnStop()Message: BN_CLICKED
  Control: IDC_STOP
```

8. Add the following variable with the Class Wizard to the CHandsOn13_3Dlg class:

```
Name: m_CDSlider   Type: CSliderCtrl
```

9. Edit the OnInitDialog() function in the CHandsOn13_3Dlg class in the CHandsOn13_3Dlg.cpp file as follows:

```
BOOL CHandsOn13_3Dlg::OnInitDialog()
{
 CDialog::OnInitDialog();
 .
 .
 .
```

```
m_CDAudio.Open ();

SetTimer (1, 2000, NULL);

m_CDSlider.SetRange (0, 500);

return TRUE;
}
```

10. Edit the OnPlay() function in the CHandsOn13_3Dlg class in the CHandsOn13_3Dlg.cpp file as follows:

```
void CHandsOn13_3Dlg::OnPlay()
{
int nSliderPos, nSliderSecs;
int nMinutes, nSeconds, nTotalSecs;

// Get the current slider position
nSliderPos = m_CDSlider.GetPos ();

// Get the total length of the CD in seconds
m_CDAudio.GetTotalLength (&nMinutes,
 &nSeconds);
nTotalSecs = (nMinutes * 60) + nSeconds;

// Figure out the slider position in seconds
nSliderSecs = (nTotalSecs/500) * nSliderPos;

// Calculate the minute and second
nMinutes = nSliderSecs / 60;
nSeconds = nSliderSecs % 60;

// Seek to that position and play
m_CDAudio.SeekTo (1, nMinutes, nSeconds, 0);
m_CDAudio.Play ();
}
```

11. Edit the OnStop() function in the CHandsOn13_3Dlg class in the CHandsOn13_3Dlg.cpp file as follows:

```
void CHandsOn13_3Dlg::OnStop()
{
m_CDAudio.Stop ();

m_CDSlider.SetPos (0);
}
```

12. Edit the OnTimer() function in the CHandsOn13_3Dlg class in the CHandsOn13_3Dlg.cpp file as follows:

```
void CHandsOn13_3Dlg::OnTimer(UINT nIDEvent)
{
 // Only update the slider position if the CD
 // is playing
 BOOL bPaused;
 if (m_CDAudio.IsPlaying (&bPaused)){
  int nSliderPos;
  int nMinutes, nSeconds;
  DWORD dwCurrentSecs, dwTotalSecs;

  // Get the total length of the CD in seconds
  m_CDAudio.GetTotalLength (&nMinutes,
   &nSeconds);
  dwTotalSecs = (nMinutes * 60) + nSeconds;

  // Get the current position of the CD in
  // seconds
  dwCurrentSecs = 0;
  int nCurrentTrack =
   m_CDAudio.GetCurrentTrack ();
  for (int i = 1; i <= nCurrentTrack; i++){
   if (i == nCurrentTrack){
    nMinutes = m_CDAudio.GetMinutes ();
    nSeconds = m_CDAudio.GetSeconds ();
    }
   else{
    m_CDAudio.GetTrackLength (i, &nMinutes,
     &nSeconds);
    }
   dwCurrentSecs += (nMinutes*60) + nSeconds;
   }

  // Figure out the new slider position
  nSliderPos = (dwCurrentSecs * 500) /
   dwTotalSecs;

  // Update the slider position
  m_CDSlider.SetPos (nSliderPos);
  }

 CDialog::OnTimer(nIDEvent);
}
```

13. Compile and run the program.

You are now ready to play the CD. Simply use the Play and Stop buttons to play the audio. Adjusting the slider bar will skip you to different positions on the disc.

ON THE WEB

There is a wealth of information on the Web about multimedia and CD audio. There is everything from CD audio players to C++ libraries, as well as original and creative CD applications. Here are a few sites to get you started:

Voyager CD Link

www.voyagerco.com/cdlink

Voyager CD Link, shown in Figure 13-6, is an excellent example of what can be done with CD audio. CD Link allows Web pages to send commands through your computer and control your CD drive. This creates an opportunity for Web page developers to have real-time CD audio accompany their Web pages and Web applications.

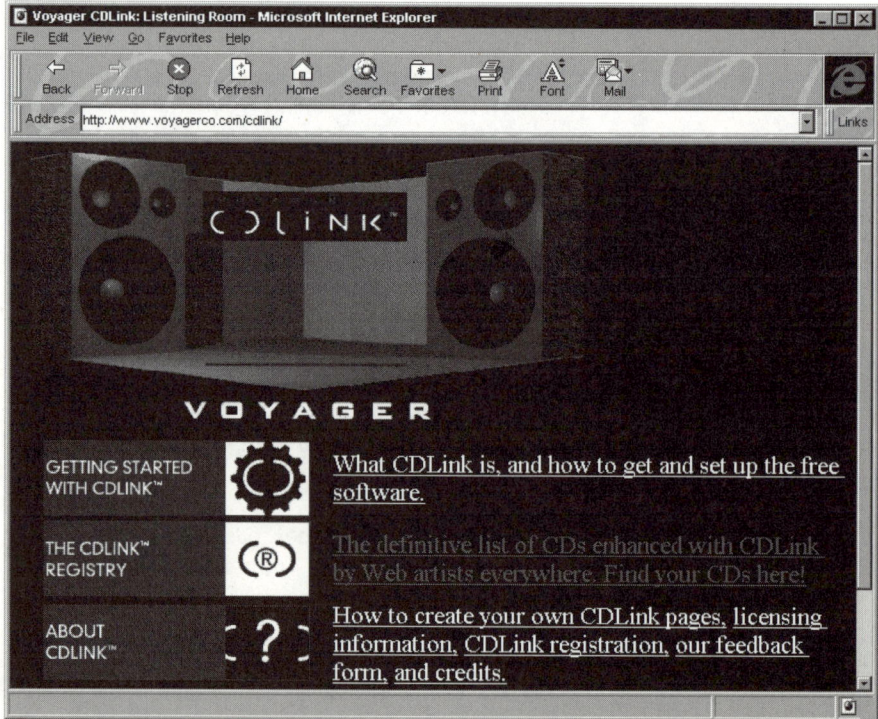

Figure 13-6: Voyager CD Link is an excellent CD audio Web application.

TegoSoft

www.tego.com/ocxkit.html

TegoSoft offers ActiveX and OCX controls for software developers on many platforms. This Web site lists some of the kits they have available for Visual C++ programmers, including controls for playing CD audio and other multimedia devices.

CDRunner

www.cdrunner.com

CDRunner offers both CD audio and CD-ROM players with a rich feature set. Support for enhanced CD, removable drives, and multidrive changers is built in (see Figure 13-7).

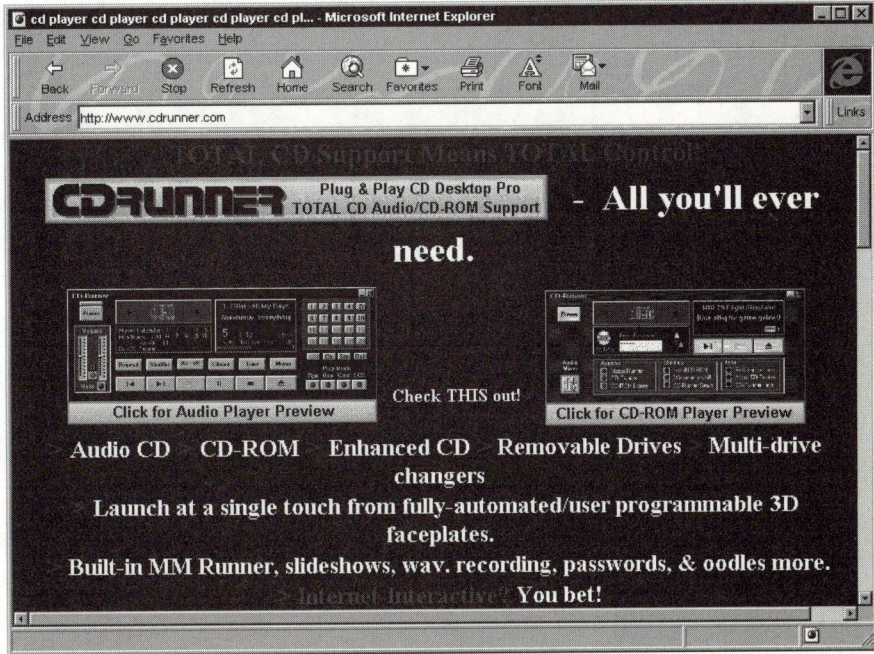

Figure 13-7: CDRunner offers both audio and CD-ROM players.

SHAREWARE & COMMERCIAL DEMOS

If you don't have access to the World Wide Web, don't fret. There are plenty of shareware and commercial CD audio applications and libraries available. We've included a few on the CD, so feel free to take a look.

Pro Audio CD Player

The Aldrige Company has developed a very solid and efficient CD audio player. The demo can be found in the CDAUDIO\DEMOS directory with the filename PROCD3.EXE. You can also find the Aldridge Company on the Web at www.aldridge.com. (See Figure 13-8.)

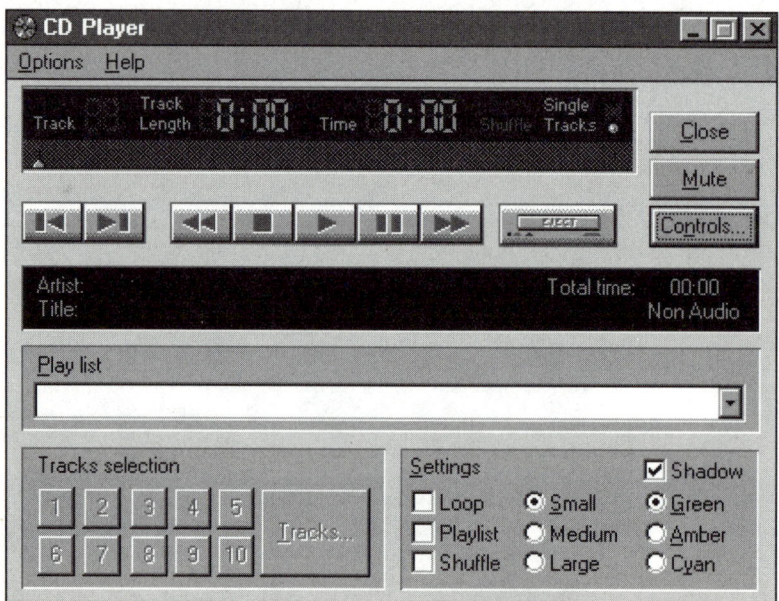

Figure 13-8: The Aldridge Company's Pro Audio CD Player.

Multi Media Mixer

Multi Media Mixer is a great little shareware application. It allows you to play AVI, MIDI, WAV, and CD audio all at the same time. This means you could sing into a microphone while you are playing a CD and record it as a WAV file. Very cool! This piece of shareware can be found in the CDAUDIO\DEMOS directory with the filename MMM.ZIP.

CD Worx

CD Worx is a great utility if you are planning on creating your own audio CDs. It allows you to digitally record audio from a CD and save it as a WAV file with no loss of quality. From there, you can write your own CDs if you have access to a recordable CD drive. It can be found in the CDAUDIO\DEMOS directory with the filename CDW9521X.ZIP. (See Figure 13-9.)

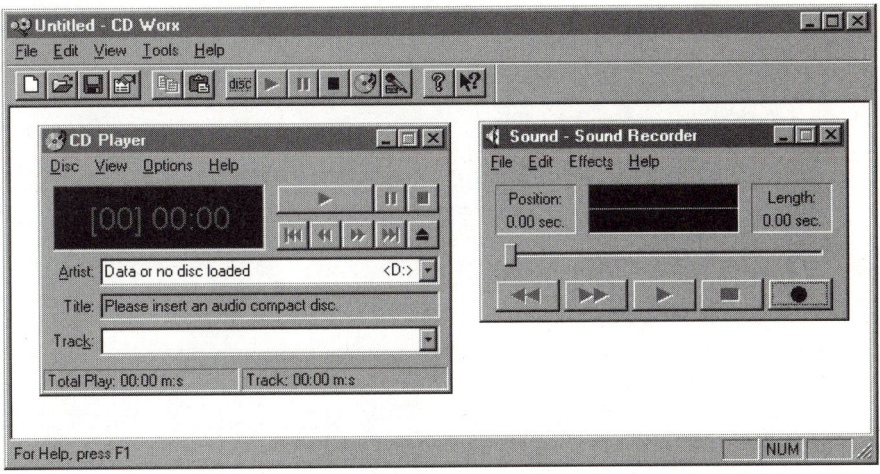

Figure 13-9: CD Worx lets you save CD audio tracks as WAV files.

Moving On

You have now gained the capability to make your applications sound as good as a CD bought in your local record store. Along with the earlier chapters on sound and MIDI, you now have everything you need to create dynamic multimedia applications. Just link in the CDAudio class library, add a few lines of code, and you're ready to go.

If you use your imagination, there is no limit to the CD audio-based applications you can develop. Send me your applications at ivt-rcl@interpath.com if you come up with something you would like to share.

Chapter 14

Modem, Network & Internet Communications

20 years ago, I helped start the personal computer revolution. Today, thanks to high-speed modems, the personal computer is revolutionizing the world.

—*Steve Wozniak*

It's time to take a ride on the highway. The information superhighway, that is. This chapter covers communications, and gives you the tools you need to build applications that communicate over modems, networks, and the Internet. These tools can empower your programs with all of the computer-accessible information in the world.

The communication class is named *CMessage*, because it's written especially to send text-based message packets. Everything that's being sent to another computer is treated as a message.

With this class library, you can create simple applications that do nothing more than connect to a remote location and send messages. You can also use the class library to construct fully functional telecommunications programs that access Internet sites around the world. Only your needs and your imagination will limit the final product.

Common uses of remote communications are business applications that link different sites in order to keep tabs on inventories and transactions. For example, I wrote a large drug-dispensing program in which many clinic sites automatically receive new orders and updated pharmacy information each evening from a central host location. The central host gets inventory levels and transaction information from each site during evening hours. A large part of my time was spent constructing telecommunications routines that sent and received information packets. If I had had the class library that's included on the CD-ROM included with this book, my development time would have been reduced significantly.

Multiplayer games that can be played over a modem, network, or Internet connection are fun. Several years ago, I wrote a bridge game that included modem and network play. Of course, playing against a real person is much more fun than playing against a silicon opponent who doesn't get mad when you trump his ace or beat his redouble bid. But if you're a game developer, consider adding modem, network, and Internet play, if it's appropriate, and be prepared for a wave of additional popularity as a result. But what an enormous task figuring everything out. Even to this day, there aren't many good references on the subject, and creating a class library such as you're getting can be a daunting task.

The CMessage class is derived from the CTalk class. The CTalk class handles opening the communications, reading, and writing. The CMessage class handles packaging the messages into blocks of formatted data.

The CTalk class has three virtual classes that it manages. One is for the modem, one for network connections, and one for Internet connections. This makes it easy for an application developer. Once the class is created by specifying modem, network, or Internet, all subsequent calls are identical.

THE CMESSAGE CLASS LIBRARY IN BRIEF

The CMessage class makes connecting to remote computers, sending and receiving data, and terminating connections easy. You can establish a connection, send a message, and hang up using only five functions.

All messages must be sent in ASCII text. This design decision helps make the modem-to-modem connections much more robust during noisy connections. If you want to send binary data, you'll have to convert it to ASCII text, send it as a message, then convert it back to binary data on the destination computer.

Each message that's sent has a type variable. You can define these any way you want. For instance, a game move might have a value of 2, a text message to another person a value of 3, and a request for file data a value of 4. This makes it easy for the receiving computer to interpret the data and know what to do with it.

All source code and support files to rebuild Talk.lib can be found in the Talk directory on the Companion CD-ROM.

TYPES OF COMMUNICATIONS

You might be wondering why it's important to know some of the technical details behind the CMessage class. To answer that question, let me give you an anecdote.

Several years ago, I was asked to provide modem and network functions for a military simulator. I spent several weeks writing functions according to the specifications I was given, then I turned over the library, along with example programs showing how to use it.

The programmers who then had to implement it were clueless, even with the example programs. As they asked me questions about why some things were the way they were, I soon realized it was because they didn't understand the basics of serial and network communications.

I spent several hours bringing the programmers up to speed with some over-the-phone tutoring. Soon things clicked for them and they understood. From that point on, it wasn't long before they had enough intuition about communications to easily incorporate the library into their code.

Even though the CMessage class library is simple and can be used with a few lines of code, it's good to have a background on what's behind it. This makes it easier to understand what's going on and therefore easier to implement the library.

Serial Communications

The PC communications port uses *asynchronous communication*, or *asynch* for short. Each byte of data is potentially a separate unit. The PC sending data can pause between any two bytes of a message. The receiver, however, may have to catch the data as quickly as it arrives.

To accomplish this trick, asynch data requires one extra bit's worth of time to announce the beginning of a new byte (the "start" bit) and one extra bit's worth of time at the end (the "stop" bit). A 2400 baud modem can transfer only 240 bytes of data per second, because each byte requires a minimum of 10 bit times. At one time, this was also called "start-stop" communication by those who thought that "asynchronous" was too fancy a word.

Modern high-speed modems do not actually transmit the start and stop bits. They are squeezed out as parts of the general data compression. However, the start and stop bits will still be generated on the wire that connects a COM port to an external modem (the RS-232 interface). Because of this, and the general availability of data compression, the modern COM port is usually configured to use a higher speed (between the COM port and the modem) than the actual data transmission will support (between the two modems over the phone line). Modems may operate at 14,400 bits per second, but the COM port will be configured for 38,400 bits per second.

This is just an example of older conventions adapted to new requirements. The standards for asynchronous communication go back to the days before computers. The first modems were used by Teletype machines to send cablegrams. When the first computers were developed, the existing population of Teletype machines provided convenient terminals.

The standards made sense up to the point where it became possible to put computer chips inside the modems. "Smart" modems can dial the phone, send a fax, compress data, and correct transmission errors. None of these functions were even imagined when standards such as "RS-232" were originally developed. Although the rules have been adapted (or subverted) to accommodate modern technology, some of the old junk still pops up occasionally to cause trouble.

Sorting Out the Terminology

What is Xon/Xoff Flow Control? XON and XOFF are byte values. The Teletype had a device to read punched paper tape. The XON character turned the tape reader on, and the XOFF character turned it off. Long after the last paper tape was burned, computers have maintained the tradition that XOFF can optionally mean "stop sending data," in which case XON means "begin sending again." What is parity? Before modems did error correction, parity provided a simple mechanism to detect characters corrupted by phone line noise. Today it is unnecessary and is typically disabled.

So, in current use, the correct setting for the COM port is always 8-bit characters, no parity, 1 stop bit, hardware pacing (more about that later), and some speed faster than the native transmission speed of the modem. The panel in Windows to configure the COM port is left around because everyone is scared to get rid of it. The user should not be scared when presented by a large package of useless options.

Network Communications

When Novell created NetWare in the early 1980s, PC networks were small and predominantly homogeneous. PC LAN workgroup communication was new, and the idea of a "personal computer" was just becoming popular.

Today, NetWare coexists with many other protocols in large, global intranets. NetWare's market share as of September 1993 was between 50 and 75 percent (depending on the market research group performing the study) of what has been called the network operating system (NOS) market. With over one million NetWare networks installed worldwide, and the accelerating movement to connect networks to other networks, NetWare and its supporting protocols often coexist on the same physical channel with many other popular protocols, including TCP/IP, DECnet, and AppleTalk.

Internet Packet Exchange (IPX) is Novell's network-layer protocol. When a device on one network communicates with a device located on a different network, IPX routes the information to the destination through any intermediate networks that might be present.

Although IPX was derived from the Xerox Network Services (XNS) protocol, it has several unique features. For example, IPX packets can employ various LAN encapsulation schemes, depending on the media access protocol.

Routing within Novell IPX networks usually is accomplished using the Routing Information Protocol (RIP). Novell recently specified the NetWare Link Services Protocol (NLSP) for routing in large intranets. Although both are dynamic routing protocols, RIP has distinct limitations when used in large networks. NLSP is based on the same technology as the Intermediate System-to-Intermediate System (IS-IS) routing protocol created for and used in OSI and IP networks.

Novell includes the Service Advertisement Protocol (SAP) as part of its IPX protocol family. SAP allows nodes that provide services (such as file servers and print servers) to advertise their addresses and the services they provide. Later in this chapter, Figure 14-2 shows how IPX, RIP, NLSP, and SAP relate to the OSI reference model.

Internet Communications (Winsock)

WinSock is short for Windows Sockets, and is used as the interface between TCP/IP (Transmission Control Protocol/Internet Protocol) and Windows. TCP/IP has been called "the language of the Internet," and rightly so—most of the Internet is composed of systems that use TCP/IP to talk to one another.

The WinSock specification was born at one of the "Birds of a Feather" sessions at the Interop conference (a meeting to establish specifications) in the fall of 1991. The current version of the specification is 1.1, but work continues on the WinSock 2.0 specification.

Berkeley Sockets is the standard programming model for TCP/IP networking under UNIX. Windows Sockets was designed to be very similar to Berkeley Sockets, so that those experienced in programming with sockets in UNIX will be able to easily make the transition to Windows Sockets. However, there are a few deviations in the WinSock standard that take advantage of Windows-specific features not supported in UNIX.

WinSock is a DLL (dynamic link library) and runs under Windows 3.x, Windows for Workgroups, Windows NT, and Windows 95. The WINSOCK.DLL is the interface to TCP/IP and, from there, on out to the Internet. The following diagram illustrates how it works:

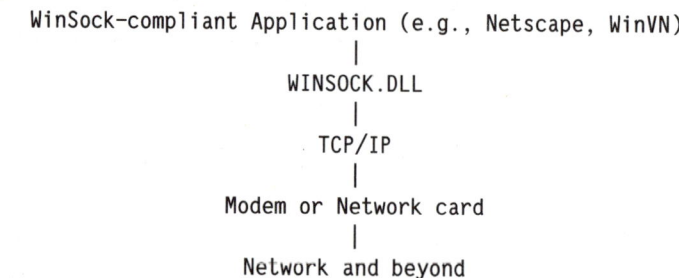

```
WinSock-compliant Application (e.g., Netscape, WinVN)
                        |
                  WINSOCK.DLL
                        |
                     TCP/IP
                        |
            Modem or Network card
                        |
             Network and beyond
```

WINSOCK.DLL actually acts as a "layer" between your WinSock applications and your TCP/IP stack. Your WinSock applications tell WINSOCK.DLL what to do, WINSOCK.DLL translates these commands to your TCP/IP stack, and your TCP/IP stack passes them on to the Internet.

But the most important thing for you to remember about WINSOCK.DLL is that the WINSOCK.DLL you're using must match the version of TCP/IP you're running. Don't assume that because all WinSocks are called WINSOCK.DLL they're all the same—they're not. So, for example, if I'm using Microsoft's TCP/IP, I can't use Trumpet Winsock.

Similarly, if I'm running on a SLIP connection, and I want to switch from Chameleon Sampler's WinSock to Trumpet Winsock, I first need to remove Chameleon's version of WINSOCK.DLL before installing the new one.

If you end up with multiple versions of WINSOCK.DLL floating around your hard disk, you're asking for trouble. Before you come screaming at alt.winsock, take a couple of minutes to check your hard disk for multiple WINSOCK.DLLs.

Requirements for Accessing the Internet

Using WinSock applications to access the Internet requires the following:

- ❑ A suitable connection to the Internet.
- ❑ A TCP/IP stack (which includes its own WINSOCK.DLL).

Your connection to the Internet may take the form of a direct connection via a network card, or a dial-up account using a modem. Most users will be using the latter. You'll probably need to set up an account with an Internet service provider (or else get an account through work or school, if available). Either a SLIP or a PPP account (protocols for communicating with the Internet via modem) is fine, though PPP is generally preferred. Or you can get a shell account that allows you to run a SLIP emulator.

The TCP/IP stack you use depends upon your needs. Some operating systems include stacks, such as Microsoft Windows 95, Microsoft Windows NT, and IBM OS/2. For other operating systems, like Microsoft Windows 3.1/3.11 or Microsoft Windows for Workgroups 3.11, you'll need to add a stack. Some are free, some are shareware (if you continue to use them after an evaluation period, you must pay a small fee), and others are commercial. Some include no WinSock applications, while others include all the basic apps you'll need.

A fast computer, 8MB or more of memory, and a high-speed modem for dial-up connections (at least 14.4K) are also recommended.

There are several different ways individual PC users can get access to the Internet. Of all the access methods available, SLIP (Serial Line Interface Protocol) and PPP (Point-to-Point Protocol) accounts give you the most options, as far as applications are concerned.

SLIP has been around since the mid-1980s. It was originally designed to allow UNIX machines to connect to one another over the phone. It essentially "tricks" your computer into thinking its modem connection is a dedicated network connection (the kind you would usually need a network card for).

PPP is based on SLIP, but it is a more sophisticated protocol. It contains additional error-checking and authentication, which makes it more reliable than SLIP. For most PC users, there really isn't much difference between the two. Because PPP is more reliable and is generally accepted to be the standard of the future, you should get PPP if you're offered a choice between the two.

WinSock works well with SLIP and PPP. Most WinSock versions come with dialer programs to do the actual connection over your modem.

THE CHECKERS DEMO

The Checkers program demonstrates communication over the modem. Later in the chapter, there's a section that shows how to alter the program to communicate over a Novell-compatible network and a section that shows how to alter the program to communicate over the Internet.

The program can be found in the Modem\Checkers directory of the Companion CD-ROM. Using Explorer or Program Manager, run the program named Checkers.exe. When it first runs, you'll see a checkerboard with a new game, as shown in Figure 14-1. You won't be able to move any pieces until you're connected with another computer.

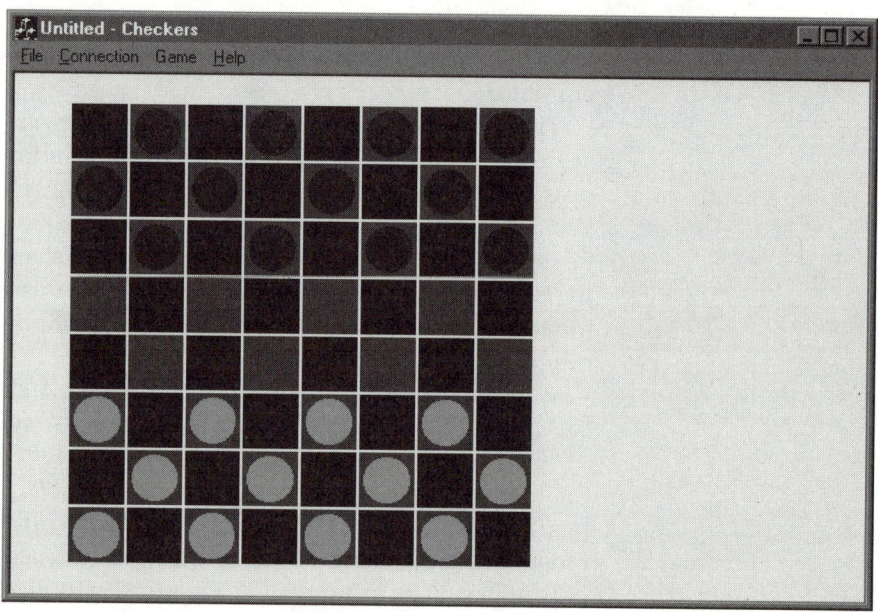

Figure 14-1: When you first run Checkers, you'll see a new game.

To connect with another computer, you have two choices. You can initiate a call or await a call. I have several computers in our lab, so it's easy for me to carry out the connections. I simply set one computer to answer mode, then walk across the room and have another computer dial the awaiting computer. Most people can't do that since they only have one computer and one phone line. If you're in this situation, you'll have to find a friend at another location to connect with. Both computers must have the Checkers program. Decide in advance who will answer and who will initiate. Then, at a preset time, have the initiating machine call the answering machine.

The first thing both checkers players must do is set communication parameters. This is done from a dialog box when either Dial or Wait for Call is selected from the Connection pull-down menu (the dial option is shown in Figure 14-2). Set to either tone or pulse dialing and select a communication port. The baud rate is set automatically in the Checkers program, but it would be easy for you to add a baud rate selection if you use the CMessage class for an application of your own. If your computer is the one to answer, leave the phone number field blank in the dialog box.

Once you click on the OK button, the program tries to open the communication port and either wait for a call or dial and try to connect to a remote computer.

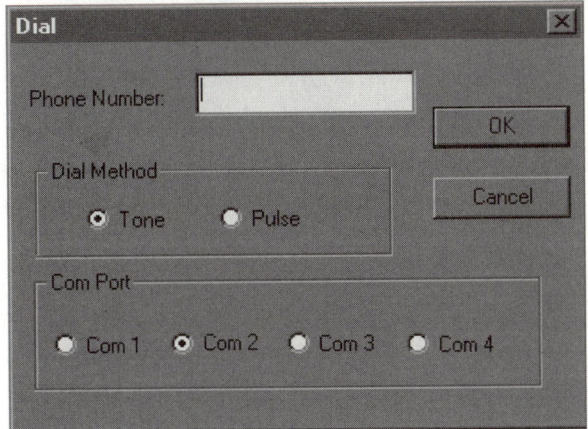

Figure 14-2: You'll need to set the communications parameters before establishing a connection.

Once the connection has been made, you'll be notified that you're connected, as you can see in Figure 14-3.

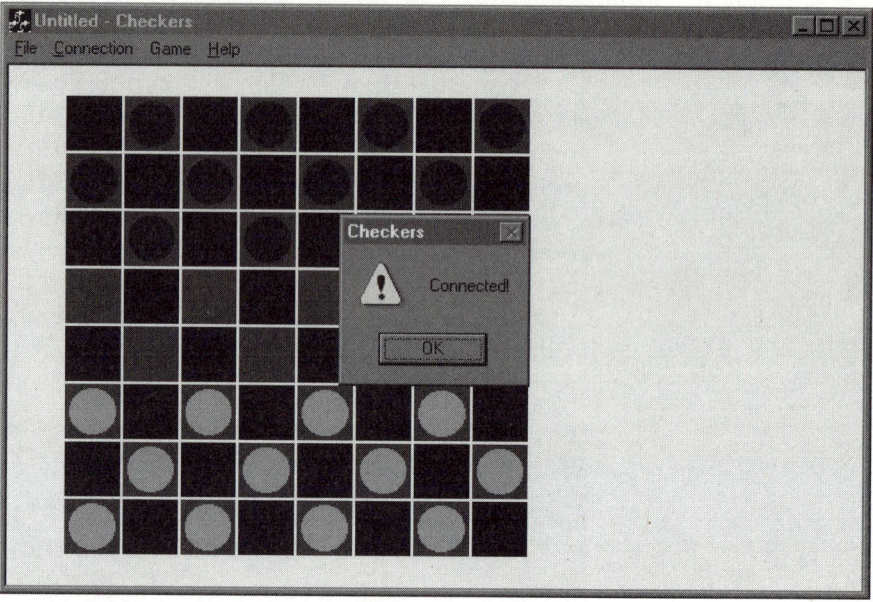

Figure 14-3: You'll be notified once the connection has been made.

This is a very simple implementation of a checkers game. You can't drag the pieces. They're moved by clicking the left mouse button on the piece that's to be moved. The empty destination square is then clicked on. If the move is legal, the piece will be moved to that square.

To jump pieces, begin in the same manner by clicking the left mouse button on the piece that's to move and do the jumping. If it's a single jump, simply click the left mouse button on the destination square. If it's a multiple jump, click the right mouse button on each destination square until you get to the final destination square, in which case you should click the left mouse button. Figure 14-4 shows a checkers game in progress.

You can send text messages to the other computer by selecting Send Message from the Connection pull-down menu. A dialog box will appear in which you can type your message, as shown in Figure 14-5.

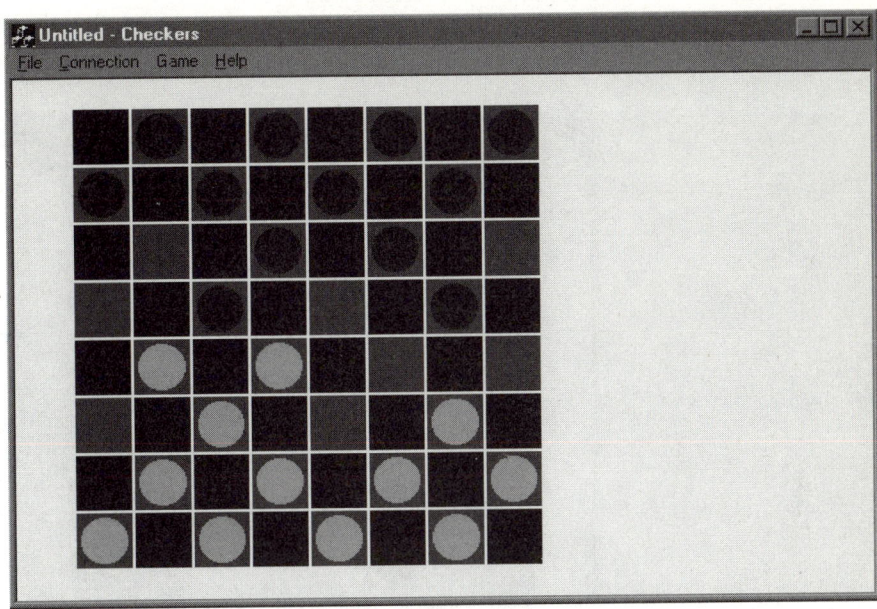

Figure 14-4: The game is simple—no bells and whistles. The few commands are easy to learn.

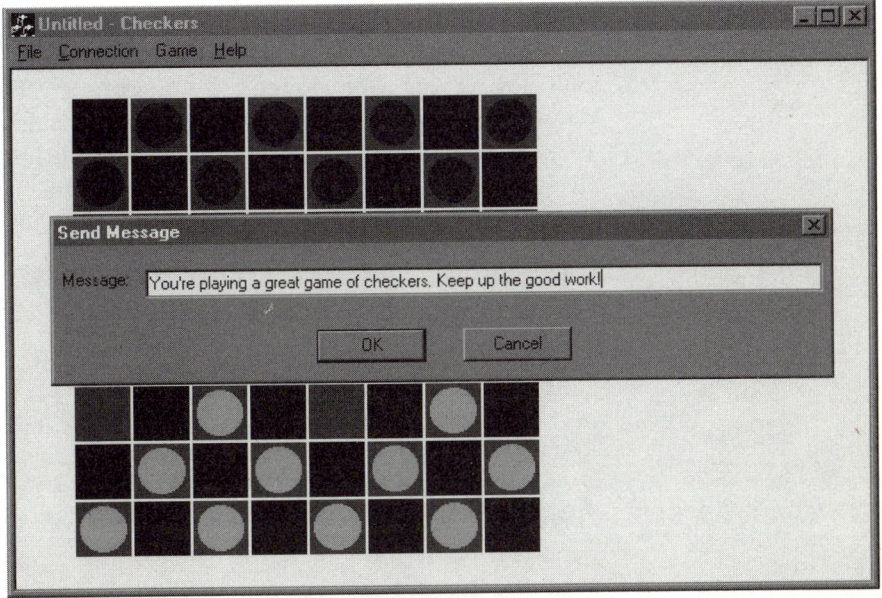

Figure 14-5: You can send a text message to the other player.

If the other player sends you a message, it'll appear in a message box on the screen, as shown in Figure 14-6.

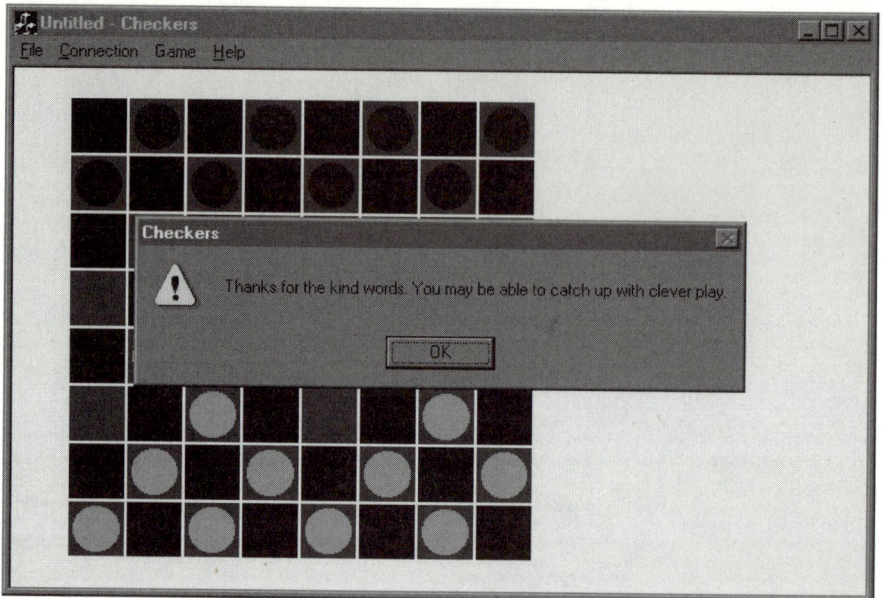

Figure 14-6: You might receive a text message from the other player.

You can ask for a new game by choosing New Game from the Game pull-down menu. A message box will appear asking you if you want a new game. If you reply yes, your opponent will be asked. If he answers yes, a new game will be started. You can quit the game by selecting Resign Game from the Game pull-down menu.

CMESSAGE CLASS LIBRARY FUNCTION CALLS

This section is provided as a reference to the public function calls offered by the CMessage class library. Since the class library was designed with simplicity as a major goal, the calls are simple and easy to use. To connect and communicate with a remote computer is easy—it just takes a few lines of code.

You may want to skip over this section and read the section entitled "Behind Checkers," which shows how the calls are used. (For some people, it's better to look at the usage of function calls before actually studying the syntax.)

CMessage()

Prototype: `CMessage();`

Purpose: This is the CMessage class constructor. There are two versions of it. This one does not assign the message type but simply creates the class. If you use this constructor, when you try to connect to a remote computer, you'll have to use the Create() function to let the CMessage class know what kind of communications you're using. This is different than the next constructor in which you do everything in step, create the CMessage class, and tell it what kind of communications you'll be trying to establish.

Arguments: None

Returns: Nothing

CMessage()

Prototype: `CMessage( int nTalkType );`

Purpose: This version of the CMessage class constructor not only creates the CMessage class but also creates the internal class that communicates with a remote computer. Using this version of the constructor is the same as the following code:

```
CMessage *pMessage = new CMessage();
pMessage->Create( MODEM );
```

Arguments: int nTalkType
Define types are MODEM, NETWORK, and INTERNET

Returns: Nothing

Create()

Prototype: `BOOL Create( int nTalkType );`

Purpose: This function creates the internal virtual class that knows how to communicate with the remote computer. This doesn't need to be used if the communication type was passed to the CMessage constructor.

Arguments: int nTalkType
Define types are MODEM, NETWORK, and INTERNET.

Returns: BOOL: TRUE if successful, FALSE if unsuccessful

GetTalkType()

Prototype: `int GetTalkType( void );`

Purpose: This function returns the communication type that a CMessage class has been assigned. The values it returns are MODEM, NETWORK, or INTERNET.

Arguments: None

Returns: int nTalkType

Open()

Prototype: `BOOL Open( int nPort );`

Purpose: This function opens the communication port for the specified device. This function must be called before the Dial(), Answer(), Hangup(), SendMessage(), and GetNextMessage() functions are used.

Arguments: int nPort

For modems, this nPort integer represents two things: port number and baud rate. The port number is in the lower 16 bits and should be a value from 1 to 4. The baud rate is in the upper 16 bits and must be 300,1200, 2400, 9600, 19200, 38400, or any other legal baud rate. For Novell-compatible networks and Internet connections, the value in nPort represents whether the socket will be opened as a server or whether the socket will be opened as a client. The server will be the connection that waits for calls; the client will be the connection that initiates calls. Two defines, CLIENT and SERVER, are defined to make it clear when you call the Open() function. If you pass no argument, a default value of CLIENT will be given.

Returns: BOOL: TRUE if successful, FALSE if unsuccessful

Close()

Prototype: `BOOL Close( void );`

Purpose: This function closes the connection with the communications device. If necessary, it disconnects from the remote computer.

Arguments: None

Returns: BOOL: TRUE if successful, FALSE if unsuccessful

Dial()

Prototype: `BOOL Dial( const char *pDialString );`

Purpose: This function attempts to make a connection with a remote computer that's awaiting the attempt.

Arguments: const char *pDialString
For modems, the dial string must be in the proper format for a Hayes-compatible modem. For example, to dial the number 800-222-3333 using tone dialing, the string "ATDT18002223333\15" must be used. Note the carriage return at the end of the string. All modem dial strings must end with a carriage return. For network connections, the dial string is ignored. For internet connections, the dial string must be a legal and valid IP address. An example of this is 199.72.81.1.

Returns: BOOL: TRUE if successful, FALSE if unsuccessful

Answer()

Prototype: `BOOL Answer( const char *pAnswerString );`

Purpose: This function instructs the communication device to wait for a remote computer to initiate a connection.

Arguments: const char *pAnswerString
For modems, the answer string should be "ATS0=1\15."
For network and Internet connections, the string is ignored.

Returns: BOOL: TRUE if successful, FALSE if unsuccessful

Hangup()

Prototype: `BOOL Hangup( void );`

Purpose: This function disconnects from the remote computer.

Arguments: None

Returns: BOOL: TRUE if successful, FALSE if unsuccessful

IsConnected()

Prototype: `BOOL IsConnected( void );`

Purpose: This function tells you whether a connection has been established with a remote computer. It works the same for both initiating and awaiting computers.

Arguments: None

Returns: BOOL: TRUE if successful, FALSE if unsuccessful

MessagesWaiting()

Prototype: `int MessagesWaiting( BOOL bFlag );`

Purpose: This function tells you whether there are any messages waiting. It gives you the number of messages if any are waiting.

Arguments: BOOL bFlag, Defaults to FALSE

Returns: int nCountOfWaitingMessages

GetNextMessage()

Prototype: `int GetNextMessage( void *pData, int *nSize );`

Purpose: This function retrieves the data of the next message and returns the message type. As a convenience, the message size is returned as well.

Arguments: void *pData
int *nSize

Returns: int nMessageType

SendMessage()

Prototype: `BOOL SendMessage( void *pMessageData, int nSize,    int nType );`

Purpose: This function sends a message to the remote computer.

Arguments: void *pMessageData
int nSize
int nType

Returns: BOOL: TRUE if successful, FALSE if unsuccessful

CTalk Function Calls Accessible Through CMessage

The following functions belong to the CTalk class but are accessible for special needs. Mainly you'll use them if you want to send and receive data without going through the CMessage class.

In order to use the functions (except for static functions) you must use the m_pTalk member of your CMessage class. Here's an example of calling the WriteData() function.

```
CMessage *pMessage( MODEM );
pMessage->m_pTalk->WriteData( "Hello", 5 );
```

WinsockInit()

Prototype: `static BOOL WinsockInit( void );`

Purpose: This function must be made once when the application first runs if any of the connections are going to be of the Internet variety.

Arguments: None

Returns: BOOL: TRUE if successful, FALSE if unsuccessful

WinsockUninit()

Prototype: `static BOOL WinsockUninit( void );`

Purpose: If WinsockInit() was called, this must be called before exiting the application.

Arguments: None

Returns: BOOL: TRUE if successful, FALSE if unsuccessful

NetworkInit()

Prototype: `static BOOK NetworkInit();`

Purpose: This function must be made once when the application first runs if any of the connections are going to be of the network variety.

Arguments: None

Returns: BOOL: TRUE if successful, FALSE if unsuccessful

NetworkUninit()

Prototype: `static BOOL NetworkUninit( void );`

Purpose: If NetworkInit() was called, this must be called before exiting the application.

Arguments: None

Returns: BOOL: TRUE if successful, FALSE if unsuccessful

WriteData()

Prototype: `int WriteData( void *pDataBuffer, int nDataLength );`

Purpose: This function writes data to the communication device. It doesn't package the data into a message packet as the message class does.

Arguments: void *pDataBuffer
int nDataLength

Returns: int nNumberOfBytesWritten

IsDataWaiting()

Prototype: `BOOL IsDataWaiting( void );`

Purpose: This function tells you whether there is data waiting that has come in from the communication device.

Arguments: None

Returns: BOOL: TRUE if successful, FALSE if unsuccessful

ReadData()

Prototype: `int ReadData( void *pDataBuffer );`

Purpose: This function reads data from the remote communications device into a buffer.

Arguments: void *pDataBuffer

Returns: int nNumberOfBytesRead

Special Network Communication Device Items in the CMessage, CTalk, CNetwork & CInternet Classes

This section contains information that's specific to network communication devices.

SetSocketNumber() (CTalk Class)

Prototype: `void SetSocketNumber( SOCKET sSocketNumber );`

Purpose: This function must be called to set the socket number over which your program will communicate. Examples are hex values of 0x4242, 0x4444, and 0x5555. Calling this function is required for network communications to work correctly. Both initiating and awaiting computers must be set to the same socket number.

Arguments: SOCKET sSocketNumber

Returns: Nothing

CNetwork::CreateUserList() (CNetwork)

Prototype: `BOOL CreateUserList( void );`

Purpose: This function calls a special DLL which in turn creates a user list based on everyone who's logged on to the network. The list is created as a text file and is saved into the current directory.
The file format is as follows:

Bytes 0-1 are both zero unless this entry is the current user, in which case bytes 0-1 will be a "/" character followed by a zero.

Bytes 2-51 are the user name.

Bytes 51-54 are the network number.

Bytes 56-61 are the node number.

Bytes 62-63 are the socket number.

Bytes 64-68 are a five-digit ASCII value representing the connection number.

Bytes 69-70 are a carriage return/line feed pair.

Arguments: None

Returns: BOOL: TRUE if successful, FALSE if unsuccessful

479

CTalk::m_RemAddr (CTalk Class)

Variable: SOCKADDR_IPX m_RemAddr

Purpose: Two members of this data structure must be assigned before calling the Dial() function. They are sa_netnum and sa_nodenum. These are the network number and the node number that are associated with a given connection number.

Special Network Communication Device Items

This section contains information that's specific to Internet communication devices.

SetPort() (CTalk Class)

Prototype: `void SetPort( int nPortNumber );`

Purpose: This function sets the communication port for the Internet communications. Common examples are 80 for WWW and 21 for FTP. It's best to use your own port above 125 so you don't conflict with the common ones.

Arguments: int nPortNumber

Returns: Nothing

GetPort() (CTalk Class)

Prototype: `int GetPort( void );`

Purpose: This function returns the port that the Internet communications device is currently set to.

Arguments: None

Returns: int nCurrentInternetPort

GetThisInternetAddress() (CTalk Class)

Prototype: `void GetThisInternetAddress( char *pszIPAddress );`

Purpose: This function returns the Internet address for the local machine.

Arguments: char *pszIPAddress

Returns: Nothing

GetThisHostName() (CTalk Class)

Prototype: void GetThisHostName(char *pszHostName);

Purpose: This function returns the host name to which a local machine is connected.

Arguments: char *pszHostName

Returns: Nothing

BEHIND CHECKERS

This section goes through the Checkers program code and provides explanations. By reading through this section, you'll gain an understanding of the CMessage class and its functions.

Initializing Variables

The CCheckersView class constructor initializes variables used for the Checkers program. The CMessage class isn't created until later, when a connection is made to a remote computer.

The CCheckersView() Constructor Code

```
CCheckersView::CCheckersView()
{

  m_pMessage = NULL;

  m_nPulse = 0;
  m_nComPort = 1;
  m_nSideColor = 0;
  m_nGameOver = FALSE;
  m_nGotPiece = -1;
  m_nGotSq = m_nOnSq = 0;
  m_nMultiple = 0;

}
```

481

Cleaning Up Before Program Termination

Before terminating the Checkers program, you need to make sure that the modem is hung up, the modem port is closed, and the CMessage class has been deleted. The ~CCheckersView() destructor takes care of all of these details.

The ~CCheckersView() Destructor

```
CCheckersView::~CCheckersView()
{

if( m_pMessage != NULL ){
m_pMessage->Hangup();
delete m_pMessage;
}
}
```

Drawing the Checkerboard & Pieces

The checkerboard is drawn in the view class's OnDraw() function. It creates several brushes and pens of the correct color so that it can draw the board and pieces in the correct colors.

First, the board is drawn. Its colors are black and red. Once the board is drawn, the CCheckers class which performs all game-related activities is interrogated to get the position of all pieces on the board. Once this information is obtained, the pieces are drawn.

The OnDraw() Code

```
#define SQWT 40
#define SQHT 40

void CCheckersView::OnDraw(CDC* pDC)
{
CCheckersDoc* pDoc = GetDocument();
ASSERT_VALID(pDoc);

int sq, col = 1;
CBrush *pOldBrush, Brush[5];
CPen *pOldPen, Pen[5];
CBitmap *pOldBitmap, Bitmap;
CDC DC;
```

```
DC.CreateCompatibleDC( pDC );
Bitmap.CreateBitmap( SQWT * 8, SQHT * 8,
 pDC->GetDeviceCaps( PLANES ),
 pDC->GetDeviceCaps( BITSPIXEL ), NULL );
pOldBitmap = DC.SelectObject( &Bitmap );

Brush[0].CreateSolidBrush( RGB( 0, 0, 0 ) );
Brush[1].CreateSolidBrush( RGB( 255, 0, 0 ));
Brush[2].CreateSolidBrush(RGB(255,255,255));
Brush[3].CreateSolidBrush( RGB( 0, 255, 0 ));
Brush[4].CreateSolidBrush( RGB( 0, 0, 255 ));

pOldBrush = DC.SelectObject( &Brush[0] );
Pen[0].CreatePen( PS_SOLID, 1, RGB(0,0,0));
Pen[1].CreatePen( PS_SOLID, 1, RGB(255,0,0));
Pen[2].CreatePen(PS_SOLID,1,RGB(255,255,255));
Pen[3].CreatePen( PS_SOLID, 1, RGB(0,255,0));
Pen[4].CreatePen( PS_SOLID, 1, RGB(0,0,255));
pOldPen = DC.SelectObject( &Pen[0] );

for( sq=0; sq<64; sq++ ){
 if( sq && !( sq % 8 ) ) col ^= 1;
 col ^= 1;
 DC.SelectObject( &Pen[col] );
 DC.SelectObject( &Brush[col] );
 DC.Rectangle( ( sq % 8 ) * SQWT,
  ( sq / 8 ) * SQHT,
  ( sq % 8 ) * SQWT + (SQWT-1),
  ( sq / 8 ) * SQHT + (SQHT-1) );
 DC.SelectObject( &Pen[2] );
 DC.SelectObject( &Brush[2] );
 DC.MoveTo( ( sq % 8 ) * SQWT,
  ( sq / 8 ) * SQHT );
 DC.LineTo( ( sq % 8 ) * SQWT + (SQWT-1),
  ( sq / 8 ) * SQHT );
 DC.LineTo( ( sq % 8 ) * SQWT + (SQWT-1),
  ( sq / 8 ) * SQHT + (SQHT-1) );
 DC.LineTo( ( sq % 8 ) * SQWT,
  ( sq / 8 ) * SQHT + (SQHT-1) );
 DC.LineTo( ( sq % 8 ) * SQWT,
  ( sq / 8 ) * SQHT );
 }

int Color[64], King;
m_Checkers.GetBoard( Color );
col = 0;
```

483

```
                    for( sq=0; sq<64; sq++ ){
                     if( sq && !( sq % 8 ) ) col ^= 1;
                     King = FALSE;
                     switch( Color[sq] ){
                      case WHITEKING:
                       King = TRUE;
                      case WHITE:
                       DC.SelectObject( &Brush[3] );
                       DC.SelectObject( &Pen[3] );
                       break;
                      case BLACKKING:
                       King = TRUE;
                      case BLACK:
                       DC.SelectObject( &Brush[4] );
                       DC.SelectObject( &Pen[4] );
                       break;
                     }
                     if( Color[sq] != NEUTRAL &&
                     Color[sq] != ILLEGAL ){
                     DC.Ellipse( ( sq % 8 ) * SQWT + 4,
                      ( sq / 8 ) * SQHT + 4,
                      ( sq % 8 ) * SQWT + (SQWT-4),
                      ( sq / 8 ) * SQHT + (SQHT-4) );
                     if( King )
                      DC.TextOut( ( sq % 8 ) * SQWT + 14,
                       ( sq / 8 ) * SQHT + 14, "K", 1 );
                     }
                    col ^= 1;
                    }

                  pDC->BitBlt( 40, 20, SQWT * 8,
                   SQHT * 8, &DC, 0, 0, SRCCOPY );

                  DC.SelectObject( pOldBrush );
                  DC.SelectObject( pOldPen );
                  DC.SelectObject( pOldBitmap );

                  }
```

Checking To See If the Mouse Was Clicked on a Square

When the mouse buttons are clicked, a way of determining if the mouse is pointing to one of the board's squares is needed. A function called OnSquare() does this. It returns a square number given X and Y coordinate arguments.

The OnSquare() Code

```
int CCheckersView::OnSquare( int mx, int my )
{
int sq;

 for( sq=0; sq<64; sq++ ){
  if( mx >= 40 + ( sq % 8 ) * SQWT &&
   my >= 20 + ( sq / 8 ) * SQHT &&
   mx <= 40 + ( sq % 8 ) * SQWT + (SQHT-1) &&
   my <= 20 + ( sq / 8 ) * SQHT + (SQHT-1) )
    return( sq );
  }
 return( -1 );

}
```

Setting the Timer in Motion

The OnTimer() function is an essential ingredient to the workings of the program. It's started in the OnCreate() function of the view class.

The OnCreate() Code

```
int CCheckersView::OnCreate(LPCREATESTRUCT lpCreateStruct)
{
 if (CView::OnCreate(lpCreateStruct) == -1)
  return -1;

 SetTimer( 1, 250, NULL );

 return 0;
}
```

Housekeeping in the Timer Code

A majority of the maintenance of the CMessage class occurs in the OnTimer() function. The first thing it does is look for a new connect. First, it checks to see if the Boolean variable m_pMessage->m_pTalk->m_bConnected is TRUE. If it is, a connection has already been established and we don't need to look for a new connection. If it's FALSE, we call the IsConnected() function. This function returns TRUE if we have a new connection.

The next thing that happens is that a new disconnect is looked for. If the variable m_pMessage->m_pTalk->m_bDisconnect is TRUE, the modem connection has been lost. The CMessage class is deleted and a message box alerting the user to the disconnect is displayed.

If the user has made a multiple move, an ASCII text message is generated with a wsprintf() call. This message is then sent to the remote computer with a SendMessage() function.

The next thing that's done is a search for incoming messages with the MessagesWaiting() function. If any messages are waiting, they're retrieved and acted upon. The messages supported in this game are TEXT_MESSAGE, HANG_UP, MAKE_MOVE, MAKE_MULTIPLE_MOVE, NEW_GAME, CONFIRM_NEW_GAME, and RESIGN_GAME.

The OnTimer() Code

```
void CCheckersView::OnTimer(UINT nIDEvent)
{

 if( m_pMessage != NULL ){
  int i;
  if( !m_pMessage->m_pTalk->m_bConnected ){
   if( m_pMessage->IsConnected() )
    AfxMessageBox( "Connected!" );
   }
  else if( m_pMessage->m_pTalk->m_bConnected
   && m_pMessage->m_pTalk->m_bDisconnected ){
   delete m_pMessage;
   m_pMessage = NULL;
   AfxMessageBox( "Disconnected!" );
   return;
   }
  else{
   if( m_nMultiple && !m_nGameOver ){
    m_nButtonTicks++;
    if( m_nButtonTicks > 40 ){
     m_nMQueue[0] = m_nMultiple;
     m_nMultiple = 0;
     char *pBuffer = new char[2000];
     char Temp[50];
     memset( pBuffer, 0, 2000 );
     for( i=0; i<m_nMQueue[0]*2+1; i++ ){
      wsprintf( Temp, "%05d ", m_nMQueue[i] );
      strcat( pBuffer, Temp );
      }
```

```
   m_pMessage->SendMessage( pBuffer,
    strlen( pBuffer ), MAKE_MULTIPLE_MOVE );
   delete [] pBuffer;
   m_Checkers.ChangeSide();
   IsGameOver();
   }
  }
int Moves[5], nNumMoves;
if( m_pMessage->MessagesWaiting() ){
 int nSize, nType;
 char *pBuffer = new char [2000];
 memset( pBuffer, 0, 2000 );
 nType =
  m_pMessage->GetNextMessage( pBuffer,
   &nSize );
 switch( nType ){
  case TEXT_MESSAGE:
   AfxMessageBox( pBuffer );
   break;
  case HANG_UP:
   m_pMessage->Hangup();
   delete m_pMessage;
   m_pMessage = NULL;
   break;
  case MAKE_MOVE:
   Moves[0] = atoi( pBuffer );
   Moves[1] = atoi( &pBuffer[6] );
   m_Checkers.MakeHumanMove( Moves[0],
    Moves[1], TRUE );
   InvalidateRect( NULL, FALSE );
   UpdateWindow();
   break;
  case MAKE_MULTIPLE_MOVE:
   nNumMoves = atoi( pBuffer );
   for( i=0; i<nNumMoves; i++ )
    Moves[0] = atoi( &pBuffer[6+i*6*2] );
    Moves[1] = atoi( &pBuffer[6+i*6*2+6] );
    m_Checkers.MakeHumanMove( Moves[0],
    Moves[1], FALSE );
   m_Checkers.ChangeSide();
   InvalidateRect( NULL, FALSE );
   UpdateWindow();
   break;
  case NEW_GAME:
   if( MessageBox( "Want a new game?",
    "NEW GAME", MB_OKCANCEL ) == IDOK ){
```

```
                    m_pMessage->SendMessage( "", 1,
                     CONFIRM_NEW_GAME );
                    m_nGameOver = 0;
                    m_Checkers.Restart();
                    InvalidateRect( NULL, FALSE );
                    UpdateWindow();
                    }
                  break;
                case CONFIRM_NEW_GAME:
                  m_nGameOver = 0;
                  m_Checkers.Restart();
                  InvalidateRect( NULL, FALSE );
                  UpdateWindow();
                  break;
                case RESIGN_GAME:
                  AfxMessageBox("Your opponent resigned!");
                  m_nGameOver = ( m_nSideColor ^ 1 ) + 1;
                  break;
                }
                delete [] pBuffer;

            }
          }
        }
    CView::OnTimer(nIDEvent);
    }
```

Seeing If a Game Is Over

There must be a way to determine if a game is over. The IsGameOver()
function does this. It sets the m_nGameOver variable to a nonzero value
if the game has ended.

The IsGameOver() Code

```
void CCheckersView::IsGameOver( void )
{
 int Color[64];

 m_Checkers.GetBoard( Color );

 int i, black = 0, white = 0;
 for( i=0; i<64; i++ ){
  if( Color[i] == WHITE ||
  Color[i] == WHITEKING ) white++;
```

```
    else if( Color[i] == BLACK ||
     Color[i] == BLACKKING ) black++;
    }
  if( !white ){
   AfxMessageBox( "The Blue side won!" );
   m_nGameOver = WHITE + 1;
    }
  else if( !black ){
   AfxMessageBox( "The Green side won!" );
   m_nGameOver = BLACK + 1;
    }
  }
```

The Left Mouse Button

When the left mouse button is pressed, the program looks to see if it's part of a legal move on the checkerboard. If the user has completed a legal move, a string with the move information is created and sent to the remote computer with the SendMessage() function.

The OnLButtonDown() Code

```
void CCheckersView::OnLButtonDown(UINT nFlags, CPoint point)
{

 if( !m_nGameOver && !m_nMultiple &&
  m_pMessage != NULL &&
  m_pMessage->IsConnected() &&
  m_Checkers.GetSide() == m_nSideColor ){

  m_nOnSq = OnSquare( point.x, point.y );
  if( m_nOnSq != -1 ){
   if( m_nGotPiece == -1 ){
    if( m_Checkers.GetColor( m_nOnSq ) ==
     m_Checkers.GetSide() ){
     m_nGotSq = m_nOnSq;
     m_nGotPiece =
      m_Checkers.GetPiece( m_nOnSq );
     }
    }
   else{
    if( m_Checkers.GetColor( m_nOnSq ) ==
     m_Checkers.GetSide() ){
     m_nGotPiece =
      m_Checkers.GetPiece( m_nOnSq );
```

```
          m_nGotSq = m_nOnSq;
          }
      else if( m_Checkers.IsMoveLegal( m_nGotSq,
        m_nOnSq ) ){
        m_Checkers.MakeHumanMove( m_nGotSq,
         m_nOnSq, TRUE );
        int Moves[5];
        Moves[0] = m_nGotSq;
        Moves[1] = m_nOnSq;
        char *pBuffer = new char[100];
        wsprintf( pBuffer, "%05d %05d ",
         Moves[0], Moves[1] );
        m_pMessage->SendMessage( pBuffer,
         strlen( pBuffer ), MAKE_MOVE );
        delete [] pBuffer;
        InvalidateRect( NULL, FALSE );
        UpdateWindow();
        IsGameOver();
        m_nGotPiece = -1;
        }
      }
    }
  }

  CView::OnLButtonDown(nFlags, point);
}
```

The Right Mouse Button

When the right mouse button is clicked, the program looks to see if the user has made a legal jump move. If the user has completed a legal jump move, a string with the jump move information is created and sent to the remote computer with the SendMessage() function.

The OnRButtonDown() Code

```
void CCheckersView::OnRButtonDown(UINT nFlags, CPoint point)
{

  if( !m_nGameOver && m_pMessage != NULL &&
   m_pMessage->IsConnected() &&
   m_Checkers.GetSide() == m_nSideColor ){

   m_nOnSq = OnSquare( point.x, point.y );
```

```
if( m_nOnSq != -1 ){
 if( m_Checkers.IsMoveLegal( m_nGotSq,
  m_nOnSq ) ){
  m_nButtonTicks = 0;
  m_Checkers.MakeHumanMove( m_nGotSq,
  m_nOnSq, FALSE );
  InvalidateRect( NULL, FALSE );
  UpdateWindow();
  m_nMQueue[1+m_nMultiple*2] = m_nGotSq;
  m_nMQueue[2+m_nMultiple*2] = m_nOnSq;
  m_nMultiple++;
  if( !m_Checkers.CanJump( m_nOnSq ) ){
   m_nMQueue[0] = m_nMultiple;
   char *pBuffer = new char[2000];
   char Temp[50];
   memset( pBuffer, 0, 2000 );
   for( int i=0; i<m_nMQueue[0]*2+1; i++ ){
    wsprintf( Temp, "%05d ", m_nMQueue[i] );
    strcat( pBuffer, Temp );
    }
   m_pMessage->SendMessage( pBuffer,
    strlen( pBuffer ),
    MAKE_MULTIPLE_MOVE );
   delete [] pBuffer;
   m_Checkers.ChangeSide();
   IsGameOver();
   m_nGotPiece = -1;
   m_nMultiple = 0;
   }
  else m_nGotSq = m_nOnSq;
  }
 }
}
 CView::OnRButtonDown(nFlags, point);
}
```

Dialing the Remote Computer

This is an important function. It dials a remote computer that's waiting for a call. This function should be studied and understood because it's so important for your own applications.

The first thing the OnConnectionDial() function does is make sure there isn't already a connection in progress. If there is, it tells the user and returns without doing anything.

491

If there's no connection already in progress, a dialog box appears allowing the user to enter the phone number, COM port, and whether they want to pulse dial or tone dial. If the user selects the Cancel button in this dialog box, nothing further happens and no connection is attempted.

Once the OK button has been pressed, a CMessage class is created with MODEM as a parameter. The modem port is opened for a 2400 baud connection on the selected COM port. The expression for this is Open((m_nComPort + 1) | (2400 << 16));

The last thing that's done is to make a call to the Dial() function. A Hayes-compatible dialing string must be created. An example is "ATDT19195449404\15."

The OnConnectionDial() Code

```
void CCheckersView::OnConnectionDial()
{

if( m_pMessage != NULL &&
 m_pMessage->IsConnected() ){
 AfxMessageBox("You are already connected!");
 return;
 }
CDialDlg DialDlg;
DialDlg.m_ToneOrPulse = m_nPulse;
DialDlg.m_PhoneNumber = m_PhoneNumber;
DialDlg.m_ComPort = m_nComPort;
if( DialDlg.DoModal() == IDOK ){
 m_nComPort = DialDlg.m_ComPort;
 m_PhoneNumber = DialDlg.m_PhoneNumber;
 m_nPulse = DialDlg.m_ToneOrPulse;
 if( !DialDlg.m_PhoneNumber.GetLength() )
  return;

 if( m_pMessage ) delete m_pMessage;
 m_pMessage = new CMessage( MODEM );
 if( m_pMessage != NULL &&
  m_pMessage->Open( ( m_nComPort + 1 ) |
  ( 2400 << 16 ) ) ){
  if( !m_nPulse )
   m_pMessage->Dial( "ATDT" +
    m_PhoneNumber + "\15" );
  else
   m_pMessage->Dial( "ATDP" +
    m_PhoneNumber + "\15" );
  m_nSideColor = 0;
  }
```

```
    else AfxMessageBox("Couldn't create class!");
  }
}
```

Hanging Up

At some point, you're going to want to hang up. A menu choice lets users do that. The code that's called is found in the OnConnectHangup() function.

The OnConnectionHangup() Code

```
void CCheckersView::OnConnectionHangup()
{

  if( m_pMessage ){
   m_pMessage->Hangup();
   delete m_pMessage;
   m_pMessage = NULL;
   }


}
```

Sending a Text Message

It's always fun to send your opponents messages during a game. You might want to congratulate them on a great move, or taunt them after you've outwitted them.

Users can send text messages by selecting Send Message from the Connection menu.

The OnConnectionSendmessage() Code

```
void CCheckersView::OnConnectionSendmessage()
{

  if( m_pMessage == NULL ||
   !m_pMessage->IsConnected() ){
   AfxMessageBox( "You are not connected!" );
   return;
   }
  CMessageDlg MessageDlg;
  if( MessageDlg.DoModal() == IDOK ){
   m_pMessage->SendMessage(
    MessageDlg.m_Message.GetBuffer( 100 ),
```

```
            MessageDlg.m_Message.GetLength(),
            TEXT_MESSAGE );
        }
    }
```

Waiting for a Call

When a user selects Wait for Call from the Connection menu, the OnConnectionWaitforcall() function is called. This function first looks for a connection in progress, in which case it alerts the users that there's already a connection established.

If there's no connection currently established, it creates a CMessage class, opens the modem port, and sends the string "ATS0=1\15" to the modem so that it will auto-answer after one ring.

The OnConnectionWaitforcall() Code

```
void CCheckersView::OnConnectionWaitforcall()
{

    if( m_pMessage != NULL &&
        m_pMessage->IsConnected() ){
        AfxMessageBox( "You're already connected!");
        return;
    }
    CDialDlg DialDlg;
    DialDlg.m_ToneOrPulse = m_nPulse;
    DialDlg.m_PhoneNumber = m_PhoneNumber;
    DialDlg.m_ComPort = m_nComPort;
    if( DialDlg.DoModal() == IDOK ){
        m_nComPort = DialDlg.m_ComPort;
        m_PhoneNumber = DialDlg.m_PhoneNumber;
        m_nPulse = DialDlg.m_ToneOrPulse;

        if( m_pMessage != NULL )
            delete m_pMessage;
        m_pMessage = new CMessage( MODEM );
        if( m_pMessage == NULL ){
            AfxMessageBox("Could not create CMessage");
            return;
        }
        if( m_pMessage->Open( ( m_nComPort + 1 ) |
            ( 2400 << 16 ) ) ){
            m_pMessage->Answer( "ATS0=1\15" );
            m_nSideColor = 1;
```

```
        }
    else
     AfxMessageBox( "Couldn't open the port!" );
    }


  }
```

Starting a New Game

If a user decides to start a new game, he or she needs to select New Game from the Game menu. The OnGameNewGame() function is called. This function sends a request for a new game message.

The OnGameNewGame() Code

```
void CCheckersView::OnGameNewgame()
{
 if( m_pMessage == NULL ||
  !m_pMessage->IsConnected() )
  AfxMessageBox( "You're not connected!" );
 else if( MessageBox( "Ask for new game?",
  "NEW GAME", MB_YESNO ) == IDYES )
  m_pMessage->SendMessage( "", 1, NEW_GAME );
}
```

Resigning From a Game

To resign from a game, the user simply selects Resign Game from the Game menu. The OnGameResignGame() function sends a message to the remote computer letting it know that this player has resigned.

The OnGameResignGame() Code

```
void CCheckersView::OnGameResigngame()
{
 if( m_pMessage == NULL ||
  !m_pMessage->IsConnected() )
   AfxMessageBox( "You're not connected!" );
 else if( m_nGameOver )
  AfxMessageBox( "The game is already over!");
 else m_pMessage->SendMessage( "", 1,
  RESIGN_GAME );
}
```

MAKING CHANGES TO THE CHECKERS DEMO PROGRAM FOR NETWORK COMMUNICATIONS

A directory named Network\Checkers can be found on the Companion CD-ROM. It contains the project for the altered version of Checkers that communicates over Novell-compatible networks.

This section describes the changes that were made. This will help you understand the CMessage class and the related functions better.

Selecting From a User List

The first thing you must do is select the user you'll connect to. This is true for both awaiting connections and initiating connections. A special DLL named USERLIST.DLL must be in the current directory—or, better yet, the WINDOWS\SYSTEM directory. This allows a call to the static function CNetwork::CreateUserList() to create a data file in the current directory. The name of the data file will be USERLIST. Then, you can read the data file and find out who's logged on to the network.

The first thing done to the Checkers program was editing the CDialDlg dialog box. The only two items that were kept were the OK and Cancel buttons. A ListBox was then added. This ListBox will contain the user list. Figure 14-7 shows the new dialog box from the resource editor.

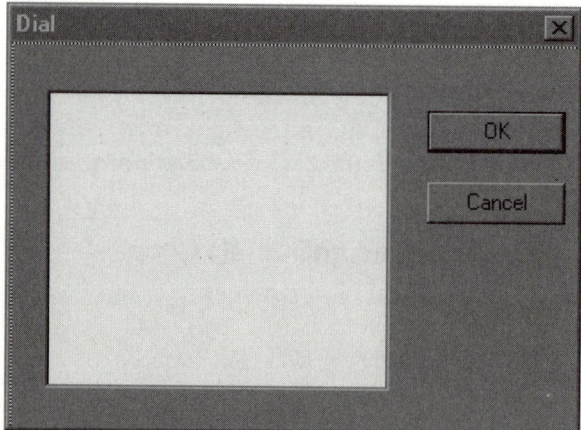

Figure 14-7: The altered dialog box has OK and Cancel buttons, and a ListBox.

In order to populate the ListBox, code had to be added to the OnInitDialog() function (which was also added with the Class Wizard).

The code that was added follows:

```
CNetwork::CreateUserList();
CFile cf;
if( cf.Open( "USERLIST",
 CFile::modeRead ) ){
 int fs = cf.GetLength();
 int records = fs / 71;
 char junk[200];
 for( int i=0; i<records; i++ ){
  cf.Read( junk, 71 );
  if( junk[0] != '*' &&
   memcmp( &junk[2], "NOT_LOGGED_IN", 13 ) )
   m_UserList.AddString( &junk[2] );
  }
 }
```

Besides adding an integer variable to the CDialDlg class named m_Index, an OnOK() function was added. The small amount of code put into the OnOK() function is as follows:

```
m_Index = m_UserList.GetCurSel();
CDialog::OnOK();
```

Initializing & Uninitializing the Network DLLs

To the CMainFrm constructor the following line was added:

```
CTalk::NetworkInit();
```

To the CMainFrm destructor the following line was added:

```
CTalk::NetworkUninit();
```

Getting the Node & Address From the USERLIST File

A special function to retrieve the network number and network address for a given connection was added to the view class. This information must be copied into the m_RemAddr data structure which is a member of the CTalk class. The code follows:

```
BOOL CCheckersView::GetNetworkInfo( int nIndex, void *pNetnum, void *pNetaddr )
{
 CFile cf;
```

497

```
if(!cf.Open( "USERLIST", CFile::modeRead ))
 return( FALSE );

if( nIndex * 71 > (int) cf.GetLength() )
 return( FALSE );

cf.Seek( nIndex * 71 + 51, CFile::begin );
cf.Read( pNetnum, 4 );
cf.Seek( nIndex * 71 + 56, CFile::begin );
cf.Read( pNetaddr, 6 );

return( TRUE );

}
```

Dialing the Remote Computer

The OnConnectionDial() function changed slightly. The main differences between the OnConnectionDial() function in this program and the modem-based program are: 1) creating the CMessage class with NETWORK as an argument, 2) making a call to SetSocketNumber() so that the CNetwork class knows what socket number to use to connect, 3) making a call to GetNetworkInfo() so that the m_RemAddr.sa_netnum and m_RemAddr.sa_nodenum data structure members have the correct information for the connection to which the program will connect, 4) making the call to Open() with CLIENT as the argument, and 5) making a call to Dial() with an empty string. The code follows:

```
void CCheckersView::OnConnectionDial()
{

 if( m_pMessage != NULL &&
  m_pMessage->IsConnected() ){
  AfxMessageBox("You are already connected!");
  return;
  }
 CDialDlg DialDlg;
 if( DialDlg.DoModal() == IDOK ){
  if( m_pMessage ) delete m_pMessage;
  m_pMessage = new CMessage( NETWORK );
  if( m_pMessage == NULL ){
   AfxMessageBox("Could not create CMessage");
   return;
   }
 m_pMessage->m_pTalk->SetSocketNumber(0x4242);
  GetNetworkInfo( DialDlg.m_Index,
```

```
      m_pMessage->m_pTalk->m_RemAddr.sa_netnum,
      m_pMessage->m_pTalk->m_RemAddr.sa_nodenum);
    if( m_pMessage->Open( CLIENT ) ){
      m_pMessage->Dial( "" );
      m_nSideColor = 0;
      }
    else
      AfxMessageBox("Couldn't create CMessage!");
    }
  }
```

Waiting for a Call

The OnConnectionWaitforcall() function changed slightly. The main differences between the OnConnectionWaitforcall() function in this program and the modem-based program are: 1) creating the CMessage class with NETWORK as an argument, 2) making a call to SetSocketNumber() so that the CNetwork class knows over what socket number to connect, 3) making a call to GetNetworkInfo() so that the m_RemAddr.sa_netnum and m_RemAddr.sa_nodenum data structure members have the correct information for the connection to which the program will connect, 4) making the call to Open() with SERVER as the argument, and 5) making a call to Answer() with an empty string.

The code follows:

```
void CCheckersView::OnConnectionWaitforcall()
{

  if( m_pMessage != NULL &&
    m_pMessage->IsConnected() ){
    AfxMessageBox( "You're already connected!");
    return;
    }
  CDialDlg DialDlg;
  if( DialDlg.DoModal() == IDOK ){
    if( m_pMessage != NULL )
      delete m_pMessage;
    m_pMessage = new CMessage( NETWORK );
    if( m_pMessage == NULL ){
      AfxMessageBox("Could not create CMessage");
      return;
      }
  m_pMessage->m_pTalk->SetSocketNumber(0x4242);
    GetNetworkInfo( DialDlg.m_Index,
      m_pMessage->m_pTalk->m_RemAddr.sa_netnum,
```

```
        m_pMessage->m_pTalk->m_RemAddr.sa_nodenum);
    if( m_pMessage->Open( SERVER ) ){
    m_pMessage->Answer( "" );
    m_nSideColor = 1;
    }
    else AfxMessageBox("Couldn't open socket!");
    }


}
```

MAKING CHANGES TO THE CHECKERS DEMO PROGRAM FOR INTERNET COMMUNICATIONS

A directory named Internet\Checkers can be found on the Companion CD-ROM. It contains the project for the altered version of Checkers that communicates over Novell-compatible networks.

This section describes the changes that were made. This will help you understand the CMessage class and the related functions.

Identify Your IP Address

The first thing you'll need to make sure of is that your dialer is connected to your Internet service. Then, the computer that's going to await a call needs to find out its IP address. The calling computer uses the IP address just as the modem version used the phone number. It's the destination address the computer will connect to. You can find out the IP address of a computer by selecting This IP Address from the Connection menu.

The CDialDlg dialog box was altered so that the OK and Cancel buttons and the phone number editable field remained. The phone number label was then changed to "IP Address." The dialog box as it appears in the resource editor can be seen in Figure 14-8.

Figure 14-8: The altered dialog box has OK and Cancel buttons and an IP Address editable field.

Initializing & Uninitializing the Network DLLs

To the CMainFrm constructor the following line was added:

```
CTalk::WinsockInit();
```

To the CMainFrm destructor the following line was added:

```
CTalk::WinsockUninit();
```

Dialing the Remote Computer

The OnConnectionDial() function changed slightly. The main differences between the OnConnectionDial() function in this program and the modem-based program are: 1) creating the CMessage class with INTERNET as an argument, 2) making a call to SetPort() so that the CNetwork class knows over what port number to connect, 3) making the call to Open() with CLIENT as the argument, and 4) making a call to Dial() with an empty string. The code follows:

```
void CCheckersView::OnConnectionDial()
{
 if( m_pMessage != NULL &&
  m_pMessage->IsConnected() ){
  AfxMessageBox("You are already connected!");
  return;
  }
 CDialDlg DialDlg;
 DialDlg.m_PhoneNumber = m_PhoneNumber;
 if( DialDlg.DoModal() == IDOK ){
  m_PhoneNumber = DialDlg.m_PhoneNumber;
  if( !DialDlg.m_PhoneNumber.GetLength() )
   return;

  if( m_pMessage ) delete m_pMessage;
  m_pMessage = new CMessage( INTERNET );
  if( m_pMessage == NULL ){
   AfxMessageBox("Couldn't create CMessage!");
   return;
   }
  m_pMessage->m_pTalk->SetPort( 80 );
  if( m_pMessage->Open( CLIENT ) ){
   m_pMessage->Dial( m_PhoneNumber );
   m_nSideColor = 0;
   }
  else AfxMessageBox( "Could not open port!");
  }
}
```

Waiting for a Call

The OnConnectionWaitforcall() function changed slightly. The main differences between the OnConnectionWaitforcall() function in this program and the modem-based program are: 1) creating the CMessage class with INTERNET as an argument, 2) making a call to SetPort() so that the CNetwork class knows over what port number to connect, 3) making the call to Open() with SERVER as the argument, and 4) making a call to Answer() with an empty string. The code follows:

```
void CCheckersView::OnConnectionWaitforcall()
{

  if( m_pMessage != NULL &&
   m_pMessage->IsConnected() ){
   AfxMessageBox( "You're alread connected!" );
   return;
   }
  if( m_pMessage != NULL )
   delete m_pMessage;
  m_pMessage = new CMessage( INTERNET );
  if( m_pMessage == NULL ){
   AfxMessageBox( "Could not create CMessage");
   return;
   }
  m_pMessage->m_pTalk->SetPort( 80 );
  if( m_pMessage->Open( SERVER ) ){
   m_pMessage->Answer( "" );
   m_nSideColor = 1;
   }
  else AfxMessageBox( "Could not open port!" );

  }
```

USING THE CMESSAGE CLASS IN A NUTSHELL

This section has a simplified version of connecting and answering with the CMessage class over a modem. Start by including "Message.h" in the view class include file. Then declare a CMessage class variable named m_pMessage.

Create a Timer & Get It Started

With the Class Wizard, create an OnCreate() and an OnTimer() function. In the OnCreate() function, start the timer with the following code:

```
SetTimer( 1, 250, NULL );
```

The following timer code is very simple—it merely looks for connections and disconnections:

```
if( m_pMessage != NULL ){
 if( !m_pMessage->m_pTalk->m_bConnected ){
  if( m_pMessage->IsConnected() )
   AfxMessageBox( "Connected!" );
  }
 else if( m_pMessage->m_pTalk->m_bConnected
  && m_pMessage->m_pTalk->m_bDisconnected ){
  delete m_pMessage;
  m_pMessage = NULL;
  AfxMessageBox( "Disconnected!" );
  }
 }
CView::OnTimer(nIDEvent);
}
```

Answering

One computer must answer while the other dials. The following simple code causes the computer to answer:

```
m_pMessage = new CMessage( MODEM );
m_pMessage->Open( ( m_nComPort + 1 ) |
 ( 2400 << 16 ) ) ){
m_pMessage->Answer( "ATS0=1\15" );
```

Dialing

The other computer must dial. The following simplified code shows you how to dial a remote computer:

```
m_pMessage = new CMessage( MODEM );
m_pMessage->Open( ( m_nComPort + 1 ) |
 ( 2400 << 16 ) ) ){
m_pMessage->Dial( "ATDT3334567\15" );
```

CREATING PROGRAMS THAT COMMUNICATE WITH THE CMESSAGE CLASS

This section provides you with some hands-on exercises that start simple and get a little more complicated. The reason they start simple is so that you have every opportunity to understand the CMessage class and learn how to use it completely.

Hands-On 1: Connecting Two Computers Over a Modem

In this first hands-on exercise you'll create a program that either dials another computer or awaits a call from another computer.

To keep things easy, the phone number is part of the compiled code. Later, you'll want to make the phone number a variable that's read in from the registry or entered in a dialog box.

The baud rate and COM port are hard-coded and compiled right into the program code. Both of the test computers that this program was run on operate on COM 2, so that's what is in the program code. Change it if you have a different COM port you'll use to connect.

You'll have to compile the program twice: once for the dialing computer and once for the awaiting computer. Source code comments show you where the change must be made to each version.

1. Create a Visual C++ project named HandsOn14_1 with the following attributes:

   ❏ Single-document interface

   ❏ English language

   ❏ No database support

   ❏ No compound document support

   ❏ No automation or ActiveX control support

   ❏ 3D controls, but no other features

   ❏ No source file comments

   ❏ Link MFC as a static library

2. Select Settings from the Project menu. Choose the Link tab. Add the following libraries to the Object/library modules field. The libraries for the release and debug versions are different. Both are listed below.

Release Project Libraries	Debug Project Libraries
wsock32.lib	wsock32.lib
undock32.lib	undock32.lib
Talk.lib	TalkD.lib

3. Set the Active Configuration to Win32 Release.

4. Add the following include to the HandsOn14_1View.h file:

```
#include "Message.h"
```

5. Add the following variable declaration to the CHandsOn14_1View class in the HandsOn14_1View.h file:

```
CMessage *m_pMessage;
```

6. Add the following code to the CHandsOn14_1View constructor:

```
CHandsOn14_1View::CHandsOn14_1View()
{

m_pMessage = new CMessage( MODEM );

// For awaiting computers...
m_pMessage->Open( ( 2400 << 16 ) | ( 2 ) );
m_pMessage->Answer( "ATS0=1\15" );

// For dialing computers...
m_pMessage->Open( ( 2400 << 16 ) | ( 2 ) );
m_pMessage->Dial( "ATDT2743691\15" );

}
```

7. Add the following code to the CHandsOn14_1View destructor:

```
CHandsOn14_1View::~CHandsOn14_1View()
{

delete m_pMessage;

}
```

8. Add the following functions with the Class Wizard to the CHandsOn14_1View class in the HandsOn14_1View.h file:

```
Name:OnCreate()  Message:WM_CREATE
Name:OnTimer()   Message:WM_TIMER
```

9. Edit the OnCreate function in the CHandsOn14_1View class in the HandsOn14_1View.cpp file as follows:

```
int CHandsOn14_1View::OnCreate(LPCREATESTRUCT lpCreateStruct)
{
 if (CView::OnCreate(lpCreateStruct) == -1)
  return -1;

 SetTimer( 1, 250, NULL );

 return 0;
}
```

10. Edit the OnTimer function in the CHandsOn14_1View class in the HandsOn14_1View.cpp file as follows:

```
void CHandsOn14_1View::OnTimer(UINT nIDEvent)
{

 if( m_pMessage != NULL ){
  if( !m_pMessage->m_pTalk->m_bConnected ){
   if( m_pMessage->IsConnected() )
    AfxMessageBox( "Modem Connected!" );
  }
  else if( m_pMessage->m_pTalk->m_bConnected
   && m_pMessage->m_pTalk->m_bDisconnected ){
   delete m_pMessage;
   m_pMessage = NULL;
   AfxMessageBox( "Modem Disconnected!" );
  }
 }

 CView::OnTimer(nIDEvent);
}
```

11. Compile and run the program.

When the awaiting program runs, it'll simply set for auto-answer in the background. A noise will be heard when the modem answers and sends a carrier signal. You'll be notified with a message box when an incoming call has been answered, as shown in Figure 14-9.

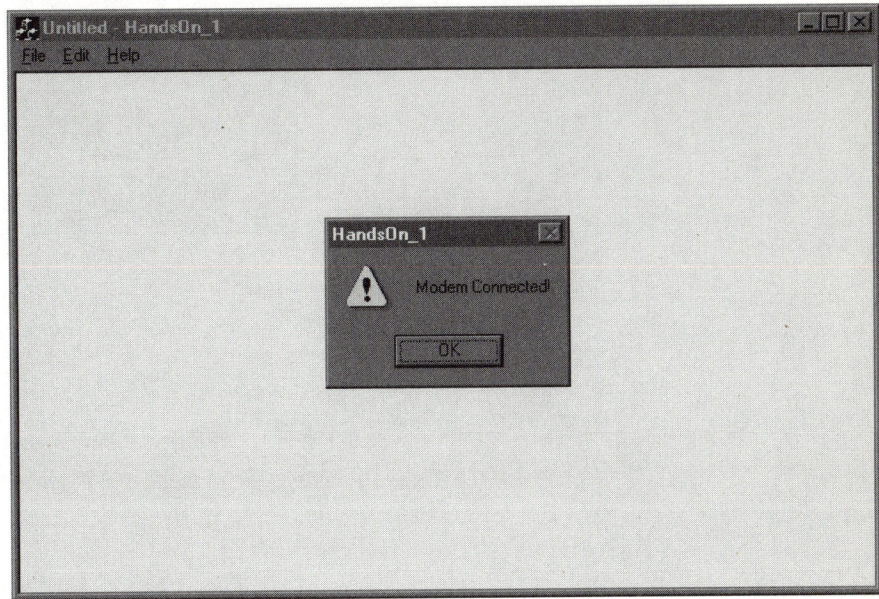

Figure 14-9: A message box will alert you when the computers are connected.

When the dialing program runs, you'll hear the modem dialing the number and you'll hear the ring before the remote computer answers. The carrier noise will then sound and the computers will connect. A message box will appear (as in Figure 14-9) to let you know that the computers are connected.

The only way for the computers to disconnect is for one to terminate. When this happens, the other computer will display a message, as in Figure 14-10, alerting you to the disconnect.

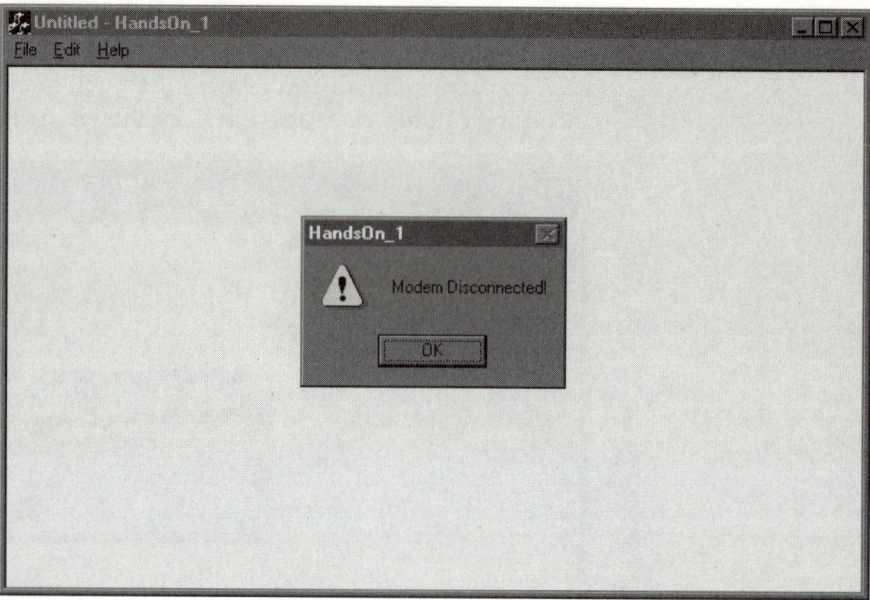

Figure 14-10: If the computers disconnect, you'll get a message to that effect.

Hands-On 2: Connecting Two Computers Over a Novell-Compatible Network

In order to connect over a Novell-compatible network, you'll need to make some small changes in the code that's found in the view class constructor, and you'll need to add a new function to fill in the m_RemAddr data structure fields.

As in the Hands-On14_1 exercise, this one makes some assumptions based on the test machines that were used to develop the exercise. Make changes accordingly for your situation.

The dialing computer is on connection 1. You can find out which connection you are on by typing WHOAMI from the DOS prompt. WHOAMI is a Novell command-line utility. The awaiting computer is on connection 2.

The program must be compiled twice: once with the code for the awaiting computer and once with the code for the dialing computer.

1. Create a Visual C++ project named HandsOn14_2 with the following attributes:

   ❒ Single-document interface

   ❒ English language

   ❒ No database support

   ❒ No compound document support

   ❒ No automation or ActiveX control support

   ❒ 3D controls, but no other features

   ❒ No source file comments

   ❒ Link MFC as a static library

2. Select Settings from the Project menu. Choose the Link tab. Add the following libraries to the Object/library modules field. The libraries for the release and debug versions are different. Both are listed below.

Release Project Libraries	Debug Project Libraries
wsock32.lib	wsock32.lib
undock32.lib	undock32.lib
Talk.lib	TalkD.lib

3. Set the Active Configuration to Win32 Release.

4. Add the following include to the HandsOn14_2View.h file:

```
#include "Message.h"
```

5. Add the following variable declaration to the CHandsOn14_2View class in the HandsOn14_2View.h file:

```
CMessage *m_pMessage;
```

6. Add the following code to the CHandsOn14_2View constructor:

```
CHandsOn14_2View::CHandsOn14_2View()
{

CTalk::NetworkInit();

CNetwork::CreateUserList();
```

```
m_pMessage = new CMessage( NETWORK );
m_pMessage->m_pTalk->SetSocketNumber( 0x4242 );

// For awaiting computers...
SetRemAddr( 1 );
m_pMessage->Open( SERVER );
m_pMessage->Answer( "" );

// For dialing computers...
SetRemAddr( 2 );
m_pMessage->Open( CLIENT );
m_pMessage->Dial( "" );

}
```

7. Add the following code to the CHandsOn14_2View destructor:

```
CHandsOn14_2View::~CHandsOn14_2View()
{

delete m_pMessage;

CTalk::NetworkUninit();

}
```

8. Add the following functions with the Class Wizard to the CHandsOn14_2View class in the HandsOn14_2View.h file:

```
Name:OnCreate()  Message:WM_CREATE
Name:OnTimer()  Message:WM_TIMER
```

9. Edit the OnCreate function in the CHandsOn14_2View class in the HandsOn14_2View.cpp file as follows:

```
int CHandsOn14_2View::OnCreate(LPCREATESTRUCT lpCreateStruct)
{
 if (CView::OnCreate(lpCreateStruct) == -1)
  return -1;

 SetTimer( 1, 250, NULL );

 return 0;
}
```

10. Edit the OnTimer function in the CHandsOn14_2View class in the HandsOn14_2View.cpp file as follows:

```
void CHandsOn14_2View::OnTimer(UINT nIDEvent)
{
 if( m_pMessage != NULL ){
  if( !m_pMessage->m_pTalk->m_bConnected ){
   if( m_pMessage->IsConnected() )
    AfxMessageBox( "Network Connected!" );
   }
  else if( m_pMessage->m_pTalk->m_bConnected
   && m_pMessage->m_pTalk->m_bDisconnected ){
   delete m_pMessage;
   m_pMessage = NULL;
   AfxMessageBox( "Network Disconnected!" );
   }
  }
 CView::OnTimer(nIDEvent);
}
```

11. Add the following function declaration to the HandsOn14_2View.h file:

```
void SetRemAddr( int );
```

12. Add the SetRemAddr function in the CHandsOn14_2View class in the HandsOn14_2View.cpp file as follows:

```
void CHandsOn14_2View::SetRemAddr( int nConnectionNumber )
{
 if( cf.Open( "USERLIST", CFile::modeRead ) ){
  int records = cf.GetLength() / 71;
  for( int i=0; i<records; i++ ){
   char junk[100];
   cf.Read( junk, 71 );
   if( atoi( &junk[64] ) ==
    nConnectionNumber ){
    memcpy(
     m_pMessage->m_pTalk->m_RemAddr.sa_netnum,
     &junk[51], 4 );
    memcpy(
     m_pMessage->m_pTalk->m_RemAddr.sa_nodenum,
     &junk[56], 6 );
    return;
    }
   }
  }
}
```

13. Compile and run the program.

This program will look the same as the first exercise when it runs. You won't, however, hear the modem carrier. When the computers connect, you'll get a message box alerting you to the connection. When they disconnect, another message box will appear to let you know.

Hands-On 3: Connecting Two Computers Over the Internet

In order to connect over the Internet, you'll need to make some small changes in the code that's found in the view class constructor.

As in the HandsOn14_1 exercise, this one makes some assumptions based on the test machines that were used to develop the exercise. Make changes accordingly for your situation.

The answering computer is at IP address 199.72.119.68. If you're unsure of the IP address of the answering computer, you can run the Internet version of the Checkers program (found in the Internet\Checkers directory on the Companion CD-ROM) and select This IP Address from the Connection menu. If your dialer has you correctly connected to your Internet service, the IP address will be displayed in a message box.

The program must be compiled twice: once with the code for the awaiting computer and once with the code for the dialing computer.

1. Create a Visual C++ project named HandsOn14_3 with the following attributes:
   - ❏ Single-document interface
   - ❏ English language
   - ❏ No database support
   - ❏ No compound document support
   - ❏ No automation or ActiveX control support
   - ❏ 3D controls, but no other features
   - ❏ No source file comments
   - ❏ Link MFC as a static library

2. Select Settings from the Project menu. Choose the Link tab. Add the following libraries to the Object/library modules field. The libraries for the release and debug versions are different. Both are listed below.

Release Project Libraries	Debug Project Libraries
wsock32.lib	wsock32.lib
undock32.lib	undock32.lib
Talk.lib	TalkD.lib

3. Set the Active Configuration to Win32 Release.

4. Add the following include to the HandsOn14_3View.h file:

```
#include "Message.h"
```

5. Add the following variable declaration to the CHandsOn14_3View class in the HandsOn14_3View.h file:

```
CMessage *m_pMessage;
```

6. Add the following code to the CHandsOn14_3View constructor:

```
CHandsOn14_3View::CHandsOn14_3View()
{

CTalk::WinsockInit();

m_pMessage = new CMessage( INTERNET );
m_pMessage->m_pTalk->SetPort( 80 );

// For awaiting computers...
m_pMessage->Open( SERVER );
m_pMessage->Answer( "" );

// For dialing computers...
m_pMessage->Open( CLIENT );
m_pMessage->Dial( "199.72.119.68" );

}
```

7. Add the following code to the CHandsOn14_3View destructor:

```
CHandsOn14_3View::~CHandsOn14_3View()
{

delete m_pMessage;

CTalk::WinsockUninit();

}
```

8. Add the following functions with the Class Wizard to the CHandsOn14_3View class in the HandsOn14_3View.h file:

```
Name:OnCreate()  Message:WM_CREATE
Name:OnTimer()  Message:WM_TIMER
```

9. Edit the OnCreate function in the CHandsOn14_3View class in the HandsOn14_3View.cpp file as follows:

```
int CHandsOn14_3View::OnCreate(LPCREATESTRUCT lpCreateStruct)
{
 if (CView::OnCreate(lpCreateStruct) == -1)
  return -1;

 SetTimer( 1, 250, NULL );

 return 0;
}
```

10. Edit the OnTimer function in the CHandsOn14_3View class in the HandsOn14_3View.cpp file as follows:

```
void CHandsOn14_3View::OnTimer(UINT nIDEvent)
{
 if( m_pMessage != NULL ){
  if( !m_pMessage->m_pTalk->m_bConnected ){
   if( m_pMessage->IsConnected() )
    AfxMessageBox( "Internet Connected!" );
   }
  else if( m_pMessage->m_pTalk->m_bConnected
   && m_pMessage->m_pTalk->m_bDisconnected ){
   delete m_pMessage;
   m_pMessage = NULL;
   AfxMessageBox( "Internet Disconnected!" );
   }
  }

 CView::OnTimer(nIDEvent);
}
```

11. Compile and run the program.

This program will look the same as the HandOn14_1 exercise when it runs. You won't, however, hear the modem carrier. When the computers connect, you'll get a message box alerting you to the connection. When they disconnect, another message box will appear to let you know.

Hands-On 4: Sending Simple Messages

Now that you've gotten experience connecting over the modem, a Novell-compatible network, and the Internet, it's time to send some messages. This exercise connects over a modem and then sends text messages when the 1, 2, 3, or 4 key is pressed.

1. Create a Visual C++ project named HandsOn14_4 with the following attributes:

   ❏ Single-document interface

   ❏ English language

   ❏ No database support

   ❏ No compound document support

   ❏ No automation or ActiveX control support

   ❏ 3D controls, but no other features

   ❏ No source file comments

   ❏ Link MFC as a static library

2. Select Settings from the Project menu. Choose the Link tab. Add the following libraries to the Object/library modules field. The libraries for the release and debug versions are different. Both are listed below.

Release Project Libraries	Debug Project Libraries
wsock32.lib	wsock32.lib
undock32.lib	undock32.lib
Talk.lib	TalkD.lib

3. Set the Active Configuration to Win32 Release.

4. Add the following include to the HandsOn14_4View.h file:

   ```
   #include "Message.h"
   ```

5. Add the following variable declaration to the CHandsOn14_4View class in the HandsOn14_4View.h file:

```
CMessage *m_pMessage;
```

6. Add the following code to the CHandsOn14_4View constructor:

```
CHandsOn14_4View::CHandsOn14_4View()
{
m_pMessage = new CMessage( MODEM );

// For awaiting computers...
m_pMessage->Open( ( 2400 << 16 ) | ( 2 ) );
m_pMessage->Answer( "ATS0=1\15" );

// For dialing computers...
//m_pMessage->Open( ( 2400 << 16 ) | ( 2 ) );
//m_pMessage->Dial( "ATDT3492741\15" );
}
```

7. Add the following code to the CHandsOn14_4View destructor:

```
CHandsOn14_4View::~CHandsOn14_4View()
{
 delete m_pMessage;
}
```

8. Add the following functions with the Class Wizard to the CHandsOn14_4View class in the HandsOn14_4View.h file:

```
Name:OnCreate()  Message:WM_CREATE
Name:OnTimer()  Message:WM_TIMER
Name:OnChar()  Message:WM_CHAR
```

9. Edit the OnCreate function in the CHandsOn14_4View class in the HandsOn14_4View.cpp file as follows:

```
int CHandsOn14_4View::OnCreate(LPCREATESTRUCT lpCreateStruct)
{
 if (CView::OnCreate(lpCreateStruct) == -1)
  return -1;

 SetTimer( 1, 250, NULL );

 return 0;
}
```

10. Edit the OnTimer function in the CHandsOn14_4View class in the HandsOn14_4View.cpp file as follows:

```
void CHandsOn14_4View::OnTimer(UINT nIDEvent)
{
 if( m_pMessage != NULL ){
  if( !m_pMessage->m_pTalk->m_bConnected ){
   if( m_pMessage->IsConnected() )
    AfxMessageBox( "Connected!" );
   }
  else if( m_pMessage->m_pTalk->m_bConnected
   && m_pMessage->m_pTalk->m_bDisconnected ){
   delete m_pMessage;
   m_pMessage = NULL;
   AfxMessageBox( "Disconnected!" );
   }
  else if( m_pMessage->MessagesWaiting() ){
   int nSize, nType;
   char *pBuffer = new char [2000];
   memset( pBuffer, 0, 2000 );
   // Only text messages...
   nType =
    m_pMessage->GetNextMessage( pBuffer,
     &nSize );
   AfxMessageBox( pBuffer );
   delete pBuffer;
   }
  }

 CView::OnTimer(nIDEvent);
}
```

11. Edit the OnChar function in the CHandsOn14_4View class in the HandsOn14_4View.cpp file as follows:

```
void CHandsOn14_4View::OnChar(UINT nChar, UINT nRepCnt, UINT
nFlags)
{
 static char *szMessages[] = {
  "This is message one.",
  "This is the second message.",
  "Hi there, Visual C++ is great!",
  "CMessage class is for communications."
  };
```

```
    if( nChar == '1' )
     m_pMessage->SendMessage( szMessages[0],
       strlen( szMessages[0] ), 1 );
    else if( nChar == '2' )
     m_pMessage->SendMessage( szMessages[1],
       strlen( szMessages[1] ), 1 );
    else if( nChar == '3' )
     m_pMessage->SendMessage( szMessages[2],
       strlen( szMessages[2] ), 1 );
    else if( nChar == '4' )
     m_pMessage->SendMessage( szMessages[3],
       strlen( szMessages[3] ), 1 );

    CView::OnChar(nChar, nRepCnt, nFlags);
    }
```

12. Compile and run the program.

When the program first runs, you'll hear the modem making noise, then you'll see the message box alerting you to the connection. Either side responds to a keypress of 1, 2, 3, or 4 by sending a text message to the other computer. Figure 14-11 shows you the first text message; Figure 14-12 shows you the fourth text message.

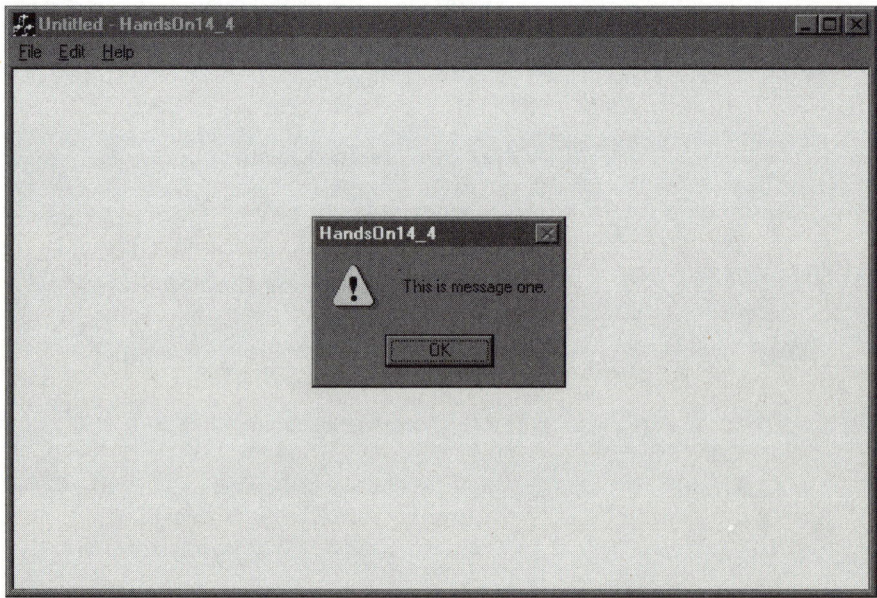

Figure 14-11: When you press the 1 key, this is the message you'll send to the remote computer.

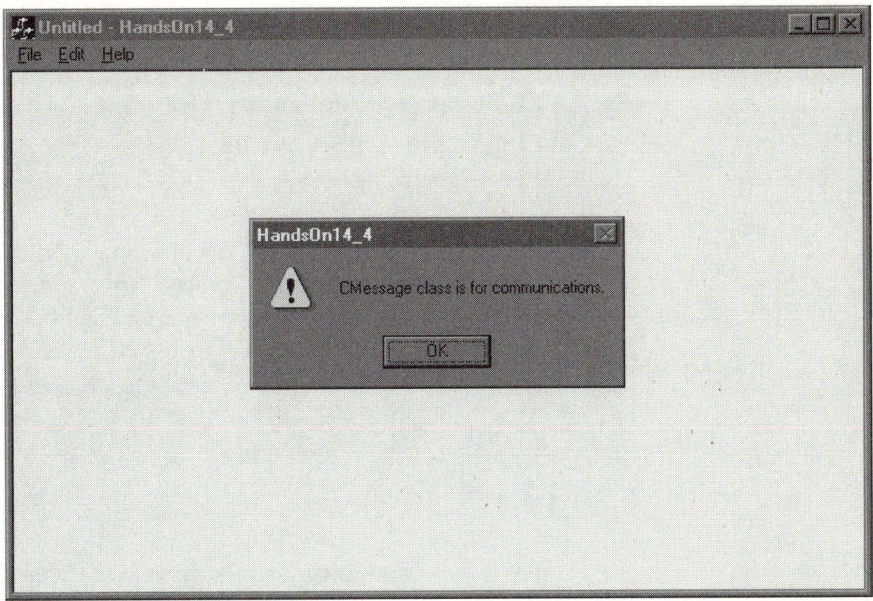

Figure 14-12: When you press the 4 key, this is the message you'll send to the remote computer.

 ## Hands-On 5: Reading Information From a Remote Computer

Suppose your company wants to keep its employees aware of current events. You can create a special program that answers a modem call and sends a text file to the remote computer. Then, employees can just dial in and read current information. The information might be about special events, altered work hours, or reminders for tomorrow's workday.

This exercises waits for a call, reads in a text file, then sends it to the remote computer. The user at the other end can then read the information. This is a great way to make current information available to people who aren't on-site. You can use the answer version of the HandsOn14_4 program to dial in. It'll get a text message and just display it in a message box.

1. Create a Visual C++ project named HandsOn14_5 with the following attributes:

   ❏ Single-document interface

   ❏ English language

   ❏ No database support

- ❑ No compound document support
- ❑ No automation or ActiveX control support
- ❑ 3D controls, but no other features
- ❑ No source file comments
- ❑ Link MFC as a static library

2. Select Settings from the Project menu. Choose the Link tab. Add the following libraries to the Object/library modules field. The libraries for the release and debug versions are different. Both are listed below.

Release Project Libraries	Debug Project Libraries
wsock32.lib	wsock32.lib
undock32.lib	undock32.lib
Talk.lib	TalkD.lib

3. Set the Active Configuration to Win32 Release.

4. Add the following include to the HandsOn14_5View.h file:

```
#include "Message.h"
```

5. Add the following variable declaration to the CHandsOn14_5View class in the HandsOn14_5View.h file:

```
CMessage *m_pMessage;
```

6. Add the following code to the CHandsOn14_5View constructor:

```
CHandsOn14_5View::CHandsOn14_5View()
{
m_pMessage = new CMessage( MODEM );

m_pMessage->Open( ( 2400 << 16 ) | ( 2 ) );
m_pMessage->Answer( "ATS0=1\15" );
}
```

7. Add the following functions with the Class Wizard to the CHandsOn14_5View class in the HandsOn14_5View.h file:

```
Name:OnCreate()  Message:WM_CREATE
Name:OnTimer()  Message:WM_TIMER
```

8. Edit the OnCreate function in the CHandsOn14_5View class in the HandsOn14_5View.cpp file as follows:

```
int CHandsOn14_5View::OnCreate(LPCREATESTRUCT lpCreateStruct)
{
 if (CView::OnCreate(lpCreateStruct) == -1)
  return -1;

 SetTimer( 1, 250, NULL );

 return 0;
}
```

9. Edit the OnTimer function in the CHandsOn14_5View class in the HandsOn14_5View.cpp file as follows:

```
void CHandsOn14_5View::OnTimer(UINT nIDEvent)
{
 if( m_pMessage != NULL ){
  if( !m_pMessage->m_pTalk->m_bConnected ){
   if( m_pMessage->IsConnected() ){
    CFile cf;
    if( cf.Open( "DATAFILE.TXT",
     CFile::modeRead ) ){
     char *pBuffer;
     int fs = (int) cf.GetLength();
     pBuffer = new char [fs];
     cf.Read( pBuffer, fs );
     m_pMessage->SendMessage( pBuffer,
      fs, 1 );
     delete [] pBuffer;
     }
    }
   }
  else if( m_pMessage->m_pTalk->m_bConnected
   && m_pMessage->m_pTalk->m_bDisconnected ){
   delete m_pMessage;
   m_pMessage = new CMessage( MODEM );
   m_pMessage->Open( ( 2400 << 16 ) | ( 2 ) );
   m_pMessage->Answer( "ATSO=1\15" );
   }
  }

 CView::OnTimer(nIDEvent);
}
```

10. Compile and run the program.

When the program runs, you won't see anything. The message boxes don't appear telling of connections and disconnections. That's because the assumption is made that this program will need to run unattended.

As people connect, you will hear the modem carrier sound as connections are being made. You could easily add a connection counter to the program that displays from the view window.

On the Web

There are tons of places on the Web where you'll find resources for telecommunications. Some of them are featured here so that you can sample them.

A list of practically everything you'll need in the way of telecommunications resources can be found at this site, located at http://www.wgta.org/teledir/teledir.htm. It covers everything from long distance carriers to education and training. (See Figure 14-13.)

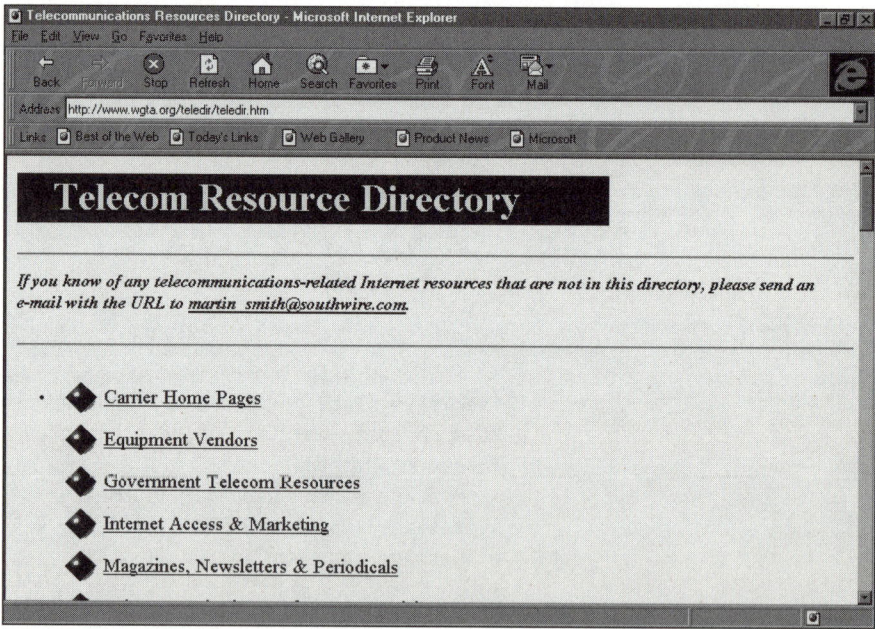

Figure 14-13: This site links to many valuable resources.

This site features, among other things, hardware and software vendors. It's located at http://ext.usu/edu/resource/techres.html. If you follow the links, you'll find yourself looking at a very comprehensive list. (See Figure 14-14.)

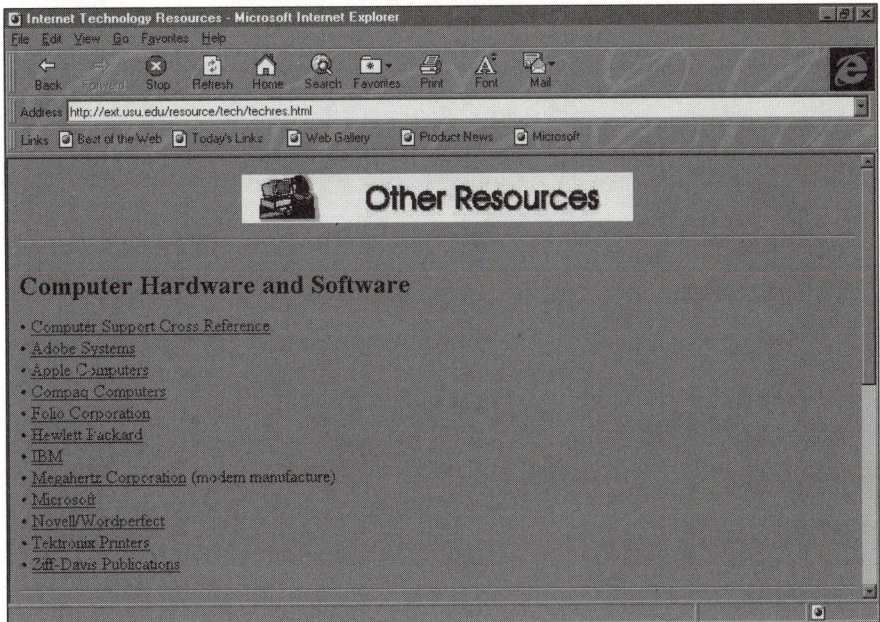

Figure 14-14: This site has mostly software and hardware resources.

For service providers galore, check out this site, located at http://www.cablelabs.com/NR/telco_page.html. These links will bring you to virtually every service provider there is. And that's an advantage if you're trying to comparison-shop. (See Figure 14-15.)

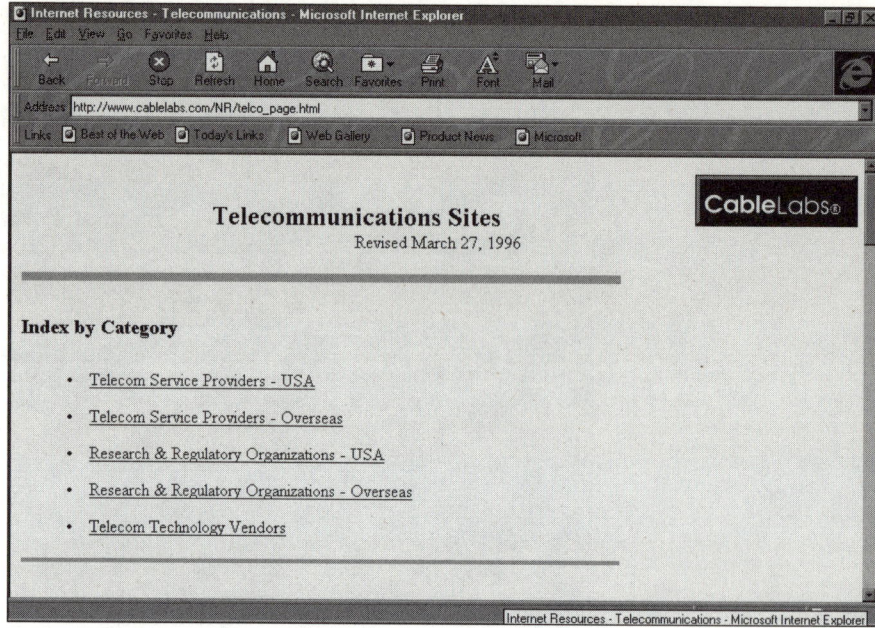

Figure 14-15: This site specializes in service providers.

Moving On

You've learned about telecommunications. You've learned about important ways to use them and ways to apply the technology. You've also learned how to easily communicate over modems, networks, and the Internet using the CMessage class library. It's an easy next step to create your own applications that use the CMessage class library.

The next chapter talks about data compression. It's a good topic for today's data-intensive applications. You can even use it in conjunction with the CMessage class. You can compress data before you send it to a remote computer to reduce connection time.

Chapter 15

Data Compression

> *I concluded, we kinotropists must be numbered among
> Britain's most adept programmers of Enginery or any
> sort, and virtually all advances in the compression of
> data have originated as kinotropic applications.*
> —*William Gibson and Bruce Sterling*

Today computers have average hard drives that are 100 to 200 times larger than the average hard drive of 10 years ago. That's good news for consumers who want more hard-drive space to allow more applications to fit on their systems. Application developers, though, seem to have risen to the challenge by creating programs that do their best to consume as *much* hard drive space as possible. Therefore, the net gain for most computer users is minimal.

In addition, developers have stopped compressing data. Most of them figure that hard drives are big, so they don't have to fool with compressing data. The worst offenders are graphics and sound files. Windows' native graphical format is the BMP file, which is completely uncompressed. A full-screen BMP in 640 X 480 with 256 colors requires 300K of disk space. Windows' native sound format is the WAV file, which is also completely uncompressed. These files can easily be as large as several hundred kilobytes.

In the early 1980s, when most applications came on a single floppy disk, developers went to great lengths to cram in all they could. There was no question about whether to compress data—the only question was which method to use. Time passed and current applications are now very sophisticated. But large applications with lots of data are no excuse for consuming more hard drive space than is necessary. Developers need to start compressing data on a regular basis and stop cutting that corner just because hard drives have gotten larger.

The CompressedFile class library gives you the tools you need to compress and decompress data. It's easy, so you won't have any excuses. Go ahead and crunch things down!

THE COMPRESSEDFILE CLASS LIBRARY

This data compression class library can be linked in with the Visual C++ program. The library is simple to use. Replacements for the CFile class library are given. You can open a file, read data, and close the file just as if it was a normal open, read, and close sequence of operations. The same thing goes for writing data. You can create, write, and close just as if you were using the standard file class library.

All source code and support files to rebuild the CompressedFile.lib file can be found in the DATACOMP\CompressedFile directory on the Companion CD-ROM.

The Data Compression Demo

We've built a simple demonstration program that shows what the class library can do. The program can be found in the DATACOMP\CompressDemo directory on the Companion CD-ROM. Using File Manager or Program Manager, run the program named CompressDemo.exe. It's a multiple-document program. When it first runs, all you'll see is an empty application window. (See Figure 15-1.)

The first thing you'll need to do is load a file. Any file or file type will do, but text, BMP, and WAV files compress well, so you might want to try one of those file types. To load a file, select Open from the File menu, then use the standard Windows file selector to select a file. The file will load and a window will appear with some relevant information about the file. Unless the file you load has been compressed with the data compression library, it will be labeled as "no compression" in the win-

dow, since it wasn't compressed with the data compression libraries that come on the Companion CD-ROM. (See Figure 15-2.)

Figure 15-1: The empty application window you'll see when the data compression demo first runs.

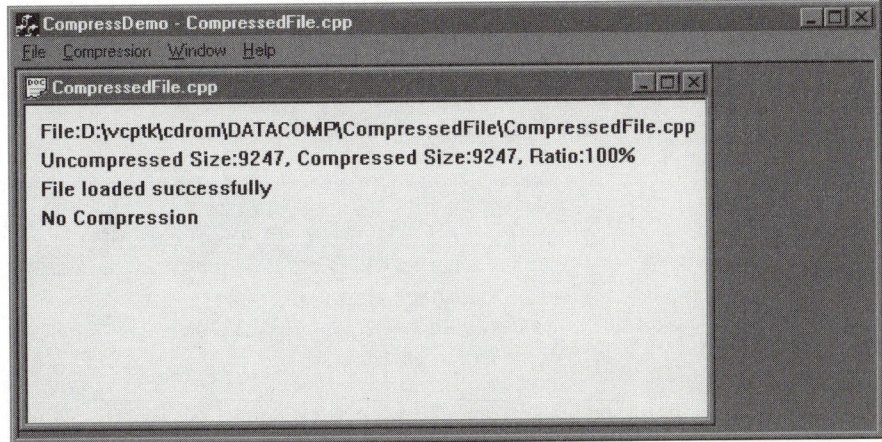

Figure 15-2: Once a file is loaded, a window opens and displays information about the file.

The next thing to do to test the program is select a compression type from the Compression menu. The choices offered are Huffman, LZSS, LZW, and None. LZW is the default choice and usually produces the best results. Leave this choice selected for now. (See Figure 15-3.)

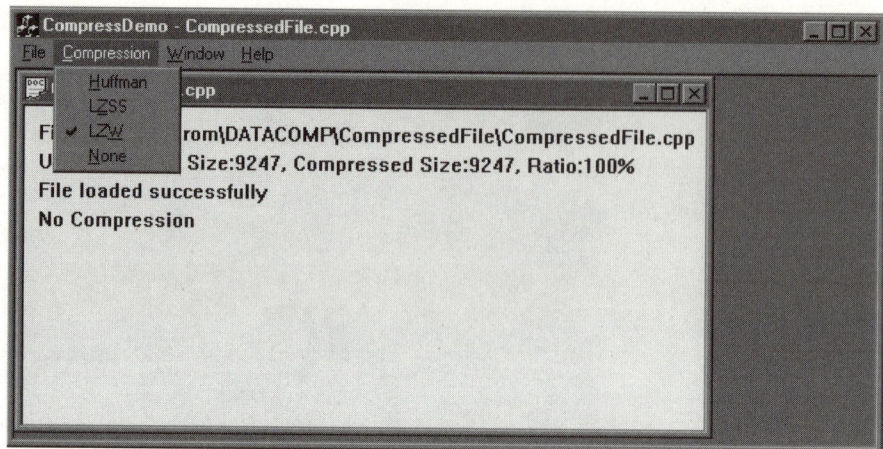

Figure 15-3: You can select from several types of compression methods.

To save the file with the chosen compression method, select Save As from the File menu. A standard Windows file selector will appear. Type a filename and click on the OK button. For this example, we saved our file as TEST.CMP using LZW compression. After the file saves, the information in the window will update to reflect the saved file size and the compression type, as shown in Figure 15-4.

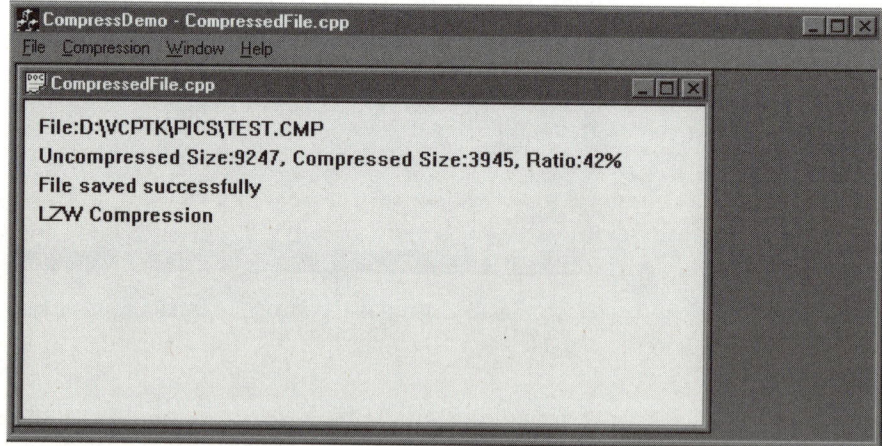

Figure 15-4: The window is updated with new information after the file is saved.

Different Types of Data Compression

Some explanation on the three different compression methods supported by the compression library will help you understand the rest of the chapter. This section gives a short description of each one.

Huffman Data Compression

The Huffman coding takes a probabalistic approach to data compression. It depends on knowing the probability of each symbol's appearance in a message. Given the probabilities, a table of codes is constructed with different codes having different numbers of bits. The codes with the greater probabilities have the smallest numbers of bits, and the codes with the lesser probabilities have the largest numbers of bits.

The Huffman compression algorithm starts off by looking at a list of characters and developing a corresponding list of probabilities (or frequency counts). This way, the frequency of occurrence is known for each character.

The list is sorted by frequency count, the highest at the top of the list and the lowest at the bottom. A binary tree is developed with which the binary token for each character can be accessed.

The individual symbols in the tree are laid out as a string of leaf nodes that are going to be connected by a binary tree. Each node has a weight, which is simply the frequency or probability of the symbol's appearance.

The two free nodes with the lowest weights are located. A parent node for these two nodes is created and assigned a weight equal to the sum of the two child nodes. The parent node is added to the list of free nodes, and the two child nodes are removed from the list. One of the child nodes is designated as the path taken from the parent node when decoding a 0 bit. The other is arbitrarily set to 1 bit. These steps are repeated until only one free node is left. This free node is designated as the root of the tree.

LZSS Data Compression

LZSS compression uses previously seen text as a dictionary. It replaces phrases in the input text with pointers into the dictionary to achieve compression. The amount of compression depends on how long the dictionary phrases are, how large the window into previously seen text is, and the entropy of the source text with respect to the LZSS model.

The main data structure in LZSS is a text window, divided into two parts. The first consists of a large block of recently decoded text. The second, normally much smaller, is a look-ahead buffer. The look-ahead buffer has characters read in from the input stream but not yet encoded.

The normal size of the text window is several thousand characters. The look-ahead buffer is generally much smaller, maybe 10 to 100 characters. The algorithm tries to match the contents of the look-ahead buffer to a string in the dictionary.

The code to implement this compression algorithm is fairly simple. It merely has to look through the entire text window for the longest match, encode it, then shift.

The decompression algorithm is even simpler, since it doesn't have to do comparisons. It reads in a token, outputs the indicated phrase, outputs the following character, shifts, and repeats. It maintains the window but it does not work with string comparisons.

LZW Data Compression

LZW is a dictionary-based compression scheme. It stores phrases in a potentially unlimited dictionary. It is different than LZSS in that it abandons the concept of a text window.

LZW outputs a series of tokens similar to LZSS. Each LZW token has two components: a phrase location and a character that follows the phrase. Each token consists of a code that selects a given phrase and a single character that follows the phrase. The phrase length is already known by the decoder and doesn't have to be part of the token.

When using the LZW algorithm, both the encoder and decoder start off with a very small dictionary consisting of 256 phrases, each a single character. As each character is read in, it is added to the current string. As long as the current string matches some phrase in the dictionary, this process continues.

But eventually the string will no longer have a corresponding phrase in the dictionary. This is when LZW outputs a token and a character. Remember that the string did have a match in the dictionary until the last character was read in. The current string, therefore, is defined as that last match with one new character added on.

The compression algorithm outputs the index for the previous match and the character that broke the match. It then takes an additional step. The new phrase, consisting of the dictionary match and the new character, is added to the dictionary. The next time the phrase appears, it can be used to build an even longer phrase.

LZW can arbitrarily set the size of the phrase dictionary. This may cause two effects that must be dealt with. First, you have to consider the number of bits allocated in the output token for the phrase code. Second, and more important, you have to consider how much CPU time managing the dictionary will take.

CCompressedFile Class Library Function Calls

This section is provided as a reference to the public function calls the data compression library offers. Since the library was designed with simplicity as a major goal, there aren't many calls. That's good because using data compression is easy—it just takes a few lines of code.

You may want to skip over this section and read the section entitled "Behind CompressDemo," which shows how the calls are used. (For some people, it's better to look at the usage of function calls before actually studying their syntax.)

CCompressedFile()

Prototype: `CCompressedFile( int nType );`

Purpose: This is the CompressedFile class constructor. The nType argument that can be given determines the data compression type that will be used. If you don't give the constructor an argument, it defaults to LZW compression.

Arguments: int nType, Defaults to LZW
The choices are HUFF, LZSS, LZW, and UNCOMP

Returns: Nothing

Open()

Prototype: `BOOL Open( const char *pszFileName, unsigned int nOpenFlags );`

Purpose: This function is almost exactly like the Cfile::Open() function. It opens a file for reading or writing. At the same time, it initializes all arrays and variables for the data compression or decompression.

Arguments: const char *pszFileName
unsigned int nOpenFlags

Returns: BOOL: TRUE for success, FALSE for failure

Close()

Prototype: `void Close( void );`

Purpose: This function closes the file and flushes all buffers.

Arguments: None

Returns: Nothing

GetPosition()

Prototype: `DWORD GetPosition( void );`

Purpose: This function returns the position the file pointer points to. If 500 bytes have been written to a newly created file, the value returned will be 500. If 2048 bytes have been read from a newly opened file, the value returned will be 2048.

Arguments: None

Returns: DWORD dwCurrentPointer

GetLength()

Prototype: `DWORD GetLength( void );`

Purpose: This function returns the byte length of the file.

Arguments: None

Returns: DWORD dwFileLength

FindFileInArchive()

Prototype: `BOOL FindFileInArchive( int nIndex );`

Purpose: Compressed archive files that are created with the CompressedFile class library can have more than one file stored in each archive file. Before this function is called, the compressed file must be opened with the Open() function. The FindFileInArchive() function then seeks to the file specified by nIndex. If there are five files in the archive and an argument of 2 is passed in, the file at index 2 will be sought. This is the third file in the archive, and that's the one that will be decompressed.

Arguments: int nIndex

Returns: BOOL: TRUE for success, FALSE for failure

ReadByte()

Prototype:	`int ReadByte( void );`
Purpose:	This function reads a single byte from an opened file.
Arguments:	None
Returns:	int nByteValue

WriteByte()

Prototype:	`void WriteByte( int nByte );`
Purpose:	This function writes a single byte to an opened file.
Arguments:	int nByte
Returns:	void

Read()

Prototype:	`unsigned int Read( void far *pBuffer, unsigned int nBytes );`
Purpose:	This function reads a specified number of bytes into a buffer. It returns the number of bytes actually read. This functions almost exactly like the Cfile::Read() function.
Arguments:	void far *pBuffer unsigned int nBytes
Returns:	unsigned int nBytesRead

Write()

Prototype:	`void Write( void far *pBuffer, unsigned int nBytes );`
Purpose:	This function writes a specified number of bytes that are in a buffer to the file. This functions almost exactly like the Cfile::Write() function.
Arguments:	void far *pBuffer int nBytes
Returns:	Nothing

Behind CompressDemo

Complete source code for CompressDemo can be found in the DATACOMP\CompressDemo directory of the Companion CD-ROM. This section shows the highlights of the program's source code and gives explanations for each. You will notice that the Open(), Read(), Write(), and Close() functions are called in exactly the same way as those in the Cfile class. An effort was made to keep the CCompressedFile class as compatible with the Cfile class as possible.

ImageView was created with the Visual C++ AppWizard with the following settings:

❏ Multiple-document interface
❏ English language
❏ No database support
❏ No compound document support
❏ No automation or ActiveX control support
❏ 3D controls, but no other features
❏ Yes source file comments
❏ MFC linked as a static library

Opening a File

The code that loads a file from disk into memory can be found in the CCompressDemoView class. The function in which it's placed is the OnDraw() function. Every time a file is opened, a new MDI window is opened and drawn. The file can then be loaded the first time the OnDraw() function is called.

Once the file is loaded, information about it is drawn to the child window. That way, the user can see the details about the file, its compression method, its size, and its compression ratio.

The first thing to do in the OnDraw() function is to see whether or not the file has been loaded. The Boolean variable m_bLoaded is FALSE if the file hasn't been loaded, TRUE if it has been loaded.

Obtaining the filename from the document class, a CCompressedFile class object is created with the MakeNewFile() static function. When the file is loaded, a determination is made whether or not the file has been compressed with the CCompressedFile compression class. This is transparent to the programmer, but it's nice to know that you don't have to worry about it.

A buffer is allocated for the data that will be read. The size that's needed for the uncompressed data can be obtained by examining the CCompressedFile member variable named m_dwUncompressedSize.

Once the buffer is allocated, a single call to the Read() function is made. The Read() function looks exactly like the Read() function of the Cfile class. It takes two arguments: a pointer to a buffer and the size to read.

The compressed and uncompressed sizes are stored into the view class from the CCompressedFile class. This is just so that the information can be displayed in the view window after the CCompressedFile object is deleted.

The file is closed and then deleted. No further CCompressedFile read operations are performed in the application.

Information about the file is displayed at the end of the OnDraw() function. The file name, compression type, compresssed and uncompressed sizes, the compression ratio, and the status of the read operation are all drawn.

The OnDraw() Function

```
static char *szComps[] = {
"No Compression            ",
"Huffman Compression       ",
"LZSS Compression          ",
"LZW Compression           ",
"Companding Compression    "
};

void CCompressDemoView::OnDraw(CDC* pDC)
{
 CCompressDemoDoc* pDoc = GetDocument();
 ASSERT_VALID(pDoc);

 if( !m_bLoaded ){
  CString PathName = pDoc->GetPathName();
  strcpy( m_szFilename,
   PathName.GetBuffer( 3 ) );
  strcpy( m_szSaveLoad,
   "File loaded unsuccessfully     " );

  m_pFile =
   CCompressedFile::MakeNewFile(m_szFilename);

  if( !m_pFile )
   AfxMessageBox(
    "Could not create File class!" );
```

```
    else{
     m_dwUncompressedSize =
      m_dwCompressedSize = 0L;

     if( m_pFile != NULL ){
      if( m_pFile->Open( m_szFilename,
       CFile::modeRead ) ){
       strcpy( m_szCompression,
        szComps[m_pFile->m_nCompressionType+1]);
       hGlobal = ::GlobalAlloc( GMEM_FIXED,
        m_pFile->m_dwUncompressedSize + 100L );
       if( hGlobal ){
        m_cbDataBuffer = (unsigned char *)
         ::GlobalLock( hGlobal );
        BeginWaitCursor();
        m_pFile->Read( m_cbDataBuffer,
         m_pFile->m_dwUncompressedSize );
        EndWaitCursor();
        m_bSuccess = TRUE;
        m_dwUncompressedSize =
         m_pFile->m_dwUncompressedSize;
        m_dwCompressedSize =
         m_pFile->m_dwCompressedSize;
        strcpy( m_szSaveLoad,
         "File loaded successfully     " );
        }
       else AfxMessageBox( "Couldn't create!" );
       m_pFile->Close();
       }
      else AfxMessageBox("Couldn't open file!");
      delete m_pFile;
      m_pFile = NULL;
      }
     }
    m_bLoaded = TRUE;
    }

  char junk[200];
  wsprintf( junk, "File:%s          ",
   m_szFilename );
  pDC->TextOut( 10, 10, junk, strlen( junk ) );
  wsprintf( junk, "Uncompressed Size:%ld,
   Compressed Size:%ld, Ratio:%ld%%        ",
   m_dwUncompressedSize, m_dwCompressedSize,
  ( m_dwCompressedSize*100 )
```

```
   / m_dwUncompressedSize );
pDC->TextOut( 10, 30, junk, strlen( junk ) );
pDC->TextOut( 10, 50, m_szSaveLoad,
 strlen( m_szSaveLoad ) );
pDC->TextOut( 10, 70, m_szCompression,
 strlen( m_szCompression ) );

}
```

Saving Files

Saving files is done in the CCompressDemoView class, in the
OnFileSaveAs() function.

The first things that must happen in the OnSaveAs() function are
checks to make sure there is an allocated buffer and that the size of the
data is not zero. Either one of these situations will create an unsuccessful
write operation.

The next thing the code does is create a CCompressedFile object with
the static MakeNewFile() function. This function takes as its second
argument the compression type for the file.

The Open() function is then called. It is called in exactly the same way
as the Open() function of the Cfile class. It takes a filename as its first
argument and the file attributes as its second argument. It returns TRUE
if successful or FALSE if unsuccessful.

A single call to the Write() function is made. Doing this causes the
CCompressedFile to write all of the data to disk. This Write() function is
called in exactly the same way as the Write() function of the Cfile class. It
takes a buffer pointer as its first argument and an integer value representing the number of bytes to write to disk.

The display variables are all updated so that any change in file status,
size, or compression type is reflected in the view window.

The OnFileSaveAs() Function

```
void CCompressDemoView::SaveAs(char *Filename)
{
 CCompressDemoDoc *pDoc = GetDocument();

 if( !hGlobal ){
 AfxMessageBox( "No buffer to save!" );
 return;
 }
```

```
                              if( !m_dwUncompressedSize ){
                               AfxMessageBox( "There is no data!" );
                               return;
                               }

                              m_pFile = CCompressedFile::MakeNewFile( NULL,
                               pDoc->m_nCompressionSelected );
                              if( !m_pFile )
                               AfxMessageBox( "Couldn't create!" );
                              else{
                               strcpy( m_szSaveLoad,
                                "File saved unsuccessfully     " );
                               if( !m_pFile->Open( Filename,
                                CFile::modeWrite | CFile::modeCreate ) )
                                 AfxMessageBox( "Couldn't create!" );
                               else{
                                BeginWaitCursor();
                                m_pFile->Write( m_cbDataBuffer,
                                 m_dwUncompressedSize );
                                m_pFile->Close();
                                EndWaitCursor();
                                m_dwCompressedSize =
                                 m_pFile->m_dwCompressedSize;
                                strcpy( m_szFilename, Filename );
                                strcpy( m_szSaveLoad,
                                 "File saved successfully     " );
                                strcpy( m_szCompression,
                                 szComps[m_pFile->m_nCompressionType+1] );
                                InvalidateRect( NULL );
                                UpdateWindow();
                                }
                               delete m_pFile;
                               m_pFile = NULL;
                               }

                             }
```

COMPRESSING & DECOMPRESSING DATA IN A NUTSHELL

This section gives you the bare bones of saving and loading files using the CCompressedFile class. These short examples do no error checking or anything fancy. They're given only to help you understand the basics of using the CCompressedFile class.

Reading a File

Start off by creating a CCompressedFile object by calling the static MakeNewFile() function. The first parameter is not necessary. It's the name of the file, but you'll usually give the filename when you open the file. The second argument is the compression type. This can be either HUFF, LZSS, LZW, or UNCOMP. The second argument will default to LZW if you don't pass it a value.

```
CCompressedFile *pFile = MakeNewFile( NULL, LZW );
```

Next, you have to open the file. Here's the code to open a file named TEST.TXT:

```
pFile->Open( "TEST.TXT", Cfile::modeRead );
```

If you're dynamically allocating a buffer into which the data will be read, use the pFile->m_dwUncompressedSize variable to obtain the size of the buffer. The following code allocates a buffer for reading:

```
char *pBuffer = new char[pFile->m_dwUncompressedSize];
```

Now, you can read the data with a call to the Read() function. The code to do this follows:

```
pFile->Read( pBuffer, pFile->m_dwUncompressedSize );
```

Finally, you must close the file. Here's the code for that:

```
pFile->Close();
```

Writing a File

Once again, start by creating a CCompressedFile object by calling the static MakeNewFile() function.

```
CCompressedFile *pFile = MakeNewFile( NULL, LZW );
```

Next, you have to open the file. Here's the code to open a file named TEST.CMP:

```
pFile->Open( "TEST.CMP", Cfile::modeWrite | Cfile::modeCreate);
```

Now, you can write the data with a call to the Write() function. The code to do this follows:

```
char szBuffer[] =
"This is a test of this compression class.";
pFile->Write( szBuffer, strlen( szBuffer ) );
```

Finally, you must close the file. Here's the code for that:

```
pFile->Close();
```

CREATING PROGRAMS THAT USE DATA COMPRESSION

No instruction would be complete without providing some warm-up exercises so that you can easily get familiar with the CCompressedFile class. Here are some hands-on exercises. If you work your way through them, you'll be an expert in using the CCompressedFile class.

Hands-On 1: Compressing Data to a File

The first hands-on exercise creates ASCII data in an allocated buffer. Once the buffer is populated with ASCII text, it's compressed to a file.

The code that creates the data and saves it to disk is all in the OnDraw() function of the view class. Once the compression process is over, the display window will show how much compression was achieved, as seen in Figure 15-5.

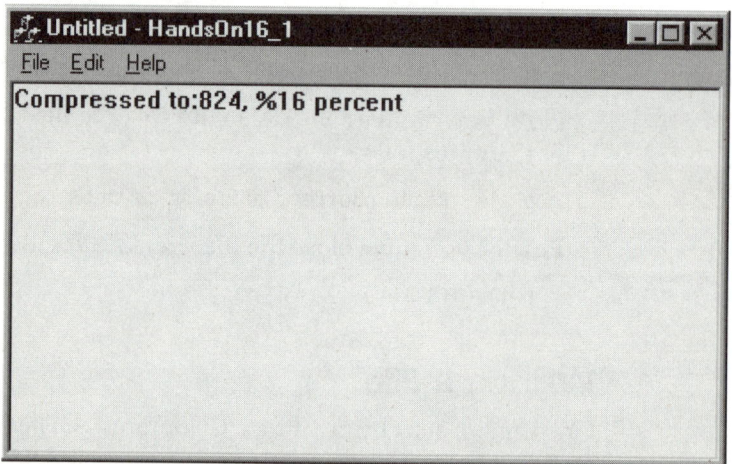

Figure 15-5: This file compresses well with LZW compression.

1. Create a Visual C++ project named HandsOn16_1 with the following attributes:

   ❑ Single-document interface

   ❑ English language

   ❑ No database support

   ❑ No compound document support

   ❑ No automation or ActiveX control support

❑ 3D controls, but no other features

❑ No source file comments

❑ Link MFC as a static library

2. Select Settings from the Project menu. Choose the Link tab. Add the following libraries to the Object/library modules field. The libraries for the release and debug versions are different. Both are listed below.

Release Project Libraries	Debug Project Libraries
CompressedFile.lib	CompressedFileD.lib

3. Set the Active Configuration to Win32 Release.

4. Add the following include to the HandsOn16_1View.h file:

```
#include "CompressedFile.h"
```

5. Add the following variable declarations to the CHandsOn16_1View class in the HandsOn16_1View.h file:

```
BOOL m_bFileCreated;
DWORD m_dwCompressedSize;
unsigned char *m_pBuffer;
```

6. Add the following code to the CHandsOn16_1View constructor:

```
CHandsOn16_1View::CHandsOn16_1View()
{

m_bFileCreated = FALSE;
m_pBuffer = NULL;

}
```

7. Add the following code to the CHandsOn16_1View destructor:

```
CHandsOn16_1View::~CHandsOn16_1View()
{

if( m_pBuffer != NULL )
  delete [] m_pBuffer;

}
```

8. Edit the OnDraw function in the CHandsOn16_1View class in the HandsOn16_1View.cpp file as follows:

```
void CHandsOn16_1View::OnDraw(CDC* pDC)
{
CHandsOn16_1Doc* pDoc = GetDocument();
ASSERT_VALID(pDoc);

 if( !m_bFileCreated ){
  CCompressedFile *pFile;
  pFile =
   CCompressedFile::MakeNewFile( NULL, LZSS );

  m_pBuffer = new unsigned char[5000];
  for( int i=0; i<100; i++ ){
   for( int j=0; j<50; j++ ){
    m_pBuffer[i*50+j] = 'A' + j;
    if( j == 48 ) m_pBuffer[i*50+j] = 13;
    else if( j == 49 ) m_pBuffer[i*50+j] = 10;
    }
    }

  pFile->Open( "TEST.CMP",
   CFile::modeWrite | CFile::modeCreate );
  pFile->Write( m_pBuffer, 5000 );
  pFile->Close();

  m_dwCompressedSize =
   pFile->m_dwCompressedSize;

  delete pFile;
  m_bFileCreated = TRUE;

  }

 char junk[200];
 wsprintf( junk,
  "Compressed to:%ld, %%%ld percent",
  m_dwCompressedSize,
  ( m_dwCompressedSize * 100 ) / 5000 );
 pDC->TextOut( 0, 0, junk, strlen( junk ) );

}
```

9. Compile and run the program.

Hands-On 2: Decompressing a File

The second program you'll create takes the file created in the first hands-on exercise and uncompresses it into a memory buffer. After the program runs, you'll see text on the screen telling you about the file compression, as shown in Figure 15-6.

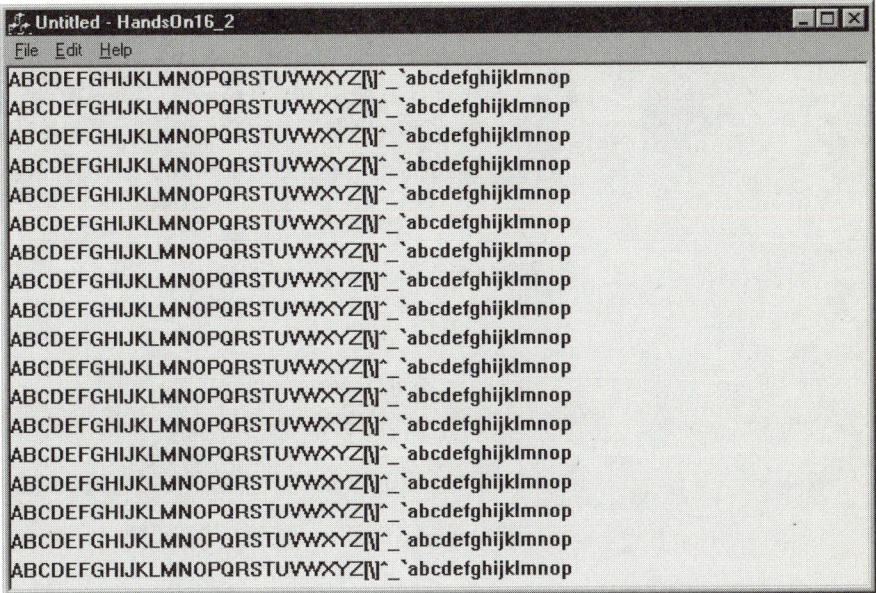

Figure 15-6: This program uncompresses the file that was compressed in the first hands-on exercise in this chapter.

1. Create a Visual C++ project named HandsOn16_2 with the following attributes:

   ❐ Single-document interface
   ❐ English language
   ❐ No database support
   ❐ No compound document support
   ❐ No automation or ActiveX control support
   ❐ 3D controls, but no other features
   ❐ No source file comments
   ❐ Link MFC as a static library

2. Select Settings from the Project menu. Choose the Link tab. Add the following libraries to the Object/library modules field. The libraries for the release and debug versions are different. Both are listed below.

Release Project Libraries	**Debug Project Libraries**
CompressedFile.lib	CompressedFileD.lib

3. Set the Active Configuration to Win32 Release.

4. Copy the file TEST.CMP from the HandsOn16_1 directory on the Companion CD-ROM to the newly created project directory.

5. Add the following include to the HandsOn16_2View.h file:

```
#include "CompressedFile.h"
```

6. Add the following variable declarations to the CHandsOn16_2View class in the HandsOn16_2View.h file:

```
BOOL m_bFileLoaded;
DWORD m_dwUncompressedSize;
unsigned char *m_pBuffer;
```

7. Add the following code to the CHandsOn16_2View constructor:

```
CHandsOn16_2View::CHandsOn16_2View()
{
 m_bFileLoaded = FALSE;
 m_pBuffer = NULL;
}
```

8. Add the following code to the CHandsOn16_2View destructor:

```
CHandsOn16_2View::~CHandsOn16_2View()
{
 if( m_pBuffer != NULL )
  delete [] m_pBuffer;
}
```

9. Edit the OnDraw function in the CHandsOn16_2View class in the HandsOn16_2View.cpp file as follows:

```
void CHandsOn16_2View::OnDraw(CDC* pDC)
{
 CHandsOn16_2Doc* pDoc = GetDocument();
 ASSERT_VALID(pDoc);
```

```
if( !m_bFileLoaded ){
 CCompressedFile *pFile;
 pFile =
  CCompressedFile::MakeNewFile( "TEST.CMP" );
 pFile->Open( "TEST.CMP", CFile::modeRead );
 m_pBuffer =
  new unsigned char[
   pFile->m_dwUncompressedSize];
 pFile->Read( m_pBuffer,
  pFile->m_dwUncompressedSize );
 pFile->Close();

 m_dwUncompressedSize =
  pFile->m_dwUncompressedSize;
 delete pFile;
 m_bFileLoaded = TRUE;
 }

char junk[200];
DWORD dwCurrent = 0;
int i, y = 0;
while( dwCurrent < m_dwUncompressedSize ){
 i = 0;
 while( m_pBuffer[dwCurrent] != 13 )
  junk[i++] = m_pBuffer[dwCurrent++];
 while( m_pBuffer[dwCurrent] < ' ' )
  dwCurrent++;
 pDC->TextOut( 0, y, junk, i );
 y += 20;
 }

}
```

10. Compile and run the program.

Hands-On 3: Compressing Multiple Files Into One Archive

One of the best uses for data compression is in install programs. You can take a large number of files and crunch them into one single file. Then, when users install the software, the installation program decompresses each file in the archive to the hard drive.

This technique will save a software publisher as much as 75 percent in disk production costs. It's well worth the effort.

When the program runs, you'll see it compress each file. It'll show you compression ratios for each one as it goes through the list. Figure 15-7 shows the program during compression.

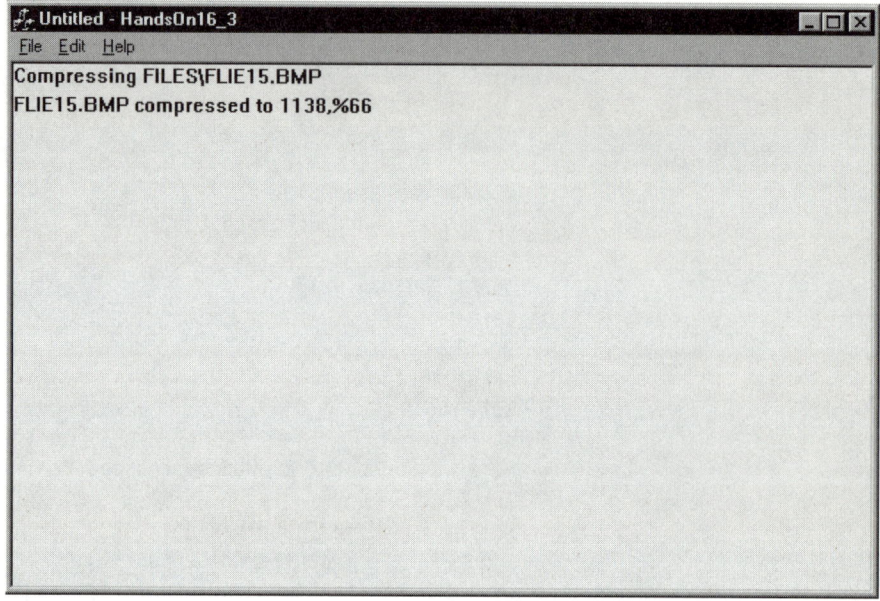

Figure 15-7: A series of 16 files are compressed into one archive file.

1. Create a Visual C++ project named HandsOn16_3 with the following attributes:

   ❏ Single-document interface

   ❏ English language

   ❏ No database support

   ❏ No compound document support

   ❏ No automation or ActiveX control support

   ❏ 3D controls, but no other features

   ❏ No source file comments

   ❏ Link MFC as a static library

2. Select Settings from the Project menu. Choose the Link tab. Add the following libraries to the Object/library modules field. The libraries for the release and debug versions are different. Both are listed below.

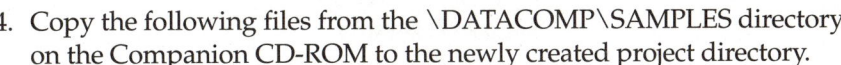

Release Project Libraries	Debug Project Libraries
CompressedFile.lib	CompressedFileD.lib

3. Set the Active Configuration to Win32 Release.

4. Copy the following files from the \DATACOMP\SAMPLES directory on the Companion CD-ROM to the newly created project directory.

> FLIE0.BMP
>
> FLIE1.BMP
>
> FLIE2.BMP
>
> FLIE3.BMP
>
> FLIE4.BMP
>
> FLIE5.BMP
>
> FLIE6.BMP
>
> FLIE7.BMP
>
> FLIE8.BMP
>
> FLIE9.BMP
>
> FLIE10.BMP
>
> FLIE11.BMP
>
> FLIE12.BMP
>
> FLIE13.BMP
>
> FLIE14.BMP
>
> FLIE15.BMP

5. Add the following includes to the HandsOn16_3View.h file:

```
#include "CompressedFile.h"
```

6. Add the following variable declarations to the CHandsOn16_3View class in the HandsOn16_3View.h file:

```
 BOOL m_bFileCompressed;
```

7. Add the following code to the CHandsOn16_3View constructor:

```
CHandsOn16_3View::CHandsOn16_3View()
{
 m_bFileCompressed = FALSE;
}
```

547

8. Edit the OnDraw function in the CHandsOn16_3View class in the HandsOn16_3View.cpp file as follows:

```cpp
void CHandsOn16_3View::OnDraw(CDC* pDC)
{
 CHandsOn16_3Doc* pDoc = GetDocument();
 ASSERT_VALID(pDoc);

 if( !m_bFileCompressed ){
  char szFilename[200];
  char szDisplay[200];
  unsigned char *pBuffer;
  BOOL bResult;
  DWORD dwFileLength, dwCompressedSize;
  CFile LoadFile;
  CCompressedFile *pSaveFile;

  for( int i=0; i<16; i++ ){
   wsprintf( szFilename,
    "FILES\\FLIE%d.BMP", i );
   if( LoadFile.Open( szFilename,
    CFile::modeRead ) ){
    dwFileLength = LoadFile.GetLength();
    pBuffer =
     new unsigned char [dwFileLength];
    if( pBuffer != NULL ){
     LoadFile.Read( pBuffer, dwFileLength);
     LoadFile.Close();
     pSaveFile =
      CCompressedFile::MakeNewFile(NULL,LZSS);
     if( pSaveFile != NULL ){
      if( i == 0 )
       bResult =
        pSaveFile->Open( "INSTALL.CMP",
         CFile::modeWrite|CFile::modeCreate);
      else bResult =
```

```
                pSaveFile->Open( "INSTALL.CMP",
                 CFile::modeWrite );
               if( bResult ){
                wsprintf( szDisplay,
                 "Compressing %s          ",
                 szFilename );
                pDC->TextOut( 0, 0, szDisplay,
                 strlen( szDisplay ) );
                pSaveFile->Write(pBuffer,dwFileLength);
                pSaveFile->Close();
                dwCompressedSize =
                 pSaveFile->m_dwCompressedSize;
                wsprintf( szDisplay,
                 "FLIE%d.BMP compressed to %ld,%%%ld",
                 i, dwCompressedSize,
                 ( dwCompressedSize * 100 ) /
                 dwFileLength );
                pDC->TextOut( 0, 20, szDisplay,
                 strlen( szDisplay ) );
                }
              delete pSaveFile;
              }
            delete [] pBuffer;
            }
          }
        }
      m_bFileCompressed = TRUE;
      for( int k=0; k<600; k++ )
       pDC->TextOut( k, 0, " ", 1 );
      for( k=0; k<600; k++ )
       pDC->TextOut( k, 20, " ", 1 );
      }

    pDC->TextOut( 0, 0, "Done!", 5 );

    }
```

9. Compile and run the program.

Hands-On 4: Uncompressing a Multiple-File Archive

The last hands-on exercise in this chapter takes the multiple-file archive file created in the third hands-on exercise and extracts each file to disk in its original state. While the program runs, you'll see in the view window which file is being uncompressed and its compression ratio. Figure 15-8 shows the program as it's uncompressing.

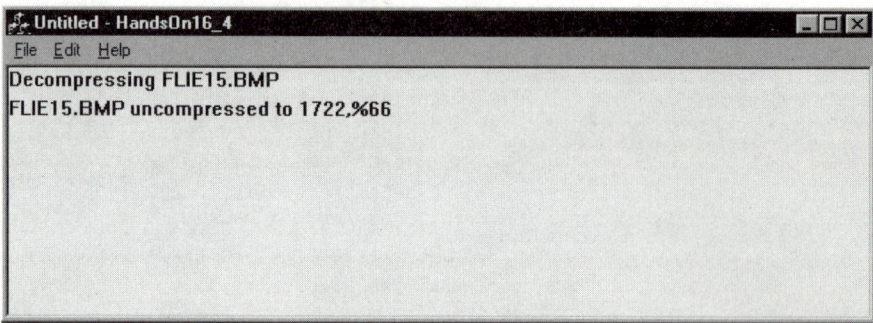

Figure 15-8: You'll see the file that's being extracted during the uncompress process.

1. Create a Visual C++ project named HandsOn16_4 with the following attributes:

   ❏ Single-document interface

   ❏ English language

   ❏ No database support

   ❏ No compound document support

   ❏ No automation or ActiveX control support

   ❏ 3D controls, but no other features

   ❏ No source file comments

   ❏ Link MFC as a static library

2. Select Settings from the Project menu. Choose the Link tab. Add the following libraries to the Object/library modules field. The libraries for the release and debug versions are different. Both are listed below.

Release Project Libraries	Debug Project Libraries
CompressedFile.lib	CompressedFileD.lib

3. Set the Active Configuration to Win32 Release.

4. Copy the INSTALL.CMP file from the HandsOn16_3 directory on the Companion CD-ROM to the newly created project directory.

5. Add the following includes to the HandsOn16_4View.h file:

```
#include "CompressedFile.h"
```

6. Add the following variable declarations to the CHandsOn16_4View class in the HandsOn16_4View.h file:

```
BOOL m_bFilesUncompressed;
```

7. Add the following code to the CHandsOn16_4View constructor:

```
CHandsOn16_4View::CHandsOn16_4View()
{
 m_bFilesUncompressed = FALSE;
}
```

8. Edit the OnDraw function in the CHandsOn16_4View class in the HandsOn16_4View.cpp file as follows:

```
void CHandsOn16_4View::OnDraw(CDC* pDC)
{
 CHandsOn16_4Doc* pDoc = GetDocument();
 ASSERT_VALID(pDoc);

 if( !m_bFilesUncompressed ){
  char szFilename[200];
  char szDisplay[200];
  unsigned char *pBuffer;
  CFile SaveFile;
  CCompressedFile *pLoadFile;

  pLoadFile =
  CCompressedFile::MakeNewFile("INSTALL.CMP");
  if( pLoadFile != NULL ){
   if( pLoadFile->Open( "INSTALL.CMP",
   CFile::modeRead ) ){
    for( int i=0; i<16; i++ ){
     if( pLoadFile->FindFileInArchive( i ) ){
      wsprintf( szFilename,
       "FLIE%d.BMP", i );
      if( SaveFile.Open( szFilename,
      CFile::modeWrite | CFile::modeCreate)){
       pBuffer = new unsigned char[
        pLoadFile->m_dwUncompressedSize];
```

551

```
              if( pBuffer != NULL ){
               pLoadFile->Read( pBuffer,
               pLoadFile->m_dwUncompressedSize );
               wsprintf( szDisplay,
                "Decompressing %s           ",
                szFilename );
               pDC->TextOut( 0, 0, szDisplay,
                strlen( szDisplay ) );
               SaveFile.Write( pBuffer,
                pLoadFile->m_dwUncompressedSize );
               SaveFile.Close();
               wsprintf( szDisplay,
              "FLIE%d.BMP uncompressed to %ld,%%%ld",
                i, pLoadFile->m_dwUncompressedSize,
               ( pLoadFile->m_dwCompressedSize*100)/
                pLoadFile->m_dwUncompressedSize );
               pDC->TextOut( 0, 20, szDisplay,
                strlen( szDisplay ) );
               delete [] pBuffer;
               }
              }
             }
            }
           }
          pLoadFile->Close();
          delete pLoadFile;
         }
        m_bFilesUncompressed = TRUE;
        for( int k=0; k<600; k++ )
         pDC->TextOut( k, 0, " ", 1 );
        for( k=0; k<600; k++ )
         pDC->TextOut( k, 20, " ", 1 );
        }

      pDC->TextOut( 0, 0, "Done!", 5 );
      }
```

9. Compile and run the program.

On the Web

This section shows you various Web sites that are related to data compression. Check them out, and you'll probably find most of them useful.

A complete course in data compression can be found online at http://www.ics.uci.edu/~dan/pubs/DataCompression.html. Figure 15-9 shows the site. Although it looks plain, it's jam-packed with an effective presentation of practically every aspect of data compression.

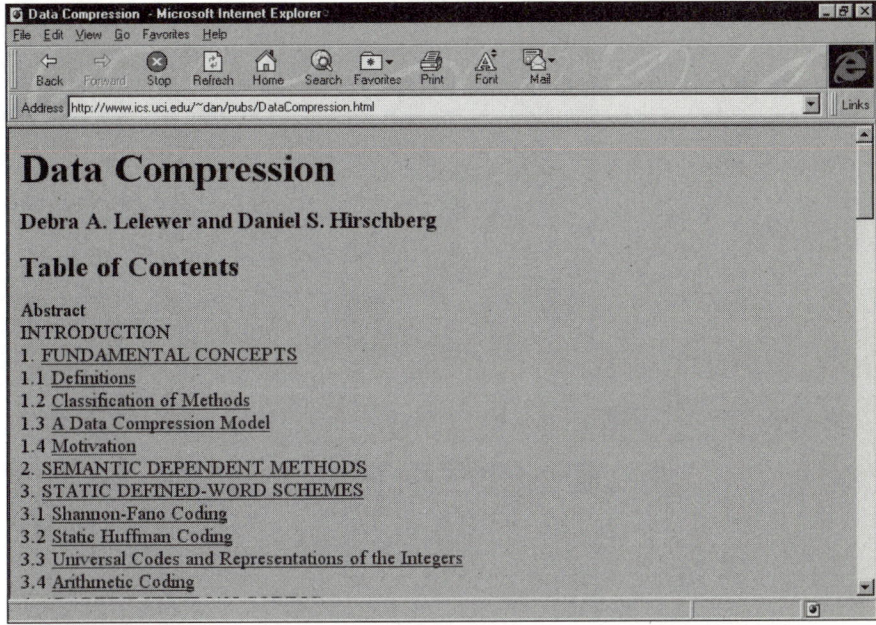

Figure 15-9: This site provides a complete course in data compression.

You can find a comprehensive study comparing data compression algorithms at http://mjcs.fsktm.um.edu.my/MJCS/Volume_8_No1/Vol_8_No1.8. Figure 15-10 shows the site and some of what it has to offer.

For the authority on data compression, visit the PKWARE site, which is shown in Figure 15-11. The PKWARE products have been leaders for more than 10 years.

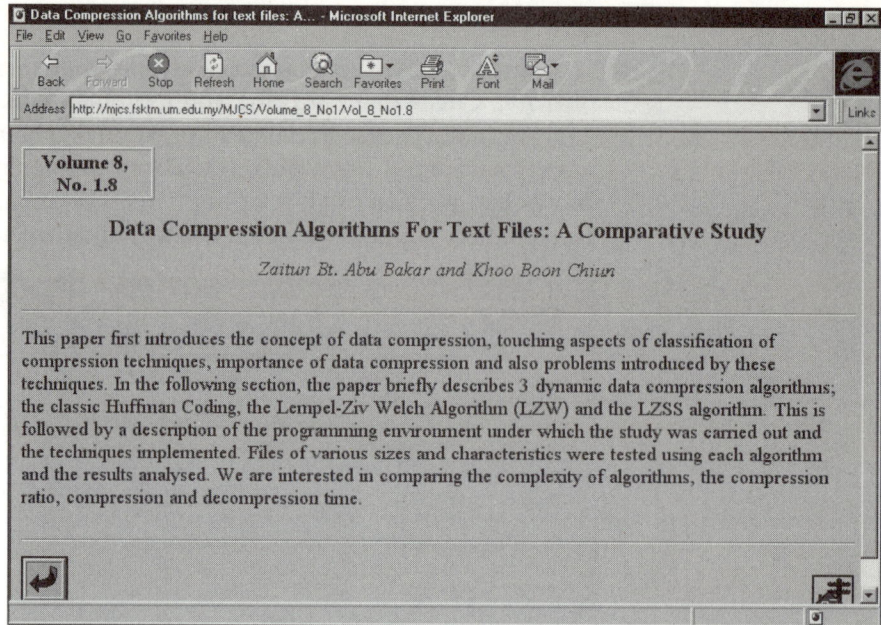

Figure 15-10: A comparison of data compression schemes can be seen at this site.

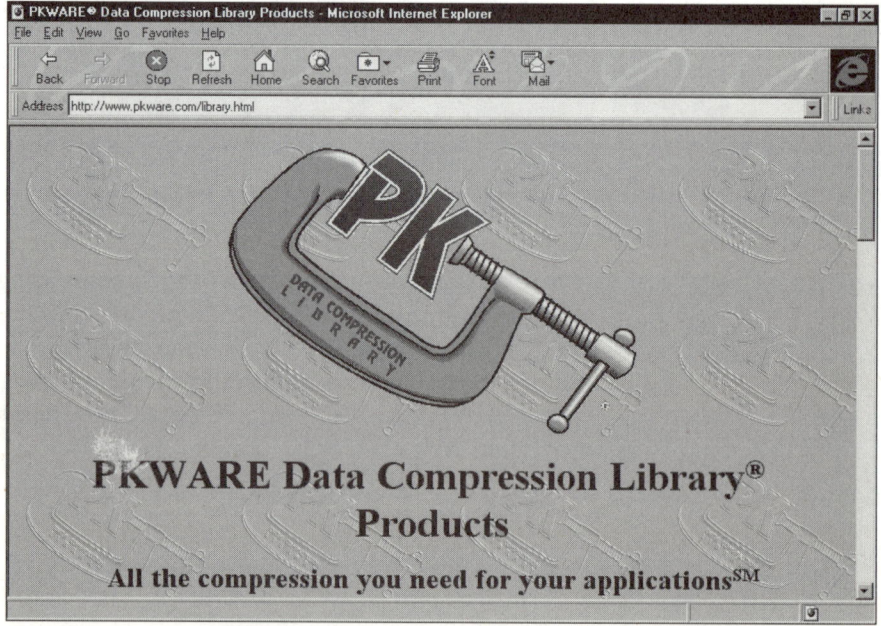

Figure 15-11: The PKWARE site is a good first stop to make if you're looking for a commercial library.

Conclusion

In this chapter you've learned how to use the CCompressedFile class to compress your data files to disk and decompress the data when reading it in. Use this whenever possible to save your users valuable hard drive space.

This book has given you tools that'll take your programs from average and functional, to above average and professional. The class library API sections of each chapter have given you handy reference sections that you can refer to any time you use the class libraries. The hands-on sections provided valuable training in using the class libraries.

You now have all the tools you need to transform your programs into professional-looking applications. And don't stop with these class libraries. Create your own from scratch or based on the ones in the book. Send them to me via e-mail and ivt-rcl@interpath.com. I'd love to use them in the next book I write.

About the Companion CD-ROM

The Companion CD-ROM included with your copy of *Visual C++ 5 Power Toolkit* contains valuable software plus class libraries, DLLs, and "include" files that were written to be used in conjunction with the book. Please note that there is a separate folder for Windows NT 3.5.1 users. This Appendix includes a listing of the Directory structure that will help you find what you need. To use the author-generated files properly, it is important to know how to make sure the Compiler can find "library" and "include" files. You will find instructions on this in this book's Introduction.

DIRECTORY STRUCTURE OF THE CD-ROM

LIB	Contains class libraries and DLLs
INCLUDE	Files for Visual C++ 5
IMAGES	
\ImageObject	Source code for the class library
\ImageView	Source code for the ImageView demo
\Demos	Software
IMAGEPR1	
\ImagePointProcesses	Source code for the class library
\ImageView	Source code for the Image View demo
\Demos	Software
IMAGEPR2	
\ImageAreaProcesses	Source code for the class library
\ImageView	Source code for the ImageView demo

SEFFECTS
   \ScreenEffects .... Source code for the class library
   \ScreenEffectDemo .... Source code for the book demo

ANIMATION
   \Animation .... Source code for the class library
   \AnimationDemo .... Source code for the book demo
   \Samples .... Sample images

DATACOMP
   \CompressedFile .... Source code for the class library
   \CompressDemo .... Source code for the book demo
   \Demos .... Software

MIDI
   \Midi .... Source code for the class library
   \MidiPlayer .... Source code for the book demo
   \Samples .... Midi samples
   \Demos .... Software

RGNMAP
   \RgnMap .... Source code for the class library
   \RegionMap .... Source code for the book demo

TWAIN
   \TWAINLib .... Source code for the class library
   \TWAINDemo .... Source code for the book demo

SOUND
   \DirectWave .... Source code for the class library
   \Wave .... Source code for the class library
   \WaveStudio .... Source code for the book demo
   \Samples .... Sound samples
   \Quack .... Software

CDAUDIO
   \CDAudio
   \CDAudioPlayer
   \demos .... Shareware

DATAENC
   \DataEncryption
   \DataEncryptionDemo

MODEM
   \Checkers
   \demos .... Shareware

INTERNET
   \Checkers

NETWORK
   \Checkers

SPLASH
  \Splash
  \SplashDemo

EXTRAS .... Extra shareware goodies.

WINNT351 .... A separate folder of auther files designed to be used with Windows NT 3.5.1. The files in this folder function the same as the "normal" author files but have had the filenames changed to be compatible with Windows NT 3.5.1.

Software on the CD-ROM

ACDSee (IMAGEPR1 Folder)   Image viewer for Windows 95

Amazing JPEG Screen Saver (EXTRAS Folder)   A screen saver that allows you to display floating JPEG images that automatically change.

Amazing AVI Screen Saver (EXTRAS Folder)   Livens up your screen with AVI animations.

CDWorkx 2.10.0579 for Windows 95 (SOUND Folder)   A program for grabbing digital audio from CDs.

CommLib demo (DATACOMP Folder)   Greenleaf Software's CommLib 5.1 is a terminal program for MS Windows examples. See more info about the full version of CommLib at http://www.gleaf.com/~gleaf.

Comm++ 3.0 demo (DATACOMP Folder)   A Windows demo of Comm++. The full version of Comm++ is a program that will accommodate interrupt-driven, circular buffered service for 35 ports at baud rates to 115,200. For more information and pricing on the full version, go to http://www.gleaf.com/~gleaf on the Web.

Crusher! (DATACOMP Folder)   A versatile and portable C/C++ data compression library. VBX and OCX custom controls are included for use with Visual Basic and similar environments.

Fractal Design Painter (EXTRAS Folder)   Painter is a paint and image creation program.

Zlib 1.04 (DATACOMP Folder)   The official PNG compression library, C source code, Version 1.0.4, in zip file format.

MIDIART v3.0 (MIDI Folder)   MIDI music bursts with color! MIDIART plays standard MIDI music files and simultaneously creates beautiful psychedelic images that are synchronized to the music. The images are created and controlled by the music itself. The user can also interact withMIDIART to control the images. Requires Windows 3.1 and a sound card or an external MIDI sound generator. Includes full online help. Shareware by AJF Consulting, Inc.

MultiMedia Mixer (CD Audio Folder)   A multimedia program that supports AVI, MIDI, WAV, and CD. With MultiMedia Mixer, you can do all four of these at the same time! For example, you could play a MIDI file or a CD while recording it to a WAV file, or watch an AVI video while listening to your favorite CD. For more info about MMM, visit http://ourworld.compuserve.com/homepages/b_mcbride/programs.htm on the Web.

Pro Audio CD Player 1.350 (SOUND Folder)   A fully featured and self-contained audio CD player for your computer with the following characteristics: 1) A small executable file; 2) Special attention is paid to the impact on system resources and memory; 3) Only minimal system intrusion occurs even when the system is not "asleep."

QUACK 2.0a Sound Effects Studio (SOUND Folder)   Creates an infinite variety of sound effect WAV files by plugging together components such as oscillators, filters, and envelope generators.

Quinn-Curtis Software (IMAGES Folder)   1) Charting Tools for Windows—a 2D Charting Function Library; 2) Real-Time Graphics Tools for Windows—Real-Time Graphics Function Library; 3) Graphics Class Library for MFC—Class library add-on to 1) and 2); 4) 3D++ Class Library—Class Library for 3D Scientific Charting and Visualization.

Installation: When these programs install, the icon they install on the Windows Start Menu or Program Group does not work. You will have to launch each program by double-clicking on its executable file from File Manager (Windows 3.x) or Windows Explorer (Windows 95 or NT), and then change the properties so you can launch them from the Start Menu or Program Group.

VideoCraft GIF Animator (EXTRAS Folder)   Features seven powerful effects editors to create stunning Web animations and video special effects. Besides animated effects such as morphing and distorting, VideoCraft can be used to convert existing ALL files to GIF animations.

Vidfun 2.2 (IMAGEPR1 Folder)   VidFun is an easy-to-use, value-added Multimedia viewer, graphics toolkit, and screen saver. Its Explorer-style interface works even in Win3.1. Win95/NT features include long filenames and 32-bit video. It integrates as a helper app for Web browsers, too. 100% functional (no crippled functions). Fast JPEG support plus Photo-CD, MPEG/VideoCD, AVI, MOV, FLI, MIDI, WAV, CD music, BMP, DCX, CMP, KQP, MAC, PICT, PCX, PNG,PSD (PhotoShop), RAS, TGA, TIF, WPG, and Multipage fax files. You may register this shareware at http://users.aol.com/lgozum/vidfun.htm on the Web.

Way Cool Screen Saver Engine 1.7 (EXTRAS Folder)   A freeware Screen Saver engine. Runs on Win95, WinNT3.51, and WinNT4.0 proprietary sound API, which is capable of adjusting the perception level of your ears by simply looking at the computer screen while adjusting a slider control. By Full Volume Studios.

TECHNICAL SUPPORT

Technical support is available for installation-related problems only. The technical support office is open from 8:00 A.M. to 6:00 P.M. Monday through Friday and can be reached via the following methods:

Phone: (919) 544-9404, extension 81

Faxback Answer System: (919) 544-9404, extension 85

E-mail: help@vmedia.com

FAX: (919) 544-9472

World Wide Web: **http://www.vmedia.com/support**

America Online: keyword *Ventana*

LIMITS OF LIABILITY & DISCLAIMER OF WARRANTY

The authors and publisher of this book have used their best efforts in preparing the CD-ROM and the programs contained in it. These efforts include the development, research, and testing of the theories and programs to determine their effectiveness. The authors and publisher make no warranty of any kind expressed or implied, with regard to these programs or the documentation contained in this book.

The authors and publisher shall not be liable in the event of incidental or consequential damages in connection with, or arising out of, the furnishing, performance, or use of the programs, associated instructions, and/or claims of productivity gains.

Some of the software on this CD-ROM is shareware; there may be additional charges (owed to the software authors/makers) incurred for their registration and continued use. See individual programs' README or VREADME.TXT files for more information.

Index

N

S

W

X

Y

VENTANA

http://www.vmedia.com

VENTANA

HTML Publishing on the Internet, Second Edition

$39.99, 700 pages, illustrated, part #: 625-4

Take advantage of critical updates and technologies that have emerged since this book's bestselling predecessor was published. Learn to create a home page and hyperlinks, and to build graphics, video and sound into documents. Highlighted throughout with examples and templates, and tips on layout and nonlinear organization. Plus, save time and money by downloading components of the new technologies from the Web or from the companion CD-ROM. The CD-ROM also features HTML authoring tools, graphics and multimedia utilities, textures, templates and demos.

The HTML Programmer's Reference

$39.99, 376 pages, illustrated, part #: 597-5

The ultimate professional companion! All HTML categories, tags and attributes are listed in one easy-reference sourcebook, complete with code examples. Saves time and money testing—all examples comply with the top browsers! Provides real-world JavaScript and HTML examples. The CD-ROM features a complete hyperlinked HTML version of the book, viewable with most popular browsers.

VENTANA

Principles of Object-Oriented Programming in Java

$39.99, 400 pages, illustrated, part #: 530-4

Move from writing programs to designing solutions—with dramatic results! Take a step beyond syntax to discover the true art of software design, with Java as your paintbrush and objects on your palette. This in-depth discussion of how, when and why to use objects enables you to create programs—using Java or any other object-oriented language that not only work smoothly, but are easy to maintain and upgrade. The CD-ROM features the Java SDK, code samples and more.

The Comprehensive Guide to Visual J++

$49.99, 792 pages, illustrated, part #: 533-9

Learn to integrate the Java language and ActiveX in one development solution! Master the Visual J++ environment using real-world coding techniques and project examples. Includes executable J++ sample projects plus undocumented tips and tricks. The CD-ROM features all code examples, sample ActiveX COM objects, Java documentation and an ActiveX component library.

VENTANA

The Mac Web Server Book

$49.95, 662 pages, illustrated, part #: 341-7

Get the most from your Internet server with this hands-on resource guide and toolset. *The Mac Web Server Book* will help you choose the right server software; set up your server; add graphics, sound and forms; and much more. The CD-ROM includes demo software, scripts, icons and shareware.

The Windows NT Web Server Book

$49.95, 680 pages, illustrated, part #: 342-5

A complete toolkit for providing services on the Internet using the Windows NT operating system. This how-to guide includes adding the necessary web server software, comparison of the major Windows NT server packages for the Web, becoming a global product provider and more! The CD-ROM features Alibaba™ Lite (a fully licensed web server), support programs, scripts, forms, utilities and demos.

The UNIX Web Server Book, Second Edition

$49.99, 752 pages, illustrated, part #: 480-4

Tools and techniques for building an Internet/intranet site. Everything you need to know to set up your UNIX web site—from basic installation to adding content, multimedia, interactivity and advanced searches. The CD-ROM features Linux, HTTP, CERN Web Server, FTP daemon, conversion software, graphics translators and utilities.

VENTANA

The Windows NT 4 Server Book

$49.99, 760 pages, illustrated, part #: 495-2

Optimize your Windows NT 4 network with this definitive, easy-to-read reference. Packed with figures, examples, diagrams, and illustrations, it focuses on the unique needs of NT Server users. An indispensable guide covering installation, add-in systems, advanced security, maintenance and more. Plus, extensive appendices—tools, online help sources, glossary of terms.

Microsoft BackOffice 2.5: The Complete Solution

$49.99, 864 pages, illustrated, part #: 296-8

Link desktops with data via BackOffice's integrated suite of server software. Features tips and tools for devising network solutions and managing multiple systems. Indispensable for IS professionals, network managers and programmers. The CD-ROM features all sample applications, configurations and code in the book; plus sample custom controls and demos.

VENTANA

Net Security: Your Digital Doberman

$29.99, 312 pages, illustrated, part #: 506-1

Doing business on the Internet can be safe . . . if you know the risks and take appropriate steps. This thorough overview helps you put a virtual Web watchdog on the job—to protect both your company and your customers from hackers, electronic shoplifters and disgruntled employees. Easy-to-follow explanations help you understand complex security technologies, with proven technologies for safe Net transactions. Tips, checklists and action plans cover digital dollars, pilfer-proof "storefronts," protecting privacy and handling breaches.

Intranet Firewalls

$34.99, 360 pages, illustrated, part #: 506-1

Protect your network by controlling access—inside and outside your company—to proprietary files. This practical, hands-on guide takes you from intranet and firewall basics through creating and launching your firewall. Professional advice helps you assess your security needs and choose the best system for you. Includes tips for avoiding costly mistakes, firewall technologies, in-depth reviews and uses for popular firewall software, advanced theory of firewall design strategies and implementation, and more.

VENTANA

TO ORDER ANY VENTANA TITLE, COMPLETE THIS ORDER FORM AND MAIL OR FAX IT TO US, WITH PAYMENT, FOR QUICK SHIPMENT.

TITLE	PART #	QTY	PRICE	TOTAL

SHIPPING

For orders shipping within the United States, please add $4.95 for the first book, $1.50 for each additional book.
For "two-day air," add $7.95 for the first book, $3.00 for each additional book.
Email: vorders@kdc.com for exact shipping charges.
Note: Please include your local sales tax.

SUBTOTAL = $ _____

SHIPPING = $ _____

TAX = $ _____

TOTAL = $ _____

Mail to: International Thomson Publishing • 7625 Empire Drive • Florence, KY 41042
☎ **US orders 800/332-7450 • fax 606/283-0718**
☎ **International orders 606/282-5786 • Canadian orders 800/268-2222**

Name _____

E-mail _____ Daytime phone _____

Company _____

Address (No PO Box) _____

City _____ State _____ Zip _____

Payment enclosed ___ VISA ___ MC ___ Acc't # _____ Exp. date _____

Signature _____ Exact name on card _____

Check your local bookstore or software retailer for these and other bestselling titles, or call toll free:

800/332-7450

8:00 am - 6:00 pm EST